STAIRWAY TO HEAVEN

STAIRWAY
TO HEAVEN

Led Zeppelin
UNCENSORED

RICHARD COLE with RICHARD TRUBO

HarperEntertainment
An Imprint of HarperCollins*Publishers*

A hardcover edition of this book was published in 1992 by HarperCollins Publishers, and a mass market edition was published by HarperPaperbacks in 1993.

First HarperEntertainment edition published 2002.

The Library of Congress has cataloged the hardcover edition as follows:
Cole, Richard.
    Stairway to heaven : Led Zeppelin uncensored / Richard Cole with Richard Trubo.
      p. cm.
    Originally published: New York : HarperCollins Publishers, 1992.
    Includes discography (p.) and index.
    ISBN 0-06-018323-3 (hc)—ISBN 0-06-093837-4 (tp)—ISBN 0-06-109021-2
      1. Led Zeppelin (Musical group).   2. Rock musicians—England—Biography.
    I. Trubo, Richard.   II. Title.

ML421.L4 C64   2002
782.42166'092'2—dc21
[B]   2001039441

06 DC/RRD 20 19 18 17 16

To Claire and Daylen,
*best wishes on your wedding
and for the happiest of
lives together in the years ahead.*

—R C

To Donna, Melissa, and Mike ...
*years ago, when I would dream about a
family, you were exactly what I had in
mind.*
—R T

CONTENTS

ACKNOWLEDGMENTS

Many people have played important roles in helping me reach the point of writing this book.

Thanks to my mother and father, who gave me love and steered me in the right direction; to Jenny Carson for Ibiza in the summer of 1984; and to Dr. Brian Wells, Mickey Bush, and Andrew Lane, who shared their experience, strength, and hope with me.

I am also appreciative of Richard Trubo for his writing talent and perseverance; Tom Miller and Jim Hornfischer, our original editors at Harper-Collins, plus Josh Behar and April Benavides, who have guided us in creating this new edition; Jane Dystel, my agent, and her partner, Miriam Goderich; Skip Chernov for his encouragement and faith in the book; and Bernie Rhodes and Roger "Snake" Kline, as well as Toni Young and Carol Arnold, who helped with the transcripts. Taylor and his fine publication, *Zoso,* proved to be an excellent resource of Led Zeppelin history; and Allison Caine planted the seed for the afterword in this edition.

Thanks go to business manager Bill McKenzie and Debbie Mathews; my lawyer, Michael Hecker; Eric Wasserman; Michelle Anthony; publicist Laura Kaufman; and Black Sabbath. Thanks also to Sharon and Ozzy Osbourne for all their help, kindness, and opportunities over the years—and to the London Quireboys and Lita Ford as well. Appreciation also goes to Lisa Robinson, and to Tony, Mario, Michael, Mo, Miguel, and Steady at the Rainbow Bar and Grill in West Hollywood.

For their love and friendship, special mention to Tony Roman, Leslie St. Nicholas, Judy Wong, Jenny Fernando, Geoffrey Sensier, Marilyn Cole, Marguerite DeBenedict, Marty Brenner, David George, Ian Peacock, my computer angel and friend Julia Negron, and my oldest friend Percy Raines-Moore.

I appreciated the assistance and camaraderie of Led Zeppelin's road crew over the years: Kenny Pickett, Clive Coulson, Joe "Jammer" Wright, Mick Hinton, Ray Thomas, Sandy McGregor, Briane Condliffe, Andy Leadbetter, Manfred Lurch, Henry "The Horse" Smith, Perry, Cracky, and Pepe. Our sound engineers were Rusty Brutsche, David "Cyrano" Langston, and Benji Le Fevre. Ian "Iggy" Knight oversaw production, and Kirby Wyatt and Ted Tittle handled lighting.

ACKNOWLEDGMENTS

Assistants to the band included Dennis Sheehan, Rick Hobbs, Johnny Larke, Rex King, John Bindon, Mitchell Fox, Dave Northover, Brian Gallivan, and Ray Washburn (Peter Grant's assistant). Our office staff consisted of Liz Gardner, Carol Browne, Cynthia Sacks, and Unity MacLaine in the U.K., and Shelley Kaye, Genine Saffer, and Sam Azar in the U.S. Steven H. Weiss was our attorney.

The band's security staff included Patsy Collins, Wes Pommeroy, Captain Bob DeForest, Bill and Jack Dautrich, Johnny Czar, Fat Fred, Don Murfett, Gerry Slater, Jim Callaghan, Paddy the Plank, Alf Weaver, Joe Tuths, Willie Vaccar, Gregg Beppler, Steve Rosenberg, Jack Kelly, Lou McClery, George Dewitt, and Bill Webber.

Since the original printing of this book, some friends who worked with me and Led Zeppelin have passed away, and it seems fitting for them to be remembered here (some were mentioned above). They include Peter Grant (Zeppelin's manager); concert promoters Tom Hulett and Phil Basile; lighting designer Kirby Wyatt; assistant John Bindon and security man Johnny Czar; and road crew members Raymond Thomas and Kenny Pickett; as well as my oldest friend, songwriter Lionel Bart; journalist Alan McDougal; my wonderful friend Nicky Bell, who made me feel part of his life and community by inviting me to his one-year-sober party when I was just a few months sober myself, and who tragically died of AIDS from IV drug use; and writer Stuart Werbin (who courageously helped me in my time of need, even when he was very sick himself). Also, my dear friend and neighbor Gloria Scott (a great inspiration who helped so many people get clean and sober). Last in this list, but certainly not least, is my dear mother, who was always there for her little devil of a son.

In this new edition, I'd like to thank a few others, including some who, in recent years, have helped me get work or employed me, including Bob Timmins, Jack Carson, and Tony Morehead. Thanks also go to Black Uhuru and Kyso, along with managers Nita Scott and Terry Rindal, and, of course, Valerie and Bruce. Charlie Hernandez, Nick Cua, Blaine Brinton, and Rhian Gittins are Ozzfest 2001 staff who were a great help to me, and old friends Bobby Thompson, Tony Dennis, and Michael Guarracino. Ron Geer, my Ozzfest bus driver, was a fantastic help.

Special mention also goes to Michael Lewis, Gary Quinn, and Peter Rafelson, my comanagers of Fem 2 Fem; the lovely Julie Ann, Christina, Lynn, Michelle, Lezlee, Alitzah, and LaLa, as well as Carl Strube and Gerry Brenner of Critique Records (who signed Fem 2 Fem), and Michael White for producing the Musical Voyeurz at the White Hall Theatre in London. I'm also appreciative of my friend and writing inspiration, Julia Cameron, whose book, *The Artist's Way*, got me back to writing. Also, many thanks go to my hairdressers, Sacha and Aaron Quarles.

I must also thank Danny Goldberg and David Silver for their support and encouragement; and Ed Gerrard, Daniel Markus, and Peter Himberger for hiring me to work with the Gipsy Kings (along with Pascal Imbert), and Sparky Neilson, the production manager. I am grateful for the wonderful time I had working with Olu Dara and the Okra Orchestra, Fu Manchu and Dan DeVita, along with crew Curly and Woody, and of course, Paul Rodgers and my present employers QPrime management and Crazy Town, especially Peter Mensch, H.M. Wollman, Tony DiCioccio and Randi of QPrime NY and Michelle and Erica of QPrime West, who've been invaluable in setting things up. Thanks also to Howard Wuelfing, Todd Horn, and Lee Ganz of Columbia Records New York and Stephanie Igunbor and Stephan Lange of Sony Europe for their help in guiding us smoothly through Europe. Much appreciation also for the Crazy Town road crew—Chris Warndahl, Skip Payatt, Jeff Chase, and Craig Underwood—along with band assistant Boom Boom Kaluna and crew bus driver Ted Foltman. Thanks also to Crazy Town travel agent Jason Ashbury of Lindon Travel in New York, and Julie Zemil of Uniworld Travel in Los Angeles.

Most of all, thanks to Jimmy Page, Robert Plant, John Paul Jones, John Bonham, and Peter Grant for the opportunity to work with the greatest rock and roll band of all time.

This book has been inspired in large part by the loving memory of John Henry Bonham. Bonham was a dear friend and the most talented drummer that rock music has ever seen.

—Richard Cole

Numerous people contributed to the research, organization, writing of and inspiration for this book, but several of them deserve special mention.

Richard Cole, of course, is foremost among them. He submitted to seemingly endless work sessions, dug up facts, went back to original sources—including his own astounding memory—and allowed the entire project to come together in a timely fashion.

Tom Miller and Jim Hornfischer, editors at HarperCollins, jumped into the manuscript with sharp pencils and even sharper suggestions. Josh Behar and April Benavides at HarperCollins were very helpful in preparing and editing this new edition of *Stairway to Heaven*.

My agent, Jane Dystel of Jane Dystel Literary Management, introduced me to Richard Cole. Throughout the duration of the research and writing, Jane provided constant encouragement and insightful input.

Finally, thanks to my parents, Bill and Ida, who have always believed in me; and to Donna, Melissa, and Mike for their love, affection, and support.

—Richard Trubo

INTRODUCTION:
THE ROCK REVOLUTION

On New Year's Day, 1962, when the Beatles walked into Decca's West Hampstead Studio Number Three on Broadhurst Gardens, rock music was forever changed. By the time they had finished recording an audition tape—with Paul McCartney crooning "Till There Was You" and John Lennon warbling "To Know Him Is to Love Him"—the Beatles had climbed aboard a musical fast track that literally revolutionized the cultural and social fabric stretching from Abbey Road to Hollywood and Vine.

Hundreds of British bands followed in the Beatles' wake. The Dave Clark Five. Herman's Hermits. The Rolling Stones. Finally, by the end of the sixties, the raw, back-breaking music of Led Zeppelin elevated the rock revolution to an absolutely manic pitch.

Before the dawning of the Zeppelin era, I had worked as tour manager with nearly a dozen other rock bands, helping to cultivate their talents, attend to their eccentricities, and nurse their egos. It was hard, often stressful work, but never boring. At times, I became exhausted; more often, I felt exhilarated. From the Who to Unit 4 + 2 . . . from the New Vaudeville Band to the Yardbirds . . . they were my boot camp that prepared me for my twelve-year tour of duty with Zeppelin.

I had grown up in Kensal Rise, a working-class neighborhood light years removed from Zeppelin's recording sessions at Headley Grange or the prestigious stage of Royal Albert Hall. My father was a metal architect who, just before World War II, helped build the elaborate doors on the Bank of England. He then went to work for Rolls-Royce making cars, and when the war began, he moved to the assembly line that manufactured aircraft. He could work miracles with his hands, but he was also much more of a scholar than I ever was, reading history just for the joy of it. While he reveled in stories about Gladstone and Disraeli, I was more interested in Presley and the Everlys. While I wanted to spend time in record stores, he took me to the British Museum and to the halls of Parliament.

My parents finally accepted where my real interests lay, and they bought me a record player when I was thirteen. Immediately, I began building a library of 45s by artists like Elvis, Ricky Nelson, Buddy Holly, and Chuck Berry. A few British singers captured my interest, too—Lonnie Donegan had several contagious tunes like "Rock Island Line"—but no one in England was quite as daring or provoked quite as much youthful hysteria as Little Richard when he sang "Good Golly, Miss Molly (She Sure Likes to Ball)."

Although I did reasonably well in school—particularly in subjects that I liked—education had never been a passport to success in my neighborhood. In fact, at age fifteen, as the new school term started, the headmaster suggested I might be better off going to work. As I soon discovered, however, the real world was hardly glamorous, at least not for a teenager with minimal skills. My first job was welding milk churns at a dairy supply company in Acton in Northwest London. It was hard, often dreary work, and it wasn't making me rich: For a forty-six-hour week, I earned just a little over three pounds, or about ten dollars.

All the while, however, my interest in rock music flourished. Songs like Roy Orbison's "Cryin'" and the Tokens' "The Lion Sleeps Tonight" got my adrenaline flowing and, for a time, even made me think that perhaps I could make a living as a musician. I finally bought myself an old drum set, hoping that I could unearth some latent musical talents.

Like millions of other teenagers, I developed a rich fantasy life. I could picture myself sprinting onto a stage, perching myself behind a kit of drums, and performing to the cheers of thousands of screaming fans, returning to the stage for encore after encore. It was a vision I replayed in my mind, again and again. Unfortunately, my talent was no match for those dreams. Much to my chagrin, after just a few hours of banging skins and crashing cymbals, I realized that Gene Krupa and Buddy Rich had no need to worry. Years later, neither would John Bonham.

With some apprehension, I began looking for a job with a future, which was a challenge for a kid from the wrong side of London. I jumped from one occupation to another, first delivering groceries, then working as an apprentice sheet-metal worker, and finally a carpenter. By age eighteen, I had gotten a job on the scaffold seven days a week—hard, dirty work that often involved the demolition of old buildings, mostly in Wembley and West End of London. The pay: Thirty pounds a week.

Eventually, it was my lust for club life that opened the doors to the music business. Beginning in 1962, I started hanging out at dance clubs in the West End, which were a crowded Mardi Gras of music and delicious-looking girls. Six nights a week, I binged and boozed from the State Ballroom to Saint Mary's Hall, from the 100 Club to the Marquee. It was wonderful just to be part of the action.

The early sixties were an exciting time when hundreds of rock and roll bands were descending upon London from throughout England, when the Rolling Stones and the Who still traveled in minivans and often played almost unnoticed for a handful of pound notes a night, and when Led Zeppelin was not even a figment of someone's imagination. In those days, from the outside looking in, I thought the rock music world looked incredibly glamorous, and I felt a bit of jealousy from my vantage point on the periphery. The young, aspiring musicians who would eventually evolve into bands like Zeppelin would crowd into the London clubs in those days, looking for a piece of the action, salivating at the chance to realize their own dreams, and aching to make connections that might turn them into the next Rock Superstars.

I routinely overdosed on this nightlife, never growing weary of the partying, the alcohol and drugs, the loud music, the easy girls. I also became absorbed in the youthful trends of the style-conscious young men of the times—some called Mods, others Rockers—who became as much a part of the London scene as Buckingham Palace and Westminster Abbey. We were kids from poor neighborhoods, most from the East End, others from South London. When the media were in a kind mood, they called us "trendsetters"; more often, we were "hoodlums" or "troublemakers," "malcontents" or "provocateurs." No matter what was written, the emotions running through this movement were universal: We were bursting with anger, furious about our economic circumstances. If you were to gather together a group of Mods or a group of Rockers, the energy created by their rage could have blown the Clock Tower off the Houses of Parliament.

As a way of setting ourselves apart from mainstream society, we conformed to particular types of fashions and aggressive, renegade attitudes and behavior. The Rockers were an outgrowth of the teddy boy hoods of the fifties. They were jeans and leather jackets and saw themselves as Brando-like nomads on their motorcycles. Their rivals, the Mods, had shorter hair and were impeccably dressed, with clothes custom-made at Carnaby Street shops, where a mass-produced, tailor-made pair of flared trousers cost about four pounds, and Fred Perry knit shirts became the "only" brand to wear.

I embraced the Mod look and lifestyle, one of thousands of Mods saturating the English landscape. We felt as if we were on the cutting edge of a social revolution, like we were Somebody. In Britain's class system, we may have been "have-nots," the forgotten generation, even outcasts, but together, we believed we were VIPs. We'd flex our rebellious muscles, sometimes impressing, sometimes intimidating others. We'd live for the moment, spending whatever money we had and ridiculing our parents' warnings to "save for a rainy day." And when my friends would say, "All I want to do is get drunk and have fun," I couldn't think of any better way to spend the night.

Neither the Mods nor the Rockers ever shied away from violence. The worst of it erupted at seaside resorts like Clacton, often on bank holidays or during Easter weekends. There really weren't any good reasons for those ugly confrontations; the violence was an end in itself, a chance to vent our frustrations and let off some steam. On one July night, we arrived in Clacton knowing the Rockers would be waiting for us, and we were equipped to fight with more than our fists. Our arsenal of weapons, in fact, might have made General Montgomery envious, with armor ranging from knives to pickaxes. The Rockers and the Mods congregated on opposite sides of the street, shouting epithets and then finally approaching one another. There were a few isolated confrontations here and there, and then a full-fledged brawl exploded in the middle of the street over the length of a block. For twenty minutes, it was absolute chaos. Brass knuckles connected with chins. Knives cut into skin. Blood splattered on the pavement. There were wails of anger and screams of pain.

Those kinds of riots made national and even international headlines ("The war of the teenage misfits"). One newspaper columnist warned, "The social fabric of England itself is disintegrating." But the more attention the Mods and the Rockers got, the more committed we became to a life-style—and to the rock music—that millions in Britain found repugnant.

About this same time, while the musicians who would eventually become Led Zeppelin were finding their niches in the music industry, I was finally getting my own initiation into the business. In 1964, I had just returned from a summer-long vacation in Spain—my first real exposure to what life was like beyond working-class London. And I came back feeling restless and hungry to find an escape from the hard, dirty life on the scaffold.

That opportunity finally presented itself at a club called the Flamingo in Soho, which was actually quite out of step with the times. While other clubs were preoccupied with the latest rock and pop music trends, the Flamingo was addicted to a soul and jazz sound. While its competitors were partial to the Beatles and the Dave Clark Five, the Flamingo embraced the music of Ray Charles and Marvin Gaye.

One of the Flamingo's regular bands was Ronnie Jones and the Nighttimers. The Nighttimers played a host of Otis Redding and Bobby "Blue" Bland tunes—"Respect," "Mr. Pitiful," "That's the Way Love Is," "Call on Me"—and other songs that reflected a rhythm and blues influence. I enjoyed their music, would hang around them before and after their gigs, and occasionally would talk to their road manager. I never really understood everything that he did, but his life seemed glamorous—certainly more exciting than my seven days a week on the scaffold.

One evening, I noticed that the Nighttimers themselves were packing their equipment into their van, a task that had always been taken care of by their road manager. I walked over to Mick Eve, a tall, thin saxophonist who was the Nighttimers' leader. Mick had once played with Georgie Fame and the Blue Flames, but just about the time Georgie started making big money—400 pounds a night as a headliner—Mick decided that the music had become too pop-oriented for his taste, and he broke away to start his own band.

"What happened to your roadie?" I asked.

"He's gone on to something else," Mick said.

"I'm looking for a job as a road manager," I told him.

"Do you know anything about it?"

Of course, I knew almost nothing. But I was desperate not to let this opportunity slip away. "Well, I can drive the van," I said, groping for some way to peak his interest. "I've traveled and I certainly know how to get around."

Then I remembered that for four weeks, I had once worked at a job soldering transistors. "And I know a lot about electronics, too," I added.

Mick gave me one of those looks that said, "Can't you do any better than that?" Then he said, "Well, I really don't feel that we need a road manager any longer."

"But you must need someone," I pleaded. "Otherwise, you wouldn't have had a road manager in the first place."

"But we never could pay him very much, Richard. He got one pound a night, and two pounds on the nights we did two shows. He averaged about seven pounds a week. The guy was always broke."

It wasn't a very appealing picture, particularly for someone like me who was already making thirty pounds a week on the scaffold. Even so, I had this seductive image of a road manager's life brimming with travel, heavy drinking, and lots of beautiful girls. And at the time, I couldn't think of a more perfect way to live.

"I'll take the job, Mick," I exclaimed, reaching to shake his hand before he could say a word. He nodded, although I'm not sure he was certain what he was agreeing to. But I couldn't have been more excited; I was finally in the music business.

The first show I did with the Nighttimers was on Boxing Day 1964, at the Carlton Ballroom on Kilburn High Road. We were one of the few rock bands that had ever been booked there, since the facilities were usually rented for Jamaican weddings or bar mitzvahs. In that initial gig, I told Mick, "I don't know whether we should be wearing dreadlocks or yarmulkes!" I don't think he ever got the joke.

Within those first few days, I discovered that the job as the Nighttimers' road manager wasn't that difficult for someone with a good head on his shoulders. There were hundreds of little clubs throughout England, and in my six months with the Nighttimers, we played a lot of them. I drove the band to and from their gigs in a small van, then set up their equipment and collected their box-office receipts, which were enough to pay expenses and not much more. Nevertheless, the job seemed to have much more potential for glamour than the scaffold.

After just two weeks with the Nighttimers, I was thoroughly won over by the music business—but I also knew that I wanted something more than to work for a small band. A friend of mine played with a group called the Chevelles, and one Sunday night, I went to see them open at the London Palladium for the Rolling Stones. That was the first time I had seen the Stones live, my first exposure to the fury, the frenzy, and the power of truly great performers. Girls in the audience were absolutely hysterical—screaming, crying, moaning, lunging toward the stage. Some even peed in their knickers, actually creating streams of water that, like the tributaries to the Mississippi, converged into a single river where the sloping seats joined the front of the stage. I had heard about bands making a splash, but this was unbelievable.

As I walked out of the Palladium that night, I muttered to myself, over and over, "Shit, that is some fucking band." I promised myself to reach higher than the Nighttimers. Even the Beatles need road managers, I reasoned, so I set my goals at the top.

Before long, I had moved on to other bands, first Unit 4 + 2, a bunch of middle-class kids who had turned a recording contract into a number one record, "Concrete and Clay," in 1965, followed by another hit, "I've Never Been in Love Like This Before," that reached number eight. They weren't the Stones, but it was definitely a move up for me.

During my tenure with Unit 4 + 2, I continued to keep in contact with the Nighttimers, who had acquired a new keyboard player named John Paul Jones. John Paul was the first future Zeppelin member who I got to know, although at the time our relationship consisted of little more than "hellos" and small talk. Even back then, Jonesy was quiet, never had much to say, never wasted words. But his talent and intuitive skills on the Hammond organ were impressive. "You're too good for this band," I told him. "One of these days, you're going to hook up with a group where you can really show off your talents." At the time, neither of us realized how prophetic that statement would be.

On my nights off, I went back to club-hopping in the West End. One night at the Scene, I caught a band called the High Numbers. The drummer, Keith Moon, attacked his drums like a madman. The guitarist, Peter Townshend, had arms as animated as a windmill, whipping, wheeling, and then leaning into C chords with the energy of a hurricane. He would strike the guitar strings so forcefully and wildly that his fingertips were worn ragged, occasionally even oozing with blood. It was a hemophiliac's nightmare.

Before long, the High Numbers became the rage among the Mods. Later, they would change their name to the Who and help write an important chapter in rock history. When I began working for them in 1965 and 1966, it was like going from junk food to caviar.

I never really got tired of watching the Who perform. In the course of a ninety-minute performance, they could electrify crowds with their music and shock audiences with their antics, while sending critics scouring their thesauruses looking for just the right adjective, just the right verb to describe what was taking place. Just when you thought the Who was the most disciplined, masterful band you had ever seen and heard, the musicians had a chameleon's gift for instantly transforming themselves into raving, deranged lunatics. All in a night's work.

At times, the anarchy that accompanied the music often became frightening. Consider the night in 1965 when the Who was performing at a London club called the Railway Tavern, not far from the tube station at Harrow & Wealdstone. As a couple hundred fans jammed into the tiny hall, tempers in the audience flared and there was pushing and shoving throughout the show. Since I was responsible for the safety of the band, the unrest in the crowd had me pacing backstage, nervous that a full-blown riot might erupt.

Near the end of the performance, Peter whirled his guitar and accidentally struck its neck on a very low ceiling above the stage. It happened with such force that the neck fractured. Peter stood stunned for just a moment, surveying the damage. Then he shouted, "Goddamn it!," gritted his teeth, and erupted in wild anger, suddenly flailing the guitar furiously and recklessly. Like a ballplayer armed with a Louisville Slugger, he swung it first in one direction, then in another, striking it on the ground, then smashing it on the amplifiers, banging the floor once more, then using the guitar as a battering ram against the amps, pummeling them again and again, progressively obliterating both the guitar and the sound system. As the demolition continued, the crowd—already on the brink of hysteria—roared its approval.

After that initial outburst, Townshend never looked back. In the closing number of subsequent shows—as the final chords of "My Generation" or "Anyway, Anyhow, Anywhere" were reverberating—audiences began to expect Peter to decimate his high-voltage, high-priced guitars, hammering them into the amplifiers, splintering them onto the floor, pulverizing them with the subtlety of a 747 slamming into the Empire State Building. Peter came to get a real kick out of it, amused that he could incite the crowd, work them up, and push them over the edge, just for the price of a guitar or two.

On occasion, Moonie would escalate the frenzy for the fun of it. He'd heave his drums across the stage, kick holes in the skins, snap drumsticks, stomp on cymbals, and annihilate what was left into toothpicks. It was a scene more appropriate for an insane asylum than a rock club.

Although audiences relished these frenzied episodes of destruction, they weren't something the Who could really afford to do every night. Perhaps a band like Led Zeppelin, or even the Who after it had achieved more fame, could absorb the costs of those kinds of outbursts. But in 1965 and 1966, when I was on the road with the band, these hurricanes of destruction ran up enormous debts. It wasn't like replacing a few guitar strings a week; Townshend and Moonie were mutilating expensive instruments and, in the process, the band's balance sheet, too. In those days, the Who was earning about 300 to 500 pounds a night, but that could be eaten up quickly by the replacement of a guitar (200 pounds), a kit of drums (100 pounds), and new amps (350 to 400 pounds). At one point, the Who was nearly 60,000 pounds in debt. You don't have to be Einstein to figure out that the band was committing fiscal suicide. And it created enormous tension within the band.

Particularly in the beginning, John Entwistle and Roger Daltrey were horrified at the destructive onslaughts and what they were costing the band. "This is absolutely ridiculous," John shouted at Peter one evening. "We lose money every night we play! We'd come out ahead just by not showing up!"

Peter couldn't be bothered with that kind of logic. "Fuck off!" he yelled back at Entwistle. "This is something we do! It's part of the show. The fans love it. So accept it!"

I stayed out of those battles. I knew Entwistle was right, but I was in no position to intervene. The dissension within the band, however, concerned me. How long can a band last, I asked myself, when everyone is at each other's throat?

Eventually, Entwistle stopped complaining, figuring that he was wasting his energy and that he'd never be able to control Townshend anyway. Fortunately, as the band began to earn more money, the destruction became a more tolerable business expense and little stood in the way of the Who's success.

In the early months of 1966, drugs and alcohol were becoming as important as anything else in my life. As exhilarating as the Who's music was, it was taking a backseat to the next handful of pills, which were an easy source of pleasure. In the process, however, the drugs were starting to seriously affect Moonie and me in particular, with both of us experiencing frequent and frightening blackouts. At that point, I began to feel that my days with the Who were numbered.

In August 1966, I was driving through London at high speeds, swerving past everyone else on the road—except for a policeman whose siren and flashing red light convinced me to pull over to the curb. It was my third speeding ticket, and two days later in court, my driver's license was revoked. Because so much of my job with the Who consisted of driving the van and transporting the band from one gig to another, they had to find someone to replace me. I was furious about losing the job, but if anyone was to blame, it was me.

In my last few days with the Who, they performed at a charity event at the 10,000-seat Wembley Empire Pool, sharing the bill with the biggest acts in rock music: the Beatles, the Rolling Stones, the Yardbirds, the Animals, the Walker Brothers, and Lulu. The Who performed just before the Stones, and they were magnificent—from "La La La Lies" to "The Good's Gone," from "Much Too Much" to "My Generation." Even so, when the Stones and the Beatles closed out the show, performing back-to-back, almost everyone forgot that the other bands had shown up at all. As Mick Jagger pranced across the stage, unleashing his high-energy Lucifer of Rock spectacle, I thought to myself, "How can anyone top this?"

Thirty minutes later, the Beatles did. John, Paul, George, and Ringo came onstage, and the roof nearly lifted off the hall. "I Feel Fine" . . . "Ticket to Ride" . . . "We Can Work It Out" . . . "She Loves You" . . . "A Hard Day's Night." Fortunately, they played only a twenty-minute set; if it were any longer, the crowd of 10,000 might have experienced a communal cardiac arrest. It was an exciting, exhilarating, and thoroughly exhausting evening.

Once again, my appetite was whetted for something bigger. I knew I wanted to stay in this business, and felt I was ready for more than the Who. Led Zeppelin was still two years away, and until then, I worked with a number of other artists and bands, including the Yardbirds, the Jeff Beck Group, Vanilla Fudge, the Young Rascals, the Searchers, the New Vaudeville Band, and Terry Reid. But they were all just stepping-stones to Zeppelin. For me—and for millions of fans—Led Zeppelin would ultimately evolve into the best that rock music had to offer.

CRASH LANDING

Richard, something bad has happened to one of your Led Zeppelin boys."

Julio Gradaloni had a grim expression on his face as he nervously shuffled through his briefcase, finally pulling out a newspaper and placing it on the table in front of us.

"What do you mean?" I asked him, feeling some anxiety starting to chill my body. "What's happened?"

Julio was my attorney, a stocky, no-nonsense lawyer in his middle fifties. He was sitting across from me in the visiting room at Rebibia Prison near Rome. I had been imprisoned there for nearly two months—on suspicion of terrorism, of all things. During those weeks behind bars, I was bewildered and frustrated, desperately and futilely trying to convince the police and prosecutors that my arrest had been some kind of blunder, that I was no more likely to blow up buildings in Italy than would the Pope himself. But on this particular morning in late September 1980, Julio took my mind off my own problems.

"One of your musicians has died," Julio said, trying to remain as composed as possible.

"Died!" I froze. After nearly twelve years as tour manager of Led Zeppelin, the four members of the band—Jimmy Page, Robert Plant, John Paul Jones, and John Bonham—had become like brothers to me.

Neither Julio nor I said anything for a few seconds. Then I stammered, "Was it—was it Pagey?" Jimmy is so frail, I thought, so weak. Maybe the cocaine, the heroin had finally taken their toll. Jimmy's body must have just given out.

Julio wasn't making eye contact, perusing the Italian newspaper, preparing to translate the article about Led Zeppelin for me.

"No," he said in a steady tone of voice. "Not Jimmy Page. Here's what the article says. 'John Bonham, drummer of Led Zeppelin, was found dead yesterday in the home of another member of the world-famous rock band. . . .' "

Julio continued to read. But after that first sentence, I stopped hearing his words. I became numb, braced my hands against the table, and bowed my head. I swallowed hard, and could feel my heart palpitating.

"Bonham is dead," I began repeating silently to myself. "Shit, I just can't believe it. Not Bonzo. Why Bonzo?"

I leaned back in my chair. There must be some mistake, I thought. It doesn't make sense. He's so strong. What could possibly kill him?

I interrupted Julio in midsentence. "Does the newspaper say what he died of? Was it drugs?"

"Well," Julio said, "they don't know yet. But they say he had used a lot of alcohol that day. It sounds like he drank himself to death."

Julio tried to change the subject. He wanted to talk with me about my own case. But I just couldn't. "Let's do it another day, Julio," I mumbled. "I'm not thinking too clearly right now."

I barely remember walking back to my cell. I crawled onto my bunk and stared silently at the sixteen-foot-high ceilings. I had this queasy feeling in my gut while pondering life without Bonham . . . without those high-voltage drum solos, his contagious laugh, and the sense of adventure that propelled us through many long nights of revelry.

"Are you all right?" one of my cell mates, Pietro, finally asked over the din of a nearby transistor radio.

"I'm not sure," I told him. "One of my friends has died."

My cell mates tried to be comforting, but I wasn't particularly receptive to their words. Finally, with an onslaught of emotions rushing through me, I snapped. Throwing a pillow against one of the walls, I shouted, "Damn it! Here I am rotting in this fucking jail for something I didn't do! I wasn't even with my friend when he died!"

I began pacing the cell. "Maybe I could have done something to help him. Maybe I could have kept him from self-destructing."

It had already been a difficult two months in that prison cell. I had been put through a forced withdrawal from a heroin addiction, enduring many uncomfortable days and nights of nausea, muscle cramps, body aches, and diarrhea, while trying to figure out how I was going to extricate myself from the bum rap that had put me behind bars. One minute, I had been relaxing at the

Excelsior, one of Rome's most elegant hotels; the next, policemen with their guns drawn had burst into my room, accusing me of a terrorist attack that had occurred 150 miles away. Since then, my day-to-day existence had become difficult—even before the stunning news about John Bonham.

In the days and weeks after Bonzo's death, I received several letters from Unity MacLaine, my secretary in Zeppelin's office. "The coroner's report," she wrote, "says that Bonzo suffocated on his own vomit. It says he had downed 40 shots of vodka that night. They call it an 'accidental death.' "

Bonham had died at Jimmy's home, the Old Mill House, in Windsor—a home Pagey had purchased earlier in the year from actor Michael Caine. The band had congregated there on September 24 to begin rehearsals for an upcoming American tour, scheduled to start in mid-October 1980. Beginning early that afternoon, John had started drinking vodkas and orange juices at a nearby pub before overindulging in double vodkas at Jimmy's home. His behavior became erratic, loud, and abrasive. He bitched about being away from home during the nineteen-date American tour.

When John finally passed out well past midnight, Rick Hobbs, Jimmy's valet and chauffeur, helped him into bed. Rick positioned the Zeppelin drummer on his side, placed a blanket over him, and quietly closed the bedroom door.

The next afternoon, John Paul Jones and Benji Le Fevre, one of the band's roadies, tiptoed into the bedroom where Bonham was sleeping. Benji shook Bonzo, first gently, then more vigorously, but was unable to arouse him. Panicking, Benji feverishly checked Bonham's vital signs. But there were none. He wasn't breathing. He didn't have a pulse. His body was cold.

When the ambulance arrived, the attendants repeatedly tried to resuscitate Bonham as his fellow musicians looked on in horror. Nothing worked. He may have been dead for hours.

After a lengthy voyage that began in 1968, Led Zeppelin had crash-landed. This was the band that had redefined success in rock music, whose record sales and concert receipts turned them into overnight millionaires and the biggest drawing card in rock music. This was the band that played such high-spirited, dynamic, wall-to-wall music—and performed with such confidence and such charisma—that concert tours were sold out just hours after tickets went on sale. Standing ovations and endless encores became ordinary. Harems of excited young girls—whose adrenaline would surge at the mere mention of Led Zeppelin—fought for the chance to fulfill the band's every sexual fantasy and fly with them on their private jet, the *Starship*, where a bedroom provided privacy, and drugs and booze helped heighten their senses.

I had been Led Zeppelin's tour manager from the beginning, since their first American concert at the Denver Coliseum in 1968, where they opened for Vanilla Fudge. Over the course of the next twelve years, I had been with them on every tour and at every concert until almost the end—scheduling flights and hotel accommodations, helping to choose concert sites, planning details from the size of the stage to the height of the crash barriers, providing show-no-mercy, paramilitarylike security, escorting girls to the rooms of the band members, and keeping Zeppelin nourished with drugs. In the process, I had seen them evolve into a powerhouse force in the music industry.

But John Bonham's death proved that there was nothing omnipotent about Led Zeppelin. Their music might live forever, but they had paid a terrible price.

THE DOWNFALL

I saw John Bonham for the last time just days before I had left for Italy in summer 1980. We met at a pub called the Water Rat on the King's Road, after an evening rehearsal in which the band was preparing for a summer European tour. While John and I drank Brandy Alexanders, I grumbled about Peter Grant, the band's manager, sending me to Italy to kick my heroin habit rather than accompanying the band on their upcoming tour.

"Don't worry," John said, "you'll get off that shit and be back with us before the summer's over."

When we left the pub, John took me for a ride in a Ferrari Daytona Spider convertible he had bought two days before. As he dropped me off in front of the pub, I turned to Bonzo.

"Do you realize that this European tour will be the first Zeppelin gigs I've ever missed?" I told John. "I hope you bastards miss me."

Bonzo smiled. "Very unlikely, Cole," he quipped. "Don't count on it." Then he asked, "How pissed off are you at Peter?"

"*Very* pissed off. But I also know that I need to get off smack once and for all. And so do you, Bonzo."

Bonham laughed. "It's not a problem for me," he said with exuberance. "If it becomes a problem, I'll just quit!"

Even though I wanted to go on the European tour, I also recognized that I was losing interest. As good as Led Zeppelin's music continued to be, I could see the organization beginning to suffocate in its own personal turmoil. For me, the hassles were starting to outweigh the joys.

In the early years of Zeppelin, we had been a close, six-man unit, with Peter and me providing the support for the four musicians. There was real joy in seeing the fame of the band mushroom so quickly, which translated into enormous financial rewards and the chance to live an incredible fantasy life-style that a bunch of musicians from mostly working-class backgrounds found irresistible and intoxicating.

But from the inside, the signs of Led Zeppelin's disintegration began to surface in the late 1970s. Jimmy, Bonzo, and I were becoming increasingly caught up in the quagmire of drugs, enough to really anger Robert and John Paul. "You're one of the people in charge of this operation," Robert once told me. "And it makes us nervous to see what's going on. Can't you see what's happening?"

I thought Robert was crazy. From the earliest years, Zeppelin's concert tours had always been drenched in alcohol . . . champagne, beer, wine, Scotch, Jack Daniels, gin . . . and brimming with drugs, even though we rarely paid for any of the illegal substances. Drugs for the band were often given to me by fans, by friends, who would knock on my hotel room door, hand me a bagful of cocaine or marijuana, and say something like, "We have a present for you." The band rarely turned anything down.

When Bonzo, Jimmy, and I began using smack, no one aggressively inter-vened, even when it started having a noticeable impact. Jimmy became so caught up in his drug habit that he sometimes showed up an hour or two late for rehearsals. Bonzo's behavior, already unpredictable, became more volatile. As for me, I was buying heroin from dealers within a few hundred feet of Peter's office in London and was becoming less attentive to my day-to-day responsibilities in the Zeppelin organization. I still felt I was in control, but I wasn't; I'm sure Bonham and Pagey were deteriorating, too.

By 1980, Peter and I were constantly at each other's throats. Peter never fired me, but we weren't getting along at all. He was fed up with my heroin habit and gave me an ultimatum.

"Pick where you want to go to clean yourself up, and I'll pay for it," Peter said. "But you're not going to bring down this organization with you."

At times, the thought of getting away actually sounded appealing. Par-ticularly while we were on tour, Peter wanted to know where I was and what I was doing at every moment of every day. I felt I was on the spot all the time, and I didn't like it. "Why are you bugging me?" I would scream at him. My drug use was making me paranoid.

I even thought of quitting. But at the same time, I was unwilling to give up the glamorous life-style of limousines, luxurious hotel suites, drugs, and groupies.

Peter was an intimidating presence, a mammoth man, overweight, with an unkempt beard and a fast-receding hairline. More important, he was a hands-on, loyal manager who knew every twist and turn of the music industry. He deserved nearly as much credit for the band's international success as the musicians themselves.

As for Bonham, I began seeing a very nasty side of him at times—an anger built on frustration—that grew out of his own mixed feelings about Led Zeppelin itself. He loved playing with the world's number one band, and he glowed when critics called him the top drummer in the business. But with increasing frequency, he resented having to go out on the road or showing up for a particular concert when he just wasn't in the mood. Like the rest of the band, Bonham no longer needed to play for the money. So when his state of mind just wasn't in sync with catching a plane to the next gig—when his big heart and his loneliness for his family would make him ache to be back home—he would say to me, "It's becoming harder to be somewhere where I don't want to be. I'll follow through because people are depending on me. But someday soon, I'm going to give it all up. I have to."

Bonham's thirty-minute drum solos—which sometimes left the drumskins torn and his hands bloodied—were a way of getting out all that anger and all that pain.

Jimmy Page was just as complex, although his commitment to the band never wavered. Because Zeppelin was his baby, his creation, his enthusiasm remained strong. But his health was a constant worry to those of us around him, thanks to a vegetarian diet that sometimes bordered on malnutrition. He appeared frail and was more prone to colds than the rest of us. Still, his passion never ebbed onstage.

Jimmy and I were very close during the early days of Zeppelin, although we spent much less time together in the later years. Offstage, we had once shared an excitement for art collecting, but as I began spending more of my money on drugs, I could no longer afford to indulge my own artistic interests, and so Jimmy and I drifted apart. He never seemed particularly impressed with his own wealth, perceiving it as a means of buying him seclusion—and maintaining his cocaine and heroin habits. But more than anything, music and Led Zeppelin were his real loves.

Through all the band's travails, John Paul Jones somehow emerged unscathed. When he dabbled in drugs, it seemed to be more out of curiosity than anything else, and never to excess. He was almost always level-headed and in control. He was also reclusive, even on the road, often content to be by himself, away from the chaos and the excesses that he may have seen bringing Led Zeppelin down. He avoided much of the band's craziness, and his marriage survived intact after all the years of touring; his wife and children seemed to be enough for him.

"Richard," he would sometimes say on the road, "here's the phone number where I'll be for the next forty-eight hours; unless there's an absolute emergency, don't tell anyone—and I do mean *anyone*—how to reach me."

Peter would become outraged when John Paul would disappear. But perhaps Jonesy was smarter than any of us, keeping his distance while the rest of us were gradually sinking in the quicksand.

Until Bonham's death, I had always felt that Robert Plant had borne most of the brunt of any negative energy that may have surrounded Led Zeppelin. From the beginning, through his soulful singing, I knew there was a sensitive side to Robert. So I wasn't surprised to see him emotionally devastated in 1975 when his wife, Maureen, nearly died from internal injuries and multiple fractures in an automobile accident on the Greek island of Rhodes or two years later, when his son, Karac, died of a serious respiratory infection. At Karac's funeral, Robert was stoic and composed through the services. But later that afternoon, Bonham and I sat with him on a grassy field on Jennings Farm, Robert's home near Birmingham. As each of us drank from a bottle of whiskey, Robert opened up, bewildered by the tragedies in his life and where Led Zeppelin was headed.

Clearly, Robert was hurt that Jimmy, John Paul, and Peter hadn't been by his side during his son's burial. "Maybe they don't have as much respect for me as I do for them," he said in a pained, monotone voice. "Maybe they're not the friends I thought they were."

A few minutes later, Robert pondered all of our pasts and futures. "We couldn't ask for any more success than we've had," he said. "Professionally, we couldn't ask for more. But where the hell has it gotten us? Why do these terrible things keep happening? What the hell is going on?"

They were questions without answers.

And then Bonham died. In my prison cell, I found myself reflecting upon the talk of a Zeppelin "jinx" that had haunted the band for years. It was something that disc jockeys and fans discussed much more than any of us did. When the subject did come up, we mostly just scoffed at it.

"It's bullshit," Jimmy once said angrily. "People take my interest in the occult and give it a life of its own."

Because the band rarely made efforts to court the press and discuss the intimate details of their lives with reporters, there was a mystique that surrounded the band that tended to fuel the rumors of a curse. "Let them think whatever they want," Jimmy said. "If the fans want to believe all the rumors, let them. A little mystery can't hurt."

The most ominous rumor was elevated to mythological status. It proclaimed that in their earliest days, the band members—except for John Paul, who refused to participate—had made a secret pact among themselves, selling their souls to the devil in exchange for the band's enormous success. It was a blood ritual, so the story went, that placed a demonic curse upon the band that would ultimately lead to the deflating of the Zeppelin. And perhaps to the death of the band members themselves.

To my knowledge, no such pact ever existed. Jimmy was a great one for spinning yarns, especially with young ladies who were fascinated with the "dark" side of the band, so maybe that's how the story got started. But despite Jimmy's preoccupation with the supernatural, he rarely discussed his dabbling in the occult with the rest of the band. One of our roadies once said to me, "I tried to broach the subject once, and Jimmy went into a rage. I'd never raise the issue again."

Jimmy was fascinated with the whole idea of black magic, and in the hours after learning of Bonzo's death, I began to wonder just how powerful his obsessions were. Jimmy owned a home that once belonged to Aleister Crowley, the British poet who experimented with spells, rituals, séances, heroin, and "sexual magick." Jimmy's neighbors were convinced that the house was haunted, and they told stories about a young man who was once decapitated there, with his head rolling down the stairs like a basketball.

After Bonzo died, the London tabloids had a field day. They blared with headlines like "A Jinx Haunts Led Zeppelin." According to one British reporter, "Bonham died as retribution for guitarist Jimmy Page's obsession with the occult."

Jimmy became furious with that kind of journalism. "They just don't know what they're talking about," he roared. "They should keep their ignorance to themselves."

As I sat in my cell, my thoughts kept returning to the possibility of a hex. Was Led Zeppelin susceptible to cataclysms because of some type of undefinable evil force? Was Jimmy's fascination with the occult somehow responsible? Or had our own hard living and personal excesses finally caught up with us?

Whatever the reason, I knew that Led Zeppelin would never be the same, if the band survived at all. Even before Bonham's death, during those first few weeks in the Italian prison, I had tried to deal with my predicament by repeatedly telling myself, "This is going to be over any day. I'll be out of here, I'll be off heroin, and I'll join the band for their American tour. Things will be good again, just like they had been in the early days."

But John Bonham's death forced me back to reality. Not only would I have to deal with my grief over the loss of a friend, but I knew Led Zeppelin itself was finished. Over the years, even though the band had never talked about anyone dying, they realized there was the possibility that one of them might decide to leave the group.

"If that happens," Jimmy said matter-of-factly, "that will be the end of Led Zeppelin. The organization will close down. Why bother going on after that?"

Bonham was such an integral part of the band. He and Robert in particular had known each other as young musicians, years before Led Zeppelin. And although they had their fights and disagreements—usually over petty matters like who was going to pay for the petrol in one of their cars—they had a strong emotional bond. I couldn't imagine Robert singing with anyone other than Bonham behind him. It would be like trying to drive a car with three wheels. When Karac died, Robert had put his arms around Bonham at the funeral and said, "You're my oldest mate, Bonzo; I can count on you to always be there for me, can't I?"

Jimmy put it bluntly: "It would be an insult to find a replacement for John Bonham in order to keep Led Zeppelin aloft."

3

ROBERT

Robert, why would you want to waste your life in a rock band? You have an opportunity for a wonderful education and a good career. Don't let yourself get sidetracked. Don't blow it."

The words were spoken by Robert Plant, Sr., whose son was itching for a life as a rock singer. For the elder Plant—a civil engineer who felt more comfortable with Beethoven than the Beatles—his son's musical ambitions were becoming his own nightmare. He could not tolerate his boy wasting his life chasing impossible dreams.

Robert Sr. spent many idle, anxious hours wondering how to steer his son back toward a more "respectable" life and career. All the while, the younger Plant was making his own homemade instruments (harmonicas and kazoos) and treating each as if it were a Stradivarius. While his dad was dejected over Robert's disinterest in making the most of his education, the teenager was poising himself in front of a mirror, teaching himself to sing by imitating Elvis records.

Most of the rock musicians—from the Beatles to the Stones to Led Zeppelin—who emerged in the sixties came from a working-class background. Their parents had survived the terrors and the heartaches of World War II—including Germany's savage bombing of London that ignited the city in flames and left much of it in ruins. The British economy had been devastated as well by years of war, and it struggled to recover. For many young musicians in Britain—who had grown up in households listening to Frank Sinatra and the Stan Kenton Orchestra—rock music became not only a way they might escape poverty, but it was their form of rebellion, too, a means of lashing out at the middle- and upper-class traditions that, to them, represented the oppression and the pain they and their families had endured. As the years progressed, rock music increasingly became one of their most potent weapons in the rebellion.

But while rock music may have primarily been the domain of the underclass, the Plants were purely middle class. Born in 1948 in West Bromwich, Staffordshire, and growing up in the west Midlands in the small rural town of Kidderminster, Robert had a background that was so highbrow that in the earliest days of Led Zeppelin, he used to look a bit disdainfully at the rest of us "commoners." He never said much that was condescending, but he sometimes seemed to breathe arrogance, as though he were a cut above us.

Robert attended King Edward VI grammar school in Stourbridge, where schoolboy pranks were part of his way of life. One afternoon, he concealed a pair of tennis shoes inside a piano, making it impossible for the teacher to play—a caper that got him expelled from the music program, which was the class he most loved.

Beginning at age fourteen, Robert let his hair grow (ostensibly to attract girls) and started playing with rock bands. He began spending less time on his schoolwork, although he did show some interest in subjects like archeology. More than anything, he felt driven to pursue his musical interests, even if his family reacted skeptically to them.

At one point, Robert Sr. hoped that his son would eventually get his musical passions out of his system. He used to drop his boy off at gigs at the Seven Stars Blues Club, where the teenager sang with the Delta Blues Band, accompanied by Chris Wood's flute and Terry Foster's eight-string guitar. When the songs were familiar, the crowd cheered and the young singer became ecstatic. But Robert was also inclined to introduce blues songs by unknowns like Blind Boy Fuller, hushing the audience and leaving them as bewildered as if he were performing *Carmen* or *Madama Butterfly*.

Robert was bright enough to realize that his odds of achieving success were slim. "Even the most talented singers usually don't make it," he said. "I'll give myself till the age of twenty; if I'm still struggling by then, I'll move on to something else."

Robert bounded from one band to another: The Crawling King Snakes (named after a John Lee Hooker song) . . . Black Snake Moan (named after a tune by Blind Lemon Jefferson) . . . the New Memphis Bluesbreakers. As he played this version of musical hopscotch, his voice began to get more attention. It literally brought people through the doors to hear that soulful, sensitive, powerful voice.

"Maybe something's starting to happen," Robert told his friends, jacking up his hopes as he sang before full houses. But despite the increasing recognition, he still had to deal with more disappointments.

In 1966, after joining a band called Listen, some scouts from CBS Records liked what they heard. They were awestruck by Robert's strong voice and nearly as impressed with his nonstop body gyrations on stage. CBS signed the band to record three singles, the first of which was a slick remake of the Young Rascals hit "You Better Run." It was released with little fanfare, however, and attracted even less attention from radio stations and record buyers. It was a brutal introduction to the music industry.

Robert was discouraged but not defeated by the lack of recognition the record received. "It'll happen," he told friends, trying to keep his own confidence level high. "I believe in myself, and that's half the battle." In fact, he was battling his own inner turmoil, beginning to wonder if anything would ever really start to break in his favor.

In 1967, CBS Records asked Robert to record two additional singles to fulfill its contract with Listen. It seemed like a wonderful opportunity—the chance to go into the studio on his own. But Robert's excitement was crushed by CBS's selection of the songs he would record. One of them, "Our Song," was a lushly orchestrated Italian ballad for which English lyrics had been written. One of Robert's friends said, "What the hell are they trying to do to him? Turn Robert into the next Tom Jones?" Robert was embarrassed by the record. He almost felt like going into hiding or personally melting down all the vinyl on which it was pressed. His instincts about it may have been correct: "Our Song" sold an unremarkable 800 copies as the record company did, in fact, try to promote him as a Tom Jones incarnate—a campaign about as successful as the Edsel. At least for the moment, a very downcast Robert saw his recording career hit a nasty brick wall.

"If my mom hadn't bought a copy of the records, the damn things wouldn't have sold at all," Robert joked. He wasn't exaggerating by much.

During this time, despite his middle-class background, Robert became a Mod, wearing Chelsea boots and snugfitting jackets and joining battles with Rockers in the borough of Margate. He also cut his long, blond locks into a French style that he patterned after Steve Marriott, the lead singer of Small Faces, who had posed the compelling musical question, "How's your bird's lumbago?" during a concert Robert attended in Birmingham.

With Robert's musical career sputtering, his parents tried again to steer him in more traditional directions. "Why don't you study to become a chartered accountant?" his worried mother suggested. Robert was dejected enough already—and now this!

Even though Robert was intelligent enough to recognize that he might be reaching for an impossible dream, he was upset with the lack of support from his parents in his musical pursuits. He still thought he had a shot at stardom, even while his mom and dad wondered whether he would ever outgrow his "fantasies" about making a career in music. He felt frustrated, hurt, and sometimes angry. At times when he was home, he sensed a growing emotional wedge between him and his parents. On some level, he desperately wanted to prove to them that he could succeed in music.

Nevertheless, to make peace in the family, Robert finally agreed to some accountant's training, even though his heart was still possessed by blues performers like Robert Johnson, Tommy McClellan, Otis Rush, Muddy Waters, and Sonny Boy Williamson, whose records he often found in the junk shops he used to scour.

After just two weeks of accountant's training, Robert threw in the towel. He was being paid a forgettable two pounds a day, but even more important, he realized that there was much more to life than ledgers and balance sheets. "I just don't want to spend my whole life counting *other* people's money!" he complained to friends. "I'd rather be the one *making* the money!"

Without any regrets, Robert shifted his full attention back to music. As before, he jumped from one band to another, ending up with a group called the Band of Joy. Like Robert's earlier musical ventures, however, this one had only minimal success. The gigs came much too infrequently, and most of them played to half-empty houses. As if Robert wasn't feeling bad enough, he was constantly at odds with the band's manager.

"Do you know what the problem is, Robert?" the band's manager asked him one day. "I don't think you sing very well! You might think seriously about leaving the band."

Robert left in a rage with his ego bruised. Yes, his voice was a bit wild, but he felt there was something unique about it, too. He tried to deflect the criticism, not let it grate upon him, but it was hard. He was determined to keep on going, even though his voice wasn't making him any money. He held onto the group's name, and the Band of Joy soon re-formed in a second—and then eventually a third—generation that went off in a number of unexpected directions. The last incarnation featured a zany, long-haired, mustachioed drummer named John Bonham, who was never fully content with the enormous power and fury he used to bring to his performing. To create even more gusto, Bonham would line his drums with aluminum foil to give them more of a crackling, explosive sound—and hopefully to attract more public attention to the group.

But, in fact, the Band of Joy had to resort to much more to win the hearts of its audiences. The members of the band sometimes performed with painted faces. They wore long tailcoats. They staged miniwars with one another, using toy machine guns. The overweight bass player, attired in a caftan and bell-bottom pants, would swan dive from the stage into the crowd, creating terror on the faces of its members, who must have thought the *Hindenburg* (or was it the *Zeppelin?*) was crashing upon them. If there was a message he was trying to communicate, no one could quite figure out what it was.

One night as the Band of Joy performed at Victoria Hall in Selkirk, an inebriated member of the audience heaved a pie at Plant. Since Robert was a constantly moving target, the pie splattered harmlessly a few feet from him.

"The Band of Joy played about two gigs a week, but we weren't making much money," recalled Robert a few years later. "If I hadn't been married by then, and my wife, Maureen, didn't have a job, I wouldn't have eaten. It was that simple. I would have been in the welfare lines."

In a sense, Maureen was Robert's savior, and he knew it. Without her financial support—not to mention her emotional support—he might have given up long before anyone had ever heard of Led Zeppelin. He had met her at a Georgie Fame concert, and they began living together shortly thereafter and eventually got married. When Robert wasn't bringing home any money, she made sure they still had a roof over their heads. When his self-confidence wavered, she helped stabilize it. He often said that if it hadn't been for Maureen, he might have gone nuts.

The Band of Joy continued to struggle. They worked their way up to about seventy quid a night, played songs by Sonny Boy Williamson and the Grateful Dead and even recorded a few demos at the Regent Sound studios. But much to their frustration, they never landed a recording contract. Finally, disheartened that the band wasn't going anywhere, Robert decided that the battle wasn't worth fighting anymore. The Band of Joy disbanded.

Once again, Robert was faced with making some hard decisions about his future. In early 1967, he did some construction work, pouring asphalt along West Bromwich High Street and using his earnings (six shillings tuppence an hour) to buy Buffalo Springfield, Love, and Moby Grape albums. Most of the British rock scene, he thought, was an embarrassment and barely worth the vinyl on which the records were pressed. But the Grape—with its combination of blues, folk, rock, r&b, country, and bluegrass—left Robert humming and itching to get back to music, much to his parents' continued distress.

Even long after Led Zeppelin had turned Robert into a millionaire, a reconciliation with his father took years. Robert's dad still had trouble accepting his son's rock music career, even with the enormous success—a fact of life that troubled Robert a lot. At a social function in Birmingham, I was chatting with the elder Plant and offered him a bottle of beer—with no glass. He looked at me with disgust, as if to say, "Who the hell do you think I am that I would drink out of a bottle?" He was from a different world.

4

BONZO

John Bonham was as down-to-earth as they came. For as long as I knew him, there weren't pretensions that needed to be peeled away to get to the real Bonham. All the loudness, all the craziness, all the wit, and all the talent were all Bonzo. What you saw was what you got.

As a child, long before John had become the drummer with the Band of Joy or Led Zeppelin, he was banging on just about anything that could make noise. Born in 1948 in Redditch—about twelve miles south of Birmingham—he would pound on his mother's pots and pans or on a round coffee tin that had a wire attached to it in an attempt to mimic the sound of a snare drum.

Bonham's mother bought him his first real drum at age ten, and before long, his father brought home a full drum kit, secondhand and a bit worn. That drum set may have been rusty, but John absolutely treasured it. He would become upset when some of his friends and fellow drummers wouldn't give their own instruments the tender loving care he felt was warranted. To Bonzo, that kind of neglect was just a rung below child abuse. Music became his first addiction, and if he went a day without playing the drums, it was like going through withdrawal.

Shortly after John left school, at a time when Ringo Starr was already the envy of every youngster in England with a set of drumsticks, Bonzo began trying to make a living with his music. He performed with Terry Webb and the Spiders, attired in a string tie and a purple coat, with his hair greased back. His playing was a bit calmer and more controlled than it would soon become.

Like Plant, Bonham was pressured by family members to give up music. "There's a lot of honest work out there, John," his father told him. "You can make a decent living if you really want to." Bonham's dad was a carpenter and a builder, and John helped him for a while, putting aside the drumsticks for a set of hammers. But he loved music—nothing he had ever done made him so happy—and before long, he was back playing in local bands: the Nicky James Movement, A Way of Life, and Steve Brett and the Mavericks.

John believed that music was the only thing he was good at, but nevertheless he became the stereotypical starving artist. At age eighteen, when he met his future wife, Pat, she was level-headed enough to think twice about marrying someone whose future might include more famine than fame. Bonham, however, was persistent.

"It's just a matter of time," he told Pat. "I'm going to make it if you have faith in me. Don't give up on me."

Despite the odds, she didn't. Pat finally relented, and they moved into a fifteen-foot trailer together. On occasion, when Bonzo was feeling dejected about the slow pace at which his career was moving—and when he'd lose his temper and lash out when reality fell short of his expectations—he might promise Pat that he would quit if things didn't soon turn around. But they were hollow promises, and both of them realized it. Music was an undeniable part of him. He never seriously thought of giving it all up.

At times, Bonzo might have done better panhandling than playing music. When he was part of the Nicky James Movement, the band was frequently so short of funds that they often performed with equipment they hadn't fully paid for; more than once, when a gig was over, their instruments or PA equipment was confiscated because they were unable to meet their payments. "This isn't the way to make good music," John told himself. But at least for the moment, he didn't have many alternatives. And he felt an unwavering loyalty to those who let him play with them; he loved being part of a group, a feeling that continued throughout the long run of Led Zeppelin. Even during those tough periods, Bonzo's notoriety spread: "He's the best drummer in England" . . . "He plays so loud that you can barely hear yourself think" . . . "He breaks more drumskins in a week than most drummers do in a lifetime."

With time, Bonzo developed more finesse and less belligerence as he played. Even though he remained a team player, he yearned for the same attention as the musicians who played in front of him, particularly as he saw other rock drummers move into the spotlight. He admired and envied Ginger Baker, dating back to the Graham Bond Organisation, when Baker never let himself become overshadowed by the others in the group despite the strong musical presence of Bond and Jack Bruce. "That's the way I want to be," Bonzo would mutter, "an equal member of the band, not someone just keeping the beat for the forward musicians." Later, when Cream's album, *Fresh Cream*, was released early in 1967, with Ginger Baker's "Toad" solo turning him into a headliner, Bonzo set his sights on stardom. Less than two years later, he was a member of Led Zeppelin.

5

JOHN PAUL

Even for those who knew John Paul Jones well, he was somewhat of a mystery man. He methodically went about making his music with a cool confidence that never was shaken. For as long as I knew him, no matter how much feeling he brought to his music, he was solid and dependable. He knew what he was capable of doing—and he did it.

John Paul's real name is John Baldwin. He came from a family that enthusiastically nurtured his musical interests. He was born in 1946 in Sidcup, Kent, where his father was a piano player and a bandleader. While still a child, John Paul performed on the piano with his old man at weddings, bar mitzvahs, and parties. John Paul realized that it wasn't Madison Square Garden or the London Palladium, but it was a good training ground for what was to come.

John Paul picked up the bass for the first time in his early teens. He had only one lesson on the instrument, but that seemed to be enough. He let his musical instincts and sensitive fingers take over, along with the influences of musicians like Charlie Mingus, Scott La Faro, and Ray Brown.

John Paul's first bass was a Dallas model ("It had a neck like a tree trunk"). But while encouraging his son's interest in music, John Paul's dad saw no future in the bass. He urged his son to concentrate on the tenor saxophone, convinced that the bass guitar's days were numbered.

Despite such ominous predictions, the bass never went the way of the accordion or the autoharp. In fact, when John Paul proved to his father that he could actually earn money with the bass, the old man had an immediate change of heart.

At age seventeen, John Paul began moving through a few bands, playing Burns guitars, performing songs by Jerry Lee Lewis and Little Richard, and wearing outfits like purple jackets and white shoes that would have embarassed him years later. The best known of these bands was the Harris/Meehan Group, fronted by Jet Harris and Tony Meehan, who had sung with the Shadows when that band had a hit record, "Diamonds." Because of his youth and inexperience, John Paul suffered some unsettled nerves during this time, but his self-confidence kept his performance level high.

Before long, John Paul found a more lucrative way to make music, namely, by becoming a studio musician. From the beginning, he was serious and methodical, and he was soon offered as much session work as he could handle, accompanying everyone from Dusty Springfield to Tom Jones to Jeff Beck. He played on the "She's a Rainbow" track for the Rolling Stones and "Sunshine Superman" for Donovan. He also became an arranger for Herman's Hermits and, in the midst of all this, released a single of his own, "Baja," whose flip side was the inexplicably titled "A Foggy Day in Vietnam." Unfortunately, the record achieved about as much popularity as the Vietnam War itself.

As successful as John Paul was in the studio, it eventually wasn't enough for him. He began looking for ways to expand his horizons beyond the four walls of the recording halls. To the general public, John Paul was unknown, but he never felt that fame was something he needed; more important, he sometimes had the urge to seek new directions for expressing himself musically.

At the same time, however, John Paul was a real homebody and earned a comfortable living in the studio that allowed him to spend a lot of time with his wife, Mo, and his two young daughters. So he'd question whether he really wanted to join a band where concerts, traveling, and being away from home were part of the bargain.

Ultimately, an opportunity would present itself that was too good to ignore. It would come from a young guitarist named Jimmy Page, whom John Paul had met in the studio. Jimmy was impressed with John Paul's work, particularly after hearing the arrangements he had done for some songs on a Yardbirds' album. Jimmy kept John Paul's name in mind and figured their paths would cross again.

6

JIMMY

Jimmy Page was born in 1944 in Heston, Middlesex, but much of his youth was spent in Feltham, a London suburb so close to Heathrow Airport that he could *feel* the airplanes land. His idle time was spent fishing and collecting stamps, until at age twelve, his life changed when he heard an Elvis record, "Baby, Let's Play House." It wasn't just Elvis's distinctive voice that caught Jimmy's attention. It was the instruments behind him—the electric guitar, the acoustic guitar, the slap bass—that compelled him to play and replay the record ad nauseum until the needle had almost worn through it.

With Elvis on his mind, Jimmy picked up a Spanish guitar with steel strings, trying to copy the sounds he had heard. His attempts were understandably rusty at first. But it didn't matter. Overnight, he was hooked. He could feel the excitement rushing through him. He couldn't have put the guitar down even if he had wanted to.

Jimmy was a star hurdler in school, but everything was soon overshadowed by the music. He asked a friend at school to teach him a few chords. He bought a self-teaching book, *Play in a Day*, at a local music shop. He would scan the backs of album covers, looking for familiar names among the guitarists—Scotty Moore, who played on Elvis's records, James Burton, who performed behind Ricky Nelson, and Cliff Gallup, who accompanied Gene Vincent. He still loved the Top 40—from "Stagger Lee" to "Jailhouse Rock" to "Save the Last Dance for Me"—but he found himself listening more to the background musicians than the lead vocalists.

Jimmy's father was an industrial personnel manager and—almost by default—began encouraging Jimmy's musical talents. Jimmy's other real love was art, which to the elder Page seemed even more of a dead end. So once Jimmy was out of school, his dad only flinched a little when, while performing at a dance hall in Epsom, Jimmy was spotted by Neil Christian, a vocalist who invited Jimmy to become part of Neil Christian and the Crusaders. Christian, ever a polite fellow, even sought the permission of Jimmy's parents. "I'll keep an eye on your boy," he promised them.

The Crusaders had the misfortune of never falling fully in sync with their audiences. Even though the band gradually built up a following, they preferred playing old Bo Diddley, Chuck Berry, and Gene Vincent songs, while the crowds wanted to hear the Top 10. To make matters worse, the Crusaders traveled in a dilapidated van that had more breakdowns than an entire ward of psychiatric patients. So despite their talent, they seemed doomed from the start in their quest to become the next Bill Haley and His Comets.

Nevertheless, their talents did not go unnoticed. Jeff Beck, whose sister introduced him to Jimmy, saw the Crusaders play one night and was awestruck by the presence of Pagey onstage. The guitar, he told friends, was almost bigger than Jimmy, who "was this skinny guy whose arms and legs projected out like toothpicks."

Even then, Jimmy dressed distinctively and created some guitar licks and melodic phrasing that sometimes almost made Neil Christian stop singing in midsong and let his young guitarist take center stage.

Jimmy was earning about twenty pounds a week with the Crusaders, but the fast pace of the band's one-night gigs finally took a toll upon his health. He may have been a star athlete in high school, but his body was no match for the physical demands of nonstop touring. Suffering from exhaustion, Jimmy developed a chronic cough that turned into a severe case of glandular fever.

One night, while standing outside a club in Sheffield, Jimmy collapsed. Doctors examined him that night and again the following day and offered a simple but firm prescription: "Slow down." Jimmy, weary and weak, was in no mood to play around with his health. He quit the Crusaders.

During his recovery, Jimmy enrolled in art college in Sutton. But as much as he enjoyed art, he wasn't happy solely with brushes and easels. He couldn't put music completely behind him and kept picking up his guitar. There were moments when he contemplated setting aside the rigors of music for the seemingly less stressful life of an artist. "Maybe art is my calling," he sometimes reasoned. "Anything I do with music should be a hobby." But before long, he began going to clubs in the West End like the Marquee and Crawdaddy, where he would jam with just about anyone who would play with him. Sometimes for hours, he would play old Chuck Berry hits until the blisters on his fingers would almost burst. He absolutely loved it.

Like John Paul, Jimmy slipped into session work—and stayed there for six years, finally putting his palette and paints aside, virtually for good. Almost overnight, he was bombarded with session opportunities, not only because he was as good as they came, but he was reliable, too, capable of playing just about any kind of music—from rock to blues to jazz. At first, he really enjoyed it, and sometimes he was in awe of the artists he backed, including the Rolling Stones, Herman's Hermits, the Kinks, and even Petula Clark and Burt Bacharach. He played on Donovan's "Hurdy Gurdy Man" and the Who's "I Can't Explain." He was once hired to play for a Muzak recording session, and there were even some commercial jingles.

Initially, because he didn't have formal musical training, Jimmy had some self-doubts about how he'd fare in the studio. No one could "feel" the music any better than he, but he was often called upon to play according to someone else's vision, not his own. And that meant following the sheet music in front of him, measure after measure.

It took Jimmy a while to learn to read music, and there were some awkward, difficult moments when his shaky skills caused embarrassing mistakes. He often said that when he first started, the sheet music looked like a bunch of crows on telephone wires. Even so, almost from the beginning, he was earning a very good living in the studio.

Not surprisingly, Jimmy's skills intimidated some of his fellow musicians. Producer Shel Talmy once told him, "The Kinks are recording a new album called *You Really Got Me*. I'd like you to sit in on it."

Shel explained that Jimmy's talents would contribute immeasurably to the recording sessions—but the band itself wasn't so sure. "What do we need him for?" an anxious Peter Quaife was supposed to have asked. "Dave Davies can handle the lead guitar work just fine. This is ridiculous, Shel!"

Shel sat back and let them vent their anger and apprehension. Then, once the emotional level had settled down, he brought in Jimmy. In short order, the Kinks became converts. Once they heard Jimmy play, no one in the band questioned Shel's judgment.

As the years wore on, and one recording session blended into the next, Jimmy developed feelings of boredom and emptiness. He told friends that the session work was robbing him of his creativity. "You go in, they tell you what they want you to play, and to keep them happy, you avoid improvising," he said. "It's all so mechanical."

At one point, when Jimmy's frustration level was particularly high, he met Andrew Oldham, the Rolling Stones' manager, who told him about the formation of a new record label. "We could use you a lot, Jimmy," Oldham told him. "Not just for session work, but for producing."

It sounded like a new challenge, a way to expand his musical horizons. So Jimmy jumped at the opportunity to become the house producer of the new label, Immediate Records, where he worked on sessions with John Mayall and Nico. It provided a surge of new enthusiasm that he desperately needed.

During this time, Jimmy bumped into Eric Clapton, literally in the lobby of a recording studio. Under his contract with Immediate, Jimmy began producing some blues cuts with Eric—songs like "Double Crossin' Time" and "Telephone Blues." The two sensed a special chemistry between them, and they would often jam with one another when their schedules allowed. One night at Jimmy's house, they played together for hours, drawing upon each other's energy, excited at the synergy of merging their enormous talents. Jimmy even recorded some of their jamming that night on a simple, two-channel tape recorder.

During those sessions, Jimmy realized that he had more to offer the music world beyond his studio work. As he looked in other directions, he was intent on making the kind of music *he* wanted to. When he joined the Yardbirds—and later formed Led Zeppelin—he demanded as much control as he could possibly get.

PRESIDING OVER A ROCK FUNERAL

What's wrong with you bastards? Don't you have any professionalism left?"

Jimmy Page had run out of patience. He was pacing the floor and lecturing Keith Relf, lead vocalist for the Yardbirds, minutes after the end of a concert in Chicago during which Relf's drinking had taken precedence over the music itself. Jimmy kicked wildly at a nearby guitar case, knocking it onto its side. His arms were crossed across his chest. The aggravation showed in his furrowed brow, his agitated voice.

"You come onto the stage, Keith, and you act as though you're spending the evening at a fuckin' pub," Jimmy shouted. "What the hell's wrong with you?"

That night, Relf had carried several bottles of booze right onto the stage with him—Scotch, brandy, bourbon, and beer. After the last chords of "Heart Full of Soul" resonated, he bent down to pick up the Scotch, then guzzled it straight out of the bottle. He did the same after "For Your Love"—in fact, after nearly every song. All the while, Jimmy glared at him from across the stage, yelled at him to "cool it," but to no avail. Keith was so sloshed that the rest of the band should have dragged him off the stage.

The Yardbirds were disintegrating, and Jimmy knew it. It kept him awake at night. And for a musician with such enormous talent and such unwavering perfectionism, Pagey seemed like an unlikely candidate to preside over the demise of one of the best-known rock bands of the sixties. Yet when I began working with Jimmy and the Yardbirds early in 1968, that was precisely what he was doing. The Yardbirds were crumbling around us.

By that point, Jimmy had been with the band for nearly two years, joining them as their bassist in June 1966. When he became a Yardbird, he saw it as an escape . . . his avenue for finally fleeing the creative straightjacket of London studio work. It also eventually provided Jimmy with the springboard that launched him into a twelve-year career with Led Zeppelin.

But first, Jimmy had to officiate at the funeral procession of the Yardbirds, where I served as one of the pallbearers. I worked as the band's tour manager on its final American tour that began in March 1968.

Peter Grant, then the Yardbirds' manager, had hired me to join the final Yardbirds tour after I had traveled with another of his acts, the New Vaudeville Band. Mick Wilshire, a drummer who I had met two years earlier while on vacation in Spain, was part of the New Vaudeville Band, and arranged for my first meeting with Peter. When I walked into Grant's office for the first time, he was sitting comfortably behind an oversized desk. It was a large office, befitting a man like Peter, who was one of the biggest fellows I had ever met. When he rose to greet me, I gulped. It seemed to take him forever just to stand all the way up. At six-foot-six, he was an imposing presence. Later, when I learned he had once been a nightclub bouncer, a professional wrestler, and a movie double for heavyweight British actors like Robert Morley, I wasn't surprised—and was a little more cautious when I was around him.

Peter was raised by his mother in a poor neighborhood in London. He dropped out of school, was scrambling for odd jobs by his early teens, and eventually stumbled into the music business. He became the British tour manager for American performers like the Everly Brothers and Little Richard, during which time he developed a show-no-mercy attitude toward anyone who crossed him. I heard the story that one evening, he pummeled a rock promoter who tried to cheat Little Richard out of a few pounds; not only did Peter's anger send the poor fellow to the emergency room, but Peter also punched out several cops who had been called in to quiet the disturbance. For Peter, it was just like being back in the wrestling ring.

I was always known as a tough guy, but Peter Grant, I figured, was in a class by himself. At that first meeting, I told Peter a little about myself and the bands I had worked for. "Well, Cole," he finally said, "the tour manager's job with the New Vaudeville Band is open. I can pay you twenty-five pounds a week. Do we have a deal?"

"Not yet," I answered without a pause. "Thirty pounds a week, that's what I need. . . . Take it or leave it!"

Peter seemed astonished by my response. Frankly, so was I, particularly since I was still feeling anxious sitting across from this oversized man. Later Peter told me, "I wasn't used to people talking to me like that. But on balance, I figured it was a good sign. I doubted you would take shit from anyone."

Peter agreed to the thirty-pound-a-week salary. We shook hands, and then as I headed for the door, he bellowed, "One more thing, Cole." I turned, and he was shaking his index finger at me. "I never want to hear that you've repeated anything that goes on in this fucking office. If you do, I'll cut your ears off! Cut 'em right off!"

At that moment, I had no doubt that he would.

"Give me a call at the end of the week, Cole. By then, I'll know when you're going to start."

That was my introduction to Peter Grant. It was also my foot in the door to Grant's organization, which eventually led me to the Yardbirds.

My tenure with the Yardbirds was a difficult experience for both me and Pagey. In the pre-Page era, the Yardbirds had enjoyed a reign of enormous popularity that began in London in 1963. Throughout the midsixties, their name alone made rock fans worldwide take notice, in large part because of their superb guitarists. Before Jimmy, the Yardbirds had provided forums for two of the finest of the era—Eric Clapton and Jeff Beck. Few guitarists could follow in those footsteps; Jimmy Page was one of them.

When Paul Samwell-Smith quit the Yardbirds in 1966, Pagey took his place. For the next two years, he was a permanent fixture in the band. But by early 1968, when I joined the Yardbirds as their tour manager, they were on their last gasp—a fact of life that everyone in the band acknowledged. If burnout can happen to rock musicians, it had definitely steamrolled its way over the Yardbirds. Of the original 1963 Yardbirds lineup of five musicians, three of them—Keith Relf, Chris Dreja, and Jim McCarty—were still hanging on at the end, although with almost no measurable enthusiasm.

From the moment Jimmy joined the Yardbirds, he ended up carrying the band as best he could. Particularly during that final 1968 tour, Relf was just going through the motions. "We've got some contractual obligations, so I'm willing to meet them," Keith told me one afternoon while sipping on a beer in his hotel room. "But I'm tired of it all. I'm just used up."

During that last tour, Relf was a shadow of what he had once been—drowning in his excessive use of alcohol and angel dust. He did a lot of acid, too, often in his hotel room with incense burning nearby. Jimmy and I would sometimes have a snort of coke together, but Keith seemed incapable of knowing when he was overdoing it. "I'm fine!" he used to shout when I showed some concern. "Damn it, you're my tour manager, not my mother!"

Throughout that tour, we traveled primarily in a leased Greyhound bus that had most of its seats removed. Canvas beds had been anchored to the floor, and that's where we slept, or at least tried to, when we weren't in hotels.

There was a single bathroom in the back, but no stereos, cooking facilities, or power outlets. It was a third-class, thoroughly cheerless operation all the way.

Jimmy had clearly assumed leadership of a band capsizing at sea. While the other musicians were suffocating in their own depression and despondency, approaching the last Yardbirds tour as thought it were a death march, Jimmy would kick them in the ass and try to get them excited about making music again. "Let's give the fans their money's worth tonight," he would plead with the rest of the band. But no matter how passionately his appeals became, he was usually ignored.

When Keith Relf was drunk, he played the harmonica like he had just picked it up for the first time. He also stumbled over song lyrics. He even yelled obscenities at the audience and at the other Yardbirds. Nevertheless, it was my job to try to keep Keith singing for an hour, get the money from the promoter, and deal with any complaints later.

Most of the complaints came from Pagey himself. "What the hell do you think you're doing?" Jimmy seethed after the disastrous Chicago concert. "These fans are paying money to hear us sing, Keith, not to watch you get drunk."

His anger fell on deaf ears. "I'm not hurting anyone, Jimmy," Keith said. "I didn't hear that anybody asked for their money back."

Despite the noticeable stress upon Jimmy, I watched him emerge as the consummate professional—the same qualities he later demonstrated throughout the reign of Led Zeppelin. Even near the final hours of the Yardbirds, Pagey would sometimes spend much of the afternoon carefully coiffing his hair and selecting stylish attire, highlighted by ruffled shirts, antique scarves, and velvet jackets. While the rest of the band was wearing jeans, beads, and caftans, Jimmy had the look of an eighteenth-century British gentleman. He felt the fans deserved something special, even if he was the only Yardbird who did.

There was another factor at work besides Jimmy's professional pride. He also hoped to do something with the name "Yardbirds" down the road. He still believed there was some luster associated with the Yardbirds name, and at one point he approached Relf and McCarty:

"If you're not going to carry on, I'd still like to. I'm thinking of forming a new band and would like the rights to use the name."

Relf laughed. "Is there actually something left that's worth anything?" Without hesitating, he added, "It's all yours. I don't want anything to do with that fuckin' name anymore!"

They signed some legal documents, and Jimmy assumed ownership of the "Yardbirds."

The last Yardbirds concert in America was on June 5, 1968, at an auto race-way on the outskirts of Montgomery, Alabama. That morning, we were sitting by the pool of our hotel while a nearby radio blared a series of news bulletins:

"Senator Robert Kennedy, who was shot last night at the Ambassador Hotel in Los Angeles, is lying near death in a hospital."

I was mortified. I felt the country was coming apart before my eyes.

For that final concert, the Yardbirds performed on a makeshift stage consisting of two thirty-five-foot flatbed trailers. The fans—spanning the dirt racetrack to the edges of the stage—were remarkably enthusiastic. Just before Jimmy went onstage, he said to me, "It's sad, isn't it? This band could have gone on for years if the enthusiasm were there. I hate to see a great band die."

But that night, it did. As a single spotlight lit up Relf, then Page, then Dreja and McCarty, they played as the Yardbirds for the last time in America: "Heart Full of Soul" . . . "Over Under Sideways Down" . . . "Shapes of Things." When the last chords of "For Your Love" faded into the night, any nostalgia that I felt was overshadowed by a sense of relief that it was finally over. Jimmy was wonderful to work with, but the tension within the band was almost unbearable at times.

A NEW START

In the wake of the Yardbirds' demise, Jimmy Page had started planning his future. Emotionally, he was exhausted from the strain of presiding over the group's death sentence and, for a time, even considered taking a hiatus.

"Maybe I need a break," he told a friend. "I'm not sure I have the stamina right now to start all over again with a new band."

But it wasn't in Jimmy's nature to sit still. He loved making music too much. He would get high from the sounds he could elicit from his guitar. Even during the times when Jimmy was using drugs, no pill or other substance could make him as euphoric, as intoxicated as music. As with any powerful, addicting drug, he was driven back to his instrument for another fix, another hit of the compelling stimulant.

There were some practical considerations as well—in particular, contractual agreements that needed to be honored. Even though the Yardbirds had disbanded, they left some unmet concert commitments in their wake—most immediately, a Scandinavian tour. That meant forming a band—the name New Yardbirds kept spinning in Jimmy's head—that could go on the road and play the remaining dates.

So in late summer 1968, in the midst of the Supergroup era, Jimmy was faced with the prospect of creating a new band. And the more he thought about it, the more intriguing the possibilities seemed. He knew about the obstacles and the land mines, of course—the huge egos and the heavy pressures that had subverted more than one Superband. "I'm not in any mood to have another band fold underneath me," he said. "I'm still feeling the repercussions from the Yardbirds."

Cream was the most recent Supergroup to go up in smoke. That band featured three of the most talented rock musicians of the times—Eric Clapton, Jack Bruce, and Ginger Baker—and they exploded with power and influence upon the release of their first album in 1967. As their name suggests, they really were the cream of the rock music crop, combining white blues with hard, driving rock. But by late 1968, the band was disintegrating, and it played its final concerts at Madison Square Garden in New York and Royal Albert Hall in London.

With Cream extinct, critics began debating who—if anyone—could fill the blues-rock void. Some talked about Ten Years After. Others looked toward Pink Floyd. But when Jimmy ultimately made the decision to form a new band that would become Led Zeppelin, he put the debate to rest.

Jimmy spent a lot of restless nights by himself at his home in Pangbourne, contemplating who he might invite to join the new band—jotting down names, adding and crossing musicians off the list, trying to picture how the band might jell with varying combinations. He was taking the whole process seriously. John Entwistle, Keith Moon, Jeff Beck . . . B. J. Wilson and Nicky Hopkins . . . they were all on Jimmy's "A" list. So were Steve Marriott and Steve Winwood, who were his top contenders to handle the lead vocals. In those early weeks, neither Robert Plant nor John Bonham was even in contention. In fact, Jimmy didn't even know who they were.

"I tried to send word to Marriott," Jimmy often recalled. "I was excited about being in a band with him. I really thought it might work. But when his management team got back to me, they said Steve felt committed to Small Faces. He wasn't interested."

Jimmy continued to scrutinize and narrow down the list of candidates. Before long, Terry Reid emerged as his frontrunner for the role of lead singer. Jimmy had seen him perform and was taken with his potent, gravelly voice. But again Jimmy's plans were undermined.

"It sounds exciting," Reid told him by phone. "But I'm afraid I'm going to have to rule myself out. I'm already under contract with Mickey Most. I guess that puts me out of the picture."

At times, Jimmy would grow weary of this winnowing process. He called Terry back and asked, "Is there anyone else you can suggest for vocals?" He wasn't expecting to hear any names that he wasn't already considering. But he was beginning to feel that perhaps this was a hopeless venture.

"Well, there's one guy you should look at," Terry said. "His name is Robert Plant. He's with a band called Hobbstweedle."

Plant's name meant nothing to Jimmy, and Hobbstweedle was barely pronounceable and certainly wasn't recognizable to Jimmy or anyone in his immediate circle. But he trusted Terry's opinion enough to track Plant down. He found him performing at a teachers' training college near Birmingham, singing before a crowd barely big enough to fill up a Volkswagen van.

Frankly, most of Plant's song selections that night didn't really excite Jimmy—tunes by Moby Grape, for example. But that voice—Jimmy got the chills listening to Robert—his strong, sexy, emotional, plaintive voice, like a cry from deep within Robert's soul.

"Why isn't this guy a star yet?" Jimmy thought to himself. "Something's gotta be wrong with him. Maybe he has one of those obnoxious personalities and no one can get along with him."

Jimmy figured he'd need to get to know Robert Plant better before offering him a place in the band. In the meantime, however, he couldn't get Robert off his mind. Overnight, he forgot about the others he had once considered—Reid, Winwood, Marriott. Unless Robert turned out to be some kind of social pariah, this was the singer he wanted.

On Robert's end, he was both excited and anxious at being contacted by Pagey. To the struggling rock singer, Jimmy Page was one of the stars in the rock stratosphere to which Robert aspired. When Jimmy told him that he was searching for a singer for a new Page-led band, Robert realized that this could finally become his ticket to fame. When Jimmy invited him to visit his Pangbourne home, Robert vowed, "I'm not going to blow this chance. This kind of opportunity may never come again."

On his way to Pangbourne, already edgy and nervous, Robert was accosted in the train station by an elderly woman offended by the singer's long hair. "Cut it! Cut your hair!" she screamed. "Don't you have any sense of decency at all?"

Before Robert could react, she slapped his cheek.

Robert was shaken by the incident. Maybe this is an omen, he thought, trying to regain his composure. Maybe this isn't meant to be. Maybe I should just turn around and go home.

But once he was at Jimmy's house, Robert's anxieties eased. The Page-Plant meeting simply couldn't have gone any better. They spent the afternoon talking about their respective musical tastes. They swapped stories. They laughed together. At one point, Jimmy said, "I want you to hear something." He walked to his stereo and put on a Joan Baez album on which she was singing "Babe, I'm Gonna Leave You."

"What do you think of this?" Jimmy asked. "Can you see us playing it?"

Robert listened. Less than midway through the tune, he nodded. When the song had ended, he picked up Jimmy's acoustic guitar and started strumming an arrangement of the song. "This might work," he said.

The chemistry was there. Robert was on board. The young singer was so happy he wanted to scream for joy, but restrained himself, at least until he was out of earshot of Pagey.

Just before Robert left for home, he put in a good word for Bonham, his old friend. Plant and Bonham lived not far from one another, and they still spent time together now and then. But they hadn't performed onstage with each other since the Band of Joy dissolved. Even so, Robert could already picture Bonzo as part of the new band, and the idea excited him. "Don't make any decisions about your drummer until you've seen him play," Plant told Page. "It's hard to describe. I don't think anyone plays the drums like him. I know no one plays them any better."

Bonzo, however, was touring with Tim Rose and seemed quite content to stay just where he was. After all, he was making about forty pounds a week, which was the most money that he had ever earned. It would have been tough for him to give up his steady income.

"When you've got a good thing going, you don't throw it out the window," Bonzo told Jimmy on the phone. "I'm content right now. Things seem to be working for me."

Nevertheless, based on the high praise from Robert, Jimmy wanted to hear Bonham perform. He traveled to the Country Club in West Hampstead where Bonzo was performing with Rose. The show began rather routinely, but about twenty-five minutes into the set, Bonham took the spotlight. Jimmy's eyes widened as Bonzo attacked the drums like a kamikaze pilot. He bombed and strafed. He blitzed and blasted. He even put his sticks down and flailed away on the drums with his hands. He did everything but pounce on them and leave them in splinters.

"I've gotta get this guy," Jimmy told himself. "There's gotta be some way to change his mind."

Jimmy started working on the drummer. "This could be a breakthrough band, John. . . . We have wonderful management. . . . I think this is an incredible opportunity for all of us. . . . Think about it and let's talk again."

Jimmy recruited Peter Grant, who would manage the new band, to help him hound Bonham. They took Bonzo to lunch. They courted him with dozens of telegrams. They got Plant to do some arm twisting, too. "We're not taking 'no' for an answer," Jimmy finally said. He wasn't kidding.

Eventually, Bonzo's resolve began to weaken. He knew about Pagey's star status and, of course, had worked with Plant. Maybe, he thought, this new band does make sense. One day, he finally threw up his hands and told Jimmy, "You win! Let's do it!"

Page was ecstatic. "You won't regret it," he told Bonham. But for weeks, the drummer lay awake at night, wondering if he had made the right decision. He was leaving behind a sure thing—forty pounds a week—for a venture that, to him, seemed risky. "I hope I didn't botch this one up," he told himself.

Meanwhile, John Paul had heard about Jimmy's efforts at putting together a new band. He had been looking for an opportunity to get away from studio work, at least for a while. So he called Jimmy with the intent of casually raising the issue of the new band. They chatted for fifteen minutes, and then near the end of the conversation, John Paul told his old session pal, "Give me a call if you need a bass player." A few days later, Jimmy did.

The band was finally in place. All that was left was to see if things clicked musically. "We've got to get together and play," Jimmy told John Paul. "I'm going to set something up for next week."

They all agreed to meet for their first rehearsal in a small, humid studio on Gerrard Street in London. Jimmy didn't sleep well the night before that first get-together, wondering if everything would finally jell as he had hoped. Robert showed up for the rehearsal with butterflies in his stomach. Everyone wanted it to work, but no one was sure what would happen. Just to be safe, Bonzo kept Tim Rose's phone number in his wallet.

At that first session, Jonesy met Plant and Bonham for the first time. Plant was a little surprised at Jonsey's appearance. After all, Page had described John Paul as "a veteran studio musician"; based on that, Plant and Bonham had wondered if they might be working with an older father figure. John Paul didn't quite fit that mold.

There was nothing in particular planned for that afternoon, but as they picked up their instruments and stared at each other nervously, Jimmy suggested that they play "Train Kept a-Rollin'," one of his favorites from his Yardbirds days. It began a little rough, but not for long. Very quickly, everything began to fall into place. They segued into "As Long as I Have You," a song by Garnet Mimms. Then "I Can't Quit You Baby." As the music bounced off the walls, Jimmy found himself smiling. By the time they were playing "Dazed and Confused," Jimmy was almost giddy with excitement.

"I think we've got something here," Jimmy announced.

No one disagreed. Four chaps whose whole lives were music all realized that they might have finally found their ultimate vehicle of expression.

When that initial jam session ended, Robert asked, "Well, what next?"

Jimmy wasn't sure. "I don't know yet, but don't stray too far from home. I want to get things moving quickly."

Two days after that jam session, Jimmy sat down with Peter. Pagey didn't try to temper his enthusiasm.

"I wish you had been there," Jimmy said. "I wish you could have heard us. It was magical. Everything just came together."

Peter could feel Jimmy's excitement. "Well, how soon can you have a polished act ready to go?"

"Peter, it's not going to take long. By the end of that rehearsal, we all felt we were in high gear. I'd like to get us out for a few live performances."

Peter pulled out the remaining Yardbirds contracts and began making some phone calls. In less than a week, the band's first minitour was arranged, beginning in Copenhagen and Stockholm in mid-September. For those first concerts, the band was billboarded as the New Yardbirds.

The band rehearsed for only a few days before heading out to Scandinavia. At the time, I was in the U.S., traveling with the Jeff Beck Group, another band managed by Peter Grant. But during my frequent contact with Peter's office, I kept hearing about the New Yardbirds. When Peter would mention them, you could hear the anticipation in his voice. "Richard, Pagey thinks this band could be incredible," he said. "It looks like things are going to move fast for them. They could be very big very soon."

In Copenhagen, the New Yardbirds' first set included "Communication Breakdown," "Dazed and Confused," "How Many More Times," "Babe I'm Gonna Leave You," and "White Summer." Bonzo later told me that there were some kinks and some equipment problems. There were false starts on a couple of songs, due more to nerves than anything else. But they left the auditorium quaking, he said. I wish I had been there.

Once back in London, Jimmy couldn't contain his excitement. "Peter, I want to go into the studio right now," he said. "Let's get some of this music on tape. Our sound is already tight enough to make some recordings."

Of course, the band didn't have a recording contract yet. But Peter trusted Jimmy's instincts. "If you're already that good, let's do it."

In October, they rented the Olympic Studios in South London and went to work. Without the backing of a record label, Peter and Jimmy had agreed to share the costs of the studio rental. And with the meter running, they didn't waste a minute.

In just thirty hours, the entire album, *Led Zeppelin*, was recorded. Jimmy and John Paul, who had literally lived in recording studios for years, pushed things along, carrying Bonzo and Robert on their coattails. Pagey orchestrated the entire event, trying to draw the best out of his colleagues. He had planned out every song. He kept the overdubs to a minimum, relying heavily on the group's live sound. Jimmy placed the microphones carefully, some just inches from the instruments, others on the opposite sides of the studio. And the results were dramatic.

"There was nothing really that complicated about it," Jimmy said. The band had sounded so good live on that Scandinavian tour that he knew they could go into the studio and make it happen there, too. He was confident, not cocky. The songs weren't altered that much from their live versions, except "Babe I'm Gonna Leave You," which he rearranged on-site.

Robert loved what he heard during the playbacks of the tapes. He felt inspired and stirred up. Having such great musicians playing behind him had spurred him on. The whole experience, he said, was so sweet.

There was no holding back Plant's phrasing and passion. And in "Babe I'm Gonna Leave You," when he crooned "Baby, baby, baby" with feeling and intensity, those words instantly became a Plant trademark that endured for the duration of the band's history.

Pagey said he felt liberated during those sessions, letting his guitar lead him as well as the other way around. He caressed a Fender 800 pedal steel guitar on "Your Time Is Gonna Come" and switched to a borrowed acoustic Gibson for "Black Mountain Side." He brought a violin bow into the studio, letting it run rampant over his guitar strings in "Dazed and Confused" and "How Many More Times." He even sang background vocals on "Communication Breakdown"—a rarity throughout Zeppelin's twelve-year career.

John Paul went about his work methodically, content to let the others gain most of the foreground attention, but still creating his own spotlight with sounds like the dramatic church organ on "Your Time Is Gonna Come." He could bring electricity to the band that could send chills quivering down your spine for hours.

And then there was Bonham. He lived up to his billing in songs like "Good Times Bad Times," where he sacrificed his single Ludwig bass drum to the gods, wrenching more out of it than most drummers could pry from a dozen of them. Jimmy would sometimes look over and became mesmerized by what John was doing on the drums.

The production costs were remarkably low—less than 1,800 pounds, including the artwork on the album jacket, that memorable scene of the zeppelin Hindenburg descending toward a catastrophic and fiery end. Ultimately, that debut album grossed a staggering 3.5 million pounds, a remarkable figure, particularly for the times.

As the recording session came to a close, the band was feeling so positive about their new undertaking that they collectively decided that they didn't need to lean on the New Yardbirds name to capture the attention they felt they deserved. "Let's go for it," Jimmy said. "The music will speak for itself."

So they changed the band's name to Led Zeppelin. It was a name that had emerged from a conversation I had months earlier with Keith Moon and John Entwistle in New York while I was touring with the Yardbirds. Moon and Entwistle were growing weary of the Who and were kidding about starting a new band with Jimmy Page. Moon joked, "I've got a good name for it. Let's call it Lead Zeppelin, 'cause it'll go over like a lead balloon."

We all roared. The next day, I told Jimmy about it, drawing a laugh out of him, too. It apparently stuck in his mind. Ultimately, Jimmy changed the spelling of "lead" to "led," thus avoiding any possibility of mispronunciation.

WELCOME
TO AMERICA

As enthusiastic as the band felt, as confident as they were in the music they could collectively make, that didn't immediately translate into universal acceptance. Peter Grant had lined up a series of gigs at British clubs like the Marquee and at a number of college campuses, including Surrey University and Liverpool University. The early audiences were sparse, however; they reacted, in fact, as though they couldn't be bothered. While the band was nearly inciting its own riot onstage, there was polite applause from the crowds but none of the raucous, shrieking enthusiasm that would soon become part of the whole Zeppelin scene. It was a sobering experience for the entire band.

Jimmy just shook his head. "I don't get it. Their response is *under*whelming. Why aren't they taking us seriously? What a joke!"

Bonzo, his ego bruised by the lukewarm reception, had a theory: "Maybe we're just too much for them, and they just don't know how to react." Their music, he reasoned, was so spirited and so potent that audiences were just stunned by it all. It measured 8.0 on the Richter scale, and the crowds were apparently just holding on, trying to ride out the convulsions and keep their beer glasses from being jolted out of their hands.

That's when Peter turned his attention to America—an American tour and a highly publicized recording contract. He had just returned from the States, where he had emerged from some tough negotiating with Atlantic Records with an unprecedented recording contract for the new band. Atlantic—the same label that had helped turn Cream into a huge although short-lived phenomenon—was looking for the next Supergroup, and Peter convinced them that Led Zeppelin was the answer. Even before Atlantic's Ahmet Ertegun had heard the tapes from that first Zeppelin recording session, he decided that he didn't want to let this band get away. Eventually, he brought out his checkbook, wrote out a $200,000 advance—the kind that only someone like Elvis Presley could command in those days. Even more important, especially for Pagey, Peter had insisted that the band itself retain full control over its music. No exceptions.

Immediately, Atlantic issued a press release that began the high-powered hype that critics of the band immediately attacked. According to the record company's initial promotion, "Top English and American rock musicians who have heard the [first Zeppelin] tracks have compared the LP to the best of Cream and Jimi Hendrix, and have called Led Zeppelin the next group to reach the heights achieved by Cream and Hendrix."

After the disappointments in the British clubs, the Atlantic contract couldn't have been more delicious. The band was ecstatic over the deal—Bonzo raced out and bought a Jaguar XK 150 with his share of the money. But as the news hit the rock press, the initial publicity was negative. Thanks in part to the Atlantic hype, columnists referred to Zeppelin as a commercial, capitalist, overly promoted group that still needed to prove itself musically. Those were the kinds of demoralizing articles that Zeppelin read—and tried to ignore—as they headed for the States for their initial U.S. tour.

My first hands-on exposure to Zeppelin came in America in December 1968. Before the debut album was yet released to support those U.S. concert dates, Peter Grant felt it was still worth the gamble to see if they could find a niche in America. "England doesn't seem to be rushing to buy tickets to see you play," he told Jimmy. "Let's see what happens across the Atlantic."

Peter painted a best-case scenario of what might happen in America. If the band could create some excitement, he said, that enthusiasm might snowball into an avalanche that could sweep not only North America, but boomerang back to England and Europe as well.

Peter realized it was an unusual, perhaps even foolish strategy. After all, the band was even less known in the States than in England. The first album would not be released until January. But Peter became convinced that waiting for something to happen in England might be suicidal.

"A new group can sit around for months in the U.K. and no one even notices," Peter told Jimmy. "There aren't that many places to play here."

By comparison, America was a potential gold mine, if not now at least in the future. Peter had five years of experience in the U.S. with bands like the

Yardbirds, the Animals, Herman's Hermits, and the New Vaudeville Band. He was a gutsy guy, willing to take risks, even with an unproven commodity like Led Zeppelin.

Peter felt he knew America inside out—which cities, which clubs, which amphitheaters to make part of that first tour. As Jimmy had done months earlier when he recruited the members of the band, Peter began making a list of his own, jotting down U.S. sites that would be critical to maximize Zeppelin's exposure. The Fillmores in New York and San Francisco. The Boston Tea Party. The Grande Ballroom in Detroit.

The list grew. By the time the itinerary was complete, it included more than twenty cities. "Let's give it a shot," Peter told his secretary.

There were some immediate complications, however. Peter had scheduled the first American gig in Denver on December 26. Peter realized he would need to fly the band out of England just before Christmas. "I'm shitting just thinking about telling the band that they'll have to be away from their families on Christmas," he said to one of his assistants. "This may turn out to be a scheduling nightmare."

Three of the band members—John Paul, Robert, and Bonzo—were married and seemingly committed enough to their relationships to perhaps send out an SOS at the mere mention of leaving their families behind at Christmas. Jimmy, the only single member of the band, was dating an American girl name Lynn whom he had met in Boston when he toured with the Yardbirds and had brought her to England to live with him; Peter figured that pulling Jimmy away from her wouldn't be easy, either. So Peter put off telling the band the details of the American tour for as long as possible.

Finally, Peter got up the nerve. He called the band together in his office and told them about the basics of the U.S. tour. "Through much of it," he said, "you'll be opening for Vanilla Fudge. Oh, and you'll be starting on Boxing Day, the day after Christmas. That means you've got to leave England on December twenty-third." Peter also told them that he wasn't going with them; he would be home for Christmas.

Peter waited for the fireworks to begin. To his surprise, no one even flinched, at least not visibly. "Well, let's just do what we have to do," Robert said. "When does the plane leave?"

Weeks later, every member of the band would swear that he'd never do anything like that again. But for the moment, they seemed determined to turn Zeppelin into the next Supergroup, and they trusted Peter's judgment.

Peter felt confident about what awaited the band across the Atlantic. "Why shouldn't it go right?" he asked himself. He couldn't come up with any answers.

Led Zeppelin packed their bags, ready to test America's waters.

"Be at L.A. airport at four tomorrow," Peter told me during a long-distance phone call. "That's when the band's plane touches down. And, Richard, don't let them get into any trouble."

I had been in Los Angeles for nearly a week, wrapping up my work with Terry Reid during his American tour. But I was eager to begin my new assignment with Led Zeppelin. Of course, I knew Jimmy Page from the Yardbirds tour earlier in the year and figured anything he touched would, by definition, be first-class. My expectations were further boosted during several phone calls with Peter, during which his enthusiasm and optimism about Zeppelin seemed to grow more profuse with each subsequent conversation.

"You better brace yourself, Richard," Peter said. "You won't believe their sound. It's sensational."

At LAX, Jimmy came off the plane first, then Robert Plant and John Bonham. Kenny Pickett, a roadie on that first tour, was with them, too. John Paul Jones planned to meet us in Denver, arriving on a separate flight from Newark, New Jersey, where he and his wife had spent the Christmas holidays with singer Madeline Bell.

Jimmy wasn't the only face in the band that was familiar to me. I had known John Paul from my early days in the music business in London. Also, back in October, as Zeppelin had begun to take shape, I had briefly met Robert and Bonzo at Peter's office on Oxford Street during a short break in my own touring with some of Peter's other bands. Since Led Zeppelin was a client of Peter's, I figured I'd be working with them someday, and we exchanged some brief pleasantries. But at that moment, the possible significance of this band didn't register. Frankly, I was only in London for ten days and was much more interested in finding an open pub than spending too much time getting acquainted with Plant and Bonham.

During those first few days in America, however, I took an immediate liking to Bonzo. He was a congenial fellow with a rich sense of humor and a contagious laugh. "Is this your idea of Christmas, Cole?" he exclaimed as we drove along the Sunset Strip in eighty-degree weather. "I didn't pack any fuckin' T-shirts or a swimsuit! You better change this weather before I get really pissed off!"

Robert, on the other hand, was harder for me to figure out. From the beginning, he had an aura of arrogance around him—arrogance coupled with anxiety—that created a shell that was difficult to penetrate. This was the first time he and Bonzo had been to America, and Robert in particular appeared nervous about what awaited him. "I'll be fine once we get that first concert behind us," he told me. Until then, however, he was moody, irritable, and tense.

While Bonham joked about America, Robert seemed genuinely upset about being there. You could feel his nervous stomach a block away.

During those three days in L.A. before we flew to Denver, the band submitted to a couple of press interviews, but they decided to forgo rehearsals. "The act is sharp," John Paul said. "We've had some time to get it into shape in England."

We ate Christmas dinner together—cooked by Bonzo—in our hotel rooms at the Château Marmont off Sunset Boulevard. There wasn't much talk as we ate, with the homesickness and the loneliness of Christmas Day really sinking in. "I hate to dwell on it, but this is really shitty being this far away from my wife on Christmas," Robert complained. "Really shitty!"

Jimmy agreed, but asked us to keep things in perspective. "It's a sacrifice," he said, "but there's going to be a payoff. This band has a lot going for it. Let's make the best of it."

The morning after Christmas, we headed back to LAX, boarding a TWA flight to Denver. That night, we met up with John Paul and assembled backstage at the Denver Coliseum, with Zeppelin's first American concert just minutes away.

Almost futilely, the band tried to stay calm backstage. Clearly, Robert and Bonzo were the most uneasy and restless. "Let's knock 'em dead, but let's get it over with, too," Robert said. There was nervous pacing and biting of fingernails.

Zephyr, a band headlined by an attractive vocalist and keyboard player named Candy Givens, opened the show. Throughout their set, the tension built backstage. Bonzo nervously tapped on some cardboard boxes piled up in our dressing room. John Paul leaned silently against a wall, his arms crossed over his chest, staring silently at the floor, lost in his own thoughts.

After forty-five minutes, Zephyr left the stage, and Led Zeppelin was announced. "Ladies and gentlemen, for their first American appearance, from London, England, please welcome Led Zeppelin!"

Jimmy, John Paul, Robert, and John glanced at one another, heaved a collective sigh, and paraded single file down the concrete stairs toward the stage. The applause was steady but not overwhelming.

Led Zeppelin performed on a revolving platform that night. Jimmy dreaded the thought of playing on a moving stage; he had done it a couple of times with the Yardbirds and despised it. For the other band members, it was their first time. "It's like a fucking merry-go-round that's out of control," Jimmy told the rest of the band just minutes before their set began. "The stage moves slowly, but it just never stops spinning. It's disorienting. When the stage finally does come to a halt, you might be facing in any direction."

As a joke, as a way of cutting the ice backstage, I asked the band if anyone wanted some Dramamine before the show began. No one even cracked a smile. All of them were feeling the strain.

Most of those Denver fans, of course, had come to see Vanilla Fudge. But Led Zeppelin didn't appear inhibited by their supporting role. Robert, his flaxen curls aglow under crimson lights, his shirt half open, pranced barefoot across the stage, striking contorted poses with Mick Jagger confidence, releasing his high-voltage voice toward the heavens.

"Good Times Bad Times"..."Dazed and Confused"..."Communication Breakdown." I could see the band begin to relax as the set progressed. After the early tunes, a gentle smirk came over Bonham's face that seemed to say, "Not bad . . . not bad!"

Jimmy, like a magician pulling surprises from his top hat, became more aggressive, teasing raw, unpredictable wah-wahs out of his Fender, his fingers dancing from fret to fret, bending the strings on the flashy guitar that Jeff Beck had given him.

"I Can't Quit You Baby" . . . "You Shook Me" . . . "Your Time Is Gonna Come." With each song, the crowd's excitement built.

While John Paul projected an aura of coolness, his calculated bass line gradually helped escalate the band to just this side of anarchy. And then there was Bonzo. More than midway through their set, he was engineering a frantic, passionate attack on his drumskins, showing no mercy, never relinquishing control. If he were a bombardier pilot, you wouldn't want to be in the line of fire.

One moment, the music was delicate and precise; the next, it was violent and reckless. It was the kind of music that almost makes your ears bleed. At the end of the set, just an hour after it started, Zeppelin had announced to the rock world that they had arrived.

As the band sprinted from the stage, perspiration dripped from their faces. But the adrenaline was still flowing. "I loved it," Robert said, reaching into a cardboard container filled with spareribs from a local eatery. "It was good, wasn't it? It was good!"

No one disagreed.

Denver was only the beginning. For me, the most memorable concert was less than a week later in Portland, Oregon. Midway through Zeppelin's set, Bonzo seemed possessed during his marathon drum solo, blasting through a powerful thunderbolt of rhythm. For ten minutes, the rest of the band was offstage, watching from the wings, stunned by Bonzo's blinding, energetic performance.

I turned to John Paul, who was standing beside me. "Jesus Christ," I said. "Bonzo is incredible! This whole band is incredible!"

A sly smile came over John Paul's face. He winked at me, nodded, and then walked back onto the stage. He knew it, too. We all felt that Led Zeppelin was going to be monstrous.

Two weeks after the opening night in Denver, Peter flew from London to San Francisco to get his first look at the band in America, performing three nights at the Fillmore West. On the way to the San Francisco airport to pick him up, I contemplated my own future and decided that if Led Zeppelin was going to be the next Supergroup, I wanted to be part of the coronation.

During the drive back to the hotel, I mustered up my courage and told Peter, "I'm fed up with fucking around with all these other bands you're sending me out with. I want to stay with Zeppelin. They're going to be big."

Peter paused for a moment. I thought he might be figuring out the best way to fire me.

Finally, he said, "Okay, Cole. When they're on the road, you'll always be with them."

I was so excited. "Damn it, thank you, Peter." For the next twelve years, Zeppelin and I were almost inseparable.

For those dates at the Fillmore West, the band opened for Taj Mahal and Country Joe and the Fish. And it was a mismatch from the beginning. Country Joe was a band whose music burst with political messages and black humor about everything from the Vietnam War to drug use. Their rebellious songs like "Feel-Like-I'm-Fixin'-to-Die Rag" became anthems for millions of young people in the 1960s. But at the Fillmore, Country Joe had to follow Zeppelin onstage, which could have triggered a nervous breakdown in just about any musician placed in the same position. As Zeppelin walked offstage, leaving behind an audience limp with exhaustion, the quieter, more cerebral sounds of Country Joe were about as appropriate as an hour of Mitch Miller or Mantovani.

During the Fillmore performances, Zeppelin didn't disappoint anyone— including themselves. After the second of the San Francisco gigs, Jimmy turned to me on the ride back to the hotel and said, "This is a turning point for us, Richard." He laughed with excitement. "When a supporting band starts overshadowing the headliner, you know something's happening. Brace yourself for a pretty thrilling ride."

Even in that first tour, I found it impossible to sit through a Zeppelin concert and not feel an emotional high, not feel moved, not feel like I was part of a special, unique experience. I told Kenny Pickett, "If this band can stick together and not let their personalities and their egos get in the way of the music, they could be one of the longest lasting in show business."

To a large degree, those three Fillmore concerts became the oil that fueled the Zeppelin machine, creating a flurry of attention not only in Northern California, but in other parts of the country as well. A New York disc jockey on an underground FM radio station talked about the band as "Beatle incarnates." Fans stormed record stores, demanding an album that didn't yet exist. Atlantic Records was being barraged with orders even before the vinyl was off the assembly line. The momentum was building.

On two occasions during that first U.S. tour—once at Detroit's Grande Ballroom and again at Miami's Image Club—John Paul left the stage during Bonham's drum solo, with a dismayed look on his face. "What's wrong with this damn equipment?" he yelled over at me. "I can't even hear my own bass!"

In fact, the music had to compete with the deafening crowd noise. And often the crowd won.

If any doubt still existed about the power of Zeppelin, it vanished at the end of January at the Boston Tea Party. The Tea Party was a converted synagogue that had become a great showcase for rock musicians. By this point in our tour, thirty-three days and twenty-eight performances into it, the band had solidified as a unit. Groups tend to either become closer on a tour, or they begin to rupture at the seams; in Zeppelin's case, as the four musicians got to know each other better, they began enjoying one another's company. And as their music really began to jell, it seemed as though they couldn't wait to get onstage.

"The other twenty-three hours of the day mean nothing," Robert said. "It's that one hour of music that I care about."

The Tea Party was sold out—in fact, the management had sold too many tickets for the 400-seat club. As Led Zeppelin began performing their sixty-minute set, both the musicians and the audience started working themselves into a frenzy. Jimmy walked to the edge of the stage, aimed the neck of his guitar at the fans as his fingers danced from fret to fret, and then extended his left leg like he was about to leap into the audience. He coaxed the crowd into an orgy of hysteria.

After an hour of playing, no one was ready for them to quit. For another fifty-five minutes, there was more ear-drum-splintering music. Standing ovations, sometimes right in the middle of songs. Fans storming toward the stage. Absolute delirium. Encore after encore. Twelve in all.

At that point, the band had only a three-month history together, and as one encore merged into the next, they simply ran out of songs to play. They would spring off the stage after each encore, with odd expressions that showed both exhilaration and panic. "What other songs do you know?" Jimmy would excitedly ask the others. "What can we play next?"

After they had performed the entire Zeppelin repertoire—some of them more than once—they moved on to "Good Golly, Miss Molly" ... "Long Tall Sally" ... old Elvis standards ... Chuck Berry songs ... anything that all of them could improvise.

Once the last note had reverberated off the walls and finally faded away, and the crowd had caught its breath and began to disperse, John Paul heaved a sigh. "It was a spectacular night, wasn't it?"

On the way back to the hotel, as Bonzo toweled off his face and howled with joy, he screamed, "The show hit them like a thunderstorm." That night at the Boston Tea Party, it really was a torrential downpour.

10

LIFE ON THE ROAD

Despite the early success that Led Zeppelin enjoyed, there was nothing very glamorous about their first American tour.

As well as providing physical security for the band and making sure that their equipment was set to go at every venue, I had the responsibility of taking charge of all the flight and hotel arrangements—and not much of it was first-class. We flew coach in commercial planes and pinched pennies on air fares by milking TWA's "Discover America" plan, which allowed us to buy airline tickets that routed us through the U.S., saving us 50 percent on every connection. It cut our travel expenses by thousands of dollars. In most cities, we stayed at Holiday Inns or other reasonably priced hotels. At the airports, there weren't limousines waiting for us, but rented cars, usually Ford LTDs from Hertz or Avis. But since none of us had credit cards, renting a car was usually a challenge.

At the airport counter in San Francisco, the clerk simply refused my request for a car. "It's a company policy," she said matter-of-factly. "No credit card, no rental car."

We argued for ten minutes. I explained that we had been able to rent them elsewhere. I offered her free tickets to a Zeppelin performance. Nothing worked. Finally, I lost my cool. I pulled $6,000 in cash out of my pocket, threw it on the counter, and shouted, "I'll buy the goddamn car! Just give me the fucking keys! Now!"

She backed away trembling, hurriedly filled out the paperwork, and pushed the keys toward me. "You guys are crazy!" she said, choking back tears. Maybe so, but we finally had a car.

The band members would drive with me in the LTD, with personal luggage squeezed into the trunk. Kenny Pickett would steer the three-ton, U-Haul truck with our equipment, including Pagey's 1958 Fender Telecaster, bass gear, Vox AC-30 amps, a kit of Ludwig drums for Bonzo, and some back-up items. They played so hard on them during the American tour that by the time we headed home, most of the equipment was wrecked.

One harrowing ride from Spokane to Seattle almost put an early end to that tour—and to Led Zeppelin—just a few days after the band had arrived in the States. We had just finished a performance at the Gonzaga Gym in Spokane and were about to depart for the Spokane airport for a flight that would eventually take us to Los Angeles. But an Arctic blizzard had moved into the region and was increasing in intensity. Our flight—and every other flight—out of Spokane was canceled.

We were stranded and cold. The state of Washington is beautiful, but being stuck there in Siberia-like weather, including eight inches of snow, is not how we had planned to spend New Year's Day, particularly since the band had a gig scheduled at the Whisky a Go Go in L.A. on January 2.

"Get us out of this fucking deep freeze!" Robert shouted at me. "Charter us a plane if you have to!"

"Charter you a plane?!" I screamed back. "And who's gonna pay for it? Should we take it out of your damn wages?"

After a couple of frenetic phone calls, I found out that we could catch a flight from Seattle to Los Angeles—if we could just get the rented LTD through the storm to the Seattle airport. As a native of London, I didn't have much experience driving in snow flurries, but escaping Washington was all the motivation I needed.

The band climbed into the car and I got behind the wheel for the 200-mile drive. Kenny Pickett was by himself in the U-Haul truck. The road conditions started out bad—slush and snowbanks—and it only deteriorated. As we slipped and slid, the visibility became worse. And I was becoming more anxious.

"Do you guys have your wills made out?" I nervously joked.

No one laughed.

To try to calm myself, I reached into the backseat and grabbed a bottle of whiskey. I handed it to Bonzo and said, "Open it! Quick! I need something to relax me!" We passed the bottle around, and everyone had a few swigs.

At about the halfway point, the road conditions became almost impossible. Through the storm up ahead, I could see some state police cars parked with their red lights flashing. They had erected roadblocks. "Shit," I thought. "These bastards better not be turning us around."

As we came to a stop, a cop on foot approached our car. I cracked the car window, and he yelled to us, "The Snoqualmie Pass is impassable. It's just snowing too hard. Take the exit off the highway and turn around."

We groaned at the possibility of spending another night in Spokane. I started thinking about other bands—the Beatles, the Rolling Stones. I doubted that they had ever gotten themselves into messes like this. And I began to wonder whether I'd ever get us out of this one.

In the time it took me to drive off the highway, however, I had already decided to keep heading for Seattle. Maybe the whiskey had given me some extra courage, but when we got to the top of the exit ramp, I announced, "We're gonna fuckin' go down the other side of the ramp and get back on the highway. I don't care what those cops say. They're never going to be able to see us or catch us."

I drove around the cloverleaf and back onto the highway, and we continued on to Seattle. I felt victorious, like I had put one over on the state police. But after just a few minutes, I realized that maybe the cops had been right.

Sheets of snow alternated with torrents of rain and hail. The winds were ferocious. We were the only car on the highway. Parts of the road were caked with ice, and the car was skidding from lane to lane. If conditions got any worse, I could have turned off the ignition and just let the car slide all the way to Seattle.

By this point, I was really scared. But I didn't dare let the band know that. Because Jimmy and I had worked together in the past, he had confidence in me and figured—probably erroneously—that I knew what I was doing. He also was struggling with the Hong Kong flu and didn't have much energy to complain about anything.

The rest of the band, however, was absolutely terrified with my driving, particularly during the hairpin curves. They had every reason to be. At one point, we approached a long, narrow suspension bridge that was actually swaying in the wind gusts. If we had taken a vote in the car, we wouldn't have gone any farther. In fact, by that point, I was finally almost ready to turn around.

We started across the bridge. I could feel it trembling beneath us, and my heartbeat quickened. We were so close to the edge—and to a drop of about 100 feet—that Bonzo and Robert became absolutely frantic.

"Richard, you fuckin' asshole, you're about to get us killed," Robert shrieked, grabbing the bottle of whiskey from John Paul's hands.

"Oh, my God," screamed Bonzo. "Can't you pull over until this storm ends?"

I shouted back, "Shut up, you fuckers, just drink some more whiskey." In fear and frustration, I pressed the accelerator to the floor and the car bolted ahead. Within another minute, we were safely on the other side of the bridge.

Another mile up the road, I stopped the car. I needed to wipe the windshield—and relieve myself of some of the booze I had drunk. It was cold so I was working fast—but obviously not fast enough. As I peed into some nearby bushes, the car started to slide backward on the icy road. The emergency brake was on, but the car was somehow skidding toward a precipice and a fifty-foot drop.

The boys were screaming. Perhaps their lives were flashing in front of them. Mine was.

Somehow, while furiously zipping up my fly, I managed to dive back into the car and jerk the steering wheel. Robert had dove into the front seat and was feverishly pressing on the brake pedal with his hands. Miraculously, we brought the car to a halt before it took flight.

Robert was absolutely livid. "I'm gonna get you fired, Cole," he shouted in exasperation. "Either that, or I'm gonna kill you."

Eventually, we made it to the Seattle airport. I turned in the rented car and all of us headed for the airport bar to thaw out and have a swig or two. We were emotional wrecks after that drive and desperately needed a drink.

"Give us a round of Scotch," I said to the bartender.

As the bartender reached for the bottle, he nonchalantly said, "Let me take a look at your IDs."

I glanced at Bonzo, whose chin had just dropped to his chest. "You've got to be kidding," he moaned. Bonzo and Robert were both under twenty-one.

"Give us a break," I told the bartender. "We've just been through hell out on the highway."

Plant and Bonham ordered some coffee and snuck a few sips of our Scotch.

Kenny Pickett, meanwhile, finally showed up at the airport, too. He had also navigated the Snoqualmie Pass by sneaking past the roadblock, but not without an eventual mishap. His U-Haul skidded off the highway, crashed through a fence, and ended up in someone's front yard. All in a day's work.

When our plane finally touched down in Los Angeles, the sight of the sunshine lifted our spirits. Even better, the three-night engagement at the Whisky a Go Go turned out to be simply spectacular—and so was the nightlife we discovered in L.A.

The band became enamored with the Whisky, which was on the cutting edge of the transformation occurring on the Sunset Strip. Old clubs like the Crescendo and Ciro's had closed down, replaced by rock venues that attracted kids as young as preteenagers—would-be tarts eager to divest themselves of innocence and join the rock and fashion revolution, even if it meant waiting in line for hours to become part of the scene inside.

The Whisky occupied a building that had once been a branch of the Bank of America. It had been painted green, and the safes and desks had been removed and replaced with a stage, oversized speakers, and glass-enclosed cages bulging with dancing girls who could keep you entranced for hours. The club soon had an international reputation, and even the Shah of Iran stopped by one night, undoubtedly wondering why there was nothing like this in Teheran.

Even when we weren't performing at the Whisky, the band just liked hanging out there, where we could drink to the point of near collapse—something which we all could do quite well. For years, I had relied on booze to relax me and numb whatever I might be feeling. John Paul liked gin and tonic. Robert would drink mostly wine and sometimes Scotch. Jimmy was attached to Jack Daniels. But Bonzo and I weren't as fussy. From Drambuie to beer to champagne, we'd drink just about anything.

Substance abuse eventually became part of the Led Zeppelin legend, and we got off to a fast start on that initial tour. Frankly, part of the rock music game was to get as stewed as possible, as often as possible. With all the stresses that come from launching a new band—and from touring in general—alcohol became our constant companion. We had plenty of marijuana, too, and occasionally a snort or two of cocaine. But alcohol was nearly an everyday indulgence. It helped pass the time. It eased anxieties. And it loosened inhibitions in all kinds of social situations.

In just five days in L.A., the band discovered that we could create a lot of good-natured mischief, particularly at the Château Marmont. The Marmont is an old hotel with an incredible history. Jean Harlow had an affair with Clark Gable there. Paul Newman met Joanne Woodward at the Marmont. John Belushi died there in 1982.

Rock musicians developed a special fondness for the hotel. Graham Nash lived there for five months. Alice Cooper's roadies played football naked on the mezzanine. Jim Morrison tumbled out a second-story window, injuring his back and legs.

Jimmy and I had stayed at the Château Marmont with the Yardbirds, and I had returned there when I toured with Terry Reid. In early 1969, as Led Zeppelin checked into the Marmont, I decided that we'd share bungalows to cut down expenses. Robert and Bonzo roomed together downstairs. Jimmy and I stayed in a room upstairs, and John Paul and Kenny were together.

Bonzo used to say that it was impossible to come back to the hotel after a performance and sip tea or hot chocolate and watch the telly. After flailing at the drums with the force of an atomic bomb, Bonzo literally needed hours to calm down and unwind. "I'm too hyper," he would complain, tapping his foot, scratching at his arms. "I gotta let loose and blow off some steam."

That's how the legendary Zeppelin high jinks got started. They weren't designed to create chaos, but rather to deal with excess energy and cope with the boredom of life thousands of miles from home.

At the Marmont, it began pretty innocently. One night, after we had played the Whisky, Jimmy and I decided to have a little fun. We prepared buckets filled with water and eggs and then waited for Robert and Bonzo to drag themselves back to their bungalow.

We were rewarded for our patience. Just as they were about to walk through their front door, we attacked. The buckets were tilted on their sides, bombarding our targets with the gooey potion. Robert and Bonzo were absolutely drenched. It was purely kids' stuff, a schoolyardlike prank that Jimmy and I should have outgrown years earlier. But we roared with laughter at the success of the practical joke.

From Los Angeles, the band flew to San Francisco, where the juvenile delinquency continued. We stayed at a hotel called the Alta Mira across the Golden Gate in Sausalito. To save a few dollars and to cater to Jimmy's vegetarian tastes, I decided to get rooms that had kitchens—which also gave us plenty of ammunition for food fights. Our rooms faced one another across a hallway, and at midday Bonzo suggested, "Why don't we serve them their lunch by air mail?"

He picked up some uncooked eggs and began throwing them from one room to the other. The eggs didn't last long, so we found other ammunition— tomatoes, oranges, potatoes, cheese, doughnuts, cookies, nuts. The mayhem continued for about fifteen minutes, with food soaring across the hallway. When it was over, there was enough cholesterol splattered on the walls and windows to clog the arteries of half of San Francisco.

Peter would sometimes become concerned about our antics, convinced that I had lost control of the band. My philosophy was that if we made it to the concert halls on time and Led Zeppelin performed up to par, there was no reason to live like nuns or librarians offstage. I saw our horseplay as harmless fun; but perhaps it was a stepping-stone to something a lot worse—the destruction of property or, ultimately, the destruction of ourselves.

During that first tour, I had been given some amyl nitrate by a friend in San Francisco, and I introduced Bonzo to it. As he and I sniffed a few amyl nitrate "poppers" one afternoon, Peter called us from London. He spoke to all the band members, one by one, asking how they were doing.

When it came Bonzo's turn, he told Peter, "It's great up here, Peter. Richard is giving me Amy's nightdress!"

Bonzo hadn't gotten the name of the drug quite right, and Peter probably didn't know what to think.

"Amy's nightdress!" roared Peter. "Get that fucker Cole and put him on the phone!"

I clutched the phone, and gave Peter my most innocent tone of voice. "Yes, Peter, how are you today?"

"What the fuck are you doing to Bonzo?" he shouted. "Amy's nightdress!"

Perhaps Peter thought that a groupie named Amy—and her nightdress—had joined us in Sausalito. Unfortunately, it was nothing quite that exciting. Not yet, that is.

Eventually, Peter realized that our horseplay was on a very juvenile level. At times over the years, he even joined us in some of our capers.

It was not all fun and games, however. In mid-January, the first real fractures within the group emerged. It resulted from a joke that Robert took the wrong way and that created a lot of animosity between him and me—feelings that lasted for many months.

We had arrived in Miami Beach to play the Image Club and checked into the Newport Hotel on Collins Avenue. Within an hour after our arrival, Jimmy and I had headed for the hotel pool, where we met and were chatting with a couple of girls. A few minutes later, Robert approached us wearing street clothes. "I'm going to take a walk through the shopping district around here," he said. "I'll see you in an hour or two."

Half jokingly, I told him, "Before you come back, Robert, pick up some sandwiches for us. I'd like a tuna on rye."

Maybe it was the way I said it, perhaps a bit too condescendingly for Robert's taste, particularly since I was supposed to be working for him, not giving him orders. "Pick up your own fucking sandwiches!" he seethed. Robert shook his head in disgust and walked away.

I learned that even in those days before Led Zeppelin had reached Olympian heights, Robert had a strong ego that I was better off not messing with.

For months after that, Robert and I were on a collision course. He seemed intent on harassing me, at times seeming to even belittle me, making it clear who was the boss and who was the employee. When we were in hotels, he would call my room with requests like "Richard, ring up room service and have them send up some tea and breakfast for me." I wanted to tell him to call the hotel kitchen himself. But he appeared to get a kick out of making me angry. I would always make the calls for Robert just to get him off my back. But it made me furious. I began to feel that my long-term relationship with him might be a rocky one.

Zeppelin's first American tour ended in New York at the Fillmore East. We stayed at the Gorham Hotel on West 55th Street, a wonderful place that Chris Stamp had discovered when managing the Who and that became a favorite among cost-conscious rock bands, thanks to its reasonably priced, kitchen-equipped suites. By this time, New York was eagerly awaiting the debut of Zeppelin. The word had spread about the band's incredible power . . . electrified performances that headline acts were finding almost impossible to follow.

At the Fillmore East, Zeppelin—along with Delaney and Bonnie—were scheduled to open for Iron Butterfly. Butterfly was a huge band in the United States. Their second album, *In-A-Gadda-Da-Vida*, was a monstrous hit—it eventually stayed on the charts for 140 weeks—and their third album was just weeks away from being released. Their music would cut audiences down to size with a sound packing the heavyweight punch of a dozen Mike Tysons. But still, Iron Butterfly was nervous about playing after Led Zeppelin, and Peter sensed that.

Peter was the kind of guy who enjoyed flexing his corporate muscles, who would go for the jugular if he had the chance. "Led Zeppelin is capable of bringing *anyone* down to size," he said. On occasion, he enjoyed watching them do it.

Although Zeppelin was scheduled to go on first that night at the Fillmore, followed by Delaney and Bonnie and then Iron Butterfly, Peter approached Bill Graham, Fillmore's impresario, for a special favor. "Bill, you have to let Zeppelin perform second," Peter pleaded. "Do it for an old friend. I want to see Zeppelin and Iron Butterfly perform back-to-back."

Graham shrugged his shoulders. "Sure, why not!"

Peter got his wish. But we heard that when the members of Iron Butterfly received the news, they freaked out. They knew the stories about Led Zeppelin rocking the rafters in one venue after another. The Butterfly's Doug Ingle and Erik Braunn, we were told by some of the backstage crew, were threatening not to take the stage at all. They were demanding that Led Zeppelin be dropped from the bill altogether.

"That's ridiculous," Graham said he told Iron Butterfly. "You have a contract to perform tonight. Hell if you're going to back out of this because you don't like the opening act. I'm the one who decides the order of appearance, not you."

Just before Led Zeppelin went onstage, Peter was almost out of control. In the dressing room, he gathered the band together and told them what was happening with Iron Butterfly. "Go out there and blow them out of this place!"

That was quite an order, but Zeppelin did just that. On consecutive nights, their sets were absolutely incredible. As they left the stage, with the final chords of "How Many More Times" resounding off the walls, the crowd chanted, "Zeppelin . . . Zeppelin . . . Zeppelin." Ingle, Braunn, and Lee Dorman were irate. The audience was still calling for more Led Zeppelin as Iron Butterfly began their set. For a headline act, it couldn't have been more demoralizing. For a new band like Zeppelin, it couldn't have gotten any sweeter.

"Iron Butterfly is a good band," said Peter, letting some arrogance shine through. "But they were no match for Led Zeppelin. Nobody is a match for Led Zeppelin."

11

BACK TO REALITY

Jimmy Page was distraught. The first American tour had ended on a remarkable high that left the band feeling euphoric for days after returning to England. But back in Peter's office, Jimmy was stunned as he sifted through some reviews of the concerts. And from the way they read, you might have thought that Led Zeppelin had invented cancer or heart disease.

"This is absurd," Jimmy muttered to himself. "These critics don't know a fucking thing about music. They're out of touch. Completely out of touch."

Peter had been right about that first American tour. Fans in the U.S. were ready for a trailblazing band like Led Zeppelin. Ironically, however, the rock critics apparently weren't.

Jimmy felt that Led Zeppelin was *his* band. And the vicious, critical comments were like witnessing the torture of his own child. In disgust, he wadded up a couple of the reviews in a ball and slammed them into a wastebasket.

Peter tried to calm Jimmy down. He was almost as angry as Pagey, but figured there wasn't much to be gained by letting a few confused critics undermine the band's well-being or confidence level.

"Let's put things in perspective," Peter said. "A lot of the press are still pissed off about all of Atlantic's hype about the signing of Led Zeppelin. And we're paying the price now."

Much of the media had proclaimed that Zeppelin was a money-hungry band being shoved down the mouths of a gullible public. They seemed to ignore the fact that during that first American tour, we played for as little as $200 per gig and rarely more than $1,500. Yet the critics had soured on us before they had ever heard a note.

The media saved their most vicious attacks for Robert, perhaps not surprisingly. The lead singer of any band always has to bear his soul a little more than anyone else. And the press collectively wondered who this young, untested singer really was. He had never performed before big crowds on big stages. And, suddenly, he was in the spotlight, at the center of the hype, in the bull's-eye of the critics' target.

Peter and I panicked, trying to hide most of the vicious attacks from Robert. When we'd buy the newspapers or when the clippings were sent to the office, we'd get rid of the reviews that I knew would really hurt. It would have been ridiculous to upset him. But some leaked through, and they had a demoralizing effect.

At first, Robert got angry. Then he got defensive. And then smug. Frankly, I think he was scared. His apparent cockiness was one way of trying to hide the pain and pretend that the attacks didn't hurt. But they did. Later, Robert would say that, in the midst of the media onslaught, the band just decided that "the best thing to do was shut the fuck up and play." Nevertheless, the press assaults bothered him a lot. You could tell it in the way he talked about reporters who used to try to corner him for backstage interviews. "Tell them no interviews until they learn something about music," he would say to me. "A lot of them are ignorant people."

When the band's debut album, *Led Zeppelin*, was released in the U.S. in early 1969, things didn't improve much. Actually, key FM radio stations throughout America already had advance test pressings of the album and had been playing them for weeks. Atlantic had also distributed seven-inch promo discs of two of the longer cuts on the album—"Babe I'm Gonna Leave You" and "Dazed and Confused."

But even though the disc jockeys seemed to like what they heard—continuing to talk about the album's vibrancy, originality, and raw energy—the print media showed no mercy. Some critics insisted that Led Zeppelin was little more than a copycat of the Jeff Beck Group, which also had emerged from the Yardbirds, with Beck and Rod Stewart at the helm.

In *Rolling Stone*, John Mendelsohn ripped the new Zeppelin album apart, song by song: "The popular formula in this, the aftermath era of such successful British bluesmen as Cream and John Mayall, seems to be: add, to an excellent guitarist who, since leaving the Yardbirds and/or Mayall has become a minor musical deity, a competent rhythm section and a pretty soul-belter who can do a good spade imitation. The latest of the British groups so conceived offers little that its twin, the Jeff Beck Group, didn't say as well or bet-ter three months ago."

Ouch!

Despite such attacks, album sales didn't seem to suffer. The record climbed the charts quickly, and as it did the same hostile press began hounding the band for interviews. They suddenly were eager for a Zeppelin headline, clam-oring for any small bit of gossip. But no one in the band was particularly ea-ger to sit through any interviews.

"It's ridiculous," Jimmy said. "If they're going to swing hatchets at us, why should we have anything to do with them? Tell them we're busy. Tell them anything."

Peter tried to stay above it all and not let it bother him. While the band was nursing its wounds from the press's barbs, he went to work planning Zeppelin's next move. Even with all the cries of commercialism, and even with all the audience enthusiasm, the band's first tour of the U.S. did no better than break even. Once we were home and tallied up the figures, I was sur-prised by the numbers.

Peter sat there, sifting through the expense records. "Plane fares . . . auto rentals . . . hotels . . . food . . . equipment upkeep . . . salaries. Whatever we made was gone before we got home."

But Peter wasn't upset. By the reactions of bands like Iron Butterfly, he knew that Zeppelin was on the fast track. At this point, he wasn't concerned about the bottom line. It would change dramatically for the better very soon, he told me.

On a personal level, none of us was making much in those days. I was being paid only $100 a week. Robert and Bonzo were making the same—a flat salary that they sent home to their wives and kids to add to the record company ad-vance. That check from Atlantic provided them a nice financial cushion—something they hadn't been used to. When the band was originally formed, Bonzo was so pressed for cash that he had asked Peter, "Can I drive the equip-ment truck for a little extra money . . . maybe about fifty pounds a week?"

Jimmy and John Paul weren't paid anything for that first American tour. The band was their investment, and they envisioned an enormous payoff down the road. Like Peter, they were familiar enough with everything else in the record stores to recognize that Zeppelin was about to blast off—at least with the fans if not the critics.

Jimmy was determined eventually to keep Zeppelin's profits where they be-longed—with the band itself. He related many horror stories—tales that used to make him furious just in the telling—of being ripped off in the past, in-cluding his time with the Yardbirds. "On one occasion, the Yardbirds toured the U.S. with the Stones, right after we had appeared in the Antonioni movie, *Blow-Up*," he said. "We were at the peak of whatever popularity we had at that time. But after five weeks of touring, do you know how much each member of the Yardbirds got? A check for a hundred and twelve pounds! That's fucking all!"

"Who got the rest of the money that you earned?" I asked.

"Hell if I know! But it wasn't us!"

It's a common story among rock musicians. The bands may attract the pay-ing customers, and have gold record on their walls, but their bank accounts are empty.

Jimmy and Peter, however, had a special chemistry between them that seemed likely to avoid those problems. When Peter took over the manage-ment of the Yardbirds in its waning days, Jimmy felt that he was actually looking out for his musicians, not just for himself. Peter was honest, and in the music business, that was almost unheard of. With Led Zeppelin, Peter acted like the fifth member of the band. Just as I was running interference for the group on the road, Peter was adamant about protecting the business side of their lives. His philosophy was simple: Since the band is drawing the fans to the concert halls, they should reap the financial rewards. It was a rare, refreshing attitude.

Jimmy was so used to having money vanish from sight that, even in Led Zeppelin's halcyon days, he couldn't break his thrifty habits. We were once in a London pub, drinking with a band called the Liverpool Scene. They were teasing Jimmy about his Jack Benny-like money management. One of them coined the nickname "Led Wallet" for Jimmy, and it stuck.

After the first U.S. tour, the phone began ringing constantly in Peter's of-fice. American promoters eagerly asked about Zeppelin's availability—a sharp contrast to what was occurring in the U.K. There was still very little interest in the band back home. Zeppelin's first album wasn't even released in England until March, and there was no huge outcry for it before then.

So as eager as the U.S. promoters were to have us back, the big British pro-moters weren't interested. One London promoter put it bluntly on the phone: "Peter, there's a new band being formed in England with nearly every tick of the clock. So why do we need another one?"

Those kinds of remarks were painful. But on some level, Jimmy and the others understood what was going on. After the debut album was released in England, the band congregated for a meeting in Peter's office, where Jimmy analyzed things this way:

"In the U.S., FM radio stations are willing to play lengthy Zeppelin-style cuts. But British radio is still hooked on singles, and so it's harder for us to get airplay here. That's just a fact of life we have to live with."

Even so, they desperately wanted acceptance at home. Although they didn't talk about it much, they resented the cold shoulder from the U.K.

To attract converts in England, the band launched a British tour in March 1969, confined to one-nighters at small clubs—Fishmongers' Hall and the Marquee in London, Mother's in Birmingham, Cook's Ferry Inn in Manchester, and Klook's Kleek in Edmonton. They were cramped little clubs, often bursting with audiences of no more than 300 or 400. Some had no dressing rooms. The fees were small, too—sixty pounds against 60 percent of the gross was typical, although they sometimes went as high as 140 pounds per night.

Amazingly, word of mouth helped sell out nearly every performance. But even with packed houses, no one would make much money. Peter was still frustrated, but insisted, "Things are going to turn around in England. In the meantime, maybe it's time to go back to the U.S."

Perhaps Zeppelin really belonged in America.

12

LED WALLET

Jimmy Page was alone in the boathouse underneath his home, inspecting the instruments and the equipment that were collecting dust. A lot of them dated back to the Yardbirds' days; some of them were even older.

Barely two months earlier, by the end of Led Zeppelin's first American tour, the group had worn out and virtually destroyed much of the old Yardbirds gear it had been using. Unlike Peter Townshend, who intentionally would smash and mutilate instruments as audiences roared their approval, Zeppelin just played them to death. But Pagey, ever frugal, didn't relish investing very much money, if any, on new gear for the upcoming second American tour, which would begin in just two weeks, in late April 1969. How could he resurrect some of this equipment, he asked himself, without crippling the band's already shaky profit and loss statements?

Some blown-out Fenders from the Yardbirds' days were being stored in the boathouse. The Rickenbacker gear from the first Zeppelin tour was next to it, and even though it was still usable, Jimmy didn't think it was up to his standards. The fans might not notice, he thought, but he would.

It was a real dilemma for a perfectionist like Page. He wanted everything to be precise and exact. At the same time, however, the mere thought of spending thousands of dollars on new gear was agonizing. Led Wallet had met Led Zeppelin head-on, and, at least for the moment, it was a stalemate.

That night, Jimmy had a brainstorm. He picked up the phone and called Clive Coulson, who was going to be joining us as a roadie on the new U.S. tour.

"Clive, I want to get some Marshall gear before we leave for America," Jimmy told him.

"That's pretty expensive stuff," Clive said. "How much can we spend on it?"

"We're not going to spend a damn thing," Jimmy exclaimed. "With some tools and a little creativity, it's not going to cost us anything."

Clive and I arrived at Jimmy's house the next day, and Pagey explained what he had in mind: He told Clive to remove the backs from both the Fender and the Rickenbacker cabinets, take the speakers out of each, and place them in the opposite cabinet. Then he instructed Clive to take the Fender cabinets—once the Rickenbacker speakers were inside them—to Sound City near Piccadilly Circus and trade them in for some new Marshall equipment.

"With the import tariffs, Fenders are the most expensive amps you can buy," Jimmy said. "They'll never know that there are Rickenbacker speakers inside the Fender cabinets."

It worked. Clive returned from Sound City with two sets of new Marshall speakers—without spending a quid. Led Wallet was the victor this time.

In the final days before the flight to the U.S. for the second American tour, Zeppelin started feeling butterflies. As I've learned over the years, no matter how many tours and concerts a band has to its credit . . . no matter how well they have played and how loud the crowds have cheered . . . there is always some apprehension at the start of every new tour. Will this one go as smoothly as the last? Will the fans fill up the seats? Will they leave the clubs and concert halls yearning for more?

But as that tour began, those anxieties proved to be unfounded. Night after night, the band left audiences in one city, then the next, spellbound. San Francisco . . . Detroit . . . Chicago . . . Boston . . . New York . . . thirty performances in nineteen cities with music that exploded with such horsepower that it eclipsed nearly everything that had ever reverberated through the Fillmores, the Guthrie Theatre in Minneapolis, the Kinetic Circus in Chicago, and Boston Garden.

That second U.S. tour started in San Francisco with some unexpected fireworks. Bill Graham, the unpredictable owner/manager of the Fillmore West, was a bright, hardworking businessman, tough and direct, who was always fair with the Yardbirds and Led Zeppelin. He made sure every detail was taken care of, giving us every frill we requested and often more.

But when we arrived at the Fillmore West on that Thursday afternoon in May, a few hours before our first performance, we received anything but a cordial welcome. Clive approached Graham, who was playing basketball with a few employees at a hoop set up in back of the club.

"Mr. Graham," Clive said, "we're here to set up Led Zeppelin's equipment. Can we get started?"

Graham glared in our direction and pointed his index finger at us.

"Who the hell are you speaking to, fella?" Graham shouted, with veins bulging from his neck. "When I'm ready to talk to you, I'll talk to you. Can't you see I'm right in the middle of something?"

Poor Clive. He turned to me as if to say, "When can I catch the next flight back to London?" He learned firsthand that when Graham wanted to put on his frightening persona, it could be an Academy Award-winning performance. We never figured out why Graham had made such a scene, but we agreed never to interfere with his basketball game again. I also was forced to recognize that although those of us in the Led Zeppelin entourage felt great about the band, others weren't quite ready to roll out the red carpet yet.

For part of that second tour, as we had done with the first, Led Zeppelin shared the bill with Vanilla Fudge. But this time, the Fudge weren't always the headliners. In any given city, the band whose albums were getting the most airplay would headline that night, based on Atlantic Records' market research. We really didn't care whether we performed first or last; the audience reaction to Led Zeppelin was always the same—sheer pandemonium.

At the beginning of the tour, Led Zeppelin was playing hour-long shows. But in response to the audiences, the performances gradually grew . . . from seventy-five minutes . . . to ninety minutes . . . and more. When the band would run short on songs, they would improvise tunes by Otis Redding and Love. Robert would even occasionally try to sneak in an old Moby Grape song or two, although the rest of the band would rarely stand for it, primarily as a way of needling Plant a little.

"No show is the same," Jimmy would say. Even though Zeppelin's own songs were becoming standards, they always left room for improvisation, from Jimmy's inventive riffs to Bonham's drum solos that made believers of the fans all the way in the back row. Sometimes, the band would surprise themselves with the creative directions their music took and the way they could push their instruments to the brink and back.

By the midway point of that tour, Zeppelin's confidence level was sky-high. They had literally come to expect the audience frenzy. They certainly weren't blasé about it, but they would have been surprised if the crowd hadn't become fanatical by the end of each evening. The band's reputation had preceded them, and the audiences appeared to be on the edge of hysteria even as the band was being introduced. Once they started playing, it was wall-to-wall madness.

"It feels great just being out there playing music," Bonham said to me one evening just before going onstage. "But once the crowd gets going, it's absolute lunacy. The energy from those fans drives me beyond the point of no return."

During the tour, however, the band didn't have the luxury of merely basking in the nonstop applause. They were being constantly pressured by Atlantic Records to move toward completion of their second album, *Led Zeppelin II*. The first album had entered the *Billboard* charts at Number 99 and then catapulted its way into the Top 10. Eventually, it would spend seventy-three weeks on the charts, including reappearances as late as 1979—ten years after its release.

"Can't Atlantic just be happy counting the money from the sales of the first album?" Robert complained one day. "I just hate being under the gun like this. It's not fair!"

"Why don't we just be more blunt about it," Bonzo suggested. "Let's just tell them to fuck off!"

Despite their anxiety over facing record-company pressures in the middle of a tour, Led Zeppelin was also thoroughly professional. They realized they had a contractual commitment that they needed to take seriously. Jimmy and Robert began frantically writing songs in hotel rooms ("Whole Lotta Love," "Ramble On"), sometimes scribbling lyrics and notes on hotel stationery. Robert wrote a complete song lyric ("Thank You") on his own for the first time, which he dedicated to his wife. On occasion, these songs were rehearsed and recorded just hours after they were written.

Whenever we had a day off, wherever we were, Jimmy would find an available studio—the Ardent Studio in Memphis, the Gold Star Studio in Los Angeles—and the band would isolate themselves there from early evening until late at night, adding one more track to the album. Robert occasionally entered the studio alone to record some voice-overs. He laid down the lead vocal for "Whole Lotta Love" in a single take ("I was right on the money the first time; there's just no way to improve upon it").

"Whole Lotta Love" got an enormous amount of Jimmy's attention in the studio. With Robert's vocal already on tape, he spent hours building everything else around it. For the descending chord structure, he used a metal slide and a reverse echo effect. The same backward echo technique also appeared on "Ramble On."

A lot of the effects in "Whole Lotta Love" and the rest of the album emerged from pure experimentation. Jimmy would sit down in the control room with the engineer on that second album, and they'd literally start playing with the dials, turning them one way, then the other, seeing what kinds of sounds they could create. For "Whole Lotta Love," they produced a dizzying onslaught of screeches, squeals, and squalls.

Jimmy also worked tirelessly by himself, mixing "Bring It On Home," then "What Is and What Should Never Be." He added twelve-string picking to "Thank You" and a barrage of Gibson overdubs to "Ramble On."

It would sometimes make me nervous just to watch Pagey in the studio. He would become much more anxious there than he ever did onstage. No matter how well prepared he was, he rarely seemed completely satisfied. He always wanted something a little closer to perfection. His confidence would ebb and flow. Sometimes, after hours of mixing, he would collapse his face into his hands, as if trying to smother the tension and hide from the reality of still more sessions, still more work on an album that never seemed to end. It was long, exhausting work, and as much as he enjoyed the creative process, it would sometimes overwhelm him.

On several occasions, Jimmy and I would catch a plane into New York from a gig in Minneapolis or Chicago. I would carry the unfinished tapes on the plane with me, wrapped in foil. We'd grab a taxi to A&R Studios, spend half a day there, and then fly out to the next concert. It was grueling, punishing, and terribly stressful. But he felt it had to be done.

As the tour progressed, we flew into Baltimore for a concert at the Merriweather Pavilion. Frank Barsalona and Barbara Skydel of Premier Talent were handling our booking for the tour, and their agency also represented the Who. "Why don't we put Zeppelin and the Who on the same bill?" Frank suggested to Peter.

Peter sat back and contemplated the idea for a moment. "Sure, let's do it." He knew the Who would be getting top billing, but he felt Zeppelin could hold its own against the more seasoned band.

Both bands were nervous about playing with the other. After the opening act—a singing comedian named Uncle Dirty—Zeppelin took the stage and did a powerful ninety-minute set. Then the Who pulled out all the stops with ninety minutes of their own, capped by a record-breaking destruction of instruments.

Near the end of the show, I went to pick up Zeppelin's money with John "Wiggy" Wolfe, who was doing the same for the Who. "I hope you guys made a lot of money," I told Wiggy. "With all those instruments that Townshend destroyed, you're gonna need a few dollars to replace 'em."

Wiggy told me that the Who was being paid $6,750 for the concert. "Really," I said. "We're getting almost as much—six thousand dollars."

Wiggy was shocked. "I can't believe you're getting only seven hundred and fifty dollars less than us."

"Well, particularly since it'll cost you ten thousand dollars just to buy new instruments, I guess Zeppelin came out ahead on this one."

■ ■ ■

Throughout that tour, as if the difficulties working on the new album weren't enough, Zeppelin and the press continued to be at odds. Even as the size of the crowds at our concerts grew, the media indifference—even antipathy—seemed to intensify. During that second tour, *Variety*'s review was typical of the ruthlessness we encountered:

"This quartet's obsession with power, volume, and melodramatic theatrics leaves little room for the subtlety other Britishers employ. There is plenty of room for dynamics and understatement in the Zeppelin's brand of ultrahard rock. But the combo has forsaken the musical sense for the sheer power that entices their predominantly juvenile audience."

When Jimmy would read bad reviews, he would become absolutely unglued. "Are these critics writing in a vacuum?" he complained one day, sitting in a hotel room in Chicago. "Don't they hear the crowd cheering for more encores?" He disgustingly tossed a review across the room. "And they write with such arrogance, as though their opinion means more than anyone else's. Just because they write well doesn't mean they know music!"

John Paul often took a more whimsical attitude toward the whole matter. "There's one advantage to them snubbing us," he said. "Because they don't hang around us a lot, we don't have to waste a lot of time answering their questions, which can be pretty idiotic at times."

Pagey began talking about refusing to do *any* more interviews with the media, something which irked the publicity forces at Atlantic Records. Ultimately, once the band had the power to make unpopular demands like that, Jimmy unconditionally rejected all requests for interviews—a policy that stayed in force for several tours. "Once the media develop a better, more balanced perspective of our music, then I'll start talking to them again," he said.

The hostility between the band and the press reached a peak during the final three weeks of the tour when Ellen Sander, a *Life* reporter, began to travel with us. It wasn't a particularly pleasant experience for anyone. Sander had actually suggested to her editors that she cover the Who's American tour instead; when that didn't work out, she turned to Led Zeppelin as a backup.

Because Zeppelin was such a new band, we probably should have welcomed attention from a magazine with the stature of *Life*. In fact, Peter sat down with us one afternoon and said, "Please give her a little polite attention. She's with a big American magazine. Whatever she writes is going to be read by millions of people."

So we tried. We took turns casually chatting with Sander, but none of us could find anything too endearing about her. She wasn't that much fun to be around. She didn't seem particularly fond of our music, and she clearly had contempt for our lifestyle.

Sander's journalism was reflective of the ongoing problems that Led Zeppelin had with the media. When she finally did write about her experiences on the tour, her recollections were thoroughly unflattering and, from our point of view, largely inaccurate. Sander's most provocative claim was that as she was departing the tour and bidding us "good-bye and godspeed," she was attacked by two members of the band (whom she did not identify). As she recalled it, they grabbed at her clothes and shredded her dress. Peter Grant, she insisted, rescued her before she was thoroughly sacrificed to these monsters/musicians.

"What a bunch of crap!" Bonzo told me later. "We may have been teasing her a little, and maybe our drunkenness offended her. But if she thought we were trying to rape her, then she's got a lot wilder imagination than most writers."

Sander's observations were brutal. "If you walk inside the cages of the zoo you get to see the animals close up, stroke the captive pelts, and mingle with the energy behind the mystique," she wrote. "You also get to smell the shit firsthand."

Peter asked me to try to find some way to help the band live with the pressures that were building up during that tour. "It's torture," Pagey once told me on a plane flight on the way to a recording studio in New York. "This band is a newborn, and I'm already ready for a break."

13

A TASTE OF DECADENCE

By the second American tour, we always had plenty of girls hanging around the stage doors and the hotels. Plant and Page seemed to be their main interests, but many of the young ladies weren't particular. While the band began to rely on me to arrange whatever late-night entertainment they desired, the girls made it easy.

Even by this early period in Zeppelin's history, I could already see recreational patterns developing that would persist throughout the band's lifetime. There were the girls, of course, whom we began to party with, sometimes to excess. And there were endless bottles of alcohol, too. Both, of course, were welcome diversions from the stresses of traveling and the record-company pressures that hit us hard during that second U.S. tour. But we soon began to overdo it. The alcohol and later the drugs, too, eventually caught up with the band and began taking their toll. And as early as 1969, there were already signs of an eventual downhill slide.

When it came to girls, Jimmy would say, "The younger, the better." More than the others, Jimmy seemed to lust after the girls whose faces were childlike and innocent and whose bodies had barely taken shape. But he wasn't the only one who enjoyed the young ones. Maybe it was a sign of our immaturity, but after all, we were only twenty or twenty-one ourselves, so a fourteen- or fifteen-year-old wasn't total madness—or at least it didn't seem so at the time. And as for the married members of the band, most were able to at least temporarily overlook the fact that they had wives waiting for them back in England; if there were ever any guilt pangs, I never saw them.

"My dream," Jimmy once told me, "is to find a young, Joni Mitchell lookalike . . . thin, angular features, long blond hair, a voice that could sing you to sleep."

I kept my eyes open, but never really filled the prescription to his satisfaction. In fact, I don't think he ever would have been content with anyone but the real thing.

"Richard, I'll tell you what I fantasize about," Jimmy said. "I'd like to have Joni Mitchell sitting on the end of my bed, playing the guitar and singing for me." He didn't elaborate on the fantasy any further, but I presumed that he would have liked a little more from Joni than guitar strumming.

I would often saunter down to the hotel lobbies where the young ladies would congregate and invite some of them up to our rooms. Even though Led Zeppelin and dozens of other rock bands were often accused of exploiting these girls, I thought it was a bum rap. We rarely went looking for them; they made themselves available to us. We never forced them into doing anything they didn't want to. They were looking for some fun—and so were we. There was no emotional involvement on either side. As a blonde in Boston told me, "I just want a good time. If any of you guys want to have some fun, I'm available." She was wearing her high school cheerleader outfit.

Some of the girls were hangers-on from the Yardbirds' days. They had been fans of Jimmy's and hadn't broken their addiction to him. They also appeared to have created their own groupie hierarchy, determined to stay on the first team rather than slip down to benchwarmers. A few became madly jealous if they sensed a decline in attention from Jimmy. And their exchanges with each other often got bitter ("Jimmy always treated me like a lady, which is more than I can say for you!"). Occasionally, their hostile words would deteriorate into hair-pulling, eye-gouging free-for-alls.

The girls and the booze usually went together. But sometimes the liquor was enough. In a few cities in those days, we did two shows a night, usually at 10 P.M. and midnight, and during the hour break between the two performances, we'd uncork some champagne, sometimes several bottles of it. "The booze helps calm my nerves," Bonzo would tell me. "I just feel better when I've had a drink or two." In actuality, he would have ten to twelve drinks.

One night in Kansas City, after the second show at a club just south of the Missouri River, I drove the band back to our hotel, the Muehlbach, one of the finest old inns in the city. We went into the hotel bar, and after a few more drinks—Scotch, champagne, gin and tonic—John Paul, Robert, and Jimmy took the elevator to their rooms. Bonzo and I decided there was still more drinking to do. So we kept the bartender company.

Eventually, we became so intoxicated that I doubted we would ever find our way to our rooms. But we tried, weaving through the hotel lobby like a couple of drunks—which we were becoming. Bonzo couldn't stay on his feet any longer and collapsed into an oversized chair and refused to budge.

"Go up without me, Cole," he said, his speech slurring one word after another. "I'll be fine here. I'll be just fine."

I wasn't in any shape to argue. I just wanted to get some sleep. Once inside my room, I took a couple of Mandrax to help me doze off and crawled into bed, expecting to snooze peacefully until morning. But Bonzo had other plans. At about 3 A.M., the phone in my room jarred me awake.

"Richard!"

"Who is this?" I mumbled.

"Hey, Richard. You gotta get me outta here!"

I recognized Bonzo's voice, but was still trying to orient myself.

"It's me, Richard. Come down and get me."

"Where are you, you cunt?"

"Where do you think? I'm in jail, that's where I am. Come and bail me out."

Bonham then apparently handed the phone to a cop, who proceeded to explain that Bonzo had been taken to jail for being drunk in a public place—namely, the Muehlbach lobby. He gave me the address of the jail, which was about two miles down the road.

I was furious, but my anger was related more to being awakened than to a concern over Bonham's well-being. Cursing under my breath, I got dressed and stuffed $5,000 in cash into my pocket. Ten minutes later, I was in the police station.

"I'm here to get John Bonham," I told the sergeant at the desk. "I'm his manager." I figured calling myself his manager sounded more impressive than tour manager. "What's it going to cost to bail him out?"

"Cost!" The sergeant snickered. "That son of a bitch isn't going anywhere. He's gonna sleep it off. Come and pick him up in the morning when he's sober."

So at nine the following morning, I returned. Bonham had a sheepish look on his face as they led him to the waiting area of the police station. His face was bruised with one contusion below his left eye and another on the cheek next to it.

"I think the cops roughed me up a little," he whispered. "I really don't remember."

None of us learned much from experiences like that. There were many more drinking episodes during that tour. Particularly when Peter wasn't with us, I was the only one to try to keep Zeppelin in line. And I was usually just as possessed with alcohol—if not more so—than the rest of the band.

In May—not long before Bonham's twenty-first birthday—Zeppelin performed two shows at the Rose Palace in Pasadena. Barry Imhoff, the promoter of the event, knew what our life-style was becoming by then. So he chose a birthday gift that John couldn't have appreciated any more—a four-foot-tall bottle of champagne!

Between the first and second shows that night, Bonzo single-handedly guzzled nearly a third of the bottle. When it was time for him to maneuver back into the drummer's stool for the second show, he dragged the oversized bottle onto the stage with him. For a sober observer, it was probably a sad sight: There, like a weightlifter pressing a barbell, he raised the bottle over his head between songs and flooded his mouth and throat with alcohol. He was so drunk that he fell off his stool twice. By the time the performance ended, the bottle was empty.

Imhoff still had one more gift for us: Four live octopuses.

"What are we supposed to do with octopuses?" I asked.

"They make great bathtub companions," he claimed. "They're much more fun than a rubber duck."

Back at the hotel, we had invited a couple of girls up to our rooms, and I figured they might be able to make better use of the octopuses than I could. "You girls look like you need a little cleaning up," I told them. "Take off your clothes and climb into the bathtub."

They agreed, and after they had jumped into the tub, Jimmy and I carried in the octopuses and tossed them into the water. "We figure you need something to keep you company," Jimmy giggled.

The girls remained remarkably calm, considering there were these creatures swimming around them. As we watched them play, the octopuses somehow instinctively knew just where to congregate and just where to place their tentacles. One of the girls, a little brunette who Jimmy couldn't take his eyes off, gasped and then sighed as one of the octopuses explored her genitals.

"Oh, my God," she squealed. "I've gotta get one of these. It's like having an eight-armed vibrator!"

"Maybe we oughta market these things," I told Jimmy. "It would probably have even more universal appeal than music."

We were in the Los Angeles area for almost a week, and at the Château Marmont we ran room service ragged with our appetite for booze. "Los

Angeles is something special," Bonzo used to say. "It's different. It's decadent."

Back in England, Zeppelin lived quite normal lives with storybooklike families or girlfriends. But the road—particularly Los Angeles—was becoming a place of excess. Of course, we probably spent many more hours in the States sitting in airports, watching television or talking about music. There were many hours spent in recording studios and even more time onstage. But it's some of the wild, reckless episodes that still stick most vividly in my mind. Seemingly overnight, we found ourselves in a position to do almost anything we wanted, and in L.A. there seemed to be a tidal wave of free-spirited girls who were always cooperative and compliant. For a group of working-class boys from London, it was like finding the Promised Land.

I was in John Bonham's bungalow at the Marmont late one night, and each of us had a girl in tow. Although we certainly weren't Casanovas, we still could have added several notches to the Marmont's cluttered bedposts. By this point, we had devoured a few bottles of booze, and Bonzo and I were each occupying one of the beds in the room, with our clothes in a single pile on the floor.

While I was intertwined pretzel-like with my girl—a bird from Santa Monica named Robin—Bonzo decided to walk into the kitchen to catch his breath and grab a drink of water. While there, he spotted two large industrial-sized cans of baked beans. The chef in him apparently took over.

Bonzo opened the cans, and then, while cradling one in each arm, he pranced into the bedroom.

"Dinnertime!" he announced. "Come and get it!"

As Robin and I looked up in horror, Bonham stood over us, held the cans over our heads, and then tilted them simultaneously on their sides, pouring their cold contents onto our naked bodies.

"You fucker," I screamed, rolling to the opposite end of the bed in a futile attempt to escape the line of fire.

Within seconds, Robin and I were swimming in a gooey, sloppy puddle of beans that covered us from our eyebrows to our ankles. It was a scene out of *Tom Jones.*

Before Robin and I could come up for air, Peter Grant had walked into the bungalow and surveyed the scene. On occasion, Peter would show anger or disgust over incidents like this. But not that night.

"Peter," yelled Bonzo, "grab a spoon and dig in!"

Peter chuckled and then was overcome with a mischievous urge of his own.

"Cole, you fucking slob, don't you have *any* class?" he roared. "Let me add a little sophistication to your life."

Peter grabbed a full bottle of champagne on the nearby dresser, shook and then uncorked it, and proceeded to spray Robin and me with its contents.

Bonham would become almost teary-eyed when we finally had to check out of the Marmont. On our last night there, he had been drinking pretty heavily and decided that he wanted to play doctor. He borrowed a white coat and a room service cart from a hotel valet and lifted a girl named Candy onto the cart. Candy was a pretty, blond teenager from Miami who we had met during the first tour. She showed up unannounced at the Marmont, salivating for some Zeppelin high jinks. We didn't disappoint her.

Bonham undressed her on the cart, cackling as he removed each piece of clothing. Once she was nude, he proclaimed, "It's time for some surgery, my dear."

He scampered into the bathroom and returned with a shaving brush, shaving cream, and razor. "This won't hurt a bit, sweetheart," he told Candy, who lay there submissively as he applied shaving cream to her pubic hair.

For the next ten minutes, the band and I took turns shaving her vagina: Robert with vitality and broad strokes . . . Jimmy with the passion of Rodin or Michelangelo. All the while, Candy giggled her way through the procedure.

When it was over, as we admired our artistic efforts, Robert suddenly interrupted the festivities with a shrill, agonizing wail. "Oh, fuck!" he screamed. "Bonham, how could you? How could you?"

Robert picked up the shaving brush and waved it in the air. "This is mine. This is my fucking brush."

Everyone in the room burst into laughter. John Paul patted Robert on the back. "Enjoy your next shave," he said.

Not all the girls we ran into during that second tour were as pretty as Candy. And, of course, we were in a position to be quite selective. For the unattractive birds—the ones who were painfully hard on the eyes—well, as Bonham said, "If you let any of those dogs up to the room, you're fired!"

The Plaster Casters were some of the most persistent girls, stubbornly overstaying their invitation despite our repeated pleas that they simply vanish. They were determined to make casts of the band members' erect penises, perhaps someday displaying them in the Rock and Roll Hall of Fame. One day at the Marmont, Cynthia P. Caster explained to us how they created the casts that had made them so famous. "First we get the musician excited, any way we can," she said. "Then my assistant does the actual casting while I keep the hard-on going. She's quite talented. You guys should try it. This is really an art form."

Maybe so. But Robert once joked, "There's no way I could keep my dick hard around those fat chicks."

I had known the Plaster Casters from my days with the Yardbirds. And they were still as hefty and as homely as ever. I think that Zeppelin would have chosen celibacy if the Casters were the only alternative. I know I would have.

One afternoon at the Marmont, we were sunning ourselves by the pool. The Casters were there, too, and they really began to torment us. They wanted to make some plaster casts; we wouldn't even entertain the idea. They wanted to make small talk; we wanted them to shut up.

Finally, Bonzo had had enough. "The only way you bitches are going to clam up is to fill your mouths with water!"

He got up from his chaise lounge, walked toward Cynthia, and pushed her toward the edge of the pool. When she was just a step away, he shoved her with the full force of his body. Cynthia became airborne and plunged into the water with the force of a pregnant whale. The resulting tsunami drenched half of the surrounding patio.

Instead of sinking to the bottom of the pool like dead weight, however, Cynthia's multiple layers of clothing—including a black velvet dress with obnoxiously gaudy frills—came to her rescue. The air trapped within her clothes kept her bobbing at the surface, providing enough support so she was able to keep her head above water, although not without a struggle and a lot of splashing.

"Get me out of here, you assholes," she gurgled, barely loud enough to be heard over our laughter.

I leaped into the pool and towed her to the ladder, where she made a rather unladylike exit from the water.

Despite such zaniness, we never lost sight of why we were really in America. "We're here to make music—that's number one," Bonzo would proclaim, often half drunk. Alcohol continued to cause some embarrassing situations, at one time or another affecting every member of the band.

Because of booze, we often became a nightmare to be with on an airplane, particularly when the crew made no efforts to limit the alcohol they served us. During that second tour, on a commercial flight from Athens, Ohio, to Minneapolis, Robert had devoured a few drinks and was feeling much too giddy for the confining quarters of an airplane. So he got up from his seat and began prancing up and down the aisle, looking like a cross between the Pied Piper and a Spanish matador. He was letting loose, allowing himself some temporary liberation from the demands of our touring schedule. He peered in one direction, then another, fluttered his arms and began singing an uncommon refrain:

"Toilets! Toilets! Toilets for Robert!"

He was so loud that the entire planeload of seventy passengers could hear him, and they stared dumbfounded at this bizarre man bounding through the plane like a raving lunatic.

"Where are the toilets? Robert needs a toilet! Toilets!"

Many of the passengers were noticeably disturbed, wondering just what might happen next. I wondered, too, but was more interested in waiting for my next drink than in helping Robert to the bathroom. Fortunately, a flight attendant took Robert by the hand and led him toward the bathroom. After he banged on the door and finally barged his way in, his "concert" came to an abrupt end.

At one point during the tour, as incidents like that began to multiply, I recognized that perhaps we all needed some R&R. I suggested that we unwind for a few days in Honolulu, where we already had a show scheduled. The vote in favor was unanimous.

There were two elegant mansions on Diamond Head, with breathtaking views of the Pacific and Waikiki Beach, that many rock bands rented from time to time. Peter was able to get us into one of them, a multimillion-dollar Spanish villa that might have made William Randolph Hearst jealous. During our four days there, we got burned to a crisp in the tropical sun and were treated to sailing expeditions and a luau. I remember relaxing on the beach, listening to Bob Dylan's *Lay Lady Lay*, which had just climbed to the top of the charts. Perhaps inspired by Dylan, we spent part of our Hawaiian visit leied with flowers and laid with female bodies.

In a sense, we found ourselves in a no-win situation. When our schedule kept us running nonstop, we yearned for a halt in the action, but during that Hawaiian stay, when there was finally time to relax, we soon found ourselves bored out of our minds. "It's hard to figure," Bonzo observed one day, popping the cap on a bottle of beer. "Either we're running so fast that we're ready to collapse, or we have so little to do that we're going crazy."

Even so, no one was better at creating something to do than Bonzo—and there was no better target for his practical jokes than Plant. Bonham played an occasional prank on John Paul, like the time he flooded Jonesy's room in Hawaii by sneaking a garden hose through the sliding glass door. But John Paul was so easygoing that even when he awoke to find his room turned into a wading pool, he just took it in stride. Those kinds of low-key responses made him a much less attractive guinea pig for the tomfoolery that the rest of us savored. It was much more fun to harass someone like Robert, who would often have hysterical reactions to the pranks aimed in his direction.

From Hawaii, we flew into Detroit for a performance at the Grande Ballroom, a former mattress-manufacturing plant that had been transformed into the city's premiere rock club. Our plane landed in the predawn hours, and it was barely daybreak when we checked into the Congress Hotel on the morning of the concert. We had flown through the night and had been drinking heavily while in the air. We were dead tired, irritable, and just wanted to check into our rooms and get some sleep.

But as we dragged ourselves and our luggage through the hotel lobby, something else besides the need for sleep captured our attention. "There's blood all over the fuckin' carpet," John Paul exclaimed, tiptoeing his way around the still damp patches of blood.

"Ahh, come on, Jonesy," I said. "America's a tough place, but don't be ridiculous."

Then I took a closer look. He wasn't being ridiculous at all.

Less than half an hour before we arrived, there had been an attempted robbery at the hotel. The bellhop had confronted the robber with a loaded pistol, and the lobby had turned into something resembling the showdown in *High Noon*.

"That motherfucker tried to come in and rob us," the bellhop told us, his voice still quivering and his hand still trembling. "I shot the bastard, and he died right here at my feet. They just took the body away."

Robert looked down at the carpet—we swore we could see some steam rising from the fresh bloodstains. "I think I'm going to throw up," Robert moaned. "I really do."

"Get hold of yourself, Robert," I said. "These things happen."

Then Robert exploded. "Jesus Christ, why are we staying in this hotel anyway, Richard? We're working like maniacs, and you put us in a hotel that's like a battlefield."

"Do you think everything that happens is my fault?" I shouted. "I didn't shoot the bastard!"

"Sometimes I wonder!" he muttered.

That night at the Grande Ballroom, things didn't improve much. As the band performed, they had to cope with blown fuses and power outages. Each time they had to stop playing—once right in the middle of "I Can't Quit You Baby," then just as they were launching into "Black Mountain Side"—the overflow crowd grew progressively agitated. Before long, rowdiness bordered on mutiny. Perhaps only the mellowing aroma of marijuana, wafting through the hall and settling upon the audience, kept them from rioting.

"What a fucked-up night!" Bonzo complained as we drove back to the hotel after the performance. "Tell Detroit we're not coming back."

I wondered for the first time whether this chaos was worth it.

As the tour wound down, the hectic pace was affecting all of us. The band began sleeping a little more and partying a little less. On airplane flights, we became more interested in being left alone than nagging the stewardesses for just one more drink. Each night, however, the music itself seemed to revitalize the band, along with an occasional second wind for some more revelry.

Even when our level of exhaustion had peaked, the Steve Paul Scene was a club that Led Zeppelin couldn't resist. Located in the heart of Manhattan at West 46th Street and Eighth Avenue, it was a place where the Young Rascals and other pop groups had found enthusiastic audiences in the mid to late sixties and where Jimi Hendrix would drop in unannounced to jam with whomever was courageous enough to join him onstage.

When Zeppelin began frequenting the Steve Paul Scene, Page and Bonham would order a row of porch climbers, potent drinks that could leave you staggering, although the bartender would never reveal exactly what was in them. And if the drinks didn't take care of you, there were plenty of girls to help while away the night.

One evening at the bar, a tall redhead approached Robert and within sixty seconds was sitting on his lap. Before Robert knew it, she was French-kissing him—with an unexpected bonus. As they kissed, she passed a Seconal from her mouth to his.

"What the hell was that?" he exclaimed.

"Swallow it, and then I'll tell you," she said. He was foolish enough to follow her instructions. Every time we went back to Steve Paul's, Plant asked if the redhead was there.

For years thereafter, if we were within striking distance of New York, Robert, Jimmy, and I insisted that we somehow find a way to get to the Steve Paul Scene—even if it meant some last-minute restructuring of the concerts themselves. We were driven to fulfill whatever crazy need was there to blow off steam. One Saturday night, the band was booked into the Philadelphia Spectrum, with Jethro Tull performing on the same bill before us. I did a little arithmetic, and the figures weren't encouraging. "By the time we finish the show and drive the ninety-three miles to New York City, we won't have much drinking time left before the bars close," I complained to Robert.

"Well, then, do something about it," he insisted.

This was one of the few instances in the band's history where merriment took precedence over music. I might have felt a little guilty about it, except that I was as interested in getting to the New York bars as anyone. So I approached Larry Spivak, the promoter at the Spectrum, with a story guaranteed to tug at his heartstrings.

"Larry, we've got a real problem here," I told him, just minutes before Jethro Tull was set to open the show. "Jimmy Page is very sick, some kind of intestinal problem. I don't think he's going to last the night. I've phoned our doctor, I've talked to the band, and for Jimmy's sake, the boys have agreed to go on before Jethro Tull so we can get Jimmy out of here and into bed for the night."

Spivak was stunned. "What the hell are you talking about? A lot more people came here to see Led Zeppelin. I can't switch the bill around."

I wasn't about to give in.

"Larry, go into the dressing room and look at Jimmy for yourself. The poor bastard looks so anemic he may collapse at any moment. We've gotta go on first. It's not even open to discussion."

Spivak was irate. Yet he finally began to believe he had no choice but to comply. At eight o'clock, we opened the show.

Meanwhile, Ian Anderson of Jethro Tull was upset that he had been bumped to a later time. He must have known the futility of trying to succeed Led Zeppelin on the stage. After the same type of incident with Iron Butterfly earlier in the year, no one wanted to even try it. It was virtually suicidal.

Jimmy didn't feel much sympathy for Anderson. "Jethro Tull is an overrated band," he said. "They get a lot more attention than they deserve." The next year when we were in Los Angeles, on hearing a radio advertisement for a Tull concert at the Forum, Jimmy created his own parody of the commercial. "Ladies and gentlemen," he said, "tonight only, Jethro Dull bores 'em at the Forum."

That night at the Spectrum, after performing ahead of Jethro Tull, we were in the car by nine-thirty, breaking the sound barrier on a reckless ride to New York City. We pulled up in front of the Steve Paul Scene a little after eleven o'clock and drank and flirted for three delicious hours.

The second American tour closed with two raucous nights at the Fillmore East. The band came away feeling that each member was defining a place for himself in the group. When Led Zeppelin had been formed the previous year, it was known primarily as Jimmy Page's Supergroup. But by the time the band headed back to London on June 1, barely more than five months after making its American debut, rock fans were beginning to perceive Robert Plant as an equal to Page, a powerful force in his own right within the band. Bonham and Jones, too, were becoming more relaxed and more confident.

On the flight home, John Paul told me, "This group could become one of the biggest bands in history. We've got a really good thing going. I hope we don't blow it."

14

FAST TRACK

Back in London, Led Zeppelin continued to operate in overdrive. We had barely unpacked our bags after the second U.S. tour when Peter Grant already began talking about a third one.

"I can feel the momentum building," Peter told me in his office in early June 1969, only three days following our return. "We could keep this band on the road year-round and never run out of bookings." Then he added, "This is the time to take advantage of all the interest that's been created."

I was worried, however, and warned Peter about the fatigue factor. "The band was starting to wilt near the end of the last tour," I told him. "If we're not careful, Led Zeppelin's not going to die from the ego conflicts that kill other bands; it's going to just collapse from exhaustion."

Even back in England, the band kept moving at a hyperkinetic pace. The second album, *Led Zeppelin II,* still wasn't completed, and unlike the debut album—which was recorded in just hours—it seemed like we would never wrap this one up.

Jimmy would have liked a couple of weeks just to step back and put the whole project in perspective. He had been running so fast in the States, dashing from one studio to the next in between concert dates, coping with blood-shot eyes late into the night in one recording studio after another, that he felt he desperately needed more planning time for the album.

Back in London, because I had a stack of paperwork and other matters to take care of in Peter's office, I spent very little time in the Olympic Studios with the band. But when I would drop in, even for just half an hour or so, I could see the battle fatigue taking its toll on Jimmy. His face seemed drawn. The circles under his eyes were getting darker. He started smoking more cigarettes than usual.

One night, Jimmy was facing several more hours in the studio to complete "Living Loving Maid (She's Just a Woman)." The song wasn't anyone's favorite—it was never played in any live concert. In the studio, Jimmy's work on that cut never quite produced anything that really excited the band. At one point, as his own frustration level grew, Jimmy moaned, "Don't we get any time to enjoy our success? Don't we ever get any time off?" He paced the floor, lit up another cigarette, and somehow talked himself into getting back to work.

To add to the pressures on the band, there were sixteen performances already scheduled in England for the month of June, at places like Free Trade Hall in Manchester ... Colston Hall in Bristol ... Guildhall in Plymouth ... Birmingham Town Hall ... Newcastle City Hall. On balance, the band could rejoice about a recent surge of interest in their music in the U.K. Back in February, we had returned home from the first American tour to a thoroughly apathetic Britain. But this time, after the second U.S. tour had ended, the response was completely different in England. *Led Zeppelin* was at the top of the charts at home. Peter began turning down many more offers throughout the U.K. than he accepted.

Still, Peter saw the end of the Yellow Brick Road leading not to London, but to cities like Chicago, New York, and Los Angeles. "I want to get back to the States as soon as possible," he said. "Now is the time to do it."

By the time the band touched down in Atlanta for the July 5 launching of the new tour, I sensed that Zeppelin was, more than ever before, a band of equals. Perhaps Pagey and John Paul were the senior partners in terms of musical experience, but they never pulled rank. Everyone respected one another's talents. Rarely did they verbally express their admiration for one another, but you could see it in the appreciative glances they offered one another onstage or the subconscious nods of their heads that seemed to communicate some regard for what each of them was contributing.

At this point, Led Zeppelin also had become close enough where they could tease and joke with one another, knowing that they probably wouldn't permanently ruffle any feathers. One night, for instance, we were sipping some wine and laughing over some of the boring shows on British TV.

"What about that bloke, *Percy Thrower?!*" John Paul said. "You know, the guy who does the gardening show. It's a whole program of watching plants grow! How exciting can you get?!"

"Hey," Jimmy interjected. "We do the same thing. We watch Plant grow, too!"

"What a perfect name!" laughed John Paul. "Percy."

From that day on, we rarely called him Robert again. Henceforth, it was always Percy. Robert never complained.

With some other nicknames, however, we showed a little more caution. Peter and I used to call Jimmy "the old girl"—but never to his face. The name grew out of a good laugh we got one night watching him in the hours prior to a concert. In Los Angeles during that summer tour, Jimmy was admiring himself in front of his hotel mirror at the Château Marmont, like a beauty contestant about to strut down the runway. He was attired in a Prince Charming-type outfit, rich in velvet and velours. He had curlers in his hair, and after he removed them he spent fifteen minutes brushing his locks. It was quite a performance.

Although Jimmy deserved some razzing for primping that was more befitting a teenage girl on prom night, Peter and I were too cowardly to poke fun directly. There were certain things Jimmy might be sensitive about on a particular day, and there didn't seem much point in risking a volcanic eruption.

But among ourselves, Peter and I rollicked over our inside joke. We'd say things like, "Tell the old girl that the limos are waiting downstairs. . . . Isn't it time for the old girl to get dolled up for the concert?" In some odd way, it was actually an affectionate term, but unless he were in an unusually good mood, I think Jimmy would have been incensed had he known about it.

During that summer tour, Zeppelin performed in nine outdoor festivals, from the Newport Pop Festival to the Woodinville Festival in Seattle to Central Park in New York. Those outdoor, multiact gigs also gave the band the opportunity to size up other bands, too, some of whom—from the Doors to the Byrds—were billed above us in those days.

"It's just a matter of time until we're the headline act, until we blow these guys right off the stage," Bonzo said on a couple of occasions.

Early in that tour, we spent one of our days off watching other rock musicians perform at an outdoor festival at the Singer Bowl on the New York World's Fair site in Flushing Meadows. Vanilla Fudge, Jeff Beck, and Ten Years After topped the bill. We viewed the concert from backstage, never straying too far from a buffet table brimming with beer, wine, and chips and mingling with a menagerie of musician friends.

Alvin Lee, the guitarist for Ten Years After, was a terrific performer, and I remember how amazed we were watching him—the lighting speed of his fingers as he cradled and nursed the guitar from one song to the next, bathing the audience with heavy rock sounds that had made him one of the most respected musicians of the late sixties.

"He's just great," Jimmy said, with his eyes spellbound by Lee's fingers. Not too many musicians could captivate Jimmy that way, and I found it almost as interesting to watch his reactions to Lee as to observe Lee himself.

As Ten Years After played, however, Bonham seemed to grow restless. He had been drinking all afternoon and was eager to leave. "Hang in there, Bonzo," I told him. "We'll be outta here in an hour or so." Finally, Bonham was almost jumping out of his skin, moving from one location to another, scratching his arms, draining still another bottle of beer.

Then, in an instant, he became like Mr. Hyde, with a devilish gleam in his eye that virtually transformed him into the mischievous Bonzo. I could see trouble on the horizon.

"Oh, no, Bonzo," I muttered. Although I had no idea what he had in mind, I knew it probably wouldn't earn him a Boy Scouts merit badge.

"I'll fucking fix him!" Bonham shouted, pointing at Lee. "Watch this!"

Bonham grabbed a carton of orange juice from the buffet table and walked just far enough onstage to get within striking distance.

"It's time for a juice break!" he screamed. "Alvin, do you want some juice?"

Without waiting for an answer, Bonham heaved the juice carton and its contents toward Lee. In an instant, the juice splashed on the guitarist and his instrument.

As the crowd roared, Lee gasped as he was bathed in the cold liquid. "What the hell's going on?" he shouted, glaring at Bonham. "You motherfucker!"

Lee had fury in his eyes. He continued to play, but kept eye contact with Bonham. Maybe it was the alcohol, but Bonham didn't seem intimidated. He shook his index finger at Lee, as if cautioning him to keep his cool.

"Don't let a little thing like this bother you," Bonham yelled. "Orange juice is good for you. Vitamin C, you know."

As Lee continued to play, he raised and pointed his guitar toward Bonham, as if it were a sword or perhaps a machine gun. I sensed that their confrontation was going to get a lot more interesting before it finally cooled down.

In fact, on that hot, 100-degree afternoon, the situation only got worse for Lee. The orange juice quickly dried and his hands and the guitar became sticky. His fingers just couldn't maneuver properly from fret to fret. He was forced to slow his pace. He struggled through the group's remaining songs.

By the time Lee left the stage, he was outraged. He steamed past us toward his dressing room.

"You're an asshole, Bonham," he mumbled. "A real asshole."

Bonzo, however, was overjoyed. He began laughing uncontrollably about the chaos he had created.

"Bonzo's got to get a grip on things," Jimmy said to me. He seemed genuinely concerned about the mayhem that often occurred when Bonham and alcohol got together. "He's his own worst enemy. Maybe he's *our* own worst enemy, too."

"He's just blowing off steam," I said. "If he didn't let it out this way, he might be punching somebody."

But Bonham wasn't finished for the day. He waited patiently for Jeff Beck to take the stage about an hour later. Beck was one of the most frantic blues guitarists I had ever seen, someone who could rouse an audience into a feverish state within minutes after his performance began. This particular afternoon, he seemed to have Bonham in a trance.

Late in Beck's set, an even more inebriated Bonham stumbled onto the stage. I desperately lunged for him and grabbed him by the shoulder, but he broke away. "Don't worry," he said. "I'll be just a minute, Richard. I'm coming right back."

Beck glanced at Bonham, but, with no orange juice in sight, continued to play, styling his way through "Rice Pudding," seemingly undisturbed by the unannounced walk-on.

Bonham gyrated for a minute or two and then talked Mickey Waller into relinquishing his seat behind the drums. Beck stopped playing as Bonham perched himself on Waller's stool. Bonzo grabbed the drumsticks and immediately began pounding out a stripper's rhythm.

"Oh, no," I thought to myself. "This is getting out of control."

The drums thundered. The cymbals vibrated. The crowd started clapping in time to the rhythm. As Bonham's excitement level rose, he egged on the audience to make even more noise. And they did.

Offstage, Plant and I began giggling like schoolboys. "He's a lunatic," I said. "They should lock him up."

As the crowd roared even louder, Bonzo leaped from the drummer's chair and ran to center stage. Immediately, he began peeling off his clothes. Layer by layer. Bump after grind.

First, Bonzo's shirt came off. Then his pants. By this time, Plant and I were encouraging him to keep going.

Bonham wasn't about to disappoint us. In moments, he was down to just his undershorts.

"More?" he squealed into the nearest microphone.

"More!" the crowd shouted back.

Bonham slipped off his underpants. The crowd, which had become more delirious as each piece of clothing was discarded, went absolutely berserk as Bonham stood before them in only his birthday suit. His equipment impressed the audience.

At that moment, Peter sprinted onto the stage like an Olympic runner charging out of the starting blocks. "You son of a bitch!" he shouted as he rushed toward Bonham. At the same moment, a half-dozen uniformed policemen were climbing onto the stage to make an arrest.

Peter reached Bonham before the police did, picked up his naked drummer, and raced backstage. They ducked into an empty dressing room, slammed the door, and locked it.

"You fucking bastard!" Peter roared. "If you aren't dressed by the time the police break down this door, you're out of the band!"

Bonham, suddenly acting quite sober, sheepishly followed orders. He grabbed a pair of pants and a shirt that didn't even belong to him but were sitting on a shelf within arm's reach. The clothes were a couple of sizes too small for Bonham, but Peter didn't care.

"Do you know what you're doing?" Peter fumed. "Do you realize that you're jeopardizing the future of this entire band by the way you behave? What's wrong with you, John? Are you trying to ruin things for everyone?"

Bonham didn't answer. Once he was dressed, he and Peter opened the door and paraded politely past the policemen, neither uttering a word. The rest of the band joined up with them at the rear entrance to the stage, and we headed toward a car that was waiting for us. We hurriedly left, hoping that the entire incident would be forgotten by the time Bonham had sobered up. Fortunately, it was.

At the Woodinville Festival, Bonham was on much better behavior. He knew that he'd have to face Peter's wrath if there were other wild outbursts. Also, like the rest of us, he was in awe that day of Chuck Berry, who performed just before us. The bill was crammed with artists—Vanilla Fudge, the Byrds, the Chicago Transit Authority, the Doors. But Berry was the artist who most intrigued us, beginning with his meticulously timed entrance and ending with an exit that lasted not much longer than the blink of an eye.

"It's amazing how little time Berry spends at a show," Peter advised us in advance. "He'll show up just minutes before he goes onstage and leave before the applause has faded."

Berry drove up in a mauve Cadillac about twenty minutes before his set began, looking thinner than I had imagined him, with his familiar mustache trimmed to perfection. He brought his guitar with him and picked up a local band in Seattle, a three-piece combo that had been rehearsing Berry's tunes on their own for three days. "I've been playing 'Sweet Little Sixteen' since I was seven years old," the keyboard player told me. "I can't believe I'm playing it with Chuck Berry himself today! This is a day I'll never forget."

What a contrast to the way Zeppelin operated. Although the band wouldn't arrive at a venue until perhaps thirty minutes before the curtain rose, our crew would usually show up at eight or nine in the morning, a half day before the concert was scheduled to begin. They'd work nonstop until about four-thirty in the afternoon—tuning Jimmy's guitars, setting up the drums for Bonham's brutal attack, making final adjustments to John Paul's bass. They would test the special effects rack and run sound checks until they felt absolutely confident that Robert's voice would resonate with the same intensity captured in the recording studio. The crew were artists in their own right, creating the technical environment that the band demanded. Yes, they took occasional breaks during their eight hours of preparation—snatching some Jack Daniels or Blue Nun wine stored in Zeppelin's dressing room. But even so, there was none of the nonchalance that we saw with Chuck Berry.

Three years later, I was in Birmingham, England, with Bonham and Plant. It was between tours, and we were barhopping, drinking beer and flirting with the girls. Chuck Berry happened to be performing at a club called Barbarella's, and we sat down to listen.

Midway through "Johnny B. Goode," Bonham was experiencing one of his fidgety, nervous fits. "I can't believe the drummer!" he groaned. "Chuck Berry's a rock 'n' roll legend, and they got this worthless drummer backing him. Richard, I gotta do something. This guy can't play worth a damn!"

"Well, what the hell can you possibly do?" I yelled at him. "Sit tight. We'll leave soon."

As the show dragged on, Bonham's anxiety began to overtake him. Finally, he had had enough. "I can't take it anymore. The fucking drummer is *useless*! I gotta get him out of there!"

Bonham suddenly climbed onto the stage, grabbed the drummer by the shirt, and exclaimed, "Chuck wants me to take over!"

Berry was startled, but didn't say a word. Bonham sat down behind the drums, grinned at Berry, and looked eager to start playing. I presume Berry knew who his new drummer was, but we'll never know for sure. As Berry began twanging the opening bars of "Roll Over Beethoven," Bonham slid into a drum accompaniment that was so seismic, so potent, that Beethoven himself may have felt the vibrations. Bonham sat in for three songs, waving to the cheering crowd when he finally left the stage. Berry gave him a wink that said, "Now *there's* a real drummer!"

That was a sentiment that a lot of people felt. At one time or another, all of us worried whether Bonzo was operating too close to the edge. He often acted as though he were one of the original escapees from the cuckoo's nest. But when you can play drums the way he could, people are willing to put up with a lot more crap than they would from someone with less talent. As a result, Bonzo's erratic behavior continued almost unabated.

FISH STORIES

Cole, I know it's four in the morning, but have all the fucking sharks in Puget Sound fallen asleep?"

John Bonham was growing impatient.

"I'll give 'em another ten minutes, Cole. Just ten more minutes. Then I'm going into the water myself."

Bonham was talking nonstop, the meaningless kind of chatter that after a while was starting to drive me crazy. I was trying to keep my cool, not to respond at all. Maybe if I don't say anything, I thought, Bonham will just shut up.

"I'm really starting to get bored, Cole. If I have to, I'll swim out and wrestle those little bastards to the shore. With my bare hands. I mean it. I'm gonna do it!"

Finally, I had had enough. "Shut the fuck up, Bonzo! If you don't keep your voice down, you're going to wake up half of Seattle! You're probably scaring the goddamn sharks away!"

We were sitting on the balcony of Bonham's second-floor room at the Edgewater Inn, with our fishing poles positioned over the dark, still waters of Puget Sound at the edge of Pier 67. The Edgewater was an extraordinary hotel—a motor inn, really—and its novelty never wore off for Led Zeppelin. There was nothing elegant about it, but the four-story structure hung directly over Elliott Bay and the fishing could be exciting. The hotel gift shop supplied the fishing rods, and if the mud sharks were biting, it was as much fun as a big-game hunt in Africa.

In fact, Bonham and I really didn't know much about how to fish. Just stick some bait on the end of the hook and wait for something to happen. Still, we had heard enough fishing terms to keep the conversation lively—at least for a while—although we weren't exactly sure what any of it meant.

"What are we doing wrong here tonight, Cole? Are we jigging when we should be spinning? Should we be angling from a different angle?"

"Hell if I know. We never have this much trouble in the Thames, do we?"

Even the one-liners, perhaps because they were so weak, couldn't amuse us for long. "Have those fucking sharks simply left town?" I asked at one point while taking the lamps from our hotel rooms and, with the help of extension cords, perching them on the balcony ledge to light up the water below. "I don't see any of those sons of bitches out there!"

Earlier that evening, Jimmy Page had been fishing from the adjacent balcony, but had given up as the night wore on. "He obviously doesn't have the blood of a fisherman running through his veins," Bonham quipped. More likely, Jimmy may have drowned himself in so much alcohol that he had finally become weary and turned in for the night. Throughout the tour, we indulged in a little more cocaine than in the previous trip to America, but I also made sure that all of us had plenty of booze available, and no one stayed sober for long.

Bonham picked up a bottle of champagne—our third that night. "Let's pour a little of this on the bait," he said. "Let's get 'em drunk. Make 'em a little more cooperative."

By this point, Bonham had consumed way too much champagne himself. In fact, we were both pretty inebriated—so much so that it's somewhat of a miracle that neither of us stumbled off the balcony into the forty-five-degree water. We really didn't know what our limit was—how much we could drink and still remain somewhat functional—and, frankly, we rarely cared. On this summer tour, Bonzo and the others had learned to try to temper their alcohol consumption in the hours immediately before a concert, but beyond that, the word "limit" really had no place in their drinking vocabulary.

Maybe it was the music that brought us to America, but fishing (and drinking) at the Edgewater Inn were clearly some of the more interesting diversions we had found to kill the long hours from one concert to the next. At this juncture in Zeppelin's history—its third American tour—we could have afforded to stay in any hotel in the city. But in Seattle, the Edgewater Inn—despite its modest accommodations and the lingering, fishy aroma that seemed to have become entrapped in even the towels and the bed sheets—was clearly our sentimental favorite.

"If you ever put us up anywhere else but here, Richard, you'll be looking for other work," Robert told me one day, jabbing his index finger into my chest. He probably was only half joking.

My own familiarity with the Edgewater Inn dated back to 1968 when I had toured with Terry Reid. He was opening for the Moody Blues one night in Seattle, and before the show, I was chatting backstage with Ray Thomas, the Moody Blues' flute player, and Pete Jackson, their tour manger. "Where are you staying?" Pete asked. "Next time you come to Seattle, you gotta stay at the Edgewater Inn. It's unbelievable. You can fish right from your hotel room!"

I was skeptical. "Fish from your hotel room! I find that hard to believe, Pete."

"He's telling the truth," Ray said. "The Beatles used to stay there. They're the ones who told us about it. When you're there, go into the gift shop. They've got pictures of the Beatles fishing."

So when Led Zeppelin launched their third American tour, we had fishing on our minds. In the three weeks it took us to weave our way to the West Coast by way of Atlanta, Philadelphia, New York, Chicago, Milwaukee, and Saint Paul, the band often seemed preoccupied with reaching Seattle.

"How many more days until we get to the Edgewater?" Jimmy would ask.

"I'm itchin' for some fishin'," Bonham roared one night in a drunken stupor at the Steve Paul Scene in New York.

Everyone groaned. Bonham's rhymes weren't the kind that would have intimidated Cole Porter. "It's comforting knowing that Jimmy and Robert, and not you, are writing the songs for this band," I told him.

When we finally reached Seattle, I called a local market and ordered five pounds of fresh salmon and five pounds of steak. That was our bait for the next two nights.

On that first attempt at fishing, however, Bonham and I were well into our third hour and just about ready to give up. Then suddenly, he got a bite.

"My God, Cole, it's happened," he bellowed. "I got one!"

He leaped from his chair and furiously began reeling in the line.

"It's a huge one, Cole! I can feel it! Get the camera ready! It might be Moby Dick."

I urged him on. "Do you need a hand? Bring that fucker in!"

We were shouting loud enough to arouse the entire hotel. Lights came on, one by one, in many of the rooms. "Grab the harpoon!" Bonzo shrieked. "Thar she blows!"

As Bonham continued to grapple with the fishing line, I lifted up one of the lamps, holding it farther out over the water to give us a clearer look when the monstrous catch came into view. "Hang on, Bonzo," I shouted. "Don't let that bastard get away!"

In the excitement, I lost my grip on the lamp. It plunged into the water, sinking faster than an anchor.

"Fuck the lamp! What did you catch, Bonham? Do you think it's a shark?"

As the fish got within a few feet of the balcony, I realized that Bonzo's flair for the dramatic had consumed him. It wasn't Moby Dick after all. Nor the Loch Ness monster. Bonzo had hooked a rather anemic-looking red snapper that had stopped struggling long before it left the water.

Bonham wasn't the slightest bit disappointed. "Richard, it's a start," he exclaimed, almost giddy with excitement. "We can fish until dawn. We'll have a dozen bigger ones by morning."

He was right. Over the next three hours, we caught one after another, mostly red snappers, but a couple of mud sharks, too. And with each catch, we made even more noise than with the previous one—particularly when we'd shriek upon cutting our fingers on the hooks. Pity the poor folks in the hotel who were trying to sleep.

The next day, we were bragging to a roomful of people—including Pagey, Plant, and a couple of the roadies—about our success the night before. "Charles Atlas couldn't have reeled in a couple of those suckers," Bonham boasted. "They grow 'em big in America."

"So what are you gonna do with the fish now?" Plant asked, pinching his nostrils and peering into the wastebasket that we had filled with water and dead fish. "I bet they can smell these things all the way back to London."

"We'll find something to do with them," I said.

That night, we did. And it turned into probably the most notorious off-stage incident ever associated with Led Zeppelin. It became known as the Shark Episode, the subject of gossip in rock clubs and concert halls around the world. As with any piece of gossip, the story got twisted and distorted every time it was told. But here is what really happened.

We had some girls in our rooms, and one of them seemed particularly playful. Her name was Jackie, a tall redhead from Portland, seventeen years old, who was one of the few birds I had ever met who could drink us under the table. She was chugging champagne from the bottle, talking openly about sex, spicing up her sentences with salty language. And she seemed to be trying to bait us into doing something daring.

"Are you guys into bondage?" she asked at one point. "I really like being tied up. I really do."

I looked at Jimmy, and we smiled at one another.

"Well, let's give the girl what she wants," I announced. "Let's do what we can to make her happy."

I got on the phone to the front desk.

"Pardon me, this is Richard Cole. We need some rope up in Room 242 as soon as possible. Have you got any?"

There was a long pause on the phone line.

"What do you need rope for?" the desk clerk asked in a startled tone of voice.

I was afraid he'd want to know. "What do we need the rope for?" I was groping for an answer. "Well, luggage, of course. We've got a couple pieces of luggage coming apart here, and unless we tie them up tightly, they're going to come apart on our plane."

Ten minutes later, we had the rope. "Not too tight," Jackie giggled as she took off her clothes and made herself comfortable, waiting for us to tie her to the bed. We bound her hands, then her feet, and wrapped the rope through the bed frame.

"Just relax," I told her. "I think you're going to like this."

I picked up one of the red snappers and gently inserted it into Jackie's vagina.

"What the hell is that," she shrieked.

I was almost too busy to answer. "I'm putting this red snapper into your red snapper!" I roared.

Then I inserted the fish into her ass. She let out a gasp.

The proceedings were filmed by Mark Stein of Vanilla Fudge. The Fudge had performed with us at the outdoor festival in Woodinville, and Mark had a home-movie camera with him. "Smile!" Mark laughed as the camera continued to run. "Everyone look at the camera and say 'Cheese.' "

The whole incident was something that I just wanted to do and that I had never done before. Perhaps it was a cheap thrill. I knew we could get away with it simply because we had gotten away with most things. And no one ever said, "That's enough!" or "Give the girl a break!"

Jackie certainly never complained. Her only words were exclamations, seemingly in response to the physical sensations she was experiencing. "Oh, my God!" she shouted at one point. "Shit! This is fuckin' amazing!" At one point, she asked me not to stop. When I finally did, it was because I had finally become bored with the whole thing. Even the kinkiest type of sex loses its appeal after a while.

Word about the escapade spread quickly. Rumors circulated that the girl had been raped . . . that she had been crying hysterically . . . that she had pleaded for me to stop . . . that she had struggled to escape . . . that a shark had been used to penetrate her. None of the stories was true. But for years, when people wanted to criticize Led Zeppelin, they referred to the incident as a metaphor for the worst of rock music's personal vandalism. The thirty-minute episode was used as the definitive example of the "debauchery" and "depravity" running rampant through the rock music world. And Led Zeppelin was cast as the worst of the lot.

That kind of behavior really was more the exception than the rule for us. When it occurred, Bonham and I were clearly the gang leaders; if the others participated, they were often coaxed into it, or they joined in more as a breather from the boredom or the frantic pace of life on the road.

GREAT DANE

When Zeppelin reached Los Angeles during the summer 1969 tour and checked into the Château Marmont for a six-day stay, there was something about that hotel that put us in the mood for some disorderly conduct. And in L.A., there were plenty of girls around who were game for just about anything we wanted to try.

One afternoon, a friend of mine showed up at the Marmont with a Great Dane—a large male that probably weighed 150 pounds, with a dark gray coat. The dog seemed pretty easygoing, and I figured we could get it to do just about anything—or at least it was worth a try.

I approached a girl named Jamie, who had been sitting near the hotel pool for two days, hoping for a little attention from us. "Have you ever made love to a dog?" I asked.

A stunned expression came over her face. I didn't blame her.

"Not lately," she answered.

"Well, John Bonham and I have this bet. We've bet that this Great Dane we have will find you so attractive—and get so turned on—that he'll want to eat you."

Jamie was startled.

"I know it sounds crazy," I said, "but it would be fun to try, wouldn't it?"

Jamie thought about it for a moment. She probably flashed back on all those Sundays she had spent in church and everything she had learned as a child at Girl Scout meetings. Then she shrugged her shoulders in a what-the-hell gesture. "Okay, I guess so. But I can back out whenever I want to. Okay?"

"Of course," I said as we walked back toward Bonham's room.

Jamie and the dog sized one another up. As she began to disrobe, she giggled. "This is insane."

When she was naked, Jamie sat down on the floor and spread her legs. My friend pointed his dog in her direction.

"Come on," he said, kneeling down beside the girl, trying to coax the dog closer to her vagina. "Come on, boy."

The scene was like an outtake from a very bad pornographic movie. The dog wouldn't budge.

"I've got an idea," Bonham said. "We've got some bacon strips in the kitchen that are left over from breakfast. Does the dog like bacon?"

Bonham went to the kitchen and returned with the bacon, placing it in front of her vagina. "Come on, poochie," he said, attempting to entice the dog forward.

The dog howled, then turned and walked away. The game was over.

Like the Shark Episode, the incident was something to do, something we had never done before. After some initial hesitation, the girl was cooperative. Later, Bonham rationalized the whole episode. "The girl wasn't that pretty anyway," he said. "The dog had a lot better taste than we did."

As a rock band with soaring popularity, we all knew that we had power that most people don't. At times, maybe we intimidated girls to do things that they might not have otherwise done. But we were young and crazy enough to take advantage of our position—in both sexual and non-sexual situations.

The Zeppelin wives joined us for a few days during that tour, including some of the shows in Las Vegas and other West Coast cities. Their presence was rather uncommon over the years, since they were generally quite content to remain at home, away from the hectic pace of touring. When they were around, however, the boys' behavior improved dramatically; the groupies, for instance, vanished almost instantaneously.

On this particular tour, I figured that by pulling a few strings, I could get us some front-row seats to Elvis Presley's show at the International Hotel. Elvis was one of the few performers the band looked up to. "There's nobody better," Jimmy said. "Nobody."

That afternoon, I had called Bill Miller, the entertainment director at the International, whose son, Jimmy, produced records for the Rolling Stones, Traffic, and Spencer Davis.

"My name is Richard Cole," I told him. "I'm a close friend of your son's." I really wasn't, but Pagey knew Jimmy Miller, and I figured that was close enough. "Jimmy told us that whenever we came to town, you could arrange for us to see Elvis."

Bill never hesitated. "No problem," he said. "Jimmy speaks very highly of you, Richard."

I tried to contain my laughter.

"How many seats do you need?" he asked.

That night, we had front-row tables. It was the first time any of us had seen Elvis perform. And we weren't disappointed.

Perhaps the only dissatisfied person among us that night was John Paul, but it was good-natured despair. Before entering the showroom to see Elvis, we had spent a few minutes in the International's lounge, watching Ike and Tina Turner perform. And as Tina sang "River Deep, Mountain High" and "Come Together," sensually and seductively teasing the audience with dozens of bumps and grinds, John Paul fell in love.

He turned to his wife. "Mo," he said, "what would I have to buy you so I could sleep with Tina Turner? I've always wanted to screw her. Please, Mo. Name your price! Anything!"

Mo decided that it was a deal she wasn't interested in making.

Once the wives were gone, there were plenty of other opportunities for just about anything we were interested in doing. Back in L.A., we had spent many hours drinking at both the Whisky and a new club, Thee Experience. Jimmy and I had met Marshall Brevitz, the owner of Thee Experience, the year before at his club in Miami. He was a sweet guy, a little overweight and losing his hair. Jimmy liked Marshall, and when the new L.A. club opened on Sunset Boulevard, Pagey suggested that we give it some immediate notoriety by hanging out there.

Although the lines in front of Thee Experience often wound into the darkness when Zeppelin was in town, the club never enjoyed the success of some of the more famous rock establishments in L.A. Marshall made the mistake of locating his club at the corner of Sunset and Gardner, a few blocks west of La Brea, but too far away from most of West Hollywood's nightlife. The Whisky, the Roxy, the Rainbow, and Gazzari's were always packed because they were within a block of one another, and people often went to all four clubs in the same night. Thee Experience was just too isolated.

So we tried to help out. "Just keep giving us free drinks, and you can tell the world that this is where Led Zeppelin's going to be," I told Marshall.

After a night of drinking, there wasn't much that we weren't willing to try, even in a public place like Thee Experience. We were becoming even kinkier, even more uninhibited and bizarre, as the days and weeks passed. It seemed as if we were willing to attempt anything, knowing that if necessary we could flash the name Led Zeppelin and probably wiggle out of just about any situation.

One night, I was flirting heavily with a young blonde at Thee Experience, and I figured she was a likely candidate to come back to the Château Marmont with me. We began kissing and touching one another, and in the natural course of events I decided it was a shame to wait until we got back to the hotel.

"Let's push two tables together and do it right here!" I suggested.

At first, she thought—or perhaps hoped—that I was kidding. When she realized I wasn't, she began laughing nervously. "Okay," she said, "but let's find some tables in the corner."

She helped me rearrange the furniture, and then we pulled off just enough of our clothes to screw right there on top of the tables, in full view of half of the club. It may not have shown good judgment, but not a single person complained. It was not a G-rated performance.

The next night, as we drove back to Thee Experience, Robert joked, "I don't know how we could top the show you put on last night." But, somehow, we almost did. While we were waiting for our third round of drinks to arrive, two girls volunteered to crawl under the tables and perform oral sex on the band. They did it in record time.

As Bonzo zipped up his fly, he said, "Marshall, I think we've found a big drawing card for your club. These girls have a special talent that could bring in a lot of new customers every night. Once the word gets out, you'll have the most popular club in Los Angeles."

In those days, lots of women just weren't timid or self-conscious about anything. We saw no reason to show any self-restraint ourselves. The flesh was out there for the taking, and it was easy to become a hedonist. There seemed to be no reason not to.

PHANTOM PERFORMANCE

Led Zeppelin's summer 1969 tour of America ended on the last day in August with a performance at the Texas International Festival in Dallas. Peter Grant had negotiated a fee of nearly $14,000 for the hour-long set, which was more than we had earned for any single show to date. Still, we were counting on the second album, finally scheduled for release in late October, to drive our asking price much higher.

We returned to London and scattered for a long-awaited but short-lived vacation. Six weeks after the curtain fell on the U.S. tour, the band reluctantly reassembled in Paris to begin the promotion of *Led Zeppelin II*. The relationship between the band and the press, of course, already had a nightmarish history, and anything that smacked of courting the press was almost more than the band could handle.

"I guess it's part of the game," Robert said. Nevertheless, he despised this aspect of the business—to have to sit there politely and chat or answer questions with people whose knowledge of music was often pretty pathetic.

Eddie Barclay, whose Barclay Records distributed Led Zeppelin's albums in France, had talked Peter into flying the band across the English Channel to perform a one-hour set at a private party, celebrating the imminent release of *Led Zeppelin II*. "Let the band do their talking with their music," Eddie said. "They'll play a few songs, and the promotion people and the media will love it."

That all sounded great. But even the best-laid plans can go awry.

We had checked into the Westminster, an expensive, 100-room hotel with marble fireplaces and parquet floors located on the Rue de la Paix. As we were settling into our rooms, the phone rang. It was Clive Coulson.

"Richard, we're down here setting up the equipment for tonight's show. I don't think the band is going to want to hear this, but the stage is a boxing ring. They've never performed in one of these before, have they? Do you think they'll want to perform in a boxing ring?"

I knew the answer without even asking the band.

"This is absurd," I said. "Take all the equipment out, Clive. The band isn't going to play tonight. If they want someone to perform in a boxing ring, let them sign Muhammad Ali to a recording contract!"

Although there was no live music that night, we did show up for the party. "Act as cordial as you can," Peter advised the band before we left the hotel. "I know it's terrible to have to endure these things. I'm going to be having just as bad a time as you are. Let's just bite our lips and make the best of it."

We survived the party, pretending that we were having a good time mingling with the press. We also discovered just how influential Eddie Barclay was with the French media. Even though the band never performed that night, our "show" was nevertheless reviewed in the papers the next day. "Zeppelin was called back for repeated encores," one critic wrote. "Even blasé record company executives couldn't get enough of them. No matter what the band played—from 'Good Times Bad Times' to 'Ramble On'—the party crowd screamed for more."

"Oh, brother," John Paul muttered when we read the reviews in the Paris newspapers. Because of Zeppelin's shaky relationship with the media, he joked that these French reviews were the nicest articles ever written about us. At that point, they probably were.

"Maybe that's the key to winning the press to our side," Jimmy wisecracked. "Let's just stop showing up for the concerts! Our phantom performances sound a lot better to the critics!"

After the Paris party had ended, we went our separate ways late that night, heading for the clubs, taking with us some of the cute birds who worked for Barclay. "Just stay out of trouble," Peter cautioned, knowing that his half-hearted advice wasn't going to be taken seriously, but feeling some obligation to offer it. "I want to get out of Paris sometime tomorrow without too many scars."

The next morning, I woke up at about eleven o'clock and called Bonham's room to ask if he wanted me to order him some breakfast. He didn't answer the phone, nor did I hear any rustling when I knocked on his door.

"That bastard is the soundest sleeper I know," I mumbled to myself. "I've got to wake him up somehow."

I climbed out the window of my own third-story room, figuring I could inch my way along the ledge to Bonham's room and enter through his window. But as I began the sixty-foot journey from my room to his, I looked down at the street for the first time. Suddenly, I realized that an unexpected slip or a sneeze that threw me off balance could pose some serious risk to my life expectancy. Instantly, the trip became a much more cautious, more deliberate one. Step by step.

"Just take it slow, Richard," I told myself. "There's no hurry. I've got all day."

At about the halfway point, I heard shouts from the street level. "Oh, shut the fuck up down there," I thought. The last things I needed at that moment were distractions.

The chatter from the street was all in French, and I lost most of it in the translation. I hesitated to look down at all, focusing instead on getting to my destination without injury. When I finally did glance down, there was a small but growing crowd of people who were watching my every move. In the midst of my cheering section were two very vocal gendarmes.

Finally, their French started to make sense. "Get down from there as quickly as possible," they were yelling. "If you're headed for Cartier, the store has been secured. Come down, we'd like to question you."

Cartier! What the hell were they talking about?

Then I realized that Cartier was next door to the Westminster. Apparently, the gendarmes were convinced that I was a Parisian cat burglar on my way to steal a few thousand francs' worth of jewelry.

I suddenly became very nervous—something that's not usually recommended on a ledge three stories above street level. "If they shoot and ask questions later," I thought, "I'm in trouble." I shifted directions and crept back to my room. Along the way, I smiled at them and occasionally waved politely, hoping to forestall any warning shots.

A few minutes later, when I climbed back into my room, I heaved a sigh of relief. The gendarmes were there waiting for me, and I tried to explain that I had only been trying to awaken a friend. They, however, were skeptical. They gave me one of those looks that said, "Is that the best story you can come up with?" But when they searched me and discovered that my pockets weren't packed with gems and stones, there was nothing they could arrest me for. After half an hour of questioning, they let me go.

Ironically, I apparently risked my life in vain. Bonham wasn't even in his hotel room at the time. About three hours later, a cab dropped him off in front of the Westminster.

Back in Jimmy's room, John tried to make some sense of his own night. "I just don't understand it," he said, with a perplexed expression on his face. "I guess I had too much to drink last night and somehow ended up on a farm about twenty kilometers outside of Paris. I have no idea how I got there or who I was with. When I woke up this morning, I was all by myself, sleeping on a sofa in this farmhouse, with these cows mooing off in the distance. I used the phone to call a cab and get the hell out of there."

Just another boozy adventure!

Once we were back in England, Peter Grant couldn't get America off his mind. There were no more savvy managers in the rock music business than Peter. He could taste an opportunity from thousands of miles away. He could evaluate its pros and cons and reach an instant conclusion about its viability that was nearly always right on target. And whenever the band was home, he was salivating to get them back to the States.

"It's purely a dollars and cents game," he said one afternoon in the fall of 1969. "This band can make a lot of money and get a lot of attention by spending as much time as possible in America. At this point, I don't think we have to worry about overkill. And with the new album coming out, now is the perfect time for another tour."

Peter spent the rest of the day calling each of the band members, explaining his rationale for getting Zeppelin back on the road. He didn't have to arm-twist too aggressively, particularly when he explained what was already tentatively on the agenda. "The band's been offered a two-night gig at Carnegie Hall," he told Jimmy. "It's just too tempting and too prestigious to turn down. The Stones played Carnegie Hall in the midsixties; no rock band has played there since. I think this is something we should do."

As good as it sounded, there were mixed feelings among the band. "Not America again!" Bonzo thought. "We're all tired. Give us some time off!" They all wanted to spend more time with their girlfriends or their wives. At one point, a frustrated Robert echoed a complaint that had been heard before: "We're making all this money now; isn't money supposed to buy you some relaxation time?"

But after all, this was Carnegie Hall. The more Peter talked to them about it, the more irresistible it sounded. "Let's go for it!" Jimmy finally said. With that, Peter and I spent a week on the phone, patching together a three-week, seventeen-city tour. It would take us from the East Coast through the Midwest and out to the Western states, as well as give us a few engagements in Canada.

With the new album set for release in the States in the midst of the tour, the band concentrated on the music from *Led Zeppelin II* in its set: "Whole Lotta Love" . . . "Bring It On Home" . . . "What Is and What Should Never Be."

"Thank You" was built around a keyboard solo by John Paul. "Moby Dick" became a part of their act, featuring a drum solo by Bonzo that, over the years, eventually extended to twenty minutes, then thirty minutes, and sometimes even longer. When the band performed songs from the first album, there was often a new twist to them, like variations on "Dazed and Confused," with Jimmy taking the song in imaginative directions—eventually even inserting small pieces of other songs by Joni Mitchell or the Eagles and letting the band follow his lead. "Let's keep it loose," Jimmy used to tell the band. "Nothing needs to be very structured."

Everyone in the group had the latitude to grab onto a song and shape and sweeten it into what he wanted it to be on any given night. They had developed confidence in each other's musical instincts. As a result, they often hit paydirt.

About midway through that fall tour, Zeppelin performed at Boston Garden to a throng of fans—nearly 20,000 paying customers. The Garden was sweltering that night, and the air-conditioning system had melted down within the first half hour. But it didn't matter. The fans were maniacal from the first song to the last.

"This is the performance that puts Zeppelin over the top for me," Peter said backstage. "This band could be just as big as the Beatles or the Stones. Or even bigger."

Peter's judgment, of course, was usually worth paying attention to. I decided to brace myself for Led Zeppelin's ascent into the rock heavens.

That night after the Boston concert, fans stopped Peter in our hotel and talked to him about a Zeppelin "force" still echoing through their heads. "At this point in their careers," Peter told me, "even if I wanted to hold them back and take things a little slower, it couldn't be done. They're unstoppable."

When *Led Zeppelin II* was released, it hardly had the record stores all to itself. Other new albums were released at the same time—*Let It Bleed* by the Stones, *Abbey Road* by the Beatles, *The Best of Cream*, and *Crosby, Stills and Nash*. But Zeppelin's true believers couldn't be bothered with them. Once *Led Zeppelin II* had landed in the record racks, fans lined up around the block in some cities for a first-day purchase. Sales began during the third week of October, and they were so monstrous that by November tenth—two days after the end of the band's fall American tour—the Recording Industry of America had awarded us a gold album. As a Denver disc jockey proclaimed, "Hundreds of thousands of stereo needles are being sacrificed tonight playing, replaying, and then replaying again *Led Zeppelin II*."

During that fourth U.S. tour, the titanic sales of the new album put the band in festive spirits. It helped ease the fatigue that seemed to come and go with little predictability. It helped boost egos that sagged when an uncomplimentary review would strike a nerve. It also gave us one more excuse to throw a party.

In San Francisco, we rented a suite at the Villa Roma, an elegant hotel built around a courtyard, to stage a celebration of the album's success for about twenty-five guests, mostly locals. A couple of absolutely gorgeous girls showed up—tall, long hair, breathy voices, seductive body English, and virtually every other feminine quality that could snap our libidos to attention. The band members almost trampled each other in the rush to introduce themselves to these ladies.

One of the girls had brought three gray doves with her in a cage, although she kept taking them out and letting them soar around the room. One of the doves in particular was like a kamikaze pilot, banging into walls as though it were on a suicide mission. Somehow, the stunned bird would regain its strength and equilibrium and begin flying again. With the doves as entertainment, we consumed alcohol as quickly as room service could supply it. The festivities were finally called to a halt at about 3 A.M. By that time, I was so drunk that I had very little recollection of much of anything, including who ended up with the girls.

We spent the night in our own rooms at the Villa Roma, and the following morning I walked with Jimmy and John Paul through the hotel courtyard on our way to breakfast. Our attention on that stroll, however, was drawn to the sound of running water—a waterfall, really—plunging off the balcony of a second-floor room, splattering on the cement below.

"My God," John Paul suddenly exclaimed. "That's the room where we had the party last night."

I could immediately see a bill for damages flashing through my brain. In unison, we turned and sprinted up the stairs. I fumbled through my pants pocket, desperately groping for the key to the room. When I finally located it, I jammed it into the lock, shoved the door open, and stormed inside. Within the first couple of steps, we were up to our ankles in water.

"Oh, shit!" I exclaimed. "It's a fucking swimming pool in here."

I splashed into the bathroom, looking for the source of the San Francisco flood. The culprit was the bathtub, overflowing with a tidal wave of water that had probably been spewing out for seven or eight hours by then. I turned the faucet off, quickly surveyed the scene, and shook my head in disbelief. "Who in the fuck left the damn water on?"

Jimmy peered into the bathtub and saw the source of the problem. "Look at this," he sighed. "One of those fucking doves got sucked into the drain. That's what clogged it up."

I reached in and picked up the remains of the little bird. He had flown his last suicide mission. The water in the tub began to drain.

"This carpeting is a total loss," Jimmy said, sloshing through the water damage in the room. "Do you think the hotel has dove insurance?"

"This one could be costly," John Paul chimed in. "We may have to sign over the royalties from the new album to pay for this."

"I wouldn't worry about it," I told them. And, in fact, I felt confident that we had absolutely no reason for concern. After all, when we checked into the Villa Roma, I registered the band under someone else's name. My reasoning: To avoid being bothered by fans and also to minimize the paper trail if we accumulated additional charges.

A couple of days later, I told the story to Bonham, who burst into hysterics over what I had done. "That's spectacular," he said. "I can't believe you can get away with something like that." Then he asked, "Whose name was that room registered under?"

"Frank Barsalona," I said. Frank was the agent with Premier Talent who handled the band's U.S. bookings. "He should be getting the bill any day. I hope he has a sense of humor."

"If he doesn't," said Bonzo, "maybe he's good at laying new carpeting."

As the new album sales became astronomical, and with the increasing popularity of Zeppelin seeming all but inevitable, the band members would occasionally chat with Peter during their idle hours about how to protect their individual nest eggs. They were also receiving advice from the home office in London, where our accountants were offering recommendations designed to turn them into instant tax experts.

During a short break in the tour, everyone in the band made a quick exit off the U.S. mainland on the advice of our tax attorneys, who had added up the numbers on the band's likely earnings for 1969 and arrived at a figure of about $1 million. Because the band had worked in the States for a cumulative total of nearly six months, we were on the brink of having to pay both U.S. and British taxes—not an appealing thought for a band earning a seven-figure income.

Jonesy, Bonzo, and Peter decided to fly directly to London to be with their families during the break. The rest of us convened in San Juan, Puerto Rico. For tax purposes, Puerto Rico was not considered part of the States, yet it was still within striking distance of the mainland.

Jimmy, Robert, and I stayed at the Caribe Hilton Hotel in San Juan. We squeezed in as much midday sunbathing, early-evening piña coladas, and late-night revelry as possible.

One evening, I convinced Robert and Jimmy to accompany me into Old San Juan, a seven-square-block area that was the original city, with buildings dating back to the sixteenth and seventeenth centuries. A bellhop at our hotel had warned us, "Señors, Old San Juan is fine during the day. But don't go there at night. It's too dangerous for the tourists. Too much crime."

I dragged Robert and Jimmy there anyway, although you could see the anxiety etched into their furrowed brows and tight lips. I began looking for a bar where we could find some good Mexican beer and maybe relieve some of their tension. We walked into the first club we approached on Calle San Sebastián—but it wasn't what I had expected. In fact, I had the feeling that we had entered the Twilight Zone. The bar was so dark that I could barely see my companions, much less anyone else who might be in the place. As we edged our way across the bar, I could feel dozens of eyes staring at us. Then, a few seconds later, someone turned all the lights on in the club.

Clearly, we looked different from the rest of the patrons. They looked as if they had just disembarked from a pirate ship after a hard day of plundering and torture. We wore flowery shirts and earrings and had long hair—a bit too much on the effeminate side for this crowd.

"We're getting out of here," Robert announced, turning toward the door.

"Naw, Percy," I said, grabbing his arm. "Let's order some drinks."

"You're mad, Cole," Jimmy said. "I don't think they want to be our friends." He was starting to tremble.

"We're okay," I said, letting my desire for alcohol smother any fear I was feeling. "They won't touch us." I wasn't at all convinced of the truth of that statement.

The club itself was as sleazy as any I had ever seen—no wonder I wanted to stay. We sat at a table with one leg missing and ordered three beers. A few minutes later, just as Jimmy excused himself to go to the bathroom, a gorgeous brunette wearing about seven pounds of makeup—obviously a hooker—walked over to our table, sat down in Pagey's chair between Plant and me, and tried to get friendly.

Before the conversation had even gotten beyond "Cómo estás?," she reached down and put her hand on my crotch.

"Oooh," she sighed. "Grande!"

I smiled and looked over at Plant. I was really beginning to like this place.

Then she placed her other hand on Robert's crotch. "Ooooh," she moaned. "*Mucho* grande!"

For the first time that evening, Robert laughed.

"This is a very perceptive young lady," he said "*Very* perceptive."

When Pagey returned, he refused to submit to her below-the-waist evaluation. "Let's get out of here before we get killed!" he said.

Robert and I had already had our egos stroked for the night, and so we agreed to a quick exit.

At the end of the American tour, when we finally flew home to London, we talked about what an amazing year 1969 had been. The band had come out of nowhere and was on the brink of superstardom. We had toured at a merciless pace—160 performances since that very first one in Copenhagen fourteen months earlier. The group was making so much money that we had to do things like evaluate our tax status in the middle of a tour. At times, it was exhausting just to think about how far we had come.

That's me on the right in my pre-Zeppelin days, posing with Henri Harrison
of the New Vaudeville Band after a busy night on the town in
Las Vegas, 1967. *(The Richard Cole Collection)*

On the Yardbirds' final U.S. tour in 1968, Jimmy Page prepares to strum a few chords at an outdoor concert in Rhode Island. *(The Richard Cole Collection)*

Here I am collecting a gold record from Keith Moon *(left)* for Maggie Bell in 1972 for the album of *Tommy* songs performed by the London Symphony Orchestra and Chamber Choir. *(The Richard Cole Collection)*

John Bonham, with his fishing pole strategically positioned, waits for a bite on the balcony of the Edgewater Inn in Seattle, 1969. "Hurry up and cut a few more sirloin steaks, Richard; the sharks are starving!" *(The Richard Cole Collection)*

Band assistant Brian Gallivan *(left)* and head of Led Zeppelin security Bill Dautrich watch the fishing off the balcony in Seattle, 1977. *(The Richard Cole Collection)*

Members of our road crew relax before unloading equipment in New York, 1969. From left: Joe "Jammer" Wright, Clive Coulson, a friend, and Mick Turner (Eric Clapton's assistant). *(The Richard Cole Collection)*

Thousands of miles skyward, Bonzo and his wife, Pat, head for the next destination during a 1969 U.S. tour. *(The Richard Cole Collection)*

Robert Plant never looked more peaceful than during this in-flight nap after a hard night of playing music. *(The Richard Cole Collection)*

Maureen and Robert Plant
are flying high at a fair in
Texas, 1969.
(The Richard Cole Collection)

Clive Coulson *(left)* chats with
Robert outside a hotel in the
United States, 1969.
(The Richard Cole Collection)

Pat and John Bonham, with John Paul on the right, wait for a rental car arrival in Texas, 1969. *(The Richard Cole Collection)*

Robert *(left)*, Jimmy *(center)*, and Bonzo *(right)* onstage in Scandinavia, February 1970. That's me in the background. *(Photograph by Torbjorn Hansson)*

At a club in Düsseldorf, March 1970, we bumped into a fellow who called himself "The Baron" *(second from right)*. That's me *(left)*, Jimmy *(second from left)*, and Robert *(right)* posing with him.
(The Richard Cole Collection)

Jimmy's up to monkey business again in Bombay, 1972.
(The Richard Cole Collection)

Robert *(left)* and Jimmy on Keats Island, British Columbia, 1970.
Are they looking for magic mushrooms? *(The Richard Cole Collection)*

Robert with the big log on Keats Island, 1970. *(The Richard Cole Collection)*

Bonzo *(left)* and I act like tourists at the Fontainebleau in Miami, 1970.
"Where are those thirty beers you ordered for us, Richard?"
(The Richard Cole Collection)

Ricardo and Percy dance cheek to cheek at the Hyatt House, 1973. *(The Richard Cole Collection)*

Rod Stewart *(left)*, friend, and Ronnie Wood of the Jeff Beck Group enjoy
their first visit to L.A. at the Hyatt rooftop pool in 1968.
(The Richard Cole Collection)

▲ FOR YOUR ALBUM

**BONUS
PHOTO**

exclusive
with

FILM
SERVICE
BY
HITE
PHOTO

FOR YOUR WALLET

Patent Pending
©All rights reserved
K

Jeff Beck *(right)* and I watch the girls go by, Detroit, 1968.
(The Richard Cole Collection)

One of my bigger catches at the Edgewater Inn in Seattle, 1970.
"Bonzo, please hang this in the closet." *(The Richard Cole Collection)*

Here I am with a balcony full of fish at the Edgewater Inn, 1970.
The fish were particularly hungry that day. *(The Richard Cole Collection)*

Peter takes to the sea
on the waters off
Vancouver, 1970.
*(The Richard Cole
Collection)*

Jimmy enjoying the fresh air
on a sailing expedition near
Vancouver, 1970.
(The Richard Cole Collection)

Peter *(left)*, Jimmy *(center)*, and Bonzo *(right)*. "Only a few more concerts and we'll
be on our way home." *(The Richard Cole Collection)*

Jimmy, with camera in hand, visits the Emerald Buddha in Bangkok, 1971.
(The Richard Cole Collection)

Bonzo *(left)* and Robert converse at a park in Japan, 1971.
(The Richard Cole Collection)

Even in India Jimmy *(left)* and John Paul enjoyed traveling first class, 1972.
(The Richard Cole Collection)

Robert *(right)* and I balance ourselves on a camel in Bombay, 1972.
"It's a pity, Richard, that you can't go without a drink for as long as this camel!"
(The Richard Cole Collection)

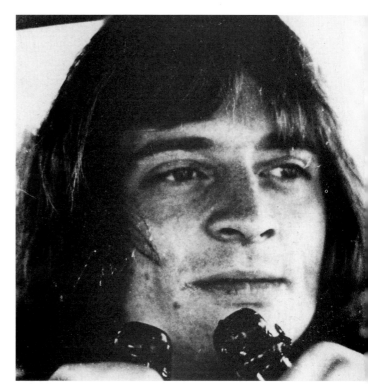

John Paul clutching his "breakfast" in Chicago. *(The Richard Cole Collection)*

"I never thought you'd make this train!"
Robert prepares for a rail trip, 1973. *(The Richard Cole Collection)*

That's me *(left)* and John Paul *(second from right)* joined by Harold *(center)*
and Al, "our boys in Chicago," 1973. *(The Richard Cole Collection)*

"NAME YOUR PRICE"

How much did you say?"

"You heard me, Cole. They offered us one million dollars!"

"And you turned it down?"

"It just wasn't right. It would have been a mistake."

Peter Grant was explaining why he had rejected one of the dozens of concert offers that had poured into the Led Zeppelin office. Because of the enormous record sales of *Led Zeppelin II,* a lot of promoters virtually said, "Name your price." They wanted the band that bad.

One of the most tempting offers had come from a group of American promoters, who proposed staging a Zeppelin concert in West Germany on New Year's Eve, using a satellite transmission to beam the performance into movie theaters throughout the U.S. and Europe.

"We'll pay the band half a million dollars," the promoters said in their initial offer. "That should start off your nineteen seventy with a bang!"

Not a big enough bang for Peter, even if it was a phenomenal sum for one night's work. Like Jimmy, Peter was a perfectionist. And the thought of subjecting his band to the satellite transmission made him shudder.

"I've heard the sound quality on those closed-circuit transmissions," he told the American businessmen. "I've never been impressed. It's just not up to our standards."

Initially, the Americans figured he was kidding. After all, for $500,000, perhaps a band could be convinced to put up with a little static or a bit more treble than they'd like. But the more they talked to Peter, the more they realized that he was serious.

"Television just isn't the best medium for a band that's conscientious about quality," Peter said. "That's why this band has never done TV. When you're talking about a satellite transmission over thousands of miles, it can't be very good."

The Americans apparently still believed that if the price were right, Peter might change his mind. They called back two days later. They raised their offer to $1 million!

Peter never hesitated. "The answer is still no," he told them. "You can raise the fee as high as you like. I'm not going to change my mind. Quality is still paramount to this band."

I had a tremendous amount of respect for Peter for making decisions like that. After all, $1 million was more money that any rock band had ever made on a single night. But he wasn't going to budge from his own artistic principles.

I also think Peter enjoyed hearing the shocked reactions of the Americans when he matter-of-factly rejected their offer, as though $1 million wasn't a significant amount of money. The egos of everyone in the organization were growing—perhaps overgrowing—and by turning down a $1 million offer, that's one way of telling the world just how big and important you are.

Still, the driving force behind his decision was an unwavering set of principles about the quality of the band's music. "There's more to life than money," he once told me. He knew that other opportunities would present themselves under terms he could live with. So on New Year's Eve, we stayed home.

Nevertheless, Led Zeppelin did its celebrating a few days later. On January 9, we eagerly anticipated the band's performance that night at Royal Albert Hall. "England finally belongs to us," Bonzo said. "After tonight, there's not going to be any doubt in anyone's mind."

It was also Jimmy Page's twenty-sixth birthday. As the crowd gathered at Royal Albert Hall, some arriving four to five hours before show time, many carried signs wishing Pagey a happy birthday. Others were more generic: "We love you, Jimmy" . . . "Zeppelin Forever."

Robert was feeling on top of the world. The extraordinary record sales were abstractions in his mind; it was hard to relate to sales figures in six and even seven figures. But when he could look out on an audience, stare into individual faces, and bring them to an orgasmic pitch within minutes, numbers became meaningless. We knew that the critics were wrong. If the press didn't like Led Zeppelin, it was their problem. Yes, those negative reviews—which still outnumbered the positive ones—angered Robert. But he knew that this band touched people's lives. He witnessed it from a vantage point that no one else had.

Royal Albert Hall was the third stop on a short, seven-concert tour of the U.K. And the band held nothing back. They planned a two-hour set, but it ran at least thirty minutes longer than that. They had added songs like "Since I've Been Loving You" and "Thank You" to the act, but more than that, the audience reaction was so overwhelming that the band spontaneously changed the show several times in midstream. During "Bring It on Home," Pagey and Bonham began dueling one another with their respective instruments—first one, then the other, in a stirring showdown that no one, neither the band nor the audience, wanted to end. The applause was so strong for some songs that even as the band would begin to wind them down, the crowd reaction inspired them to extend them even further. For instance, as they were drawing "How Many More Times" to a close, the audience hysteria became so intense that the band couldn't move on to its next number, "The Lemon Song." So instead, they began another riff of "How Many More Times" and carried on with it for another eight minutes.

There were moments of irony, too. As popular as the original Zeppelin material was, the music that really brought down the house was a medley of old rock 'n' roll songs, including "Long Tall Sally," and "Whole Lotta Shakin' Going On."

Roger Daltrey was backstage with a drink in his hand, watching the show with an astonished look on his face. "I know why no one wants to play with these guys," he said at one point. "They're just too good."

Daltrey was accompanied by his girlfriend, Heather, who had brought Jimmy a rather unique birthday present—a beautiful, successful French model named Charlotte Martin. Heather was convinced that Jimmy and Charlotte would hit it off.

I had met Charlotte in the south of France in 1966 and run into her again two years later when she was dating Eric Clapton. Charlotte was the type of girl who you couldn't look at just once. Tall. Thin. Blond. Perfect features. You had to glance a second time.

But I also knew a different side of Charlotte. At least in her relationship with me, she was aloof, unfriendly, and indifferent. It was my feeling that unless she really liked you, she had a "take it or leave it" attitude. Frankly, I wasn't impressed.

Nevertheless, Jimmy and Charlotte instantly became an item. After the concert that evening, Jimmy chatted with her for several minutes and then took me aside. "Can you drive Charlotte and me to her apartment? It's not that far out of your way." I gave them a ride, and that was the beginning of a relationship that continued for years.

During that entire time, Charlotte and I never really got along. She continued to act coolly toward me, as though we hadn't known one another from those days in France. Eventually, however, I guess she realized that I was a permanent fixture with Led Zeppelin, and she seemed to have decided that if she was going to spend time with Jimmy, she'd have to be reasonably pleasant with me, too. So our relationship became a polite one. Even so, I never found her easy to be around.

It often became a nightmare when Charlotte traveled with the band. Unlike the wives of the other band members—Maureen Plant, Pat Bonham, and Mo Jones—who were always very cooperative, Charlotte created constant problems for me, which only magnified the friction between us. As tour manager, one of my responsibilities was to oversee the band's safety, and when the wives and girlfriends attended concerts, that meant watching over eight people, not just four.

Still, I tried to keep things running as smoothly as possible. When the band went on for its encores, I would tell the girls, "Move into the limos; we're going to be departing soon." They all followed my directions—except Charlotte.

"I want to stay and watch until the show's over," Charlotte would complain.

"Like hell you will!" I'd shout at her.

"You can't tell me what to do," she'd yell back.

"You bet I fucking can! Get the hell into the limo!"

Eventually, she'd cooperate, but not until we were at each other's throats.

Back in London, I was delighted to hear that Charlotte wouldn't be part of the traveling entourage on a European tour scheduled to begin in late February, with stops in Copenhagen, Helsinki, Stockholm, Amsterdam, Cologne, Vienna, Hamburg, and Montreux. During that seven-country European tour, I had arranged for a five-ton truck to travel with us. Not only would we need it to transport Led Zeppelin's equipment from one city to the next, but I sensed that the band would be accumulating new belongings along the way. That's what new money does for you.

I hired a fellow named Manfred Lurch as one of our truck drivers; he could speak several languages, and I figured he could converse with customs officials just about anywhere. As expected, both Manfred and the truck proved indispensable. We loaded up the truck with the spoils of a dozen shopping sprees, cramming the vehicle with blues albums, Ernst Fuchs paintings, Escher lithographs, and pieces of furniture.

■ ■ ■

Nevertheless, the best planning couldn't anticipate what we encountered in Copenhagen during that tour. It should have been a positive, even sentimental performance. After all, seventeen months earlier, Copenhagen was the site of the first Zeppelin concert ever. In fact, when we touched down at the airport at Kastrup on February 19, we all felt excitement and anticipation. "This is where it all started," Jimmy Page said. "It's almost like coming home."

But rather than making a trumphant return, the band suddenly found itself in the middle of a bizarre controversy with one of Europe's more famous families. Eva von Zeppelin didn't want the band using "*my* family's name this way." And overnight, Led Zeppelin's music was over-shadowed by some highly publicized offstage hassles.

"Let this be a warning that these people who claim to be musicians had better not use the name Zeppelin and play their trashy music in Denmark," Eva von Zeppelin announced to the press. "If they do, I will see them in court."

Von Zeppelin wasn't kidding. She said she was a direct descendant of Count Ferdinand von Zeppelin, the aeronautical legend. Around the turn of the century, Count Ferdinand had pioneered the lighter-than-air vehicles that eventually carried his name. And Eva wasn't going to let a band that had "stolen" the name Zeppelin play in Denmark without a fight.

The band was incensed by her statements to the press. At this point in their careers, Led Zeppelin was feeling pretty important themselves and weren't used to having people make outrageous demands of them. "Who in the hell is Eva von Zeppelin anyway?" Robert Plant said. "*No one's* ever heard of that woman! A hell of a lot more people have heard of us!"

Maybe so. But Eva was making ridiculous public proclamations in which she labeled Led Zeppelin as a bunch of "screaming monkeys." As the rhetoric escalated, Jimmy realized the band would have to do something to control the damage.

"Let's invite her to meet with us," said Jimmy. "Maybe she'll realize that we're not raving maniacs after all."

In fact, Eva agreed to sit down and talk with the "screaming monkeys" at a rehearsal studio in Copenhagen, the day before our scheduled concert. Before Eva arrived, Peter told the rest of us, "Let's keep our cool and try not to offend her any more than she already is. Maybe we can smooth-talk her into forgetting about this whole thing."

In fact, the meeting was relatively pleasant. "We're not doing anything to defame your family name," Jimmy pleaded. "We're just playing music, and it's music that millions of people enjoy."

All the while, Eva insisted, "All I'm trying to do is protect my family's reputation!"

"Millions of people know us by the name Led Zeppelin," Jimmy said. "And I don't think any of them think it's offensive to your family."

The meeting ended in a stalemate. But the band felt they had softened the old lady's heart. The fireworks weren't over, however. As Eva was leaving the studio, her eyes became transfixed on a copy of the album jacket for *Led Zeppelin*—the one with the dirigible plunging into the ground in a horrifying inferno.

Eva von Zeppelin gasped. Her fury erupted all over again. There were epithets bouncing off the walls. There were reckless threats of imminent subpoenas. Eva finally stormed out of the studio.

Peter was exasperated. He didn't know quite what to do, but he knew that he had no interest in ending up in court. "This is the most ridiculous thing I've ever heard of," he said. "But that woman is angry enough to sue us." For the moment, he put egos aside and said, "Here's my recommendation. Let's go onstage tomorrow night under another name."

At first, the band resisted. "Let *her* change her damn name," Bonzo exclaimed. "We have just as much right to it as she does."

Before long, however, Peter won the band over to his side. He usually did. During that Copenhagen concert, Led Zeppelin performed as the Nobs—in some London circles, a slang term for the male sex organ! Fortunately, Eva von Zeppelin did not claim exclusive rights to *that*, too.

Immediately after the Copenhagen concert, the band was still seething. "Why did we give in anyway?" Robert asked as he grabbed a towel backstage and moved quickly toward the limo. "What gives her the right?"

"It's over, Percy," I told him. "Forget about it. Let's find something else to occupy our minds."

The driver of our limo that night was a friendly chap named Jann. "Would you like to see some of the sights of Copenhagen?" he asked. "How about Christiansborg Castle? Or the Stroget Mall?"

After the forty-eight hours we had just lived through, we weren't interested in the typical tourist spots. Tivoli Gardens and the *Little Mermaid* statue could wait. As the night wore close to midnight, we had women on our minds.

"I'll tell you what we'd like," I said to Jann. "We'd like to see Copenhagen's sex clubs!"

Jann suddenly became very quiet. "The sex clubs?" he mumbled in a disbelieving voice. He turned to glance at his passengers—Jimmy, Robert, John Paul, Bonzo, Peter, and me. We didn't exactly look like members of the British Royal Family. The expression on Jann's face screamed, "How did I ever get stuck with these six clowns?"

We drove for another ten minutes, and Jann pulled up in front of one of the city's most popular sex clubs. "Here it is," he said. I figured we'd have to scoot out of the limo quickly, and that Jann would speed away, embarrassed to be seen in that neighborhood. But suddenly, he became a different person.

"I'll take you inside," Jann said. "The manager's a friend of mine. I'll let him know that you're my special guests!"

Special guests! I guess Jann wasn't a prudish altar boy after all.

"Enjoy the show!" the manager told us. "Just remember, no audience participation."

We walked into a dimly lit room, almost stumbling over one another until our eyes adjusted to the darkness. "Am I seeing things," wisecracked Jimmy, "or are we almost the only ones in here with our clothes on?"

For the next two hours, the show took our minds off Eva von Zeppelin. There were plenty of girls, at least a couple dozen, and most of them were absolutely beautiful. A few were serving drinks; most were part of the performance—and they weren't performing Shakespeare. We sat just a few feet from the stage, when one of the naked girls began playing with herself in front of us. Bumping. Grinding. Moaning. Groaning.

"I think I'm in love," Bonham sighed.

"I think she is, too," Plant said. "Too bad it's with herself."

Within minutes, the girl was joined by a friend, and the two of them began making love in front of us. Before long, they were joined by a third girl. And then a fourth. And then a vibrator or two. They were like one big happy family.

"Pardon me," Bonham yelled at them. "Do you girls really get paid for this? I'd do it for free! I really would!"

Bonham moved toward the stage, grabbed a vibrator from one of the girls, and fumbled with it for a few moments until he had removed its batteries. Then he returned it to her.

"You gals have gotta work for your pay," he shouted over the loud music. "Don't let modern technology do everything for you!"

Most of the other male customers were on the timid side and seemed stunned by our rowdiness.

"One of these girls is my sister," Bonham told a startled patron. "Mom asked me to come down and make sure she's not getting into any trouble."

We had never run into anything quite like this in London. We stayed another hour, and it was more of the same—the kind of raunchy sex that's a lot more fun to do than to watch, but we certainly weren't complaining. As we rode back to our hotel, Robert said, "Next time we're in Copenhagen, Richard, make sure this is part of our itinerary."

Four months later, just before we returned to Denmark, I called the same sex club. "We want to reserve the club just for ourselves on Saturday night," I said. "Let me know how much money you take in on a typical Saturday night, and we'll give you the cash to cover it."

So on that second visit to the club, it was just us and the girls. It sounded like a perfect arrangement—but it wasn't nearly as much fun as the first time we had been there. Maybe it was because we had already seen the show once before. Or perhaps it was because we occasionally staged shows like this in our own hotel rooms—where audience participation was allowed! Also, since we were the only customers in the club, there weren't other people around to shock with our behavior. Whether at Carnegie Hall or a Copenhagen sex club, we liked being the center of attention. But there were competing interests at the sex clubs.

During that February 1970 stop in Copenhagen, our fascination with the sex clubs didn't mean that we had no other interests. In fact, we spent a lot of time in art galleries, too. Jimmy in particular was looking for some works of art to buy, although we found other ways to occupy our time there, too.

At Peter's suggestion, we had agreed to hold a press reception in a gallery adjacent to the Stroget. Reporters, critics, and music company executives crammed into the gallery, and there were plenty of hors d'oeuvres and champagne to keep them happy. At one point, a music critic cornered Bonham and me and began pontificating about one subject after another, none of which interested us. "Once a rock group achieves commercial success, I believe that they lose something," he babbled. "Maybe it's their hunger that gives intensity to their music. You guys have to watch out for that. I'd hate to see it happen to you."

Then his attention shifted to the pop art painting in front of us. He began analyzing it, placing even more of a strain on our patience. "It reminds me so much of Lichtenstein and perhaps a touch of Rauschenberg, too," he said. "I find it so moving . . . so moving."

Bonzo turned to me and whispered, "What fucking bullshit!"

"When I look at it," the critic continued, "I see such a strong statement against abstract expressionism."

Bonzo finally lost his cool.

"Do you want to know what I think of this painting?" Bonzo roared.

"Of course, I'd love to know," the critic said timidly.

Bonzo walked toward the painting, lifted it off the wall, and screamed, "This is what I think of it!"

He raised the painting over his head and snapped it downward, crashing it onto the head of the critic. The frame cracked. The canvas ripped down the middle. The critic was knocked to the ground. He grabbed his head, moaning in pain.

The stunned crowd became silent.

"Are there any other paintings you'd like me to critique tonight?!" Bonzo exclaimed as he walked toward the door.

The rest of us thought it was a perfect time to exit as well. We left Peter behind to try to mend fences. Before we had left town, we got a $5,000 bill from the art gallery to cover the cost of the painting Bonham had destroyed.

"That's the last time we ever have a press party at an art gallery," John Paul said during the drive back to our hotel.

"From now on, let's hold them in strip joints," I said. "It would be a lot more appropriate."

"THOSE ZEPPELIN BASTARDS"

Henry Smith, one of our road managers, was gathering up our equipment at the Winnipeg airport. We had just flown into the Canadian city during our fifth North American tour, which was launched in March 1970. But as Henry surveyed the equipment, he noticed that one of the guitars was missing.

"Shit," he said to himself. "It's one of Jimmy's. He's not going to be happy."

The band and I were already in our hotel when Henry called me to report the missing guitar. "It's the old black one," Henry said. "The Les Paul that Keith Richard gave him."

I knew Jimmy wouldn't be happy. I walked down to his room to tell him what had happened. As soon as he heard the news, he snapped.

"Lost a guitar!" he shouted. "How in the hell can they lose a guitar?!"

He kicked at a nearby sofa. "Richard, this is ridiculous! Do you know how much I love that guitar?"

I couldn't recall ever seeing Jimmy quite this angry. I decided just to let him talk.

"How could somebody just walk off with it?" he shouted. "Don't the airports do anything to keep things from being ripped off?"

For a full hour, Jimmy continued to blow off steam. "Where were the road managers, Richard? Don't we pay them to keep an eye on the gear? I feel like firing every last one of them!"

When I finally left Jimmy's room, I thought to myself, "If this is any sign of what the rest of this tour is going to be like, I'm ready to go home now."

Airport security never turned up any sign of the guitar. Apparently, some-one had stolen it off a baggage truck or a conveyer belt. Our chances of get-ting it back were virtually nil.

Jimmy, however, was desperate. He placed an ad in *Rolling Stone*, pleading for help in locating the guitar. We waited for someone to contact us. But no one ever did. The guitar was never recovered. Somebody, somewhere, ended up with a remarkable piece of Zeppelin memorabilia.

During the course of the tour, Jimmy never seemed to fully recover from the loss. He got through all twenty-nine performances without any noticeable impact upon his playing. But he'd look dejected at times, and I figured it was related to the guitar. It really didn't matter that every show was a sellout, that it was a guaranteed $1 million tour before it had even begun. To Jimmy, the loss of the guitar ruined everything.

In planning that 1970 trip, Peter had made the decision that Led Zeppelin would have no opening acts during the entire tour. Night after night, it would just be two and a half hours of pure Zeppelin.

"When we have a support act, there's a lot of fucking around to worry about," Peter said. "There are the gear changeovers and the worries about moving equipment and possibly damaging it. If we're out there alone, we can set up our own gear and leave it there. I don't have any doubts that the band can carry the show on its own."

Peter also knew that fans didn't come to a Led Zeppelin concert to hear supporting acts. He had a "let's give the public what they want" attitude, and that meant a long night of Zeppelinmania.

The band felt liberated by Peter's decision. As the sole act on the bill, they would have full control of the entire show. And the idea excited them. Some nights, they felt like playing until morning.

As cocky as the band sometimes behaved offstage—and as their reputation grew as a band that used and supposedly exploited the young groupies who hung around them—they never took their fans for granted. They knew who bought the records, who paid for the tickets. "If the show's going well, let's just keep playing," John Paul said. "As long as the fans will stick around, so will we."

By the midway point of the tour, many of the shows were running three hours, occasionally even longer. Individual songs would go on for ten, fifteen, or twenty minutes. "Dazed and Confused" would routinely stretch for forty minutes. Crowds burst into standing ovations in the middle of songs.

There was never an intermission. Bonham would sneak off the stage while Jimmy and John Paul would showcase a lengthy musical rush. Then Bonham would reciprocate with a twenty- or thirty-minute drum solo of his own—

ripping off his shirt, tossing his drumsticks into the audience, and pummeling the drums with his hands until they formed calluses. Bonham's interlude was so gripping that none of us would stray too far from the stage. Very simply, the band was good, every night, all night.

Jimmy couldn't stand it when he'd hear about the big-name bands that played only a fifty-minute set—and would sometimes cut it even shorter if the vibes just weren't right. "They're on and off before the audience can ever blink," he muttered. "It's just not fair to the fans." Jimmy figured that maybe those bands just didn't have much to say. By contrast, Zeppelin had a lot of different moods they tried to express during the night. You can't do that in fifty minutes.

When the tour moved into the South—Memphis, Raleigh, Atlanta—we expected life to become a little more uncomfortable for us, although it had nothing to do with fan reaction. Particularly in the South, people in airports would stare, whistle, and chuckle over our long hair. It wasn't anything we couldn't deal with, although after seeing *Easy Rider* we had become a bit more anxious about how people responded to our hair.

"If you spot some rednecks driving in a pickup truck with a rifle rack in the back window, take cover!" John Paul nervously joked.

In Raleigh, the harassment escalated to a higher plateau. Henry Smith was in the restroom backstage just before the concert began and from the bathroom stall heard two cops talking about "planting some stuff on those Zeppelin bastards and sending them up the river for a while."

Henry panicked and, while still buckling his pants, bolted out of the bathroom and darted through the auditorium until he found me. "They're gonna get us!" he jabbered. "The cops are out to get us!"

I generally wasn't as paranoid as Henry, but still became pretty unsettled by what he had told me. Not knowing quite where to turn, I found a pay phone and called the Raleigh offices of both Pinkerton's and Brink's, trying to arrange for some immediate security for the band.

"I'm the tour manager with the rock band Led Zeppelin," I told the fellow who answered the phone at Brink's. I wasn't the kind of customer he was used to, and he was skeptical of my claim that Raleigh's men in blue could have an evil plot in mind.

"Sorry, fella," the voice at Brink's said. "This story doesn't sound right to me. We protect bank presidents, not guitar players."

By this point, my own anxiety had escalated considerably. I had visions of the entire band ending up in jail by the end of the night, and I knew that was something I didn't want to deal with. As a last resort, I called Steve Weiss, our attorney, in New York City. I told him what Henry had heard and the problems I was having hiring some local protection.

"You're a lawyer," I told him. "Maybe you'll have more clout trying to get some security out here to help us. I just feel very unsafe at the moment and think we need some protection in place quickly."

Steve agreed. "The band has a lot of assets—including its reputation—that need to be protected," he told me. "I'll see what I can do."

From New York, Steve placed some calls, and within forty-five minutes, two security men—ties, coats, and short hair—arrived backstage. They were very businesslike, and if they felt out of place having to guard some long-haired musicians, they didn't show it. "We're here to make sure that your stay here in Raleigh is problem-free," one of them said.

In fact, there were no problems. One of the security men positioned himself at the entrance to the band's dressing room. Another one was in the wings of the stage, keeping the band itself under surveillance for anything suspicious. The night proceeded without a hitch. The extra security may have kept the Raleigh cops from making life miserable for Led Zeppelin.

Late that night, when I told the band about the whole incident, they were flabbergasted. "That's fuckin' amazing!" Bonzo exclaimed. "Don't these cops have anything better to do than try to bust rock musicians? People are getting killed in the streets, and they're trying to create a marijuana bust! How absurd!"

From that point on, I tried to be more careful with the illegal substances that we carried with us. We usually had some cocaine and some pills, and sometimes the anticipation of taking the drugs—and the rush of the drugs themselves—would blind me to any risks we were assuming. But when I was thinking more clearly, when I allowed the anxiety to overtake the craving, the thought of a bust hovered in the back of my mind. It was one more source of stress in my job.

20

HANDCUFFS

We're back!"

The elderly woman in the gift shop at the Edgewater Inn in Seattle looked up at Bonzo. "Who are you?" she asked.

"We were here last year," he said. "Don't you remember? We're some of your top fishermen!"

We had come down to the gift shop to get some fishing rods for the evening. I felt a little tense, wondering if the stories of the Shark Episode—which had spread literally throughout the world—had reached the Edgewater staff itself yet. This woman, however, seemed to have other priorities. Most immediately, her attention was devoted to straightening up the candy rack next to the cash register.

Within a few minutes, we were dipping our fishing poles into Puget Sound. "It's good to be home," Robert said.

Amazingly, we picked up right where we had left off the last time around. Bonzo caught a couple of mud sharks within the first half hour. Jimmy caught one, too. As the night progressed, we reeled them in like old pros.

"Someone must have just restocked the ocean," Bonzo hypothesized.

As the night wore on and our fishing expedition continued, three rather foxy teenage girls, two blondes and a brunette, knocked on our hotel room door at about 3 A.M. They wore miniskirts, their tits were falling out of their blouses, and they had "Fuck me" written all over their smiles. It may have been early Sunday morning, but they didn't appear to be on their way to church.

Bonham and I, however, were concentrating on our fishing. We looked at each other and shook our heads. "Sorry," I said. "We're fishing tonight. Come back tomorrow!"

Oddly enough, even the groupies bored us sometimes. As Led Zeppelin's fame and fortune allowed us to live out our fantasies, we were constantly looking for something new to entertain us. The fishing was all we needed for the moment. These particular girls were seductive-looking and obviously in the mood for a little recreation. But there would be girls in other cities; the fishing was a "now or never" proposition.

By this trip to Seattle, we realized that the stench of the sharks could become crippling after a day or two of sitting in the hotel room. "It's hard keeping the booze down when there's this putrid, fishy smell everywhere," Bonham complained.

"Maybe so," I said, "but you'd need a room deodorizer the size of Cheyenne, Wyoming, to freshen up this place!"

We finally decided to rent an extra "fishing room" where we could toss our catches for the day. On this particular trip, we reeled in about thirty sharks over a two-night period and threw them in a pile in the middle of the room.

"What are we gonna do with these suckers now?" Bonzo asked.

"I don't know," I said. "Let's try stacking them up in the closet. If we close the closet door, maybe the smell won't be as bad."

In a rather orderly fashion, Bonzo and I began to place one shark atop the other in the wardrobe closet, pausing every minute or two for another swig of booze. When they were finally perfectly arranged, we gently closed the closet door and turned in for the night.

The next morning, we were awakened by screams. A maid was running hysterically down the hallway, apparently having made a rapid exit from the fishing room. She had been cleaning the room and followed the odor to the closet. When she opened the closet door, a tidal wave of sharks—all thirty of them—collapsed on top of her, knocking her to the floor and sending her scrambling for her life. Perhaps she thought that she had been attacked by alien monsters.

A few minutes later, the hotel manager rushed into the room to inspect the damage. As he surveyed the carnage, he placed the palms of his hands on his balding head, apparently as a way of displaying his disgust. If he had had any hair, he probably would have pulled it out, one clump at a time.

"Don't you fellows have any sense of decency?" he said. "Don't you have any respect for private property?"

I looked at John Paul and whispered, "I think the answer's 'no' to both questions."

John Paul and I headed back to our rooms to try to get back to sleep. "Has everyone in America lost his sense of humor?" he mumbled.

When we checked out of the Edgewater later that day, the hotel had charged us a $250 cleaning fee to wash the carpets and remove the fish stains from the closet.

Our reaction to the Edgewater incident was a classic example of the band feeling its power and perhaps exhibiting some of the snobbery that can come with success and wealth. It's easy to start thinking that you can get away with things that the average person might not even consider doing, particularly since you usually can. The $250 damages charge really didn't mean anything to us. It was a small price to pay for a little fun.

As Bonzo once said, "We're in a place now where we don't have to take shit from *anyone*!" That meant coming down hard on people who seemed to run counter to our own best interests. On the '70 tour, that often translated into roughing up bootleggers when we caught them at work.

As the band's popularity mushroomed, so did the demand for bootleg tapes and vinyl of their live performances. The two albums in the record stores weren't enough. Many fans wanted a lot more of Led Zeppelin than we had given them.

During every concert on that North American tour, Peter and I were always looking for tape recorders in the crowd. "It's money out of our pocket," Peter complained. "Those bastards aren't gonna get away with it."

In the early minutes of our performance in Vancouver, Peter spotted a man crouched near the front of the stage, operating a sophisticated-looking recorder and holding a microphone overhead.

"Look at that bastard with the mike and the tape machine!" Peter growled. "He's right out in the open. What a fool!"

Some members of the crew and I stormed over, grabbed the fellow by the shirt collar, lifted him to his feet, and shouted, "You can't do that here, you asshole! If you want a recording, go to the record store and buy one like everybody else!"

The man was hoisted into the air and dropped in a heap onto the floor. We grabbed the recorder and smashed it against a security barricade, shattering it into a dozen pieces.

"Enjoy the rest of the show!" I bellowed as we turned and walked backstage.

Unfortunately for us, the man wasn't making bootleg tapes. He wasn't even an overzealous fan.

"There's a stagehand who just told me that the guy we beat up is a government official!" I told Peter. "He works for the city and measures the music's decibel level."

Before the show was over, Vancouver police showed up backstage, and questioned us for nearly an hour. Fortunately, the cops didn't seem eager to pursue a case that might draw a lot of headlines. We agreed to pay for the recorder, and the incident was forgotten.

As we left the Northwest, we made our way to Los Angeles by way of Denver. As much as we yearned to return to the Château Marmont in L.A., Peter insisted that we move down the street to the Continental Hyatt House on Sunset Boulevard. Since the murder of Sharon Tate and four of her friends by the Charlie Manson cult in 1969, Peter had become paranoid about security. The Marmont, with its isolated bungalows spread over the hotel grounds, seemed like too easy a target for someone with foul play on his mind. Peter felt that a self-contained, high-rise hotel would offer us greater protection.

On that first stay at the Hyatt House, Plant and Bonham had already renamed it the "Riot House"—for obvious reasons. Girls on a Zeppelin safari swarmed through the lobby and crowded into elevators that took them to the ninth floor where we hibernated. And with no fishing to distract us, we would have found it silly to resist their invitations. There were girls everywhere—in the lobby, in the hallways, and inevitably in our beds. Sometimes the band and I would round up a few girls and pile them into the back of our stretch limousine, weighing it down so much that the trunk would become stuck on the pavement of the Riot House driveway, requiring a push off the curb so the car could negotiate its way onto Sunset Boulevard. It was absolute madness there for almost a week.

One afternoon, a seventeen-year-old approached me in the hotel lobby. "We've heard about Jimmy's whips," she said. "Does he really use whips?"

"Do you like whips?" I asked.

"I love 'em!"

I had heard stories about Jimmy's affection for whips, too, but I had never seen them. He carried a small black box with him, and I presumed that might be where he stored them. Miss Pamela, who was one of Jimmy's girls in the U.S. during the early seventies, used to say that other girls claimed that Jimmy had used some whips from time to time, although they were never used on her.

I never found out whether Jimmy really had a weakness for whips. But there were other kinky paraphernalia that we used from time to time—most commonly handcuffs!

When we departed for a concert at the L.A. Forum, Bonham and I handcuffed two girls—a cute little brunette and her tall blonde friend—to the beds in our rooms. We wanted to make sure they'd be there when we returned. As Bonzo said, "We need something to slip into after a hard day's work! These girls look perfect for the job!"

As we snapped the handcuffs in place, you might have expected a hysterical reaction from the girls, struggling against their confinement, pleading to be released. But it never happened. They never complained about their temporary confinement.

"I've already called room service," I told the girls as we were leaving. "A valet will bring up dinner for you at eight o'clock. There are also a few joints sitting here if you want some. If there's anything else you need, let room service know. Have a nice evening!"

When we returned from the concert, the girls were in the room waiting for us. They had eaten their dinner and, except for some minor irritation around their wrists, had no ill effects from their experience.

"Can we party now?" one of them asked.

"Why not," Jimmy said, popping open a bottle of champagne.

The girls didn't leave for another twenty-four hours. No handcuffs were needed to keep them around.

21

FRIENDS

In the final days of the spring 1970 North American tour, all of us were exhausted. Too much traveling, too little sleep, too much alcohol, too many drugs.

More than anyone, Robert seemed on the brink of collapse at times. He had been plagued by a cold for days, and his voice had taken a beating. It had become so ragged and hoarse that he could barely speak, much less sing. Professional pride would get him onto the stage each night, where he would push his voice as far as it would go. "Something's got to give," he said in a gravelly voice in Salt Lake City, with frustration written all over his face. "My voice is really shot; I don't know how much longer I can last."

We had humidifers operating around the clock in Robert's hotel room to try to soothe and preserve his voice. But nothing seemed to help. Each night, he had to struggle a little more than the previous night to get through the show.

In mid-April, we were in Phoenix, staying at the Biltmore Hotel. "Maybe if I relax a little—get out of the hotel for a few hours—I'll feel better," he said. He asked me to schedule an afternoon of horseback riding.

Within an hour, he and a promotion man from Atlantic Records named Mario were out on a nearby trail with a couple of rented horses. Robert felt wonderful being out in the clean air. Ten minutes into the ride, however, it came to an abrupt end. Mario was thrown from his horse into a cactus. It took a doctor nearly half an hour to pull out all the thorns.

Later, Robert joked, "Actually, I did feel *much* better knowing it was Mario and not me who had to go through that ordeal."

A physician in Phoenix examined Robert and didn't like what he saw. He was worried about long-term damage and insisted that we cancel the final concert on the tour, planned for the next night at the Las Vegas Convention Center. But Robert was reluctant. "Let me try it," he said. "It's just one more gig. What a shame to let down the fans."

Like the rest of the band, Robert was troubled by the thought of disappointing an audience. In a voice that was barely audible, he said, "I'll try drinking a lot of hot tea tonight, and maybe my voice will be good enough for one last performance."

The next morning, however, Robert's voice was no better. Peter stepped in and took control of the situation. "That's it, Robert," he said. "There will be no show tonight. You've sung twenty-nine concerts in thirty-one days. The doctor says that if you sing without a long rest, you could ruin your voice permanently. You're not going to risk destroying your career for one concert. I've already made the decision. We're going home."

We flew directly from Phoenix to New York and then on to London. Following doctor's orders, Robert barely uttered a word on the trip home.

Back in England, Robert couldn't sit still. For a guy who often complained that the band didn't take enough time off, he was getting antsy just a week after returning home.

Robert told us he had been fighting with Maureen. Yes, life on the road was hectic, but at home, it was hell, at least for the moment. He thought maybe if he and Maureen got away—and took Jimmy with them on a working vacation—it could take the edge off their marital conflicts.

So barely more than a week after arriving back in England, Robert called Jimmy: "I'm ready to go back to work. Let's write some songs."

In the year and a half since Led Zeppelin had been created, Robert's talents seemed to have evolved more dramatically than the others. He not only sang with more confidence, but he began to believe in himself as a song-writer. No, he didn't picture himself yet on a par with Jimmy—but he was on his way. He certainly didn't feel intimidated or insecure, even though he was writing with one of the best.

Jimmy and Robert began to see what they could put together. Accompanied by Robert's family and Charlotte Martin, they drove to South Wales, staying in a mountain cottage called Bron-Yr-Aur, which means "Golden Breast" in Welsh ("Bring back a couple of those golden breasts for me," I told them).

Located near the River Dovey, Bron-Yr-Aur was a primitive setting—there was no electricity, so the lighting was provided by gaslight. Robert and Jimmy found some time for relaxation, including jeep rides through the hills. But they primarily were there to begin writing songs for Zeppelin's third album: "Out On the Tiles"... "Celebration Day"... "Bron-Y-Aur Stomp." They would take a portable tape recorder and sometimes a guitar with them on walks and would come back with both words and melody. On one of those hikes, they sat down in a small valley, Jimmy began picking out a tune, and Robert immediately improvised a verse. Fortunately, the tape recorder was running. The song quickly evolved into "That's the Way."

Robert took the lead in some of the songs for the album. His fascination with Celtic legends became the creative force behind "Immigrant Song." His dog, Strider, was the inspiration for "Bron-Y-Aur Stomp." The songs came quickly.

By mid-May, Led Zeppelin was ready to record. No one, however, was particularly interested in returning to the formality of a recording studio. "What other options do we have?" Bonzo asked.

"Let's rent a retreat somewhere and bring in a mobile studio," Jimmy suggested. No one argued with him.

Carol Browne, our secretary, made some calls and found a large country house called Headley Grange, located about forty miles from London, that we could rent. I helped the band get settled there, opening an account at the local market and bringing back the first batch of groceries and liquor. While the band was recording, I sometimes would take roadies Mick Hinton and Clive Coulson into town to a bar that would gladly serve us booze for hours.

The band's third album showed a more versatile Led Zeppelin—the same Zeppelin energy that had already brought Europe and America to their knees, but also a more romantic and softer sound at times. Jimmy played the banjo for the first time on "Gallows Pole," an old folk tune that Page and Plant arranged. The banjo belonged to John Paul. Jimmy saw it propped in a corner, picked it up, and started fooling around with it. "I love the sound," he told John Paul, and he kept returning to it at every break. Finally, he began looking for a song where he could use it. "Gallows Pole" fit the bill.

On "That's the Way," the first few renditions they recorded were electrical. "Something's not right," Jimmy kept saying. "It's just not there yet." He finally suggested that they try it with acoustic guitars. Bull's-eye. The song quickly came together.

"Tangerine" was a song dating back to Jimmy's Yardbirds' days. Robert accompanied his own singing with double-track lead vocals. Then Pagey contributed an incredible pedal steel guitar line. It was a song that jelled right from the beginning. On "Bron-Y-Aur Stomp," Jimmy did some of his best picking. At the same time, Bonzo was looking for a change of pace from his perch behind the drums and began turning whatever he could get his hands on into musical instruments, even making spoons part of the cut.

"Friends" was enhanced by the addition of strings. John Paul was broadening his own horizons in the studio, and he suggested that he write an arrangement for strings, which turned out to be magnificent. Maybe the prospect of being accompanied by violins inspired Robert; he hit high notes on that song that could have shattered glass, stretching the limits of his own voice a little more with each take. There was some debate on how to begin and end "Friends." Eventually, a bit of studio small talk was inserted at the start of the cut, and a Moog synthesizer was used at the very end.

Everyone felt that the third album was the way a record should be put together; it was a much more relaxed venture than the second, which had been written and recorded on the road with pressures that do not necessarily lend themselves to creativity. "This is the way we have to do it from now on," Pagey insisted one evening as we sat around the fireplace. "I feel energized with this kind of pace." He was worried that unless the band worked in a more leisurely environment, they were all going to burn out.

22

THE
WATER
BUG

Do you think these cars really float?"

I posed the question to John Bonham, reminding him of the Volkswagen commercials that claim VW bugs are airtight and fare almost as well in the water as Mark Spitz. I was sightseeing in Iceland with Bonham, John Paul, and roadie Jim Dobson, and as we drained the bottles of champagne we had brought with us, we concluded that, except for Ralph Nader himself, no one was better prepared to conduct a Volkswagen consumer test than us.

"Well, I'm willing to try it," said Bonham, always an enthusiastic recruit, particularly when he was a bit inebriated. "Let's find a lake or a river and get on with it!"

We were in Iceland in June 1970 at the request of the British government. Jasper Parrott, a British talent agent who was more accustomed to handling ballet dancers than rock stars, had been assigned the task of organizing a British cultural extravaganza in Iceland. He asked Led Zeppelin to represent pop music in the festival. Peter saw it as a valuable warm-up for the more important Bath Festival in England, scheduled just a week later. All of us also recognized the prestige of being chosen to represent our home country overseas.

The second day in Reykjavik was when we decided to act like tourists and rent some Land Rovers to see the sights. Hertz, however, wasn't cooperative.

"Sorry," the Hertz agent explained. "I don't think there's a single Land Rover in the country. What other cars would you like to rent?"

We settled for Volkswagens—one green, the other white. Dobson and I climbed into one of the bugs, and John Paul and Bonzo slid into the other.

While sightseeing, we kept ourselves warm by nipping on a couple bottles of Dom Perignon. Finally, after about three hours of staring at glaciers, geysers, hot springs, and volcanoes, boredom set in. That's when we decided to see if a Volkswagen really could float.

"I'll drive mine into the water," Bonham volunteered. "Let's find a lake somewhere and give it a try."

We came upon a river, and Dobson and I got out of our car to survey the scene.

"This could be a historic moment," I told Dobson. "Will it float or will it sink?"

We made sure the windows of Bonham's white car were rolled up tight. He remained in the driver's seat, with John Paul as his copilot. Bonham drove to the water's edge and stopped, looking out upon the water like Evel Knievel, concentrating on the death-defying feat to follow. He put the car in reverse and drove backward about fifty feet. The tension mounted. Finally, he shifted into first and gunned the engine, aiming for the water.

The VW left land—and hit the river with a thud. It bounced, it bobbed atop the water for a minute or two, and then it settled into a peaceful, rocking float as the engine stalled.

"The fuckin' thing's not sinking!" Dobson shouted. "I can't believe it!"

Dobson may have spoken a bit prematurely. The waterline reached above the door seals, and water began seeping into the car's interior. I suddenly got scared and felt this terrible chill running down my spine. I could envision a newspaper headline blaring, "Rock Musicians Drown While Tour Manager Looks On."

"Shit, we better get these guys out of there," I yelled at Dobson. The two of us frantically began to wade into the bitterly cold water. When we reached the car, the lake was still shallow enough for us to stand.

Dobson and I were on opposite sides of the car. Unbelievably, Bonham seemed to be enjoying himself; John Paul, on the other hand, was livid. For some reason, Jonesy had decided to wear a suit on our sightseeing expedition. I figured the poor fella was more concerned about his suit being ruined than anything else.

Dobson and I began pushing the VW to shore as quickly as we could. "Remind me never to drive one of these bugs off the Golden Gate Bridge," I gasped, trying to ignore the numbness that was overtaking my toes.

In about three minutes, we had maneuvered the car onto land. Bonzo turned the ignition key and the engine started immediately.

"It would have made a great TV commercial," I told Dobson as we drove back to our hotel. "We should have filmed it. 'From the band that brought you "Dazed and Confused" and "Whole Lotta Love" . . . now it's time to float along with Led Zeppelin!' "

Later that day, John Paul explained why he was so upset when the VW bug began to sink. "It had nothing to do with the suit," he told me. "Someone gave me some grass last night, and I had stuffed it into my socks. I didn't want it to get wet!"

The Volkswagen incident was thoroughly frivolous, even childish. But the band members were still attracted to those kinds of capers as a release from the pressures they felt—or simply as an escape from an otherwise boring situation. In Iceland, things fell into the latter category.

After a few days in Reykjavik, we were delighted when the festival ended and we could finally head home. Peter kept reminding us that the Bath Festival was right around the corner and that it would be another important turning point for the band. As usual, his plans for Zeppelin were very well thought out. "If things go well at Bath," he said, "we'll be as big at home as we are in the States. That's why this gig was worth making some sacrifices for."

What kind of sacrifices? Peter had turned down engagements in the U.S.—including a $200,000 offer to play two concerts at the Yale Bowl and in Boston—in order to perform in Bath on July 28 for just $60,000. It was an easier decision for him than you might think. Freddie Bannister, who organized the open-air concert, had promised Peter a crowd of 200,000 people. You don't get crowds much bigger than that, unless you happen to be the Pope.

Led Zeppelin wasn't the only big band on the bill. The Byrds, Jefferson Airplane, Dr. John, Country Joe and the Fish, Santana, the Flock, and Frank Zappa and the Mothers of Invention were also scheduled to perform. The Moody Blues were booked for the festival, too, but they were chased off the stage by an unexpected downpour at midday.

As much as Peter wanted Led Zeppelin to perform at Bath, he went into the negotiations with some inflexible demands. He cared about little else other than making the most of the event for his band. It was more important than money or anything else that might be promised. During the discussions with Bannister, Peter said, "Led Zeppelin *has* to close the festival on Sunday night. And I want us to take the stage at sunset. Precisely at eight o'clock. No later."

Bannister was puzzled. "Why eight o'clock?"

"That's the exact time that the sun sets," Peter explained. "If that's when Zeppelin comes onstage, we can have the lights turned on, creating an aura over the band as the sun disappears behind them." Peter certainly hadn't lost his flair for the dramatic.

Bannister agreed to Peter's starting time, and preparations began for the event. Jimmy insisted that the set feature songs from the upcoming album, not only to help promote the new record but to introduce the songs to British audiences for the first time. The band spent a couple of days locked away in rehearsals. On June 28, the day of the festival, they were ready.

The Flock preceded Led Zeppelin onstage that night. But as it neared eight o'clock, the Flock apparently had no intention of relinquishing the stage. They played one encore. Then another. As the minutes passed, Peter's impatience turned to rage.

"Get those fuckers off the stage," he howled at Bannister.

Freddie was desperately trying to keep everyone's feathers unruffled. He pleaded with Peter, "They're almost done. I'm sure they're almost done."

Peter finally couldn't control himself any longer. At ten minutes before eight, he said, "Take care of those bastards, will you, Cole?"

Tough guy was a role I still could play very well. I rounded up Henry Smith and another roadie, Sandy McGregor. Together, the three of us looked like a bunch of thugs intent on causing some serious bodily injuries. We had reputations as guys you didn't want to fuck with—and those were reputations well earned.

We marched onstage and methodically unplugged the Flock's equipment. "The party's over," I shouted at the startled band. Henry and I began moving the drums offstage, and the other equipment followed. The Flock was shouting at us to stop. So was Bannister from the wings of the stage. For about ten minutes, it was sheer pandemonium on the stage, but we accomplished our mission. Bekins couldn't have done it more efficiently.

Barely five minutes behind schedule, Zeppelin began its set, with Jimmy wearing a topcoat and a rather ridiculous yokel's hat. Robert, attired in a long-sleeve sweatshirt and jeans, had sprouted a beard that made him look more unkempt than usual. John Paul wore a leather jacket, as though he were fully prepared to join the Hell's Angels. Bonham wore a simple white T-shirt that he tore off before the night was done, even though the weather became cooler as the hours wore on. None of them seemed to have been disturbed by the commotion onstage a few moments earlier.

Zeppelin started the set with "Immigrant Song" and never looked back. It was one of the songs from *Led Zeppelin III*, scheduled to hit the record stores later in 1970. From that song to the end of the set, the crowd was incredibly responsive. As the band played song after song from the new album, the audience fluctuated between trying to listen intently to the lyrics of the new material to letting their own shouting and clapping compete with the music.

Zeppelin played "Since I've Been Loving You," then "Celebration Day," then more familiar songs from earlier albums—"Bring It On Home" and "Whole Lotta Love."

"We love Led Zeppelin," someone shouted at Robert between songs.

"We love you, too!" Robert exclaimed into the mike. "We're here to help you have fun tonight! Let us know if you are!"

Led Zeppelin seemed as though they could have played until sunrise. In the final few minutes, the band coaxed the crowd into a frenzy. The last encore consisted of "Communication Breakdown," followed by a free-form medley that included "Johnny B. Goode" and "Long Tall Sally." When they were finally finished, an MC/disc jockey named Mike Raven was swooning at the microphone, "Unbelievvvable . . . Led Zeppelin . . . You're fantassstic . . . Led Zeppelin . . . England adores you!"

England really did. When Zeppelin had finally left the stage, three hours and five encores after their set had begun, they were beside themselves. Robert was convinced they had hit a grand slam for the home folks. In fact, with nothing left to prove, Led Zeppelin would not perform in the U.K. again for nearly nine months.

23

BACKSLIDING

About a week after the Bath Festival, just as Led Zeppelin was finally catching its breath, we departed for a brief tour through Germany. In Frankfurt, the band performed before 11,000 fans at the Festhalle, the biggest crowd ever to watch a rock concert in Germany. In Cologne, about a thousand fans rioted outside the Sporthalle, throwing rocks and breaking windows when they couldn't get into the concert.

Still, as enthusiastic as the crowds were in Germany, Zeppelin was experiencing an emotional letdown after the Bath Festival. It was hard to top the 200,000 people who had seen them perform a few days earlier. The band did more than go through the motions, but there wasn't the exhilaration of the Bath performance, either.

"It's inevitable," Jimmy thought. "We can't get up for every show. We're human, too."

After the Frankfurt concert, we found a nearby bar, located a comfortable corner, and drank nonstop until the place closed its doors. During the course of the evening, our alcohol excesses became quite apparent to others in the bar. The six of us—John Paul, Jimmy, Robert, John, Peter, and I—could all tolerate liquor quite well, and before long the small table at which we were sitting was crammed with bottles and glasses. Only the bartender was keeping track of just how much we were drinking.

When I finally went to pay the bill, I was shocked. "Are you sure you added this up right?" I asked. "There were just six of us at the table."

"I know there were just six of you!" the bartender exclaimed. "But you guys almost cleaned me out. I've never seen anyone drink like you!"

During a four-hour period, we had ordered and consumed 120 slivovitzes plus about 160 beers—a total of 280 drinks among the six of us!

At one point, Bonzo exclaimed, "Let's keep running this fucking bartender ragged! By the time the bar closes, the poor bastard might be too tired to throw us out when they close!"

As immense as our alcohol consumption was, I wasn't about to lecture the band. First of all, I was just as caught up in alcohol abuse as they were. Also, I didn't yet think the alcohol was impairing the band's music or my ability to keep them moving from city to city on the road. "We're all fine," I told myself. "We're just lucky that we can hold our liquor so well."

That short German tour was a prelude to our return to the States in August for our sixth U.S. tour. Thirty-six concerts in seven weeks. Every performance was a sellout, and the band never took home less than $25,000 a night during the tour.

Most of the press was still hostile. "We're not immune to it," Bonzo said with resignation in his voice, "but their negative reviews don't hurt as much as they used to." Nearly everyone but the media, however, couldn't get enough of Led Zeppelin, even local dignitaries. Some city officials may have never heard of Led Zeppelin, but we were bringing the biggest act in rock music to their city, and they apparently felt the need to roll out the red carpet, particularly in smaller towns like Tulsa and Albuquerque that rock bands often overlooked.

Memphis was typical of the first-class treatment we got. We had played in Memphis the previous April, and the city fathers were happy to have us back. The afternoon before the concert, the mayor of Memphis presented the band with the key to the city at the Memphis City Hall.

"Memphis may be the home of Elvis," the mayor boasted, "but you boys are welcome here anytime, too."

Led Zeppelin was always well behaved during formal ceremonies like this. But none of us could ever figure out why we even bothered with them. Yes, we were flattered that we had joined the ranks of Elvis and Carl Perkins as recipients of the key to the city. And Peter told us, "I think there's some PR value to it"—but he didn't sound real convinced.

More than any of us, Jimmy thought it was a complete waste of time. As we left the mayor's office and headed back to the limos, he muttered, "These city dignitaries are probably the same guys who shout at us in airports to cut our hair. What bullshit!"

That night, the hot air soared to new levels. As with most other concerts in that tour, the band went out and worked the Memphis audience into delirium. But about midway through the performance, some fans in the crowd of 10,000 people were becoming unruly. Cups of beer were tossed into the air. Firecrackers were ignited. The sweet smell of marijuana drifted through the darkness. As the concert approached the two-hour point, the fellow who seemed to be in charge of the auditorium, a fellow we'll call Bill, was becoming increasingly agitated.

On occasion, we would encounter unpredictable and even rude treatment from the management of the halls where we played. But this particular evening, even I was surprised by what happened next. "Hey, fella," Bill shouted over to me. "This place is about to erupt into a full-fledged riot. Let's end this concert right now!"

I looked at Bill a bit bewildered, wondering whether he was joking. No one had ever asked us to cut a concert short. But apparently Bill was dead serious.

"You'll have to talk to that big guy over there," I told him, pointing to Peter.

We walked over to Peter, and Bill repeated his demand. "Your band needs to come off the stage after this song! The concert's over!"

Peter gave him a cool stare. "We don't do that," he said calmly.

"Well, you have no choice. This show's done! I'll cut the power if I have to!"

"Like hell you will!" Peter snarled. "Why in the hell are you selling alcohol in the first place, you asshole? That's what's causing all the problems!"

Bill turned to face Peter and put his right hand into his coat pocket. "I've got something that'll make you change your fucking mind, big fella."

It wasn't a bluff. Bill pulled out a .22 pistol and stuck it in Peter's ribs. "Do you believe me now?" he shouted.

At that moment, the whole scene seemed surreal. City officials were sitting in the front row, still enjoying the music of Memphis's honored guests. Yet Peter was on the verge of being blown away. It was like watching a bad B movie. But I was scared, and everyone around us was afraid to move.

Peter, however, didn't panic. "What the fuck is this?" he exclaimed. "Memphis gives us the key to your goddamn city, and now you're gonna shoot us? This is gonna be all over the national press tomorrow!"

Bill apparently had second thoughts. He backed off just as a couple of our security people grabbed and disarmed him and threw him against a wall. He slumped to the floor, with the wind knocked out of him. Zeppelin played for nearly another hour without incident.

Throughout that tour, I sensed a growing need for tighter security for the band. Zeppelin often felt claustrophobic in their hotel rooms and insisted upon going to bars and clubs, enjoying the attention and willing to put up with the occasional obnoxious fan who became too loud or intrusive. But I was becoming terribly anxious about the physical safety of the band. This, after all, was the U.S., where guns and violence were a way of life. And there were times when I was frightened and times when I probably overreacted.

After a performance at Madison Square Garden, our limos took us to Nobody's, a club on Bleecker Street. After a few beers, Bonham and I made a stop at the bathroom, where I noticed a bloke with a black leather jacket and three days' growth of beard. All that was missing was the Hell's Angels emblem and the motorcycle.

I made brief eye contact with him as I moved next to him at the sink and began to wash my hands. He was standing just a few feet to the right of me, staring at nothing in particular. He looked like an escapee from the Charlie Manson gang.

After a few seconds, he opened his jacket. Without saying a word, he quickly pulled a knife from an inside pocket. It had about a six-inch blade, clearly capable of inflicting some damage.

I didn't ask any questions. I cocked my right arm and with a closed, soapy fist lunged forward to sting him on the chin. He toppled backward, the knife flew into the air, he hit his head on the tile-covered wall, and sunk to the floor. He was out cold.

Bonham, who just then emerged from a bathroom stall, was not aware of what had happened or why.

"Holy shit! Is he a friend of yours, Richard?" asked Bonzo, with his eyes transfixed on the blood oozing out of the poor fellow's mouth and the knife resting about three feet away.

I didn't answer. We walked out of the bathroom and back to our table, leaving behind the unconscious troublemaker. We departed for our hotel a couple of minutes later without ever finding out the extent of my sparring partner's injuries.

Maybe I went overboard. Maybe not. But during that tour, I became hypersensitive to what was going on around us. Sometimes I may have made mistakes. But I felt I couldn't take chances.

That Madison Square Garden gig set a Zeppelin record—the first time the band had grossed more than $100,000 for a single concert. In fact, they did it two nights in a row.

On the flight back to London, I was sitting next to John Paul, sipping my fourth drink, wondering what kind of security arrangements we'd have to make for the next tour. John Paul was seated next to me. Zeppelin's Rock of

Gibraltar, he got the job done. On this tour more than the others, he tended to keep to himself. Maybe he was trying to back away from some of our lunacy. Perhaps he just enjoyed his own company more than ours. And although Jonesy indulged in his share of booze, he seemed more in control than the rest of us.

24

"STAIRWAY TO HEAVEN"

Two weeks after we had returned to London, *Led Zeppelin III* invaded the record stores. The American tour had whetted the public's appetite for Zeppelin, and the new album struck like a hurricane. Advance orders in the U.S. approached 750,000; in the United Kingdom, they exceeded 60,000. On its first day in the record racks, the album turned gold.

Meanwhile, *Led Zeppelin II* was still hovering on *Billboard*'s chart of the Top 100 albums. A 1970 readers' poll by *Melody Maker* ranked Led Zeppelin as the most popular rock music act, even overshadowing the Beatles. *Melody Maker* explained Led Zeppelin's success this way:

"Led Zeppelin's high places are phenomenal but not entirely unexpected. There is no doubt that Zeppelin deserves all their kudos. They have magic, ability, and the right attitude in their approach to the business of making music. . . . They combine the appeal of the traditional pop group format with the excitement, drive, and convincing validity of modern rock."

Not bad for a band that had become accustomed to being blindsided by hostile critics. When *Led Zeppelin III* was released, the band had hoped for a more positive response from the press, but Jimmy wasn't optimistic. "I haven't given up on the media," he said, "but I'm getting close."

As expected, one by one, the reviews were demoralizing. Lester Bangs, writing in *Rolling Stone*, was typical. He described having a "love-hate attitude" toward Zeppelin, "from genuine interest and mostly indefensible hopes, in part from the conviction that nobody *that* crass could be all that bad."

Bangs continued, "Most of the acoustic stuff sounds like standard Zep graded down decibelwise, and the heavy blitzes could've been outtakes from *Zeppelin II.* In fact, when I first heard the album my main impression was the consistent anonymity of most of the songs."

Perhaps even more biting was the Los Angeles *Times*'s comments that Zeppelin's popularity could be traced to heavy drug use among their fans: "Their success may be attributable at least in part to the accelerating popularity among the teenage rock 'n' roll audience of barbiturates and amphetamines, drugs that render their users most responsive to crushing volume and ferocious histrionics of the sort Zeppelin has heretofore dealt in exclusively."

Some days the reviews would sail right over the band's heads without leaving a scar. Other times, it would crush their spirits. "The critics are a bunch of fucking hacks," Robert complained one afternoon in Peter's office, showing disgust in his voice. "They're critics because they have no talent to *play* music."

In the immediate aftermath of the release of *Led Zeppelin III*, the band collectively decided to return to the studio. It was almost like a defense mechanism, a way of saying, "If the critics don't like this one, wait until they see what's next!"

Robert and Jimmy returned to Bron-Yr-Aur and began writing songs for the new LP. Away from newspapers and telephones, they were able to set aside the disappointing critical reception of *Led Zeppelin III* and get back to work. Nevertheless, Bron-Yr-Aur didn't prove to be quite the creative mecca it had been the last time around. Many of the songs for the new album were composed later right in the studio.

Part of the fourth album was recorded at Island Studio in London in December, but after Christmas Zeppelin moved to Headley Grange, again relying on a mobile recording studio. The house had a comfortable feel to it, one that allowed the band to relax and let their creative energy flow. Early on, Bonzo wandered through the house, inspecting it room by room. He finally complained, "The house seems more dilapidated than it was the last time we were here." Then I reminded him that during our last visit, we had sacrificed a banister to the gods when we needed firewood. "The owners of this place better pray for warm weather or we may reduce the house to sawdust by the end of the week," I said.

"Misty Mountain Hop" was written at the Grange. So was "The Battle of Evermore" and three others. And then there was "Stairway to Heaven." Robert improvised most of the lyrics for "Stairway" during the rehearsals as he sat in front of the roaring fireplace, looking for some way, he said, to describe spiritual perfection. Jimmy listened and was just blown away by what he heard. From the beginning, he felt that this song could be something special, that Robert had eclipsed everything that he had written before.

Late at night by himself, Pagey worked on molding "Stairway" into a cohesive unit, using the Telecaster and building guitar track upon guitar track until he had the powerful instrumental harmonies he wanted. He recorded three different guitar solos, none of them similar, and finally chose the one he thought was best after agonizing over them in the studio late one night.

The tune ultimately became one of the most popular Zeppelin cuts, even though romantic ballads were such a dramatic change of pace from the typical Zeppelin repertoire. Nevertheless, the song combined other elements identified with the band, from jazzier moments to a much heavier sound as the song built toward its conclusion. "If any song from this band has timeless qualities, I think it's 'Stairway to Heaven,' " Jimmy said, beaming like a proud father as he listened to the playbacks in the studio. He was right. The song would eventually become the most requested song on radio stations on both sides of the Atlantic.

Jimmy was so thoroughly impressed with Robert's lyrics on "Stairway" that he decided to take a hiatus from lyric writing himself. "It's not that hard a decision," he thought. "Robert has grown so much as a songwriter."

Pagey told Robert that the band had a new consummate writer of lyrics. "I'll defer to your talents for now."

As Jimmy spent more time in the studio, he became obsessive about each song on the new album and how it might be improved. He'd listen to individual moments in individual songs and then the entire product as a whole. While piecing together the folk-oriented "The Battle of Evermore," he and Robert debated how to give it a more distinctive sound. Robert felt that another voice was needed to give a richness to it. Finally, he suggested inviting Sandy Denny to sing on it with him. Denny, the soprano voice with Fairport Convention, figured Robert was kidding when she received the SOS from Plant. Zeppelin, after all, had a reputation for being a "closed shop," with other musicians rarely invited to participate in either recording sessions or live performances. But Robert convinced her that this was for real. Sandy sang counterpoint to Robert, like a town crier representing the voice of the people, supported by a rich blend of acoustic guitars and a mandolin.

The recording of the fourth album was completed in February 1971. As it was being prepared for release, there was some talk of calling it *Led Zeppelin IV*. But Jimmy was against it. He was still pissed at the critics, and perhaps as a way of retaliating against or confusing them, he didn't want the album to have a title at all. He didn't even want Led Zeppelin's name or the album's catalog number anywhere on it.

"The music is what matters," Jimmy argued. "Let people buy it because they like the music. I don't want *any* writing on the cover! Period!"

Executives at Atlantic Records were outraged at Jimmy's demand. "An album without a title!" they exclaimed. "An album without the artists' name on it! You guys are signing your own death warrant!"

Still, the band wouldn't capitulate. As a last-ditch effort, Atlantic tried to convince them to at least put "Led Zeppelin" on the spine of the album. Zeppelin refused.

The relationship between Atlantic and Zeppelin was already strained even before the debate over the album title. Peter was so upset with the record company that he was no longer on speaking terms with some of its executives. Most of the problems related to the company's continued pleas that the group begin releasing singles from its albums. Peter, however, had consistently and adamantly refused. When Atlantic had suggested "Whole Lotta Love" as a perfect choice for release as a single, Peter just scoffed at the idea. The same happened with "Immigrant Song." The list grew longer.

One of the Atlantic vice presidents called our office one day and tried to reason with me, presumably on the assumption that I could influence Peter. "These songs are already being played by radio stations as though they're singles," he argued. "Why not make it easier on them and the fans and just release them as singles?"

Peter had his own reasoning. "If we don't release a single, people will have to buy the album if they want one of the songs. Songs like 'Whole Lotta Love' are too long for singles anyway. And hell if we're going to cut it down to two and a half minutes just to make radio station program directors happy."

At the time, Peter might as well have been speaking in a foreign tongue. Atlantic's brass constantly pointed out that not only do singles get more airplay, but they are another avenue for record sales. But Peter wasn't convinced.

Nevertheless, Atlantic had made its own plans. It made an unprecedented, unilateral decision to release a single version of "Whole Lotta Love" in the States. In barely more than a month, the single had sold more than a million copies. But to Led Zeppelin, the sales figures didn't matter.

"They stabbed us in the back!" growled Peter. "We told them not to do something, and we fucking did it anyway." If the band didn't have a signed contract with the label, they might have jumped ship in 1970.

According to Phil Carson, who had just begun running Atlantic's London office, he bore the brunt of Led Zeppelin's target practice. Phil said he had a near violent confrontation with Peter, who could barely control himself one afternoon, pounding on tables and desks and letting out his anger. Phil, who had once played bass with the Springfields (Dusty Springfield's band), must have wondered at that moment why he had ever wanted to become a record company executive and have to deal with the unpredictable temperaments of musicians and their managers.

At one point, as Peter fumed and Phil backed toward a window, Phil might have become convinced that his days were numbered. After all, Phil knew about Peter's career in professional wrestling, when he used to heave opponents through the ropes and out of the ring. Phil could probably imagine himself being launched out the window, nosediving toward the ground like a disabled missile. At that moment, he might have chosen to take his chances riding over Niagara Falls in a barrel.

Phil convinced Peter that he would use his influence to ensure that no more singles would be released. And, in fact, Phil succeeded in those efforts in the U.K.

Those crises strengthened Zeppelin's resolve. In the battle over the titleless fourth album, the band wasn't going to yield. "Take it or leave it!" Jimmy told Atlantic. He was angry enough to hold up release of the entire album over the dispute.

Meanwhile, the fourth album began running into a series of delays, which ultimately postponed its release until October 1971. At one point, Jimmy had flown to Los Angeles to mix the tracks at Sunset Sound in Los Angeles. But no one, including Pagey, was happy with the way it turned out. Everything sounded fine in L.A., but when he replayed the tapes in London, the sound quality just wasn't there.

"Somehow, I got an untrue sound in L.A.," Jimmy complained. "You travel five thousand miles because the equipment is supposed to be so great there, and I could have gotten a better sound by driving ten minutes to a studio here in London. It's ridiculous." If the hassles with Atlantic weren't enough, the sound problems only made the stress levels worse.

Ultimately, Atlantic agreed to meet the band's demands. The album would be released without a title and with no words on the cover. On the front, there would be a photograph of an old hermit bracing himself with a cane, carrying a bundle of wood on his back.

For months and probably years, fans and critics alike argued over what the photograph may have symbolized; to Jimmy, who was getting deeper into metaphysical readings, the hermit represented wisdom, self-reliance, and harmony with nature.

Jimmy was accumulating a large collection of books about the occult and the supernatural. He never talked about it much with the band, and he never tried to get any of us to become believers in a particular metaphysical concept. So even though it all seemed a little weird to us, none of us ever interfered with whatever wavelength Jimmy might be on at the moment.

For the new album, however, Jimmy suggested that each member of the group choose a metaphysical symbol to put on the jacket. Most came from a book of runes that Jimmy showed them one afternoon. Robert selected a feather in a circle, the sign of peace. Bonzo settled upon a three-ring design, a sign of unity. (Later, the band would joke that Bonzo's sign bore a striking resemblance to the emblem for Ballantine beer.) John Paul's symbol—three ovals that converge within a circle—represented competence and self-confidence. Jimmy designed his own symbol, which seemed to spell the word "zoso." He denied that it was a word at all and never told any of us what, if anything, it said or meant.

Fans began calling the album by a number of names—*Four Symbols* and *Zoso* were the most popular. But as far as the band was concerned, it was nameless.

Until the new album was finally shipped to record stores, the band remained apprehensive. Would Atlantic renege on its agreement to release the album in an anonymous jacket? "I don't trust some of those bastards," Bonham said. "We're the artists. They should be listening to us instead of their market researchers."

25

NOSE JOB

It's not worth going to jail for, Bonzo. Let's get out of here."

I had my right hand on John Bonham's shoulder, trying to push him out of the kitchen of a hotel restaurant in Dublin. His hands were pressed against my chest, attempting to throw me off balance and make a lunge toward the hotel chef, who was already fully armed for combat, waving a carving knife over his head, poised like a fencer ready for battle.

"Hey, you asshole," Bonham said. "All I wanted was a goddamned meal. What kind of crap are you trying to pull?"

After a concert at Boxing Stadium in Dublin, we had returned to the hotel, and Bonham had strolled into the kitchen shortly after midnight, about thirty minutes after the restaurant had closed. He was intent on getting a meal and wasn't willing to take "no" for an answer. Bonzo could be the most headstrong, the most defiant member of the band, even though there was also a gentle, loving side to him.

It was March 1971, and Led Zeppelin was on the road. After more than a five-month hiatus from live performing, Peter had talked the band into getting back onstage, although there were mixed feelings about doing so. They certainly no longer needed the money that concerts could bring. And there was no burning enthusiasm to rekindle the excitement that inevitably comes with live performing. The band had performed live nearly 250 times in their first two years of existence, and there was a feeling that "we've done it."

But like a broken record, Peter had set his sights back on America. He hoped the band would spend at least a month there in the summer, and he didn't want them to be rusty when that tour began. Although Peter didn't control the band with an iron fist, they still trusted him implicitly and generally went along with any career move he felt strongly about. So as spring approached, Peter convinced Zeppelin to sign on for a series of concerts in Ireland and the U.K., with the possibility of a few gigs in Europe as well. "It will keep you sharp," he said. "And it won't be too taxing."

In a sense, the two concerts scheduled for Ireland were unique. Most British bands had routinely avoided Ireland since the late 1960s, when violence between Protestants and Catholics created chaos in the streets. Still, Led Zeppelin agreed to take its show on the road there, even though we were warned that kidnappings, bombings, and other terrorist acts had become almost everyday occurrences in parts of Ireland and Northern Ireland.

Jimmy, however, wasn't particularly concerned. "I don't see why Led Zeppelin would be a target," he said. "If anything, maybe we can take people's minds off the insanity that's going on around them."

Just hours before our concert in Belfast, there was a confrontation between police and demonstrators about a mile from Ulster Hall, where the band would be performing. One person died. Two policemen were hospitalized. Four cars were firebombed. As word of the violence reached us, my own anxiety level soared. The most stressful part of my job continued to be ensuring the band's safety, and the trip to Ireland seemed like walking into the lion's den. I voiced my concern to Peter, although he didn't feel any additional security was necessary. But I was a little more jittery than usual, although I didn't discuss it with the band, feeling there was no need to spread the nervousness around.

After the performance that night, a limousine was waiting for us to make a quick exit and a drive to Dublin for a performance the next night. I needed something to calm my nerves and figured no one else would complain if there was enough to go around. So earlier that day, I had stopped in a liquor store and had a bottle of Jameson's Irish whiskey waiting in the limo for each of the band members.

"It's amazing how much faster the drive goes with this stuff," Robert said. "Richard, you should buy it by the case."

I had. The trunk was filled with whiskey, ready to replenish our supplies.

We drove through some tough neighborhoods on the drive to Dublin. Tanks were parked on the sides of roads. Soldiers walked the sidewalks, ominously carrying rifles on their shoulders. Windows had been boarded up, nursing wounds from rocks thrown by rioters. A few buildings had been completely gutted by firebombs. It was a sobering sight.

By the time we finally reached Dublin, all of us had polished off a couple of bottles of Jameson's. And after the concert there, a few glasses of Irish whiskey didn't help Bonzo's self-control when he went looking for food in the hotel.

Our chauffeur had accompanied Bonham into the kitchen, and as the confrontation there escalated, he placed a frantic call to my room. "You better get the hell down here before John kills somebody or vice versa."

I raced down the stairs, and as I stormed through the kitchen doors, Bonham and the chef were facing one another on opposite sides of a table.

"I told you that we're closed, you jerk!" the chef shouted. "We can't serve food after eleven-thirty!"

"I'm not asking for a five-course meal," Bonham screamed back. "I'll settle for a fucking sandwich. I'll even make it myself if you're too damn lazy to do it!"

The chef waved his carving knife menacingly. It was big enough to engrave initials on a brontosaurus. "After I get through with you," the chef said, "you're gonna look like you went through a bread slicer!"

Bonham didn't like being threatened. He began walking around the table, moving toward his adversary. I couldn't believe what was happening. When Peter had placed Ireland on our itinerary, I had been concerned about being caught up in the country's civil war; I had never expected that the real threat would come from a chef in a hotel kitchen!

I quickly stepped in front of Bonzo and shoved him backward. He resisted and tried to push me aside. That's when I swung at him with my right fist, aiming right at his nose.

Bull's-eye! Bonham staggered back a few steps, tripped on a chair, and dropped to one knee. His nose was gushing with blood—so much blood that if this were a prizefight, it would have been stopped on a TKO.

"Fuck!" Bonzo screamed, gingerly rubbing at his nose with the back of his right hand. "Cole, who's fuckin' side are you on?"

"When you sober up, you'll thank me for that," I said, realizing there wasn't a snowball's chance in hell that he ever would. I grabbed him by the shirt and led him out of the kitchen. "That guy was ready to turn you into ground round!"

Maybe I had saved Bonham a few stitches and a scar or two, but we still had to find an emergency room. My right hand wasn't as vicious as Joe Frazier's, but I had broken Bonham's nose.

As we waited to see a doctor, Bonham said, "How can I ever thank you?" The statement oozed with sarcasm. Then the anger in his voice escalated. "Maybe I'll tell Peter to throw you out on your ass! If I had my way, Peter would fire you!"

■ ■ ■

The next day, Peter was in no mood to do much of anything. After Bonham and I had returned from the hospital, I had gone to Peter's room to explain what had happened. There were several bottles of champagne in his room—neither of us counted how many—and we finished them off in a three-hour drinking binge. Later that day, we downed thirty Irish coffees, which didn't do much for our condition.

That was the last time we used coffee to treat a hangover!

SMALL TIME

Back in England, Zeppelin was performing again, this time on a Return to the Clubs tour—an idea conceived by Peter. Amid the band's enormous success, Peter never let himself forget the band's early days when they struggled to get attention at home. In the cramped clubs in which they played in those days, they had a small but loyal following. And Peter still felt he owed them a debt.

"This new tour is a way of saying 'thank you' to those fans who have been with us since sixty-eight and sixty-nine," Peter had said when he suggested the idea. So during the remainder of March, we played in a dozen clubs, including the Marquee in London, the Mayfair Ballroom in Newcastle, the Boat Club in Nottingham, and Stepmother's in Birmingham. With audiences averaging 300 to 400 people, these dates were the ultimate contrast to the Bath Festival.

The clubs tour, however, was much better as a concept than as reality. None of us particularly enjoyed it. The clubs were small, and the demand to see Zeppelin was, of course, much larger than it had been in the early years. This was now the biggest band in the world, and literally thousands of people were turned away at the doors. Disappointed fans sometimes took out their frustrations and anger on whatever they could take a swing at—whether it was the clubs' bouncers or nearby street lamps. On a couple of occasions, the police were called to prevent a full-fledged riot from erupting.

After the scares in Ireland, I had insisted on taking two bodyguards with us on the British tour, and Peter agreed. Two brawny protectors, Patsy Collins and Jim Callaghan, gave me some peace of mind for most of those U.K. performances. Nevertheless, the Return to the Clubs tour was not incident-free. As Zeppelin performed at the Nottingham Boat Club, a fellow in his mid-twenties with a satanic face approached the stage, hovering for a minute or two as the band played "Whole Lotta Love." He had a knife tucked in his belt, and although it was still in its case, I decided not to wait to see what might happen next. I rushed toward the front of the stage and slammed my body into the bastard, wrestling him to the ground. Then with the help of Patsy, we dragged him backstage, where I confiscated the knife and then roughed him up enough to bruise his face and tear his shirt.

"What the fuck is that knife for?" I shouted as I stood over him, poised for another punch.

"My girlfriend loves Robert Plant," he mumbled. "Whenever she swoons over him, it drives me crazy. Sometimes I feel like killing both of them."

"Funny," I said. "I feel like killing *you!*"

With an open palm, I slapped him across the face and watched another welt rise on his cheek. "If you want to live to see tomorrow, you better not come within fifty feet of the stage the rest of the night." I shoved him back into the crowd.

When we played the Mayfair, just before the band went onstage Jimmy was bitching about the entire tour. "Once you've played in the big places, these small clubs are murder. It's nice to be near the audience, but you forget how small the dressing rooms are. At this point in our careers, I think we're entitled to more luxury than this. This is really hard to believe."

With the larger venues, Zeppelin had gotten spoiled very quickly. They had become used to big dressing rooms and catered food. They expected excellent sound systems, not makeshift speakers and overloaded fuse boxes that hemorrhaged and died in the middle of a set. So even though Zeppelin was eager to expose their fans to songs from their forthcoming album—songs like "Stairway to Heaven," "Rock and Roll," and "Black Dog"—I could see them cringe every time the sound system would screech, scratch, and squeal.

There wasn't much of a financial payoff, either. The band took a percentage of the door, but when you're only squeezing three hundred and fifty people into a club, the band's share covered gas money and maybe a few bottles of whiskey. "It's no Madison Square Garden," Peter said, showing a knack for understatement.

Peter still felt that the entire exercise was worth it, at least in terms of public relations. Even so, he never suggested repeating the Return to the Clubs tour. Neither did anyone else.

■ ■ ■

For me, the most memorable moment of that tour occurred offstage at a new hotel in Manchester. Zeppelin had performed at the Preston Guild Hall, but since we couldn't get hotel rooms in Preston, we drove to Manchester, planning to catch the train back to London the next day. The hotel was a couple of galaxies removed from a five-star inn, but it was the only decent place that Tony Smith, our promoter, could get us on short notice.

"You'll like it," Tony joked. "They give the rats their own rooms, so they don't bother the guests much, except during mealtime."

For some reason, at the concert in Preston, Patsy Collins and Jim Callaghan thought it would make a great practical joke to tear my jeans off. So backstage, they jumped me and went to work. As the band performed "You Shook Me" just a few feet away, my jeans were confiscated and shredded. Having an odd sense of humor myself, I could appreciate the prank, although the drive to Manchester in my undershorts became a little uncomfortable. To my recollection, freezing one's ass off was not part of the original job description for Zeppelin's tour manager.

When we checked into the hotel, I snuck up a side entrance so as not to create too much commotion in the lobby. Once I was in my room, I was delighted to find a set of waiter's clothes in the closet—much too close to my own size to leave them on the hanger. That night, when we headed to a club called Mr. Smith's in Manchester, I dressed myself in the waiter's attire. Bonham thought the outfit might get a few laughs; I figured it would be much less funny than wearing only my undershorts.

Mr. Smith's was actually a high-class club—sit-down service and wall-to-wall girls. The service, however, was dismal, and Zeppelin wasn't a band that liked to wait more than a few ticks of the clock until the first round of drinks flowed. We had ordered wine, but were still awaiting its arrival ten minutes later.

"Cole, get to work!" Bonzo finally said.

"What do you mean?"

"You've got the waiter's suit! Get us some booze!"

What the hell, I thought. I smoothed out my lapels and headed for the bar. I tried acting as though I belonged there—walking behind the bar and helping myself to some bottles of Muscadet, then French Burgundy.

There were so many people crammed into Mr. Smith's and the other waiters became so confused and puzzled by my presence that no one raised an eyebrow. To them, I must have been just the new waiter on the block.

"Oh, waiter!" Bonzo shouted in an affected, high-pitched voice. "How about some schnapps? As many as you can carry over—in about ten trips!" He laughed hysterically.

For nearly two hours, I replenished the glasses of the heavy drinkers at Zeppelin's table. At every opportunity, I'd also sneak a few drinks for myself. Naturally, the booze was on the house that night.

Before returning to the hotel, we convinced a few girls to come back with us. We were all so drunk that we had trouble finding our own rooms and ended up in Tony Smith's room, where we continued drinking from the bottles that I had smuggled out of the club. Jimmy took one of the girls into the bathroom, and we heard the bathtub water running.

"Jimmy's getting kinky again," Plant said.

A few moments later, I began smelling smoke coming from the bathroom.

"What the hell's going on," I said, peeking in and noticing that Jimmy had somehow started a fire in the middle of the sink with newspapers and towels. I shouted for some help from the other room.

Robert frantically ran into the hallway and broke the glass on the fire extinguisher case, which activated the fire alarm. He sprayed, smothered, and successfully doused the flames just as the night manager burst through the door.

"Holy shit!" he exclaimed. "What are you bastards doing?"

Robert thought a lot faster than the rest of us. "It's a religious rite," he said calmly. "My friend here is a very devout man, very spiritual. He was reciting a prayer using the ancient rituals of his ancestors. It was a moving ceremony."

Jimmy looked a little embarrassed. "Yeah. I'm sorry if I caused a disturbance. It's over now!"

The manager was furious. He didn't appear to have bought Robert's explanation. Although Zeppelin expected to get away with antics like this—and usually did—it appeared as though we might have problems this time.

"I think we ought to get out of here as quickly as possible," I whispered to Jimmy. While the night manager was in the bathroom calculating the damage, we grabbed our belongings and the girls and snuck down the stairway to the limousines. We headed directly for London, bypassing the train station on the way.

Incidentally, we never did find out what Jimmy's bathroom conflagration was all about. Of course, there was his growing preoccupation with the occult. Perhaps the fire was somehow related to that. When I asked him about it, all he said was, "I liked Percy's explanation best. Let's just say that it was an ancient rite that went up in flames."

"DICK SHOTS"

There was something lascivious about the very name Copenhagen. Maybe it was the memories of the sex clubs that brought me to attention whenever Peter even mentioned the possibility of returning to Denmark. Or perhaps it was the brothels, the bars, and the other after-dark activities.

In June and July 1971, Zeppelin had returned to playing larger venues, a refreshing rebound from the confined quarters of the Return to the Clubs tour. "It was like being in a fucking straitjacket," Robert said about those tiny clubs. So when Peter scheduled a European tour through Denmark, Sweden, Germany, Austria, and Italy, it was back to Zeppelin-sized concert halls.

Throughout Europe, audiences responded almost deliriously to "Stairway to Heaven." When the band performed at KB-Hallen in Copenhagen, the fourth Zeppelin album was still months away from its release. But judging by the audience frenzy that night as Robert guided the crowd through "Stairway" 's compelling journey, you might have thought that the song had been at the top of the charts for weeks. Word of mouth had obviously created a lot of enthusiasm about the tune. And when Plant introduced it as "something of an epic" and Jimmy gave it a distinguished touch on his red Gibson SG double-neck guitar, the performance of this single song clearly turned into an event.

"I bet there are a hundred tape recorders out there tonight trying to get 'Stairway to Heaven' on tape," Peter said backstage. "The bootleggers are going to make a killing on this one."

At the end of the show, Jimmy just shook his head. "We've got a real monster on our hands," he said, intoxicated by the audience response to "Stairway to Heaven." "It's one of those songs that is developing a life of its own," he said. Pagey knew that every musician waits for a song like this. Zeppelin had finally created one.

After the concert, Robert, Bonzo, Peter, and I were in a barhopping mood. We moved from one club to the next, having decided to prolong the night for as long as our adrenaline would keep flowing.

As we walked into one rather noisy bar, Robert said, "Let's see what we can corral here tonight." Within ten minutes, we had met a cute blonde with a lean, angular body and full lips that kept my imagination running wild. She didn't recognize the band members right away, but as soon as we introduced ourselves, she became much more friendly. Within minutes, Robert was saying, "We gotta find a place with a little more privacy." Every secluded corner was occupied, so I finally took the girl by the hand and led the three of us into the men's room.

"We'll be right out," I told Robert as I took the young lady inside one of the stalls, closing the door behind us. I lowered my pants and sat down on the toilet-seat cover. Without saying a word, the girl dropped to her knees in front of me and began giving me a blow job. It was one of the perks of being a tour manager.

I could hear Robert pacing the floor outside the stall. "Let's hurry it up, Cole," he said in a loud voice that echoed off the bathroom walls. But I was in no rush. "Patience is a virtue," I yelled out in a noticeably excited voice.

Robert continued to pace. "Relax, Percy," I hollered. "Her mouth isn't going to wear out."

Just then, Robert's patience ran out. Like a black belt in karate, he lifted and cocked his right leg and then smashed his foot into the stall door. The force of the blow ruptured the latch, swinging it inward with such a force that the blonde was shoved forward into me, propelling me backward and upward, cracking the porcelain on the toilet. In an instant, a shattered sliver of porcelain slashed against my ass, creating a three-inch-long gash that immediately began gushing blood.

"You fucking asshole!" I screamed at Robert while grabbing my butt, quickly trying to evaluate how much of it was still left. "Couldn't you have waited another minute?"

I suppose I should have counted my blessings, grateful that as the door burst open, the girl didn't bite down, leaving me with a much more serious injury than a bleeding ass.

"That'll teach you," Robert roared, chuckling as he surveyed the bizarre scene of his tour manager dabbing the gash on his ass with toilet paper and the startled blonde crawling on her hands and knees toward the bathroom exit. "From now on, let *me* go first," Robert said.

I was pissed. Not only did the girl never get the opportunity to complete her mission, but I knew I'd have to sit down very gingerly for at least a few days.

"Why don't you come back to the hotel with us?" Robert tried to convince the girl. But she seemed traumatized by what had happened. "No thanks," she said, checking to see if any of her teeth were loose. "I better get home. My friend is waiting for me in the bar. Yeah, we definitely better go home."

Robert glared at me, as though I had ruined his entire evening. Then he broke into laughter. "You look like a damn fool, dabbing your fucking ass like that." I felt like knocking him for a loop.

Back at the Palace Hotel, Robert and I paused in the lobby to continue our argument. Since the earliest days of Zeppelin, the two of us had never become particularly close. There was some ill will early on that probably got blown out of proportion, and although we certainly acted civil toward one another most of the time, an incident like this one brought all the animosity to the surface.

"I wish she had bit it off!" he shouted, turning a few heads in the lobby. We began shoving one another, then throwing elbows and spicing up our language with expletives. As hotel security arrived to separate us, the desk clerk called the police.

"They're just my sons," Peter explained to the local cops who showed up a couple of minutes later. "I can take care of them."

Peter was more amused than anyone by the whole episode. But as we headed for the elevator, he pretended as though he was going to read us the riot act. "I'll let you boys have it when we get upstairs," he said, fighting to keep a straight face, putting on a good act for the hotel management.

"Just don't whip me on my butt," I pleaded.

Frankly, I was ready to go home. But near the end of that European tour, we encountered one more traumatic incident—this one threatening to the band's life and limb. Although we hadn't run into any security difficulties throughout most of the tour, my concern over the potential for problems kept me awake nights. When we played in Milan, that concert turned into a living nightmare.

Zeppelin was booked into the Vigorelli Cycling Stadium in a government-sponsored festival on a bill with eighteen other acts. By this point in their career, Zeppelin was usually demanding—and receiving—its fee up front, including airline tickets. It was a precaution against the quicksand that can unexpectedly engulf even the most carefully planned concerts—concerts like the one in Milan. Later, Peter would say, "The Milan festival is the classic case of why you don't even bother to unpack the instruments until the check has been cashed and deposited."

Almost 15,000 people had crammed into the Italian stadium, and from my vantage point by the side of the stage, the crowd seemed well behaved for most of the afternoon. But about thirty minutes before Zeppelin began its set, a series of explosions erupted in the rear of the audience, leaving clouds of smoke hovering over the back of the stadium.

I figured the police would bring the crowd under control, but the situation seemed to be getting more, not less, chaotic as the minutes passed. "I'm going to strangle those fuckers," I told roadie Mick Hinton as I waded into the crowd. In a less than rational moment, I figured I would take care of the hoodlums myself.

But as I pushed my way toward the site of the confusion, I could barely believe my eyes. The real anarchists were the police, not the fans! In a bizarre attempt at crowd control, the riot squad was flexing its authority by wildly swinging batons and tossing tear-gas canisters into the crowd. Choking, coughing, panicky kids fled in all directions—including toward the stage. Pandemonium was beginning to break out.

Ironically, when we had arrived at the stadium, I had been impressed by the sight of dozens of police and even uniformed soldiers patrolling the gates and the grounds, gripping riot shields and seemingly prepared to keep the lid on any unruliness. "If all concerts were as well secured as this one, I'd feel a lot more comfortable," I told Peter. At the time, I didn't realize just how deeply I was putting my foot in my mouth.

As the situation deteriorated, Zeppelin decided to take the stage anyway, beginning its set with "Immigrant Song" and blasting into one tune after another from the fourth album. However, perhaps for the first time in their career, the band's music was being overshadowed by what was occurring in the crowd. I had returned to the side of the stage, and as Zeppelin continued to play, fans were literally throwing themselves onto the stage in a desperate attempt to escape the tear gas and avoid being trampled by the frantic, charging crowd behind them.

"Please!" Robert pleaded into the microphone between songs. "Don't panic! We will keep playing if you calm down!"

Peter, who was usually more prone to take these things in stride, was clearly worried. "Those fucking cops are inciting a riot," he exclaimed. "This is completely ridiculous."

At one point, a despondent Robert turned to Jimmy and yelled, "How the hell do you say 'calm down' in Italian? Shit, this is terrible."

The backstage area was suddenly jammed with people. Refuge-seeking fans were rubbing their eyes, brushing away tears, nursing their bruises, and—in a few cases—plundering whatever they could stuff into their pockets or carry out on their backs. It had become sheer anarchy.

About thirty minutes into the set, Peter and I had seen enough. Fans were running across the stage in their flight for safety. Others were seated on the stage, watching the chaos escalate throughout the stadium.

Even the bodyguards provided by the promoters to protect the band had been frightened into running for cover, leaving their positions unoccupied in front of the stage. By this point, I was absolutely terrified, literally fearing for our lives. I knew we had to get out, but had no idea where to flee.

Finally, while Zeppelin was performing "Communication Breakdown," a beer bottle sailed toward the stage and struck Mick Hinton on the forehead. He was dazed, knocked nearly unconscious, and a gash on his skin began dripping blood. At almost the same moment, a tear-gas canister exploded about twenty-five feet in front of the stage. "This place is a fucking war zone," I yelled. That's when Peter ordered Zeppelin off the stage.

"Let's get the boys out of here," Peter shouted at me as he ran toward the band. We grabbed Robert and John Paul, literally by their shirts, leading them through the tear gas that had drifted toward the stage. Bonham and Jimmy sprinted after us. By this point, the gas was so thick that it was like groping our way through an attack of London fog, with the added problem of stinging eyes. We could hear more tear-gas canisters bursting as we headed into a tunnel filled with smoke. I was becoming increasingly frantic as we searched for some kind of escape.

With the help of Gus, one of our limousine drivers, we finally found our way into a first-aid room, and I locked the door once we were inside. Jimmy was coughing, trying to catch his breath. All of us were rubbing our eyes. But at least we were safe for the moment.

We stayed in that room for an hour until the pandemonium outside had quieted down. There was occasional banging on the door, perhaps by fans desperately searching for a safe refuge. "If anyone opens that door, I'll personally wring his neck!" Peter shouted. "We'd have ten thousand people trying to squeeze in here!"

The roadies had rescued Jimmy's and John Paul's guitars and had found a secure place for them in another room backstage. But Bonham's drums had been left behind. As he paced the floor backstage, Bonzo realized that his drums were probably being pulverized in the free-for-all outside.

Led Zeppelin never returned to the stage. In fact, there wasn't much of a stage left after the rioters dismantled it. Ten well-armed policemen finally escorted us out of the stadium, an hour after we had taken shelter backstage.

On the flight home, the band became increasingly somber. "You don't expect this kind of shit at a rock concert," a downcast John Paul said. "Those fans came to listen to music, not to have their heads bashed in and their bodies trampled. Whose side are the cops on anyway?"

Robert was running his fingers through his hair and was almost in tears. "I tried to calm them down. But those fucking cops were out of control. What a nightmare. What a fucking nightmare!"

Led Zeppelin never again played in Italy. We had seen enough of Italy to last us several lifetimes.

It took us a while to recover from the Milan riot. For days, Peter kept saying, "I just don't get it. Nothing like that should *ever* happen."

We probably all could have benefited from a lengthy break in the action, a time to catch our breath and make some judgments about which directions to head in next. But Peter already had lined up dates for a summer 1971 North American tour, which was to begin in Vancouver on August 19. It was tough to get up emotionally for it, but this band always found a way to meet its professional commitments, including this one.

There were thirty-one concerts on the itinerary, including three at the Los Angeles Forum, two at Boston Garden, and one at Madison Square Garden. Ultimately, that tour would gross at least $1 million.

This was the band's seventh American tour, and the novelty of being in the U.S.—and of touring in general—was beginning to wear thin. Every concert was a sellout, every crowd seemed almost possessed in its fanaticism toward the band. Yet the incident in Milan had taken a lot out of us. Once we arrived in America, Zeppelin almost seemed to become reclusive as we moved from city to city, rarely leaving the hotels except for the concerts themselves. Occasionally, Jimmy would venture out to an antique store in New Orleans or Dallas, but those expeditions were more the exception than the rule.

"I never thought touring would become this much of a grind," Robert said. "But it has." It wasn't as much fun as it used to be for anyone.

Peter and I talked a lot about the band's safety and agreed that the more time we spent in hotel rooms, away from the maddening crowd, the better. For the most part, we could hire someone to bring just about anything we wanted to our hotel rooms, from the most expensive foods to the ripest girls. In Montreal, we were staying at the Queen Elizabeth Hotel, having checked in the day before our concert at the Forum. One evening, Bonzo was visiting the suite that Peter and I shared, and the three of us were becoming nostalgic for home comforts. We called room service and ordered a few rounds of our favorites— egg and chips, and HP brown sauce. No matter how expensive the delicacies we could afford by then, we couldn't pass up a real working-class dish like this.

As we finished our meal, there was a knock at the door, and when I answered it, there were two young girls—one a redhead, the other a brunette. "Hi," the redhead said. "We met in New York last year. I thought we'd come up and say hello."

I invited them in, and within half an hour, Peter had left and the girls and I were in bed in one of the bedrooms. Things usually happened that fast. There was little if any courtship or game-playing; it was the sex I was interested in, and apparently so were they.

Bonzo, who couldn't be bothered with our partying, was watching TV in the living room. It didn't seem to distress him that we were making love just a few feet away. However, the noise from the girls finally started to bug him. He picked up one of the girls' shoes by the front door. "Let me give her something to really shout about!" He proceeded to drop his pants—and shit in the shoe!

A few minutes later, when the brunette went to retrieve her shoe, she discovered Bonzo's memento. A horrified expression came over her face, but she seemed too frightened to say anything. She gingerly carried her shoes out the door as she and her friend left.

The next night, during the show at the Forum, Bonzo came offstage for a few moments in the middle of the concert and said, "You're not gonna believe this, Richard. The girl with the shit-filled shoe is sitting in the third row. I hope she doesn't throw it at me."

At the end of the concert, we were climbing into our limos, preparing for our getaway to the airport. Just then, the brunette appeared out of nowhere, running toward the cars. "Fuck, this is all we need," I mumbled to myself.

A security guard grabbed her a few feet from the front limo. She shouted out to us, "Remember me? You shit in my shoe yesterday! I just wanted to thank you for a wonderful night!"

You never know what's going to make people happy.

Although we didn't venture out as much as we once had, this trip to America was far from uneventful. More than in any other U.S. tour to date, we received a flurry of death threats. Even in the earliest days of Zeppelin, there had been occasional threats, but, perhaps naively, we ignored them. By 1971, however, the threats had almost become weekly occurrences. In Chicago, the promoter got a telephone call claiming that "Jimmy is going to be shot by someone in the audience tonight." In Detroit, a scrawled message was surreptitiously left on a hotel porter's desk; it read, "Two members of Led Zeppelin aren't going to get out of Detroit alive!"

Maybe some demented cranks were just having fun. But I knew we couldn't take a chance that some disturbed nut was really aiming for a member of the band. The police were always notified of the threats, and in some cities we hired extra security. But Peter and I were never confident that we had hired enough. And when we were away from our hotel suites, I was almost always paranoid, fearing that something was about to happen.

Fortunately, the tour proceeded without incident. Maybe these things are part of the price of fame. But it was terribly disturbing.

The band members themselves were generally less anxious than I. In fact, I occasionally got chewed out when they'd see me or one of our security people beat up someone in the audience. "Damn it, Richard, go easy on 'em," Robert told me one evening after I had tackled a fan in Minneapolis. But Peter and I had decided that we would never underestimate what kind of potential damage these crackpots might cause.

"You do your job and I'll do mine," I shouted at Robert. "A lot of these fans are stoned, and their state of mind is just too unpredictable. Whether you like it or not, I'm going to be aggressive if I feel I have to."

By the early seventies, our contract with every promoter stipulated that a crash barrier had to be positioned in front of the stage. We never went on without it, although on occasion it wasn't built to our specifications and fans could reach the stage just by leaning over it.

The 1971 American tour ended with two concerts in Honolulu. The band rented the same mansion at Diamond Head that we had used in 1969, but this time Jimmy insisted on having it all to himself. The rest of the band members had decided to invite their wives to join them, and Jimmy—still the only unmarried one—felt that the presence of the spouses was no reason to put a crimp in his own sexual shenanigans.

So the rest of us camped at a Hilton down the road. Some members of the crew were a little upset, having heard about the luxury of the mountaintop home. But the Hilton wasn't bad, either. We stayed in the high-rise suites, with a breathtaking view of the Pacific. We also could take full advantage of hotel room service, and by the end of our four-day stay we had literally drained their liquor stashes. It helped take my mind off my concerns over security.

One afternoon, Peter, Bonzo, and I had returned from the beach and were sitting on the balcony of my suite, plotting the rest of the day. Johnny Larke, a member of the crew whose job included keeping our room refrigerators fully stocked, came into the suite and asked if there was anything we needed.

"Larke," Bonham said, "we've been here almost twenty-four hours and we haven't gotten into any mischief yet." Bonzo hadn't changed; if there was a chance to create a little havoc or get into trouble, he'd find it. "What's there to do around here?"

"Well, the exotic drinks are good!" Johnny said.

"What kinds do they have?" Peter asked. Johnny grabbed a menu and handed it to him. Peter took a quick glance and then said, "It takes too long to read this fucking thing. Larke, have room service send up four of every drink on the menu. You can join us."

In twenty-five minutes, two room service valets were pushing their carts into our suites, bringing in enough alcohol to neutralize the senses of every sunbather on Waikiki Beach. There were nearly a hundred drinks on those carts—and we began attacking them, one after another. Not a single one went to waste. After an afternoon guzzling mai-tai's and Hawaiian highballs, green dragons and Waikiki wowees, the rest of the day was a complete blur. With the stress of this American tour, I was only too happy to lapse into a fog for a while.

Late that afternoon, we used Jonesy's camera to take a few pictures of each other. With several shots left on the roll of film and some drinks in us to warp our thinking a bit, Bonham made a suggestion.

"Let's take pictures of each other's dicks! We've got to have something to remember Hawaii by!"

And so we did. Jonesy, Bonham, Plant, and I took turns posing for the camera. Long shots. Close-ups. Even a wide angle or two now and then. It was all in good fun, and we were laughing hysterically throughout the entire episode. At one point, Bonzo suggested that we make a few bucks by selling the photos to the *National Enquirer*, but cooler heads prevailed.

Later that year, at a family party at John Paul's house, Jonesy brought out the slides of Hawaii, forgetting about the "dick shots." He showed about a dozen beach photos and a few pictures by the pool. Then the dick shots flashed up on the six-foot screen in the living room. John Paul's in-laws gasped as they got real insiders' looks at Led Zeppelin.

The next day, Mo Jones called Maureen Plant and said, "Oh, I saw a lovely photograph of your husband last night taken in Hawaii. Absolutely lovely!"

28

EASTERN ANTICS

In the early days of Led Zeppelin, Jimmy Page and Robert Plant established an ambitious goal for the band: Eventually to perform in every country in the world.

Robert had a love of traveling and exotic places. He wanted to see everything, everywhere. If he wasn't going to do it with the band, he wanted to do it on his own. But Led Zeppelin provided him with the perfect opportunity to globe-trot.

Jimmy was possessed with the same kind of wanderlust. Unlike Robert, he had the advantage of having no family ties to keep him close to home. In particular, Jimmy was attracted to the Far East, thanks to his increasing fascination with Eastern philosophy and the mystics. He wanted to suck up some of that Eastern culture firsthand and introduce the countries to rock and roll at the same time.

John Bonham and John Paul Jones were not as enamored with the prospect of traveling. They were much more comfortable as homebodies, content to spend time with their families rather than deal with airports and hotels. In fact, when you'd mention their families to them, the softer side of both Bonzo and Jonesy would surface. Particularly with Bonzo, that surprised a lot of people. After all, on the road he would sometimes behave like a raving lunatic, but his wife, Pat, provided him with stability and a haven that allowed him just to be John Bonham. A lot of people never saw Bonzo's warmth; I thought it was one of his most precious attributes.

■ ■ ■

In 1971, Jimmy and Robert wouldn't back away from pressuring their mates to explore new frontiers overseas. Finally, after weeks of discussion, John Paul and Bonzo agreed. That translated into six performances in a week in Japan—in Tokyo, Hiroshima, Osaka, and Kyoto.

We flew first-class to Japan in late September 1971, and from the opening day I could sense that this was going to be an eventful tour, however short. Yes, the music was why we were there. But offstage, things never calmed down. It was one bizarre incident, one weird episode after another.

At the very first concert at Budokan Hall in Tokyo, before Robert had even sung a single note, he was already nursing a split lip. Amazingly, the injury never really interfered with his ability to perform. But it attracted a lot of attention from reporters, although Robert consistently declined to discuss it with them.

"It's really none of your fucking business," Robert shouted at one journalist. "It's just between me and Bonzo."

Bonham and Plant had an interesting love-hate relationship. They had been pals for a long time, but sometimes they bickered like spouses who knew each other too well. Their quarrels were usually over trivial things, and any bad blood never really lasted very long.

Backstage at Budokan Hall, the two of them continued an argument they had been having for weeks—a dispute over which of them would assume responsibility for a thirty-seven-pound petrol bill for an automobile ride to Scotland they had taken together. Bonzo had paid for the gas but became tired of asking Robert to reimburse him.

Finally, in Japan, Bonzo grew weary of the debate. He figured that the most expedient way to make his point was with his fists. He swung at Robert, connecting with his lip, drawing blood and leaving it cut and swollen.

Robert was stunned, more from emotional rather than physical pain. He began cursing at Bonham while dabbing his lip with a handkerchief. Within minutes, however, the concert began. I never heard them discuss Bonzo's punch again.

"Robert and I have known each other for so long that there's never any maliciousness in these fights," Bonzo told me later. "We just lose our tempers sometimes."

By 1971, Led Zeppelin had become so successful and so wealthy that we could afford to pay the price to ensure that every show came off without a hitch. We brought Rusty Brutsche, one of the owners of Showco in Dallas, to Japan with us, along with his company's sound system, which was the best in the business. Rather than rely on local equipment and local engineers, I felt it was worth the cost to bring the best from home. It was the right decision.

Throughout Japan, Zeppelin's music was remarkably well received. Even though rock music was relatively new in Tokyo and throughout Japan, the kids obviously knew our music well. While the Japanese have a reputation for being quieter and more reserved than Westerners, fans loosened their kimonos and let their hair down when they came to Zeppelin's concerts. From the first notes of "Immigrant Song" to the final downbeat of the last encore, the audiences cheered. There was some variety in the shows from night to night. But the crowds saved their loudest response for some rock oldies, including Bo Diddley's "I'm a Man," Chuck Berry's "Maybellene," and the Isley Brothers' "Twist and Shout." Maybe they knew more about rock 'n' roll than we had figured.

For me, however, the music seemed to be overshadowed by other events on Zeppelin's agenda. Free of the paranoia that I had felt in America, we began to eagerly sample Japanese nightlife. On our first evening in Tokyo, Tats Nagashima, our promoter-host, took us to what he called the most elegant restaurant in Tokyo. "You will be quite impressed," he promised.

Tats was right. There was plenty of sukiyaki and tempura. Live, traditional music was played on the koto and the samisen. Most important, the sake flowed and the geisha girls were everywhere and very friendly.

The girls served us the sake in little white thimbles, the traditional way of drinking the winelike beverage. But Robert complained for all of us: "At this rate, we won't get drunk until we're old men!"

Bonzo seemed just as impatient. "Can we get some bigger cups?" he finally pleaded with one of the geishas. "Maybe a coffee cup. Or a beer mug. Or some buckets!"

That night, we learned that in the Japanese tradition, if you offer a geisha some sake, she has to drink it. So to be friendly, the band kept giving the girls as much sake as we were drinking ourselves. As the evening wore on, we watched them become more and more giddy.

Of course, better than most human beings, Zeppelin could hold their alcohol, whether it was sake or Scotch. But still, there were things that we didn't quite understand that night. "Here's what somebody needs to explain to me," Robert said, trying to get his equilibrium. "Usually, when we drink a lot, the women begin looking better and better. Here, while we're getting drunker and drunker, these geisha girls are looking older and more haggard!"

"He's right," I chimed in. Then I directed a question at Tats: "Why do these fucking birds seem so old and ugly?"

Perhaps I had phrased the question a little too bluntly. Tats, a tall man who fit the stereotype of the polite and proper Japanese, appeared startled. But he cleared his throat and answered, "These girls who are now serving us are the kitchen staff, not the geisha girls. You got all those girls so drunk that the restaurant had to send them home! They were too courteous to tell you that they had too much to drink."

Later that night, despite our inebriated state, the partying continued. We ended up at a discotheque called Byblos, where we started drinking Japanese beer, almost by the case. We might have also snorted some cocaine except we couldn't get it there; it seemed to be taboo in Japan. Yes, alcohol was still our primary substance of choice, but elsewhere, we had begun using cocaine more frequently, simply because it was so available. When it came to getting high, we were never too discriminating.

At one point, as we watched the action at the disco, Bonzo exclaimed, "Look at that fucking disc jockey! He's playing records inside a cage that doesn't stop moving!"

The DJ was on a mobile platform that rose and fell like a runaway elevator. "That guy is not only a fucking joke, but he also hasn't played a Led Zeppelin record the entire night," Bonzo said as we stood on a balcony watching the elevator continue to rise and fall below us. "I think we need to let him know how we feel."

"Oh, oh," I thought. "I have a feeling this could be trouble."

Bonzo unzipped his pants, and, before I could react, he began pissing on the cage—and on the disc jockey in it—as it rose toward us. John's aim was impeccable; the disc jockey would have needed an umbrella to keep from being bathed in Bonzo's bodily fluids. Fortunately, there was no law in Tokyo against urinating on a disc jockey!

I quickly led Bonham out to the street, where we jumped in a limo that had been waiting for us. The driver took us back to the Hilton, but when we arrived, Bonzo was so drunk I could barely get him out of the car, much less help him through the lobby up to our rooms. On the hotel steps, he dropped to one knee and didn't seem as though he was going to get up.

"Bonham, get your goddamn feet moving," I said, trying to drag him toward the entrance. But it was no use. Exasperated, I finally just left him there on the sidewalk, only a few feet from the gutter, and headed up to my room. Japanese passersby walked around Bonzo, letting him sleep it off. Before dawn, he had somehow found his own way up to his room.

I realized later that Peter probably would have taken a samurai sword to my midsection if he ever found out that I had left Bonham sleeping on the curb.

Although we were in Japan only a week, it seemed as if we were trying to make up for any depravity we may have missed on earlier tours. At one point, Bonzo and I decided to go shopping for samurai swords in the hotel gift shop. That night, with our swords in hand, we began swinging them at one another like a couple of maniacs. As the swords clashed against one another, I joked, "Do you have the phone number of the nearest emergency hospital? I think it's best to be prepared."

Within minutes, we had switched the target of our aggression to the hotel room itself, slashing anything in the room that would cut . . . the drapes, the bedspread and mattress, the wallpaper, the paintings. With each swing, we probably added hundreds of dollars in damages to our hotel bill.

John Paul was asleep next door, and we decided to invite him to participate in the anarchy. We knocked on his door, then banged a little louder, and finally broke in, only to find him still sleeping peacefully, having been tranquilized by an overdose of alcohol.

"Let's take him out into the hallway," Bonzo suggested. "I challenge him to keep sleeping out there."

I grabbed John Paul's legs while Bonham lifted him from under the armpits. We set him down in the hallway, threw a blanket on him, and left him there for the rest of the night.

When the hotel staff spotted Jonesy, they were too polite to awaken him. Instead, they brought three portable screens up to our floor and positioned them around him to minimize any disturbances. He slept that way until morning.

Still, the Tokyo Hilton didn't know quite what to make of us. When I checked the band out of the hotel, the manager called me into his office. In his best and most apologetic English, he said, "I know you are very good musicians, but we can't have this kind of behavior in our hotel. There was a lot of damage in your rooms. One of your people got drunk in the gutter. Another one slept in the hall. I'm sorry, but I cannot let you stay in this hotel ever again. Please look elsewhere next time you come back to Tokyo."

Sayonara!

But even lectures by hotel managers didn't have any effect on our behavior. It just never connected that we were out of line and that we needed to bring our excesses under control. Later in the tour, on the bullet train to Osaka, our high spirits hadn't been tempered at all. I had asked Tats to have some items waiting for us on the train. "Be sure the band has twelve flasks of hot sake, six bottles of Suntory whiskey, and some sandwiches for the journey."

He didn't blink an eye. "Consider it done," he said.

Once on the train, it didn't take us long to devour the liquor—and then to start creating trouble. Jimmy had met a woman in Tokyo—a cute Japanese girl named Kanuko with beautiful brown eyes who didn't seem to know much about Led Zeppelin. Jimmy invited her to accompany us on the rest of the tour, and I guess he expected us to treat her with respect. Bonham, however, had other ideas.

"She's much too sweet for Jimmy," Bonzo told me. "I'll show her what the world of rock and roll is really like."

While Jimmy and Kanuko were eating in the dining car, Bonzo found her purse in her sleeping berth and took it into the bathroom with him. When he emerged, he had a sadistic grin on his face. "Guess what!" he said. "I just shit in the handbag!" This was becoming a pattern.

Bonzo closed the purse and put it back where he had found it. Thirty minutes later, Kanuko retrieved her purse and took it with her to the ladies' room. No more than a minute later, she emerged from the bathroom—pale, stunned, crying. Bonzo whispered to me, "It looks like the shit hit the purse!"

Kanuko walked over to Jimmy and showed him Bonzo's work of art. In an instant, Jimmy went absolutely berserk. "Who the fuck did this?" he screamed, storming down the aisle of the train, frantically trying to decide whose neck to wring. All of us scattered, figuring that he was furious enough to butcher the first person he got his hands on.

Bonzo leaped into Peter's sleeping bunk, not realizing that Peter was already in it. Not only did he land on top of the oversized, burly manager, but as he did, the drink in Bonzo's hand spilled over both of them.

"You fucking asshole!" Peter growled. "Get off me! Get the fuck off me!"

Bonzo leaped up, absorbing a glancing blow to the stomach from Peter before he could extricate himself and spring away.

Robert had sought refuge in my bunk, forcing me to seek an alternate hiding place. Meanwhile, a very damp Peter began lumbering through the train, taking a swing at any familiar face he saw, including mine, causing screams from other passengers, who were convinced that terrorists had the train under siege.

"Cole, you're fired!" Peter roared. "As soon as this fucking train stops, make arrangements for the next flight back to England! You're through!"

"What did I do?" I halfheartedly pleaded, not expecting Peter really to fire me.

At about this point, Tats Nagashima was on the brink of hysteria. He was a wonderful guy, but as the pandemonium unfolded, he seemed to panic. He found a phone on the train and placed a transcontinental call to Ahmet Ertegun in New York.

"Ahmet, there's terrible, terrible trouble here." Tats's voice was trembling. "We're all on a train to Osaka, and the band has gone nuts! Mr. Grant has punched Mr. Cole and Mr. Bonham. He has started to fire people. I don't know what to do. They act like they're trying to kill each other."

Ahmet took the news in stride. "You're dealing with Led Zeppelin," he told Tats with a chuckle. "This is normal behavior for these guys. Don't worry about it. They'll be all right after they sober up and get where they're going."

And that's exactly what happened. We were like siblings who fight but whose family ties can withstand the storm. We all apologized to one another the next day and got on with the rest of the tour.

If there was any expectation that Peter's rage on the train would put an end to our tomfoolery, it never came to pass. Atlantic's Phil Carson had accompanied us on this Japanese tour, and at one point he asked me, "Don't you guys ever slow down?" The answer to his question was "No." That tour was like a nonstop Marx Brothers movie.

In Osaka, the band asked Phil if he wanted to make one of his occasional appearances on stage playing bass. He was a damn good bass player, and since Led Zeppelin rarely asked anyone to perform with them, Phil was honored at the invitation. He didn't know, however, that the band had an ulterior motive.

Phil ran onto the stage on cue. John Paul had moved to the keyboards, and Phil picked up the bass. From the start, Phil fit right in. He was feeling so wonderful, gazing out upon the crowd, thoroughly enjoying the experience. But about four minutes into the song, he suddenly realized that his bass was the only instrument he was hearing. He quickly looked around—and he was alone on the stage. As a prank, the band had snuck off in the middle of the song, leaving Phil to fend for himself. He made a valiant attempt at a bass solo, but he gave up once it was clear that the guys weren't going to rescue him. Phil put down his instrument and ran off the stage, too, as the band rollicked in laughter.

The incident was hilarious. But there was something about it that bothered me, too. Led Zeppelin had always taken its music very seriously—and still did. But this was one time that they allowed a practical joke to take precedence over the music. The Japanese audience was completely baffled by what had taken place onstage. It was very out of character for this band, and it was troubling.

The next night, Phil was "Zeppelinized" again, although this time it was *after* the second Osaka concert. We squeezed in some night-clubbing until the wee hours, and at one club, the band members collectively decided to tear off Phil's clothes. They began groping at his shirt, then his pants. Phil soon realized that he was in a losing battle, and decided to cooperate with them, systematically removing his own clothes, including his underwear. He spent a few minutes naked in the club, and as we left, he took a white tablecloth off one of the tables and wrapped it around himself.

On the limousine ride back to the hotel, Robert and John Paul became unusually apologetic about the way they had treated Phil. "I'm so sorry about what we did to you back there," Robert said. Phil should have been suspicious about their newfound compassion.

When the limousine pulled in front of the hotel, the band and Phil (still attired only in the tablecloth) exited the limo, and as they reached the revolving door at the hotel entrance, Robert extended a friendly arm and told Phil, "You go ahead and I'll follow." As Phil stepped into the door and it began to turn, Robert reached out, grabbed the tablecloth, and yanked it off Phil, while pushing the door forward to catapult Phil, stark naked, into the hotel lobby.

Even though the Atlantic Records corporate policy book didn't cover this kind of situation, Phil remained remarkably calm. He looked back at us with a startled expression on his face, but realized that he was outnumbered and would never get the tablecloth back. So he walked over to the desk clerk and asked, "Can I have the key to suite 332?" The stunned clerk handed it to him, and Phil paraded into the elevator, riding up to his room in his birthday suit.

When we reached Kyoto, I thought that Phil was trying to turn the tables on us. Late one night, he called me from his hotel room. "Richard, come down to my room quickly," he said in a frantic voice. "I've got a bird here, and she's fainted."

Oh brother, I thought to myself. Here comes his retaliation for our prank.

Jimmy and I walked down the hall, but when we got to Phil's room, there actually was a Japanese girl lying on the floor unconscious. "What the hell happened?" I said, as we all kneeled around her. I noticed that Phil's pants were unbuckled and the zipper was down. And he was terribly upset.

"I was kissing her," Phil said. "Then I got my cock out, and she fainted!"

Jimmy was patting the girl on the cheeks, trying to awaken her. Finally, she started to come to.

"Thank God," Phil said. "I thought maybe she had a heart attack or something."

We stayed there for a few minutes until the girl felt better. Finally, she said, "All I remember is that he unzipped himself, I looked down, and he had one this big." She held her hands about a foot apart—and then she fainted again.

From that moment, I figured Phil was a guy entitled to a lot more respect than we had given him.

Amid all our hell-raising, Zeppelin found out just how popular they were in Japan, with every concert a sellout. Even so, when I had finally added the numbers up, we actually *owed* money to Tats Nagashima—the first time we had ever ended a tour, big or small, in the red. We had spent so much of Tats's money on a potpourri of items—cameras, antiques, electronic equipment, hotel damage, and, most of all, Japanese beer and other alcohol—that Peter had to issue a check for much more yen than he would have liked. I hand-delivered the money—a total of $2,000—and bid Tats farewell.

Peter was philosophical about the financial realities. "If it hadn't been such an important tour for us, you might call the entire tour a disaster," he said. "But we made our presence felt in the Far East for the first time."

Yes, it was a disaster from a financial point of view, but there were other considerations.

After the last concert in Japan, John Paul, Bonzo, and Peter jetted back to England, but Jimmy, Robert, and I weren't quite ready to go home. Eager to see more of the world, we decided to take advantage of our presence in the Far East and fly to Bangkok, Thailand.

In our first few hours there, we visited the Temple of the Emerald Buddha, some of the lesser-known Buddhist temples, and a museum. We went shopping in Thai stores, where Jimmy bought an almost life-size flying horse made of gold, glass, and wood. I bought Peter a wooden Buddha, about three feet high and three feet wide. As I looked at the rotund Buddha, I said to Jimmy, "If there were a few more pounds on this statue, we wouldn't be able to tell the Buddha and Peter apart." Pagey suggested I keep the joke to myself.

That night, we had no difficulty finding Bangkok's red-light district with the help of Sammy, a driver we had hired for the duration of our stay there. The brothels were really more like bathhouses, and they were staffed by plenty of scantily clad girls. Sammy walked into one of the brothels with us. There were at least two dozen girls by the entrance, standing in rows, each with a number pinned to her negligee.

"Beautiful girls, eh?" Sammy said. "I could look at them all night."

"Well, my friends and I don't want to look at them," I told Sammy. "We want to screw them!"

"That's fine," he said, taking my request in stride. "They do that, too."

Sammy talked to one of the girls, who came over to us, smiled, and shyly asked, "We can give you what you want. Just choose the girls by the number."

Suddenly, we were like kids in a candy store. "We've got plenty of money," Robert said, calling out numbers. "I'll take eleven, nineteen, and forty-one."

"Okay," I said, "but I'd like forty-one, too, before the night is over."

For the next two hours, the three of us indulged in everything from massages to good, old-fashioned sex. When we finally ran out of stamina and left, Jimmy said, "They must have invented the term 'fucking your brains out' here."

Walking the streets in Bangkok, we got quite a bit of attention, but since no one in Thailand seemed to have heard of Led Zeppelin, it wasn't because of our music. "I think they're making fun of our long hair," Robert finally concluded. We were wearing earrings, and that was a real novelty there.

"Billy boy! Billy boy!" the kids would yell as they looked at us and pointed. Later, Sammy told us, "In Thailand, 'Billy boy' means that you are queer or homosexual. They think that's what your long hair means!"

From Bangkok, the three of us flew to Bombay for a four-day visit. We checked into the Taj Majal Hotel, directly opposite the Gateway of India archway, and then spent some time on the streets of the city. Outside the hotel, a dozen cabdrivers offered to exchange our money into rupees on the black market. "I don't think so," I told them, nervous about turning over money to an unfamiliar face.

Robert, however, finally talked me into it. "What the hell," he said. "Give one of them some bills and see what they come back with."

From the balcony of my room at the Taj Majal, I could see our designated money exchanger talking to another cabbie, and some currency changing hands. The second driver didn't look like most of the other cabbies we had seen. Although he was wearing the same khaki uniform, his slacks were immaculately pressed, his shirt was freshly laundered, there wasn't a hair out of place on his head, and his mustache looked as though it had been transplanted from Clark Gable's upper lip. "This guy should be making movies in Hollywood," I said.

After getting our money, we decided to introduce ourselves to the dapper taxi driver and ask him for a tour of the city. "Our Marathi is a little rusty," I told him. "We could use a guide if you're available."

His name was Mr. Razark, and for the next three days he became part of our entourage, taking us to Indian brothels, a disco where Jimmy jammed with some startled local musicians who couldn't believe his prowess on their Japanese-made guitars, and some shops where we bought musical instruments, scented oils, and an ivory chess set.

Razark even invited us to his own home for a meal. We were struck by the oppressive poverty in the run-down neighborhood where he lived. The streets were over-crowded with flimsy shanties that couldn't have withstood even a mild windstorm. "My home is very small," Razark said apologetically. "My wife and I share one room with our four children. My mother lives in the other room. It isn't much, but it cost me seventeen thousand pounds to buy. Bombay is a very expensive city to live in."

No wonder the poor people stay so poor, I thought.

On our last night in Bombay, we talked Razark into accompanying us to a local restaurant in his neighborhood. "We want you to take us where *you* go to eat," Jimmy said.

"No, no," he replied. "It's not good for tourists. It could be dangerous to your health."

"Don't worry about us," Jimmy said. "We'll be fine. We're tough."

So Razark drove us to a small Indian restaurant that seated about twenty people; in London or New York, it would have been condemned by the health department months earlier. At Razark's suggestion, all of us ordered chicken curry, although when it was served we had trouble finding any chicken meat on the bones.

Within an hour, we regretted not having taken Razark's warning more seriously. We had stomach cramps and nausea that kept us awake most of the night. By morning, we had vicious cases of diarrhea. I dreaded the thought of spending the better part of the upcoming day on an airplane.

During the flight back to London, all of us had to sprint to the bathroom every few minutes. Fortunately, I had a container of Johnson's baby powder with me, which the three of us shared in a desperate attempt to provide some relief for our sore asses. By the time the plane had made a stop in Geneva, the baby powder was gone, and we suffered the rest of the way home.

Throughout most of the flight back to London, perhaps as a way to get our minds off our most immediate physical problem, we talked about what we had experienced in Bombay. It had been a hard dose of reality to see the conditions in which Razark, this thoroughly decent man, and his family lived. We certainly didn't feel guilty about our own extravagant life-style; after all, the band had worked hard for their riches. But caught up in our own way of living, it was easy to overlook the distress in the world. In Bombay, we got a tough lesson about how most of the world lives. At least for those few days in India, all of us felt their pain.

29

GOING DOWN UNDER

Not long after we had returned to England, the fourth Led Zeppelin album was finally released. "It was probably more painful to get this one out than childbirth itself," Jimmy remarked.

As the band had insisted, Atlantic issued the new album without a title, which didn't deter fans from calling it *Four Symbols* or *Zoso* nor from buying it in massive quantities. The album never reached Number 1 in the U.S., but it settled into a comfortable Number 2 spot in the States. There was never any question that it would turn gold.

To support record sales, we embarked on a brief, twelve-concert British tour, highlighted by two sellout concerts at Wembley Empire Pool in London. At Wembley, all 19,000 seats were sold within minutes after they went on sale, with each ticket priced at $1.75 for a chance to see the hottest band in the world.

Throughout that short British tour, however, I had Australia and New Zealand on my mind. As soon as the tour ended, Peter had arranged for me to fly down under to lay the groundwork for the band's first concerts there, which were being planned for February 1972. So while Led Zeppelin was doing its Christmas shopping, I boarded a plane from London to Melbourne. Over the ensuing days, I hopped to Perth, then to Adelaide, Sydney, Brisbane, and Auckland. I negotiated with the local promoters and inspected, photographed, and, when necessary, changed the venues. I also lined up our hotel arrangements.

In early February, I joined Led Zeppelin for the flight to Australia on Air India. The decision to fly on the Indian airline, however, was not an easy one. Thanks to Atlantic Records becoming part of the Warner Brothers family, we could fly at a 50 percent discount because of an arrangement Warner Brothers had made with Air India. Even so, our asses had barely recovered from our last bout with Indian food, and we didn't know quite what to expect. "I'm not sure there's enough baby powder in the United Kingdom to last us all the way to Australia," Robert wisecracked. At least we had a sense of humor about it.

The plane made a stopover in Bombay, where we had arranged in advance for a break in our trip—the chance to unwind for a few days before resuming the journey to Australia. It was a blessing just to get off the plane. In Bombay, we called Mr. Razark, who drove us to a beach where we rode camels for an entire afternoon—one more Indian experience that left our rear ends feeling battered and bruised. He also took us to a music store where John Paul bought a beautiful set of drums.

Two days later, when we finally boarded an Air India jet taking us to Perth, it was like entering the Twilight Zone. This flight was so short on liquor that we were almost going through alcohol withdrawal by the time we finally arrived in Australia. "You got any cocaine, Richard?" Bonham asked. "I need something to take my mind off all of this."

The way things were going, we should have known that we'd never get through customs in Australia without a glitch. As we moved through the line, John Paul was notified that his drums were being confiscated. "These drums are made of animal skin," the customs agent told him. "I'm afraid they are illegal here."

As we climbed into the limo at curbside, Jimmy predicted, "Our lives can only get better."

Jimmy was the eternal optimist. But I had my doubts. Only time would tell.

"This is a drug bust!"

There was loud knocking at my hotel room door.

"We have a warrant to search your room! Open up!"

Only an hour after checking into our hotel in Perth, I had been trying to catch a nap when I heard unexpected loud banging on my door. The police were working their way down the hall, inviting themselves into my room and the rooms of the members of the band.

As soon as I opened the door, the cops stormed in, looking under the mattress, in the dresser drawers, and through my luggage. I sat on my bed, watching the fishing expedition, knowing that I, at least, didn't have any drugs on me. Fortunately, neither did anyone else in our entourage.

The cops were terribly disappointed. After all, busting a famous rock band is probably worth a promotion. And a band like Led Zeppelin, having built a reputation for decadence, must have seemed like a likely target. I figure we were lucky that they didn't plant anything on us. "That will probably come later in the tour," Bonzo said.

The police left as quickly as they had arrived, without an apology or an explanation, seeming not the least bit embarrassed that they had needlessly harassed us. All in a day's work, I presume.

Pagey shook his head. "Those stupid assholes!" he said. "If they had waited a day or two, we might have had something!"

The band *was* actually becoming even more involved in drug use—primarily cocaine and grass. But after the surprise visit by the men in blue, Peter offered us a warning: "We've got to be extra cautious here. I don't want anybody ending up in handcuffs in this country."

Peter thought it was important to improve our odds of avoiding arrest. But that didn't mean insisting that the band keep away from illegal substances; it meant hiring some private security to serve as a buffer between us and the local police. At Peter's request, I made a few calls, and by the next morning a local security agency had provided us with three barrel-chested, retired police detectives to accompany us on the rest of the tour.

The Australian fans were more hospitable than those original cops. Every one of the Australian and New Zealand concerts was a record breaker. They drew the biggest crowds ever to see rock performances in those countries. To attract the largest audiences possible, we had scheduled every concert at an outdoor venue, and, according to Peter's instructions, there was a rain date set for each of them. Peter adamantly refused to let the band play in the rain, fearing that with all the electrical equipment, wires, and plugs, there was the real possibility of someone being electrocuted. The Adelaide show, in fact, was postponed a day when a drizzle turned into a downpour.

At all the Australian and New Zealand concert sites, I would arrive a few hours early to make sure the stage and the surrounding crash barriers were built to specifications. On occasion, the barriers were not high enough or strong enough, and I would grab a hammer and improve upon them myself. That's what happened in Auckland, where the band was scheduled to play at Western Springs. I talked Bonham into coming out to the site early with me, and we pounded a few nails and got things into shape.

Once the repairs were made, Bonham and I started looking for something to do until the gates opened. We raided the liquor cases backstage, and after a few beers Bonzo spotted a pair of Honda motorcycles parked near the stage. "Well," he said, "don't just stand there. Let's take 'em for a spin."

The motorcycles belonged to Rem Raymond, the event's promoter, who let us ride them for a few minutes. "There's one more thing we should try," Bonham finally suggested. "I've never played chicken before. Let's do it with the bikes!"

I gulped. "Forget it, Bonzo," I said. "I don't feel suicidal today."

"Richard," he said. "Do it for your old pal. C'mon, Richard."

He was starting to whine, and I was starting to build up my courage. Finally, in a moment of total insanity, I gave in. "Okay, but I should warn you: When I play chicken, I don't flinch."

Led Zeppelin often lived by an "anything for a thrill" credo. It was an "act first, think later" attitude. This was probably the ultimate example of it.

As Bonham and I rode the bikes to an adjacent field, I told myself, "I have three beers to blame for this." We positioned ourselves about a hundred and fifty yards apart, facing one another.

"If one of us dies," I mumbled, "I hope it's me. If it turns out to be Bonzo, Peter will have me killed anyway."

I gunned the engine, turned up the throttle, and, like a couple of lunatics, Bonham and I sped toward one another. Rolling at about thirty miles per hour, we were nearly on top of each other almost immediately. But about twenty feet away from Bonzo, despite my promise, I must have flinched. My bike skidded into the dirt, and I rolled over it.

"Damn it!" I shouted, turning to look at Bonham, who by this time was fifty yards past me, obviously amused by my ungraceful landing. Other than some torn jeans and bruised pride, I was unhurt, but the motorcycle did not fare as well—either during or immediately after the crash. "It must have been the bike's fault!" I yelled to Bonham.

Just then, I spotted an ax lying near some tools about twenty yards away. I walked over, picked it up, and hovered over the bike for a few seconds. "It's like a horse with a broken leg," I said. "You gotta put it out of its misery."

Flailing the ax, I systematically dismantled the motorcycle, swing by swing. Paul Bunyan couldn't have been any more vicious.

Rem Raymond was despondent when I told him what had happened. "Sure, I got a little carried away," I explained. "But there must be a good repair shop around here. Send us the bill."

Once we were out of Rem's earshot, Bonzo mumbled, "Sure, send us the bill. We won't pay it, but go ahead and send it anyway!"

In Auckland, people traveled up to 900 miles by train to see the group perform, coming from the farthest reaches of the island. They became part of a crowd of 25,000 that paid an average of four dollars to see the band rock to the point of collapse. Western Springs was a stadium usually reserved for stock car races, but it had never seen as much horsepower as Zeppelin generated that day.

Even though Robert was a little under the weather—some mild indigestion, he said—that Auckland show was still one of the band's best concerts of the tour. "Stairway to Heaven" primed the crowd for what was to come. Then the place went nuts over "Whole Lotta Love," now part of a medley with some old rock 'n' roll songs and Zeppelin tunes ("Good Times Bad Times," "You Shook Me," "I Can't Quit You"). For a full sixteen minutes, the band pushed "Whole Lotta Love" to the point of no return, and the audience responded with its own eruption of emotions, reacting as though they were seeing history being made. As far as they were concerned, they were.

Those kinds of performances left the band feeling absolutely euphoric. They were reminiscent of the earliest American tours when fans were seeing Zeppelin for the first time. Bonzo came away from the concerts so energized that he proclaimed, "I won't be able to sleep for days." Sometimes it seemed as though he didn't.

In Adelaide, Creedence Clearwater Revival had performed the night before us and were still in town when we checked into our hotel. Creedence's drummer, Doug Clifford, had a practice drum kit in his hotel room, and Bonham and he took turns pounding out a thunderous beat until almost daybrak. Amazingly, no one from the hotel complained.

For the most part, however, except for the music itself, this tour was pure drudgery. When we had checked into the White Heron Hotel in Auckland well past midnight, not much went right. The night desk clerk had difficulty figuring out what rooms we belonged in and ended up putting Peter and me in the same suite. To be more accurate, he put Peter, me, and a married couple whom we had never met in the same suite!

When Peter and I turned the key and entered our room, the fellow was in bed with his wife, looking as though the last thing he wanted was two late-night visitors. Frankly, I couldn't blame him.

"What the hell are you doing in my room?" he shouted as his wife grabbed a blanket to cover herself.

"I was about to ask you the same fucking question!" Peter yelled back. "We'd appreciate you getting the hell out of here!"

We went down to the front desk to try to straighten the matter out. Much to our surprise, however, our roadie Mick Hinton was working at the switchboard.

"What the hell are you doing?" I asked.

"I bribed the fucking desk clerk into going into the kitchen and fetching some food for us," he said. "He told me to take care of things while he was gone."

Just then, the phone at the front desk rang.

"Front desk," Mick said as he picked up the receiver, trying to sound as if he knew what he was doing. It was our "roommate" on the other end of the line, complaining about the unannounced appearance Peter and I had made a couple of minutes earlier.

Mick sounded angry. "Look, if you don't like things around here, then go fuck yourself!" he shouted.

The hotel guest apparently tried to reason with Mick, which was a futile effort. "You asshole," Mick hollered into the phone, "this is the way we run our hotel! I suggest you get the hell out of here!"

Fifteen minutes later, the man and his wife checked out.

When we reached Sydney in the first week of March, we stayed at the Sobell Townhouses, and, for a change, we really tried to be on our best behavior. One night, I asked the desk clerk to point us toward some clubs that could withstand a Zeppelin onslaught. Our second stop was at Les Girls, owned by an American named Sammy Lee. "It's full of female impersonators," the desk clerk had told us.

Actually, Les Girls was much more . . . it had a stage show featuring transsexuals who were really quite talented—good singers, even better dancers, and they were pretty attractive, too. About midway through the show, Bonzo asked a waiter the question we all were interested in. "Are they men or women?" he said.

"Well, they've had their dicks cut off and their breasts enlarged," the waiter answered. "As far as they're concerned, they're women now!"

"Yeah, that sure doesn't sound like they're men anymore!" Robert said with a bit of understatement.

We found out that the "girls" at Les Girls were actually quite famous in Australia. And once they heard that Led Zeppelin was in the audience, they came over to greet us. We invited them to our concert the following night and then to go drinking with us after it.

Zeppelin played before 28,000 fans at Sydney's Showgrounds, and after the concert we found the "girls" to be great company and even better afternight drinkers. We were in Sydney for almost a week and had the transsexuals hanging around us most of the time. "The press doesn't know what to make of this," Peter chuckled. "A reporter asked me if all the members of Led Zeppelin were queers."

In fact, the "girls" were just pure fun, which was exactly what we were after, too. Of course, they lost some of their attractiveness by about four in the morning when the stubble had grown on their faces. One morning, the "girls" started losing their tempers, and instead of calling each other Louise and Marilyn, they regressed back to Barney and Burt. It was a show in itself.

For our departure from Australia, we booked a flight on BOAC. At John Paul's urging, we had scheduled a stop in Thailand; he had heard our stories about the trip after the Japan tour, and we decided to stop there for three days to show him Bangkok before continuing on to England. At the Bangkok airport, however, we never got past the customs officials.

"Sorry," one of them said. "Your long hair is unacceptable in Thailand. You are not allowed in the country looking like that."

We were flabbergasted. "We were just here last year," Robert said. "We probably had longer hair then. This is absurd!"

The Thai officials were inflexible, however. "We apologize," one of them said, "but this is now a rule. No long hair in the country."

We weren't used to not getting our way. Whether it was a first-class seat on an overbooked flight or the best table in a fashionable restaurant, the band expected that their name and notoriety could get them whatever they wanted.

But it didn't work this time. For more than half an hour, we argued with whomever would listen. We did everything but offer a bribe (which might have earned us time in jail). Nothing worked. Eventually, we realized that this was one debate we weren't going to win.

"You don't seem to understand," Robert ranted. "We're going to spend *money* in your country!" Maybe they didn't need any more foreign currency in Thailand.

Within an hour, we were back on the plane, heading for London.

30

BEDROOM PLAY-BY-PLAY

When you're at the top, you can get away with making demands that people would have laughed at under different circumstances."

That's how Peter Grant explained his strategy to go for the jugular when negotiating Led Zeppelin's concert contracts.

Actually, there was no real negotiating involved. In his sternest, most uncompromising voice, Peter would simply inform local promoters, "From now on, Zeppelin is going to get 90 percent of the box-office receipts. Period." It was a take-it-or-leave-it proposition. The promoters protested—and then reluctantly signed on the dotted line.

In the early 1970s, a typical big-name band playing at an open-air stadium might receive a guarantee (perhaps $50,000) against 60 percent of the gate. But Led Zeppelin wasn't typical. According to Peter, Zeppelin's ground rules were going to be different.

"After we pay for the hall, the security, the limos, the sound, and the lighting, we're taking ninety percent," Peter said. "We're not even going to bother with a guarantee."

Not surprisingly, that kind of talk did not earn Peter a place at the head of the Christmas card mailing list of most local rock promoters and agents. Some felt he was arrogant. Others said that he and his band were suffering from a bad case of swellheadedness. Most thought he was simply being unfair. All of them were incensed. But Zeppelin reaped enormous financial rewards from Peter's kamikaze style of doing business.

Under the 90 percent arrangement, the band would usually take home at least $80,000 to $90,000, often more, on a single night in the early 1970s. Later in the decade, they could have used a Brink's truck to haul away a mind-boggling $500,000 on some nights. Every concert was a sellout, which triggered a Rockefeller-style financial avalanche. They would divide the receipts five ways, with Peter as an equal partner with the four musicians.

"Look," Peter would argue with the stunned local promoters, "even when you're getting ten percent of our gate, you're making more money than you normally would for an average act where your cut is fifty percent. For us, all you're doing is handling the odds and ends anyway."

Zeppelin's summer 1972 American tour was the first time that Peter had made his no-holds-barred, 90 percent demand, which pulverized the music business's standard operating procedures.

In the weeks before that American tour, while Peter was putting his 90 percent deal on the table in cities across the U.S., the band congregated at Stargroves, Mick Jagger's country home, to lay down the first tracks for its next album. They used Jagger's mobile recording studio and may have done more experimentation than at any other Zeppelin sessions to date. Jimmy arrived with a few songs on paper, fully written and arranged, like "Over the Hills and Far Away." But there was a lot of improvising on most of the others. There was so much creative energy and everyone was feeling so up that Jimmy felt a quality album was going to come together, even without everything thoroughly prepared ahead of time.

That, at least, was Pagey's attitude at the beginning. But by the time the sessions ended, he was not content with the sound quality he was getting. Yes, he had been right about the creative energy, but he started thinking about rerecording some of the cuts elsewhere.

Still, the band had gradually made progress on the album at Stargroves. Bonzo had the original idea for "D'yer Mak'er," a song into which he incorporated a doo-wop sound. When it was finally done, it had a bit of a reggae feel as well. In trying to bring "D'yer Mak'er" to fruition, the band would congregate on the Stargroves lawn and listen to each playback, moving to the beat, dancing with a step that looked like a cross between the jerky struts of Charlie Chaplin and Groucho Marx.

As with any Zeppelin gathering, there was some ongoing horseplay at Stargroves. It cut the tension that had built up, and seemed to regenerate the band's spirits for the following day's work. In a curious way, it was also how the band members showed affection for each other. They had really grown to care for one another, although none of them was particularly good at articulating their feelings. But engaging in playful activities together, whether sharing a bottle of champagne or planning a practical joke, was a way the band could demonstrate that affection.

At Stargroves, one of our technicians who we'll call Steve was the target of some of those high jinks. He had brought a girlfriend with him, and Bonzo snuck a microphone into the bedroom that Steve and his lady would be sharing. Then we all waited for them to retire for the night.

"Great!" Bonzo exclaimed, as he monitored the noise from their bedroom, pressing the headphones so tight over his ears that I thought they might meld into his skull. "They're making love! This is going to be wonderful!"

As their heavy breathing got serious, Bonzo captured their entire sexual celebration on tape. At the same time, he was turning dials and channeling the sounds from the bedroom through the house's speaker system. Over the next thirty minutes, every room in the house—except the bedroom where Steve and his girl were performing their physical acrobatics—got a very loud, very graphic play-by-play of the activities.

As the excitement level in the bedroom escalated, so did the cheering throughout the house. "Come on, Steve! Give it to her! Go, Steve, go!"

The next morning, Steve found himself the butt of some ruthless teasing—"Steve, that girl sure could moan!"—although he never seemed to have figured out how we had ambushed him and eavesdropped at 100 decibels.

Jimmy tried to keep the recording sessions themselves as businesslike as possible. He continued to insist that the band limit their recording expenses, and that meant approaching the sessions with the seriousness of a brain surgeon probing in a cerebellum. This time around, there was not the fast pace of the debut *Led Zeppelin* effort in 1968, which was recorded with the speed of the *Concorde*, but the mood was never lackadaisical, either. Jimmy demanded that the final product have decimal-point precision.

For that reason, we finally moved to the Olympic Studios in London. In a more formal studio setting, Zeppelin got a lot more accomplished. They plunged into songs like "The Crunge," with Jimmy and John Paul following Bonzo's lead in weaving the music into a James Brown–funky sound-alike; Jimmy contributed a blues-oriented riff he had been fooling around with for seven years, finally discovering an appropriate place to use it. For "The Song Remains the Same," Robert scribbled lyrics on a pad of paper in an inspirational flurry, driven by his vision of a common denominator for all peoples and things; Jimmy had carefully crafted the rich music over many weeks, initially intending it to be an instrumental number before merging it with Plant's lyrics.

While the band remained locked away in the studio, Peter and I began seriously discussing hiring a publicist to try to make some headway against a press that still treated the band with the same respect as the bubonic plague. A few weeks earlier on our flight home from Australia, Jimmy and Robert had first broached the subject, figuring that an experienced publicist might be able to extend an olive branch toward the press in hopes of getting fairer treatment.

"If you're looking for someone who can reach the media that appeals to young audiences, try B. P. 'Beep' Fallon," I told Peter. "He did a good job getting press attention for T. Rex. He knows what he's doing."

Peter took my advice. With the band busy recording, he assumed the initiative and hired Fallon, who stayed with us for about a year. Beep was a little guy who didn't look like he had the right stuff to schmooze and manipulate the press. But operating from his office in London, he clearly had the skills and the savvy to open doors, particularly with the British press, even with those writers who had traditionally responded to Zeppelin with one big yawn.

Beep was the kind of fellow who could get on your nerves with his hyperpersonality and a corny style of speaking. But as he got us the positive press we wanted, everyone agreed that he was earning his paycheck.

When the band finally emerged from the studio in late May, the American tour was set. With the intensity of their work on the new album, Zeppelin didn't feel they had gotten much of a respite during that spring at all. And they hadn't yet even done any real thinking about the upcoming concerts themselves—what they would play, what new songs they would introduce.

But they packed their bags and prepared for the flight west. They had enough confidence in themselves to feel that these Zeppelin concerts would be as good or better than any they had ever given.

31

RISKY
BUSINESS

For the summer 1972 tour, Peter and I agreed to charter a Falcon fan-jet to transport the band from one city to the next. With a fast, hectic schedule—an itinerary that included thirty-four dates in a little more than a month—I felt that the private jet was essential. So I flew to the U.S. ahead of the band to make arrangements for a rented nine-seater.

Ultimately, I negotiated a bargain price for it. Maybe I had overheard enough of Peter's phone conversations with local promoters in which he played hardball in getting the terms he wanted. With the charter line's representative on the other side of the table, I kept hammering for a lower price. He had brought out a bottle of gin as we began talking about the details of our lease, and after ninety minutes of bargaining—and boozing—he seemed willing to agree to just about anything.

"I'm not that familiar with your music," he said, "but we'd be mighty honored to have you use this plane."

At my insistence, he gave us 4,000 free miles and slashed $5,000 off the rental fee, although for that price, we had to do without a flight attendant. "That's fine," I told him. "We'd rather have the extra seat on the jet for ourselves."

In those final days before the tour's first concert, I also devoted much of my time to Led Zeppelin's security needs. The death threats on the band members had become a way of life during the previous swing through the U.S., but they were still hard to get used to. During the '72 tour, I sometimes felt like the band was an easy target up on the stage; if some kook had wanted to take a shot at one of them, it wouldn't have been that difficult. Whenever I'd hear a loud popping noise—it could just have been a balloon bursting—I'd cringe and quickly glance to make sure the band members were okay. Without a doubt, my job was becoming much more stressful.

Throughout that tour, I tried to find ways to ease my own anxieties about Zeppelin's security. At the band's invitation, I routinely played the congas during "Whole Lotta Love," which was a welcome diversion from the routine stresses, even if it was just for a few minutes.

One night at Madison Square Garden, just before I went onstage for "Whole Lotta Love," Jerry Greenberg, a vice president at Atlantic and a former drummer himself, told me how thrilled he would be to perform with Zeppelin on that song. "Well," I said, "if you want to play with 'em, promise to give me one hundred dollars, and you can do it! I'll give you the sticks, and you can go for it!"

Jerry didn't even hesitate. "It's a deal!" He took the stage during "Whole Lotta Love," and I resorted to one of the only other ways I knew to ease the tension—taking a snort of cocaine backstage.

That Madison Square Garden concert was one of the rare instances in which the fans clearly became a risk to the band in the midst of a performance. It was the first of two electrically charged shows at the Garden, and midway through the concert, about two dozen spirited members of the crowd pushed their way toward the stage and then leaped over the crash barriers. Our body-guards rushed to meet them head-on, either pushing them aside or disabling them with a well-aimed punch. As the mayhem escalated, some fans still in their seats started to panic. They began pushing their way toward the front of the stage, as if there were some type of haven there. The bodyguards were outmanned, and dozens of fans climbed onto the stage itself. There seemed to be no malicious intent on their part, but with their combined weight, a corner of the stage actually began to collapse.

While Zeppelin performed "The Battle of Evermore," Peter became fright-ened. "Get the band off the stage," he shouted, although they were just begin-ning to disperse on their own by that point. None of us knew how much more of the stage was going to buckle, and the concert ground to a complete halt. The houselights came on, and for the next fifteen minutes a construction crew feverishly went to work, trying to reinforce the stage. At the same time, the security forces mingled among the overenthusiastic crowd, hoping to re-store a sense of calm. The concert resumed, and there were no more incidents. But those were the kinds of things that kept me awake at night.

For much of our security needs on that tour, we relied on Bill Dautrich, a former Philadelphia cop. He recommended that we keep access to the band airtight. He would fly ahead of us from city to city, meeting with the chiefs of police to arrange for escorts for our limousine fleets to and from the airports and the concert halls. Bill worked for a company called Ogden Security in Boston, and he and the company had connections with the police departments in every major city in the country. "We speak the same language," Bill would say. "They'll give me just about anything I want."

For every concert, Dautrich planned the band's rapid exit after the last song. "When done right, the 'escape' should take less than a minute," Bill used to say. Every member of the band knew in advance the route he'd be taking from the stage to the limos at the end of each concert and which car was his. Jimmy, Robert, and Peter would duck into the head limo; at the same time, Bonzo, John Paul, and I would scramble into the second one. There would be a security man riding in the front passenger seat of each limo. The last of our three limousines would carry other important members of the "inner sanctum"—Steve Weiss, our lawyer, or, in later years, publicist/Swan Song president Danny Goldberg. Usually within just thirty seconds, the limos were moving, and when they hit the top of the ramp, the sirens would begin blaring, continuing for most of the ride back to the hotel or the airport.

The day after a concert in Winnipeg, we had nothing in particular planned. As we sat around the hotel, Peter was complaining about the idle time.

"Well," I said, "why don't we go on a boat ride? Don't they have boats on the Assiniboine River?"

Peter looked at me as if I had lost my marbles. "Richard," he said, "you're not arranging an outing for a bunch of Boy Scouts. Forget the boat ride. Get us some strippers!"

I opened the Yellow Pages and made some calls. An hour later, two strippers arrived at the hotel. By that time, room service had already delivered our order for sixty screwdrivers, a third of which were gone by the time the show began. "Even if the girls are ugly," I had told Bonzo, "we can get drunk and pretend they're not here."

The girls brought their own music and a few costume changes. Both of them were brunettes in their early twenties, one of whom was extremely thin while the other could have benefited from a ten-pound weight loss. "This is your party, guys," the skinny one said as she turned on the music. "Let us know what we can do to entertain you."

Within ten minutes, I was already bored. The girls were trying hard, but we had been entertained by strippers dozens of times before, and there wasn't anything particularly exciting about these bumps and grinds.

Finally, on the brink of dozing off, I strode into the bedroom, took off my own clothes, and put on some of the apparel the girls had brought with them—G-string, bra, negligee, garter belt, nylons. Truthfully, I looked great. Gypsy Rose Lee would have been jealous.

I came back into the living room and began to strip, egged on by the band. "You're fantastic," Robert shouted. "What moves! What incredible moves!"

The girls were astonished and sat down to watch the show. It took me five minutes and a lot of gyrating, grinding, bouncing, and prancing to get the clothes off. "These garter belts are murder!" I exclaimed.

The next day, Jimmy told me, "I think you better stick with managing tours. You almost made me ill dancing in that G-string!"

I took it as a compliment.

The strippers may have been a pleasant diversion, but Pagey found someone during that tour who quickly became a much more permanent fixture in his life. Her name was Lori Maddox—tall, willowy, very attractive, with dark hair, a dark complexion, an angelic face, beautiful brown eyes, and delicious, full lips.

Jimmy was still attached to Charlotte Martin, but he became infatuated with Lori the first time they met. Beep Fallon actually took the credit for bringing Lori into the Zeppelin touring entourage. About a year earlier, he had been in the States working with a band called Silverhead, whose lead singer was Michael Des Barres (at one time the husband of Pamela Des Barres). One afternoon, Beep was browsing through a magazine and spotted a picture of Lori, a teenage model whom he knew he had met a few months earlier, although he wasn't quite sure where. Beep eventually tracked her down and then showed Jimmy her picture. Pagey nearly started salivating. "She's magnificent," he said. "Give me her phone number."

Beep knew Pagey well enough that he figured Jimmy and Lori could be a perfect fit—and that the sparks wouldn't be dampened by the presence of Charlotte back in London. After all, in addition to Lori's alluring physical attributes, she was only fourteen years old. And Jimmy, who was twenty-eight at the time, still had a weakness for girls who were struggling with their first set of false eyelashes and wobbling on their first pair of high heels.

When we finally arrived in Los Angeles during the '72 tour, Jimmy called Lori, and when they initially met at the Hyatt House, Pagey could barely contain himself. She was better than her picture, he said. He claimed he felt some magnetism coming from her eyes, and when she smiled at him—well, this was a girl he found absolutely irresistible.

Immediately, the young teenager became a principal player in Jimmy's life, which didn't sit well with the dozens of groupies who would have given their push-up bras for a chance to spend time with him. Stories floated through the

L.A. clubs about Lori and Jimmy, catty stories from girls who were outraged that this fourteen-year-old somehow was living out all their own fantasies: "Have you heard that Jimmy found a junior high school girl to play around with?" . . . "My father wouldn't even let me look at boys until I was three years older than she is!" . . . "I'd like to see someone gouge her eyes out!"

There also were rumors that the other members of the band were angry at Jimmy over his courtship of this underage girl, which continued for most of the 1970s when we were in L.A. But that was hardly the case. As Bonzo quipped, "I'm just pissed off that Jimmy got her phone number before I did." There were plenty of teenage girls to go around, and Lori wasn't the only one willing to submit to Zeppelin's spell.

Anyway, Bonham added, there were a lot of other things he wanted to do in Los Angeles besides flirt with the girls. His fascination with cars, for instance, seemed to peak during drives between L.A. International and the Riot House.

One afternoon, our limos were heading up La Cienega to Sunset Boulevard. As we passed a dealership called Old Time Cars, Bonzo and Jimmy insisted that we stop. To them, the sight of vintage automobiles—Alfa Romeos, Bugattis, Pierce-Arrows—in the window were as alluring as a beautiful girl. Well, almost as alluring.

Pagey left the limo and strode directly to an immaculate, 1937 Cord Sportsman 812. It was dark blue, with white sidewall tires and headlights sunk into the body. In less than ten minutes, he said, "I've got to have it." The asking price was $17,000, which Jimmy negotiated down to $13,500. He had a deal.

Meanwhile, Peter had seen a black and blue Pierce Silver Arrow, one of the real luxury cars of the 1930s, that he decided was a "necessity." He began bargaining over the price while Bonzo was sliding in and out of the driver's seat of a 1928 Duesenberg Model A, complete with running boards and a horn guaranteed to give cardiac arrest to the fainthearted. "I've gotta have it, I've gotta have it." Bonzo sighed. The price tag, however, was $50,000, and he thought that was just too much. "If you come down to forty-five thousand, we can start talking," he told the salesman. When that didn't happen, Bonzo backed off. "Well, we'll be back next year. If I still want it, I'll bring the cash and drive it back to England!"

Both Jimmy and Peter closed their deals within an hour, the ultimate impulsive shopping spree. Peter told me to call Atlantic Records and have them send a messenger over with a check for the cars. Both automobiles were shipped to England later in the week.

When that North American tour ended in late July, most of the band quickly jetted back to London. But Jimmy wanted to stay behind. "If it's Lori," I told him, "why don't you invite her to come back to England with us?"

He turned to me with a disbelieving look. "Lori will be just fine in L.A.," he said. "I want to do some shopping. Let's spend a few days in New York."

We got a suite at the Waldorf-Astoria, and Jimmy began shopping for antiques and browsing through bookstores. Ultimately, I had to hire two additional limos just to transport his antiques to the airport for the flight home.

32

HEROIN

Peter Grant would sometimes wonder just how he got so lucky. Not only was he managing the world's top rock band, but it had been a relatively easy ride. Most Supergroups disbanded before they ever got any momentum going. But by late 1972, with Led Zeppelin celebrating their fourth anniversary, Peter often felt that they might go on forever.

"It's really amazing," he told me. "I really haven't had to spend any time trying to settle conflicts within the band or trying to kept one member or another from jumping ship. My biggest decisions are figuring out where to book them next."

Barely more than two months after we had returned home from the States, Peter had us out on the road again, this time returning to Japan for seven concerts in Tokyo, Osaka, Nagoya, and Kyoto. We played in some of the same venues as the 1971 trip—Budokan Hall in Tokyo, Kaikan Hall in Kyoto, and Osaka Festival Hall—but this time the sellouts were instantaneous. A single advertisement, a single mention on the radio, and the kids were lined up all the way to Mount Fuji.

During a short break in the Japan tour, we had scheduled some R&R in Hong Kong. We checked into the Mandarin Hotel, and Andrew Yu, a friend of Tats Nagashima, met us there and took us to a five-star restaurant. About midway through dinner, I cornered a young fellow whom Andrew had introduced us to and asked, "My friends and I would like some cocaine. Do you think you can get us some?"

He nodded his head, although since he didn't speak much English I wasn't sure whether he understood what I had said. Fifteen minutes later, however, he had returned and waved me into the kitchen. The entire band followed.

With the passage of time, Zeppelin continued to become more enamored with cocaine. Not that we had forsaken alcohol. But people were constantly offering us cocaine, and it seemed silly to say no. Bonzo used to talk about a cocaine rush that would travel from his nose to his brain, quicker than he could blink an eye. "It's fucking indescribable," he'd say with glazed eyes. When we wanted instant gratification, cocaine would become our drug of choice.

In the restaurant's kitchen, Andrew's friend asked, "Would you like some straws?" He handed one to each of us, then unrolled the white powder on the table. "Help yourself," he said, beaming proudly.

We each took a few snorts. Something, however, didn't feel right. I finally dipped my finger in the powder and took a taste. "Holy shit!" I shouted. "What is this stuff? It sure isn't coke!"

"Couldn't find any coke," our dealer announced. "So I brought you back heroin! Do you like it?"

Years earlier, I had had a similar experience; I had been given some heroin, although I thought it was cocaine. At that time, as now, the mere mention of the word "heroin" prompted images of down-and-out junkies injecting themselves in dark alleys. It wasn't the life I wanted.

This time, within minutes after snorting it, all of us started to feel terribly ill. Maybe some of our reactions were psychological, but everyone just wanted to get back to the hotel. "Are we gonna die?" Bonzo said. I don't think he was joking.

I had already lined up some hookers for us at the hotel, but we had lost interest in them. We just wanted to lie down. "Girls," I told them, "we'll have to catch up to you during our next trip to Hong Kong. We're all going to be very sick tonight." And we were.

Fortunately, by the next day we all felt back to normal. It had been a frightening experience, but we seemed to have recovered. Another of Andrew's friends had arranged a boating trip for us that afternoon, and it seemed like a healthier pursuit than what we had undergone the previous night. I figured the fresh air would do us good.

The cruiser left from Victoria Harbor, but after just fifteen minutes in the bay, the captain seemed terribly nervous. Finally, he shut off the engine and announced, "There's a leak in the boat, and we're taking on water."

Taking on water!

At least initially it was a toss-up as to who was panicking the most. We all began waving frantically for other boats to come to our rescue. After a couple of minutes, Jimmy was almost hysterical. "I can't swim," he whined. "If we have to go overboard, someone's going to have to help me paddle to shore."

There was silence for a moment. "Don't look at me," John Paul said. "I can't swim, either."

Peter finally volunteered me for an assignment. "You're the best swimmer here, Cole. Why don't you swim to shore and get some help?"

"Fuck you!" I shouted. "I'm not swimming in there. What if there are sharks?"

Fortunately, another boat began to approach us.

"Don't get too excited," the captain told Robert as it got closer. "It's just a Chinese junk that's been turned into a floating market. He doesn't want to rescue us. He wants to sell us oranges!"

About ten minutes later, our captain finally got the bilge pump working and was able to start removing the water from the ship's interior. The cruiser began to limp to shore, with none of us even getting our socks wet.

There was a young blonde with an Australian accent aboard the cruiser whom I had noticed smiling at me through most of the trip. One of the crew members told me she was a friend of the captain's, but a lot more of her attention was directed my way. Finally, as the boat headed for land, she approached me. "You don't remember me, do you?" she said with a grin. "In Sydney earlier this year, you gave me a lift. And when you got mad at me, you shoved me out onto the street."

"Oh, my God, was that you?"

"No hard feelings," she said. "I had to walk back to the city, but I needed the exercise."

Then she pulled a small plastic bag out of her purse. "Would you like to try some of this?"

It looked like heroin. As sick as I had been the night before, my first instinct was to grab it and toss it overboard. But there was something about the sight of drugs—and a pretty woman—that I found seductive. I decided to take my chances with both. We went to the back of the boat and shared a few snorts.

Later that afternoon, Zeppelin had to catch a plane back to Japan. By that time, I was starting to feel the full effects of the heroin. As a real novice with this drug, I hadn't known quite what to expect. But this time, more than anything, I was becoming incredibly anxious—even paranoid—as we waited for the inspection of our bags at the airport.

"What's wrong with you, Richard?" Jimmy whispered as we stood in line. "You're sweating like a pig. You don't have anything on you, do you?"

"Hell, no," I said. "I'm not carrying anything. I just have this feeling that everybody is watching me. I can't explain it."

By the time we got on the plane, I was hyperventilating and feeling completely dehydrated. "Can we get some drinks?" I said to a stewardess after we sat down. I was feeling desperate for something, even just a glass of water.

"You'll have to wait until the plane takes off," she advised us.

"Fuck that!" I told Jimmy. I was breathing heavily as I walked over to the liquor locker, which they had padlocked shut. I picked up an empty food cart and began smashing it on the lock until I had broken it open. Passengers were looking on, wondering if they were getting onto a flight destined for some kind of insane asylum.

I helped myself to a couple of beers and sat down again. "Sorry if I embarrassed anyone," I said to Jimmy. "Sometimes my thirst just can't wait." If I had been smart, that was the day I should have sworn off heroin for good.

After the Japanese tour, we decided to make another attempt at entering Thailand. Our hair was just as long as it had been the previous trip when we were turned away at the airport, but this time we had an important ally working on our behalf: The King of Thailand. A few days earlier in Hong Kong, I had complained to Andrew Yu about the inhospitality we had encountered in Bangkok. "Don't worry," he said with an air of confidence. "I know the King of Thailand personally. I'll get him to write a letter that you can show to the customs officials. They wouldn't dare turn you away."

It's nice to know people in high places.

At our hotel in Osaka, we received a message from Andrew that when we changed planes in Hong Kong on the way to Bangkok, a courier carrying the King's letter would meet our plane. As promised, the letter was there waiting for us, and once Robert, Jimmy, roadie Ray Thomas, and I reached Thailand, we were escorted through customs with no questions asked. For the next three days, we got reacquainted with the decadence of Thailand.

From Bangkok, we flew to Bombay, where Jimmy and Robert had made arrangements to do some experimental recording. Jimmy had brought with him a Stellavox quadriphonic field recorder that was several generations more sophisticated than anything the Indians had ever seen. The Stellavox had been custom-made to Jimmy's specifications in Switzerland, and it produced a higher-quality sound than all of the eight-track studios in Bombay combined. Several of the Indian musicians offered to buy it, but it wasn't for sale.

Bombay's top musicians, including members of the city's symphony orchestra, were invited to participate in the recording session. Robert, Jimmy, and their Indian colleagues recorded raga-style renditions of some early Zeppelin songs, including "Friends" and "Four Sticks." There were never any plans to release these recordings, and when the overall quality of the sessions did not rise to Jimmy's perfectionist standards, there were no serious thoughts of changing those plans.

Once we were back in England, Jimmy put the tapes from the Bombay recording sessions in storage at his house. He had recently bought a new home in rural Sussex, a majestic manor called Plumpton Place. Bidding good-bye to the Thames, he had moved all his belongings—including his prized antiques and prized girlfriend, Charlotte Martin—into the new house. There were moats, terraces, and three interconnected lakes on the fifty-acre property, which had been designed by Sir Edwin Lutyens. Most important to Jimmy, there was room in the house for a recording studio. He spent extravagantly to furnish the home, adding more antiques, as well as various items from our tours to the Far East, including Buddhas and the flying horse from Thailand whose wings extended ten feet to either side and which might have become airborne if it had been outdoors when the night breezes turned to gusts.

John Paul spent the downtime after the Far Eastern tour with his wife and daughters at their home on a private estate in Northern London. It was a lovely house built in the 1920s, a cozy place that was perfect for a guy like John Paul, who was really just a homebody at heart. He remodeled it for his own needs, of course, adding a recording studio in which he spent an increasing amount of time. It felt so comfortable that he would have been quite content to rarely, if ever, leave home.

Robert retreated to his three-acre sheep ranch near Kidderminster, where he was clearly enthralled with his new baby, who was now six months old. When Robert first bought the ranch, the house on it looked as though it could have been on the brink of condemnation. But he and Maureen put their hearts into rebuilding and renovating it and furnishing it with lovely old English furniture.

Not far away, Bonzo was finding peace on his ranch in West Hagley, Worcestershire, although before long he bought a new, 100-acre spread called Old Hyde Farm. Bonzo rebuilt the existing structures there from the ground up, giving special attention to a game room, with a pool table as its centerpiece. He also began breeding and raising white-faced Hereford cattle, which immediately became a moneymaking enterprise for him as well as a source of real pride.

For a guy who made his living banging away at drumskins, I was amazed at the affection Bonzo showed for the cattle. "It's different from playing music, of course," he told me, "but I feel some of the same sense of accomplishment with what I've done with these bulls."

We were once on a commercial flight with Bill Wyman of the Rolling Stones, who was accompanied by his girlfriend, Astrid. During the flight, Bill,

Bonzo, and I were talking about Bonham's Hereford bulls, which had just swept the top prizes at a local competition. "I love those bulls, just getting up in the morning and seeing them," said John, beaming with pride like a father talking about his children. On the plane, he was wearing overalls and a wide-brimmed hat that any farmer could have put to use as a daytime shield from the sun.

A few minutes later, Bonham went to use the bathroom and Astrid turned to me and asked, "Why did you guys bring that farmer with you?" She obviously didn't recognize Bonzo. "All he talks about is those damn bulls! Does he work on one of the boys' estates?"

"Not exactly," I said, breaking the news as gently as possible. "That's our drummer! That's John Bonham!"

She seemed genuinely surprised. And embarrassed. Led Zeppelin were more than musicians, although it was hard for most people to see beyond their music.

I had always felt that, more than the others, Jimmy was much too complex an individual to be living for music alone. I knew that his dabbling in the occult continued, although he still kept that side of his life very private. On occasion, he would mention the name Aleister Crowley to me. Crowley had been a part poet, part magician, part mountain climber who conducted rituals in black magic, many at his "satanic temple" on Fulham Road. Crowley had been a real mystery to people.

I occasionally became Jimmy's unofficial chauffeur on some of his Crowley shopping sprees. Despite Pagey's love of automobiles—over the years, he owned cars like a Bentley, an Austin Champ Army Jeep, a Cord Sportsman, and an old Mercedes with running boards—he never had a driver's license ("I just never bothered to get one," he said). So several times he would call me and say, "Richard, I'm in the mood to go shopping for some Crowley artifacts." We'd drive from auction houses to rare-book showrooms, where Jimmy would buy Crowley manuscripts or other belongings (hats, paintings, clothes).

"What is it about this chap Crowley that fascinates you?" I asked Jimmy on one of our outings.

"The guy was really quite remarkable," Jimmy said. "Someday we'll talk about it, Richard."

But we never did. If the public felt there was a certain mystery surrounding Led Zeppelin, they weren't alone. As close as I was to them, I sometimes felt there was something within Jimmy that he never let anyone see. Particularly when it came to Pagey's preoccupation with Crowley, séances, and black magic, I had a lot of unanswered questions.

33

HOUSES OF
THE HOLY

It got to be painfully monotonous. No matter where Led Zeppelin performed, no matter how much advance planning we had done, it seemed like security became an overriding, nerve-racking concern. In the later months of 1972 and into 1973, the band made swings through Britain and Europe, performing at sites like Oxford's New Theatre and the Liverpool Empire and venues in Sweden, Norway, Holland, Belgium, Germany, Austria, and France. In France in particular, I began to wonder whether I'd ever have peace of mind again at a concert.

We had our worst experience in Lyon, where the security was simply atrocious. The concert was at a basketball stadium that seated 12,000. But hours before the performance, dozens of kids had already broken into the arena and were roaming through the stands. Peter warned me, "If it's necessary, you and the roadies are going to have to take matters into your own hands."

Shortly after the show began, that's exactly what happened. Some fans began throwing debris, including empty bottles, from the highest deck of seats. One of the bottles sailed directly toward the band and shattered on the stage. Slivers of glass exploded onto Bonzo and his drums.

That was all I needed to see. I looked up toward the stands, located the culprits, and then sprinted up to the top deck. A couple of our crew members followed me. We grabbed the thugs, dragged them into the aisle, and roughed them up. I think those fellas bore the brunt of years of anxiety and frustration that I had felt about the band's safety. As we tossed them out of the stadium, one of them bleeding from a cut on his forehead, I realized that force seemed to be the only option that got the message across to fans who were intent on causing trouble. Touring was stressful enough without the added concerns of whether we were going to get through each concert without any harm to the band members.

After a show in Nantes, we decided to unwind by doing some serious drinking. The band, the roadies, and a few other hangers-on—sixteen of us in all—crammed into a rented Volvo. We were literally hanging out the windows and the sunroof, with Benoit Gautier, who worked for Atlantic Records in Paris, at the wheel much of the time. It was a death-defying ride to the watering hole, and as all of us continued to shift postures, trying to find a reasonably comfortable position, we kicked in the dashboard and shredded the upholstery. Bonham and I were standing up in the trunk, leaning forward and literally pulling the sunroof off its hinges.

Before we reached the bar, a cop spotted our car, with bodies extending out of every opening, and he pulled us over. He shook his head in disbelief and finally said in French, "I'm going to arrest all of you. You all have alcohol on your breath."

"Alcohol!" Bonzo shouted. "We haven't even started partying yet. If you really want a good reason to arrest us, let us get in a few hours of drinking."

We were put into cells, and at my request, we began singing British drinking songs, doing our best to drive the cops nuts. In the meantime, realizing that there really weren't any charges that could be pressed against us, the police captain called our hotel and asked the desk clerk if we were registered there.

"They sure are," the clerk said. "But we don't want them back. The doors on their floors are all messed up, and someone threw a TV out the window!"

The cop acted as though he hadn't heard a word. "Well, we've had enough of them here. We're sending them back to your hotel. Good luck!"

A few minutes later, we were released and driven in police cars to the hotel. Once the cops were out of sight, we walked to a bar down the street and spent the rest of the night there.

In March 1973, Led Zeppelin's fifth album was finally released. It had been long delayed by endless problems with the cover artwork. Zeppelin kept looking at the prototypes coming out of the print shop and repeatedly rejected and sent them back, usually because of unacceptable, untrue, overly bright colors. Jimmy worried that the lavish colors on the album jacket would make it look like a cosmetics advertisement in a fashion magazine.

The album was called *Houses of the Holy*, an apparent reference to the spiritual aura that the band romanticized as hovering over its concert halls and audiences. Again, Zeppelin's name did not appear on the album cover. The jacket instead featured young, blond, naked children climbing up a boulder-filled mountainside. Ironically, the title song was saved for the band's next album, *Physical Graffiti*, which was not released until 1975.

The band was quite proud of *Houses of the Holy*. Five albums and more than four years down the road, they had a strong enough belief in themselves as artists to go in whatever new directions their musical instincts drew them. Firmly entrenched at the top of the rock music world, the band was expected by many fans to dig in and keep giving the public more of the same. But in *Houses of the Holy*, Led Zeppelin showed that they were willing to explore new ideas in their evolution as musicians, even if they were risky.

In "The Rain Song," John Paul single-handedly created a lush orchestration on his Mellotron that sounded as though it came from an entire symphony orchestra. "No Quarter" showed their flare for the mysterious and the dramatic. And John Bonham the songwriter was showcased on "The Ocean"; he received credit as a primary writer on the tune.

Maybe the band felt they were growing as musicians, but the critics hadn't evolved at all. Shortly after *Houses of the Holy* reached the record stores, *Rolling Stone* unleashed a savage attack upon it. Gordon Fletcher called it "one of the dullest and most confusing albums I've heard this year."

With a big American tour set to begin in May, Zeppelin didn't want to be crushed by a hostile press at every stop in the U.S. Beep Fallon was no longer working for the band, and Peter contemplated hiring a top-flight U.S. public relations firm with major media contacts to try to turn things around with the press. "The Stones are going to be touring in America at the same time as us," Peter told me. "If we don't actively go after some high visibility, the Stones will annihilate us in terms of publicity, even though we'll outdraw them at the box office."

The Stones consistently got much more—and much better—publicity than Led Zeppelin, and that grated on the egos of the band. Of course, the Stones hung out with a different crowd than us, drawn to celebrities like Truman Capote, Andy Warhol, and Lee Radziwill. Jagger & Company were the darlings of the social register, and even though Mick had a devilish image, he seemed like a choirboy next to the way the media had portrayed Led Zeppelin.

We were perfectly content to camp out relatively anonymously at local bars and strip joints, but those weren't the kinds of social activities that got the publicity we felt we needed. For the most part, the press still treated us as though we were plotting World War III.

So Peter made the initial contacts with Solters, Roskin, and Sabinson, one of the most prestigious, high-powered, and expensive PR companies in the U.S. Peter talked to Lee Solters, a straitlaced, middle-aged man who made a very nice living representing some of Hollywood's biggest stars. "We're on the final leg of a tour through France," Peter explained. "I'd like you to fly over to meet the band. Despite their image, I think you'll find them to be quite civil, quite bright young men."

Solters boarded a plane for that initial meeting with Peter and the band at the George V Hotel in Paris. He brought with him Danny Goldberg, who was in charge of the firm's rock 'n' roll division and who would be handling the Zeppelin account.

Goldberg was twenty-two years old, a tall, congenial, articulate fellow with his long hair usually tied in a ponytail. He wore his shirttails untucked over a pair of stylish, neatly pressed blue jeans. As an adolescent, he had attended a prestigious New York City prep school and then had dropped out of the University of California, Berkeley. Ironically, he had once written reviews for *Rolling Stone*, one of Zeppelin's biggest nemeses.

At that first meeting with the band, Solters suggested that Led Zeppelin needed a media face-lift. "Your music is taking a backseat to a lot of negative publicity about your offstage life, and that offstage image will require some rehabilitation," Solters pontificated. "Because you've shied away from most interviews for so long, all the press has to go on are the rumors about your maniacal behavior. We've got to mainstream you and change that outlaw image. We also have to let the population at large know that you're accomplished musicians, not savages."

They discussed nurturing a different relationship with the press. They talked about doing more interviews, although only carefully selected ones. They kicked around the idea of some benefit concerts. By the end of the meeting, Zeppelin made a handshake agreement to bring the PR firm on board, beginning with the American tour.

The band took an immediate liking to Danny Goldberg. "Everything just feels right with him," John Paul said. When Danny's hair wasn't bound in a ponytail, it was longer than any of ours. So within days, the band had nicknamed him "Goldilocks." He was a vegetarian, which won points with Jimmy, although he got some curious stares when he told us that he also stayed away from drugs and even cigarettes.

Zeppelin quickly developed a trust of Danny's media instincts and press prowess. When he arranged an interview, the band did it, no questions asked. When he recommended a press reception before or after certain concerts, they almost never said no.

As Peter and Danny ironed out a final strategy for the upcoming American invasion, Zeppelin themselves congregated in Shepperton Studios for rehearsals, mostly working on bringing songs from *Houses of the Holy* to the stage. Shepperton was owned by the Who, and it had facilities so the band could work out its lighting for the concert tour while also refining its music. I had arranged for Showco in Dallas to fly its two best technicians to London to review the final lighting and sound arrangements with the band and test them out at Shepperton. For this tour, the band was not going to leave much to chance.

Before we departed for the States, Danny Goldberg had planted a story in *Rolling Stone* calling the upcoming tour the "biggest and most profitable rock and roll tour in the history of the United States." The tour was projected to gross more than $5 million, which exceeded the claims made by Alice Cooper that he would take in $4.5 million for his current tour.

"By the end of this tour, everyone's going to say that Zeppelin is second to none," Danny promised.

We took him at his word.

"IT DOESN'T
GET ANY
BETTER"

A tangerine-colored sun lurked playfully behind a low-lying curtain of white clouds, hovering over Atlanta Stadium in Atlanta. As the sun gradually dipped toward the horizon, Jimmy Page stood out on the balcony of his hotel suite, peering into the distance. He wore faded jeans and a coal-black T-shirt and was holding a half-filled glass of red wine as he leaned against the rail. Less than a mile away, well within sight from his high-rise vantage point, he could see thousands—actually tens of thousands—of cars and people making the pilgrimage to Atlanta Stadium.

That wasn't an unusual sight around the ballpark in May 1973. But there was no baseball game that night in Atlanta. This was a night for Led Zeppelin to bring America to its knees.

As the traffic congestion around the stadium became worse, Jimmy marveled at the sight. Cars were sandwiched onto streets and highways, impatiently inching their way toward the stadium parking lots. Mustangs and Camaros, Jeeps and Volkswagens, each with its dashboard radio blaring, each filled with young people eager for a night of high-decibel music.

Since 1968, Zeppelin had performed more than 400 concerts worldwide. But for the band, this was different. This was Zeppelin's largest American concert ever, the first date on a grueling thirty-three-city, thirty-eight-concert tour.

Peter Grant was talking big numbers—the grosses of perhaps $5 million for this tour alone would add to coffers making this a $30 million year for the band, including album sales. Judging by the rush for tickets in Atlanta—a sell-out of 49,200 tickets just four hours after they had gone on sale in April—Peter was probably right on target. There were another 56,000 expected at Tampa Stadium . . . 49,000 at San Francisco's Kezar Stadium . . . 47,000 in Pittsburgh's Three Rivers Stadium. The list went on and on.

John Paul generally was pretty laid back, not prone to exaggeration or overstatement. But even he sensed that this trip to America would be unique. "This is going to be the tour that knocks America out," he had predicted on the flight over. And if the music alone didn't overwhelm the country, then maybe the lasers, smoke generators, pyrotechnics, and spinning mirrors would. We had hired a crew of thirty-three technicians and stagehands just to provide support, making sure that the special effects and the music came together on cue.

Finally, just an hour away from that Atlanta concert—as long-haired, bell-bottomed fans jostled their way into the stadium—the reasons for the hard work became apparent. "It's an absolutely incredible sight," Jimmy said as he took another sip of wine. Pagey was beyond the point of experiencing stage fright, but for the first time in quite a while he felt a sense of nervous anticipation. A lot, he believed, was riding on this tour.

Houses of the Holy was climbing fast on the record charts. But the band, whose yearning for critical acclaim had ebbed and flowed over the years, wanted to prove a point to the media and show them just how powerful and popular a musical influence they had become. And, of course, they had arrived better armed than usual, with Danny Goldberg and his publicity machine on board.

I had flown into Atlanta two days before the band to meet with Tom Hulett, the Concerts West promoter in the Southeast. In his office, I took out a notepad and sketched the specifications for the Friday night concert . . . the size of the stage (eighty feet by thirty-five feet) that we'd need . . . the height of the crash barriers (ten feet) that would keep zealous fans from overrunning the stage . . . the distance between the stage and the barriers (fifteen feet) . . . the precise location of the four towers that would support speakers powerful enough to stun the average eardrum into submission . . . and the placement of the Super-Trooper spotlights that could light up half the state of Georgia. Everything was put in writing.

On May 3, the night before the concert, the band was scheduled to fly into Atlanta. I had joined them in Miami and sensed the nervous tension as we prepared to board the flight.

Once we were at the Atlanta Hilton, we kept room service busy well into the night. With less than twenty-four hours until the Atlanta Stadium concert, we ordered everything from champagne to Irish coffee to midnight snacks. Then, before any of us could feel either anxiety or boredom, Bonham took matters into his own hands. I had told him that the technicians who would operate the lasers the next day had stored the equipment in their hotel rooms. And Bonham just couldn't contain himself. "Get those fucking lasers in here, Richard. Let's see what kind of chaos we can create."

Within minutes, with the help of the technicians, we were shining the red and green beams from our balcony onto the sidewalk below. A few pedestrians taking late-night strolls were startled by the bombardments of light that seemed to be coming from the heavens.

"The Martians have landed!" Bonham screamed out into the night. "Watch out for the Martians!" He was laughing so hard that, for him, the tour was already a success. More than four years into the history of Led Zeppelin, Bonham hadn't lost any of his childlike qualities.

By early afternoon the next day, the crew had left for the stadium to set up the lights, test the microphones, and plug in and tune the instruments. Mick Hinton assembled Bonham's drums. Ray Thomas checked Jimmy's guitar, and Brian Condliffe adjusted John Paul's Mellotron, an instrument that would be part of a Zeppelin concert for the first time. Benji Le Fevre sat at the special effects control board, running over in his own mind his responsibilities that night.

Despite my best-laid plans, the stage area wasn't constructed to specifications. The crash barrier in front of the stage had been built almost three feet too high, which might have made the security forces feel more confident, but it also would impair the view of the fans closest to the stage. I decided not to tell the band about it; at that point, it was too late to make any changes anyway.

At seven-fifteen, the limousines and police escorts had arrived downstairs. I rounded up the band, we rode the elevator down to the basement parking lot, and then moved quickly to the waiting limos. As soon as the doors slammed, the procession took off, accelerating to about forty miles per hour, with emergency lights on the police motorcycles flashing. The police had stopped traffic along our route as though we were part of a presidential motorcade. In less than five minutes, we were at the performers' entrance of the stadium, dashing for the home-team dressing room, escorted by half a dozen security men.

Even from underneath the stadium—even before the concert had started— the crowd was incredibly loud. With their enthusiasm building in intensity, the fans were already clapping, cheering, and stomping their feet.

Although Zeppelin had performed together hundreds of times, Robert described butterflies fluttering violently through his stomach. Everyone, in fact, seemed a little more strained than usual. And until Bonham hit that first drumskin and Robert warbled his first note, tension just came with the territory.

Finally, the stadium lights dimmed. The band weaved its way onto the stage. Next, with everyone in position, Bonham lifted his sticks and crashed them into the drums. Spotlights illuminated the stage. The first notes of "Rock and Roll" exploded into the Atlanta night.

As Zeppelin began to play, they saw people everywhere they looked. With "festival seating," thousands of fans had swarmed onto the field itself, packed as close to the outfield stage as possible. Even more were in the stands, on every level, down every aisle. They were on their feet, shrieking, frolicking, applauding, laughing. The noise became almost deafening. Throughout the stadium, flashbulbs burst like hundreds of fireflies that appeared and then vanished in an instant.

From backstage, Danny Goldberg thought, "If this is the sign of things to come, my job might be easier than I thought."

For three hours, neither the band nor the crowd eased up. Robert strutted across the stage, chased by white spotlights that turned red, then orange, then yellow. He held the microphone just inches from his mouth, sometimes even resting it on his lower lip. As songs ended and the crowd roared its approval, Robert extended his hand-held microphone forward, aiming it toward the crowd as if to bless them and recycle their energy through the enormous speakers.

As Jimmy played, he danced on the balls of his feet, whipping and wheeling his weight from side to side. At times, he would raise his right knee, balancing his Les Paul guitar on his thigh as he picked the strings with blinding speed, making the music sing with every bit of emotion he could draw out of himself and his instrument.

John Paul, with his page-boy haircut, was a sharp contrast to his more active mates. Wearing a kaleidoscopic-colored jacket with oversized hearts sewn to the sleeves, he was welded to the keyboards for much of the show, content to let Jimmy and Robert enjoy most of the attention. Bonham, on the other hand, was a casebook study of hyperkinetic energy. His lips were moving almost constantly, not mouthing lyrics from behind his drooping mustache, but seemingly involved in self-talk, as if urging himself to find just a little more energy, to play with even a little more precision, as he lunged between drums and cymbals. In the brief interlude between each song, he would catch his breath and wipe his sweaty palms on his jeans.

At the beginning of "No Quarter," dry ice released a thick bank of fog that quickly enveloped the stage—floating, bubbling, seeping, drifting into the crowd. As John Paul's Mellotron created an ethereal mood, Jimmy emerged from the haze, followed by Robert. With bracelets decorating his wrists,

Robert positioned his hands on his hips, then extended his fingers and projected his voice skyward.

The crowd went berserk. Green lasers soared into and seared through the night sky.

From there, the band moved into "Dazed and Confused," and the remaining special effects were unleashed. Smoke bombs exploded. Cannons burst. Lasers formed rainbow patterns that could take your breath away, if you still had any left.

In the wings to the left of the stage, Peter was shaking his head in disbelief. "It doesn't get any better," he said.

Three hours after it started, after four encores and screams pleading for even more, the band exited from the stage and raced into the idling limousines. They were absolutely euphoric as the cars accelerated, surrounded by motorcycle policemen who cleared a path from the stadium grounds.

"We showed 'em!" exclaimed Robert, referring to the critics. "Whew, what a night!"

Peter couldn't contain his excitement either. "We're the biggest thing to hit Atlanta since *Gone With the Wind!*"

Thanks to the sellout crowd, the band was $250,000 richer than they had been at the start of the day. But that was only the beginning. The crowd at Tampa Stadium the next night—56,000 people—shattered the single concert attendance record set by the Beatles at Shea Stadium in 1965, where they had been supported by several opening acts. That Beatles' concert had drawn 55,000 people and had grossed $300,000; Zeppelin's outdoor festival in Tampa grossed nearly $310,000.

There was reason to celebrate, and for Led Zeppelin, the celebrating began back at the Atlanta Hilton. Bonham ordered two Brandy Alexanders from room service to start, and when they arrived, he told the valet, "You better bring us up four more."

The first two were literally gone within seconds, and when the tray of four arrived, Bonzo suggested, "Bring us up a pitcher as soon as you can." On the valet's next trip, John's instructions were, "You better bring us two more pitchers."

Before long, Bonham and I were each drinking Brandy Alexanders right out of the pitcher. An excess of alcohol would be as much a part of this tour as it ever had been for us. Some things with Led Zeppelin never changed.

GAY BARS AND DUDE RANCHES

With the success of the opening concert, Led Zeppelin settled into a comfortable groove as the 1973 tour continued. More than in the last two American tours, the band ventured out, socializing at local clubs, drinking at nearby bars. The security risks were probably no fewer than they had been in the past. In fact, death threats surfaced almost from our first hours in America. But the band members discussed the issue and felt that *they* should call the shots and control their own actions, not the kooks who were making the crank calls. We often had a bodyguard with us on those late-night expeditions, so the band felt they had taken reasonable steps to ensure their well-being.

In New Orleans, we visited half a dozen local clubs, mostly in the French Quarter, where we created our own Mardi Gras parade down Bourbon Street, hopping from the Déjà Vu to the Ivanhoe to Fat City. We spent the most time in gay bars, where we found some of the same kind of decadence and bravado we had seen in Sydney the previous year. The New Orleans drag queens always seemed to be having much more fun than the people we'd meet in straight clubs.

As much as for any other reason, we went to gay bars because people just didn't disturb us there and we could concentrate on the alcohol. Danny Goldberg wasn't that enamored with our choice of night spots, but we also loved shocking people, and there was no better place to do that than a bar where it was often only us and a few transvestites!

One night in New Orleans, Bonham and I got so smashed that we literally couldn't remember what day it was. It was reminiscent of blackouts that Keith Moon had suffered years ago when I toured with the Who.

In the midst of a drinking binge, Bonzo suddenly began to panic and exclaimed, "Cole, what time do we go on? Are we onstage tonight?"

"Wait," I said, giving myself a moment to collect my own thoughts. "I don't think so. Not until tomorrow."

"Well, what did we do yesterday?"

I had no idea. "Maybe we were here drinking most of the day. We don't have to work until tomorrow, Bonzo. I'm pretty sure of that. Have another drink."

In a more sober moment, I would have been disturbed by that kind of disorientation. The booze was taking a toll, but I was rarely clearheaded enough to recognize it.

One night, John Paul was chatting with a couple of drag queens in a New Orleans bar. The queens were flirting endlessly with him as if they had found their "catch" for the evening. One of the "girls" eventually ended up with Jonesy in his room back at the Royal Orleans. It seems they were smoking a joint or two. The joint suddenly started the bed on fire, and within minutes sirens were blaring and firemen were tearing down the doors and taking their axes to the place.

Later, Jonesy insisted that he hadn't known the transvestite was a man. He looked sincere during his explanation, but no matter what the truth really was, we knew we had caught him in a rather embarrassing situation. "We're not going to let Jonesy forget about this one for a *long* time," I told Robert.

After Louisiana, we decided to look for less claustrophobic living accommodations when we reached Texas. On short notice, I rented a dude ranch outside Dallas, which had a private airstrip a mile away so we could easily get to and from shows in Houston, Dallas, Fort Worth, and San Antonio. We invited a few girls to stay with us at the ranch, and it was great fun. There was horseback riding and a swimming pool. We didn't ever want to leave.

One evening when we flew out to a concert in San Antonio, we left behind one of our bodyguards, Willy Vaccar, who wasn't feeling well. When we returned early the next morning, Willy was waiting for us on the steps of the house, and he was actually trembling. "The guy who owns this ranch has gone fucking mad," he exclaimed.

"What do you mean?" Peter said.

"He came into the house waving a Bible, ranting and raving about the terrible things we're doing here."

Sure enough, the owner—an elderly chap named Jim—showed up a few minutes later wearing an enormous Stetson hat, making all kinds of threats and pointing a shotgun at us through the darkness. He definitely lacked the stability you'd want in someone with his finger on the trigger.

"I don't like having you boys on my ranch!" he said in a slow Texan drawl. "You've got girls here, too, don't ya?"

I was pissed off. "You bet we do. We paid for this place. We can use it any way we want!"

"Sorry, boys! I want you OUT!"

He disappeared, and fifteen minutes later we had other visitors. The local sheriff and his deputy drove up in a patrol car. They ambled toward the front of the house. The sheriff must have been at least seventy years old. He wore house slippers and was armed with a tiny silver pistol with a pearl handle. His partner was a Gomer Pyle look-alike. They were quite a sight.

The sheriff turned to the owner of the ranch, who also had returned by then. "Jim, are you having trouble with these gents?" the sheriff asked him.

In the next few minutes, we did our best to explain our side of the story. The sheriff had trouble deciding quite what to do. Then he finally told us, "You guys better just go to bed. If there's any more trouble here tonight, I'll come back and lock you all up. We'll deal with this whole situation tomorrow."

At midmorning, Peter made a phone call to the promoters we were working with in Texas, who told him that they had overlooked sending a check to Jim. Since Jim hadn't been paid, his anger and erratic behavior suddenly became a bit more understandable.

"Why don't we get the hell out of here?" I asked the band. "Who knows what these guys are gonna do next!" We began to prepare to leave, whereupon Jim returned, standing outside waiting for us.

"I don't want you fucking me around!" he screamed. He threw a beer can into the air and fired his shotgun at it. He missed.

Peter turned to me and said, "Shit! This guy's crazy! He might've missed the fucking can, but he sure as hell ain't gonna miss me!"

Jim ran down to the gate and locked it, apparently so we couldn't leave without paying. I followed him and frantically tried to pry the gate open. But as I did, he raised his rifle and threatened to shoot me. He ordered me back into the house.

During all of this, John Paul was hiding in the bathroom, frightened that bullets were about to start flying. Robert, meanwhile, was trying his best to take things in stride, complaining that he needed a cup of tea before we departed, that he couldn't do anything until he had his hot morning beverage.

Finally, we rounded up the girls and all of us piled into our rented station wagons. I was behind the wheel of the lead car and pressed the accelerator to the floor, aiming it directly at the locked gate. I braced myself and could feel my heart rate speed up. When the car slammed into the gate, the frame shattered. We were free.

We thundered down the highway, liberally exceeding the speed limit. Expecting trouble, I had contacted our pilot two hours earlier and had him park our chartered plane at Love Field rather than at the private airstrip. As we sped toward the airport, we caught a glimpse of the sheriff and his posse of cars with their sirens wailing headed in the opposite direction back to the airstrip where they thought they could find us. We never again saw Jim and the sheriff, but I presume we hadn't won them over as Led Zeppelin fans.

CALIFORNIA BOUND

By the time the '73 tour reached Los Angeles in late May, *Houses of the Holy* had become the Number 1-selling album in the U.S. That left the entire band feeling almost giddy with excitement. Virtually everything was going our way in the tour thus far. We felt invincible.

But literally minutes after our chartered fan-jet landed at Los Angeles International, and we moved onto the airport tarmac, the mood changed. Fans had lined the fence as our plane landed, and Jimmy walked over to shake hands and sign autographs. "Give me ten minutes and then we'll be on our way," he told me. Pagey reached over and through the fence, making contact with the fans. But as he did, he caught a finger on a protruding wire and quickly pulled away. In the process, he somehow sprained the finger.

"Oh, shit!" he shouted, as much in anger as in pain. He turned and walked to the limo with his left hand in a contorted position. "I think I'm in trouble," he said as he slid into the car. He slumped down in the seat, with an exasperated look on his face.

Within an hour, Jimmy was being examined by a doctor. They concluded that he just couldn't effectively maneuver that finger on the neck of the guitar. "The best medicine for this kind of injury is rest," the doctor recommended.

Jimmy was incapacitated, at least for the next day or two. We really had no choice but to do some quick rescheduling. One of our dates at the L.A. Forum was pushed ahead four days.

We were all upset by Jimmy's accident. However, by May 31—John Bonham's twenty-fifth birthday—Jimmy insisted that we not let his injury interfere with some celebrating. That was the night of the first Forum show, and after the concert the general manager of an FM radio station in L.A. hosted a party for Bonzo at his house in the hills above Hollywood with the help of Tony Mandich of Atlantic Records and New York FM jock J. J. Jackson. Bonzo showed up wearing swimming trunks and a T-shirt. George Harrison and his wife, Patti, were there, too.

George had seen the Forum show and seemed intrigued with Led Zeppelin. He had once talked to me about coming to see the band perform at Madison Square Garden and suggested that he "pop in during intermission."

"Well," I told him, "Zeppelin doesn't take an intermission."

George was puzzled. "How long do they play?"

"Most shows run close to three hours. Never less than two and a half."

"Holy shit!" he said, letting those numbers sink in for a moment. "With the Beatles, we were contracted to play thirty minutes max! Usually, we were off the stage and gone within fifteen!"

Harrison felt there was something special about Led Zeppelin. So when Bonham wanted his picture taken with George, the former Beatle was flattered—but he was also a little hesitant. After all, he knew about Zeppelin's reputation for practical jokes and was wary that Bonham might have something else planned besides a photograph. So George decided to strike the first blow. He walked over to the birthday cake, picked up its top tier, raised it over Bonzo's head, and dumped it on the drummer.

There were gasps from the party-goers. And then laughter. John chased after George, caught him within a few steps, and then lifted Harrison up and tossed him into the pool. Almost instantly, full-fledged pandemonium broke out. Bonzo was pushed into the water, and most of the other party guests followed close behind.

Jimmy, meanwhile, rather than risk being pushed into the pool, gracefully walked down the steps into the water, wearing an elegant white suit. "Hell, I don't know how to swim," he said. "I'm going to stake out a place in the shallow water before someone pushes me in the deep end."

On June 2, 49,000 fans squeezed into Kezar Stadium in the southeastern corner of Golden Gate Park for a Zeppelin spectacle. By this point, Jimmy's finger was still in some pain, but he was becoming more mobile each day. He had toughed it out during the L.A. Forum concerts; he knew he could do the same in San Francisco.

Bill Graham, the promoter for the Kezar Stadium gig, was amazed by the ticket sales. "We could have sold three times as many tickets, maybe more, if we had the room," he told me. Scalpers were out in force, initially determined to market their tickets for $25, but soon finding themselves offered much more . . . $50, $100, even $200 a ticket.

Graham opened the gates at Kezar at five-thirty in the morning, and more than 3,000 fans who had camped out in the park for two nights stormed through the gates like someone was giving away free money rather than the Frisbees and the balloons that Bill Graham had distributed. Zeppelin didn't take the stage until midafternoon, preceded by a trio of opening acts (Roy Harper, the Tubes, Lee Michaels) who only seemed to make the audience more restless, more impatient for the band they had really come to see.

Finally, beginning at three-thirty, and continuing for two and a half hours, Zeppelin shook the city that was already much too familiar with earthquakes. They began with "Rock and Roll," and from that point on it was a foot-stomping feast of Zeppelin at their best. The crowd seemed to react most enthusiastically to "Dazed and Confused," "The Song Remains the Same," and "Whole Lotta Love." But the band could have played "Chopsticks" and brought down the house.

Blocks away on Parnassus Avenue, patients trying to rest at the University of California Medical Center grumbled that the noise from the concert kept jarring them awake. At the Presidio, more than a mile away, soldiers on guard duty swore they could feel the vibrations. Maybe only 49,000 could squeeze into Kezar, but the whole city knew Zeppelin was in town.

When I added up Kezar's box-office receipts, the gross totaled $325,000. "That's better than we did in Tampa by nearly sixteen thousand dollars," I told the band on the limo ride to San Francisco International.

"We gotta get Danny Goldberg on this story," Bonzo exclaimed, waving his right fist triumphantly in the air. "I want the fuckin' Stones to hear about the kinds of crowds we're drawing. They can't come close to us. Not even close!"

On the flight back to L.A., however, Zeppelin forgot all about ticket sales and crowd bedlam, at least for the moment. The fan-jet had just taken off when it got caught in some turbulence created by the takeoff of a jumbo jet just seconds earlier. Our plane bounced, dipped, and shook, creating high anxiety within the cabin.

No one said very much, except for an occasional expletive that you'd even forgive Mother Teresa for under the circumstances. We gripped shoulder rests, felt queasiness in our stomachs, and began to perspire.

At one time or another over the years, all of us had experienced some frazzled nerves while flying. Bonham went through a period of such crippling fear that he wouldn't get on a plane until he had a drink. Jimmy never liked flying, either, sometimes looking as though he were about to faint during turbulent flights.

On that day above San Francisco, as soon as the pilot had stabilized the fan-jet, Peter became enraged. "I've had it with these fucking little planes! This is the last time we fly them. The last time!"

Before we had touched down in L.A., Peter had given me my orders:

"We've got a month's hiatus coming up in the middle of this tour. By the time the tour resumes, I want us to have a bigger plane. I don't care what it costs. Get us something so big that it won't seem like flying at all."

37

THE
STARSHIP

As the band headed for England for their planned hiatus, I spent most of the remainder of June trying to find a jet that would meet their extravagant tastes and ease their extravagant anxieties while making traveling more comfortable.

I contacted Lou Weinstock of Toby Roberts Tours, who used to arrange for planes for Elvis. Lou passed on a brochure to me about a Boeing jet called the *Starship*. It was a 720B—a forty-seater that had been customized specifically for rock stars, although no one had yet taken a long-term lease on it. Frankly, I doubted that anyone could afford it.

The *Starship* was owned by singer Bobby Sherman and one of the creators of the Monkees. And it was elegant. A lengthy bar. Televisions. An artificial fireplace in the den and a fur-covered bed in the bedroom. A Thomas organ built into the bar. A kitchen for preparing hot food. "It's like Air Force One with satin sheets," I told Peter.

"See what kind of price you can negotiate," Peter said. "It sounds like a great way to travel. And Danny Goldberg can probably get us some great publicity out of it."

After several lengthy phone calls, I finalized the deal. The price: $30,000 for the remaining three weeks of the American tour. Yes, it was expensive. But once the band got used to the convenience, comfort, and luxury, the price wasn't important. As Robert said on our first flight, "It's like a floating palace."

When we picked up the jet at Chicago's O'Hare airport in early July, it was parked next to Hugh Hefner's plane. Thanks to Goldberg, the rock press was swarming all over the tarmac as we boarded the *Starship* for the first time. One reporter asked Peter, "How does your plane compare to Mr. Hefner's?"

Peter thought for a second, and even though he had barely seen the interior of our own plane, he answered, "The *Starship* makes Hefner's plane look like a dinky toy."

The comment made headlines in the rock press, although Bonham later told me, "I'd like to get some of those Hefner girls on the *Starship*!"

"Don't worry," I told him. "We'll have plenty of girls. I'll see to that."

The band not only fell in love with the *Starship*, but they enjoyed the status of having such an elegant plane, something that other rock bands would envy. Maybe the Stones got a lot more media attention, but no one had a jet quite like this one.

To take full advantage of the *Starship*, I devised a strategy to minimize the exhaustion—physical and mental—that had become an almost inevitable part of touring. For this and the remaining American tours, we based ourselves in a limited number of U.S. cities—New York, Chicago, New Orleans, Dallas, Miami, and Los Angeles—in hotels where we felt comfortable. From those launching pads, we would use the *Starship* to fly to concerts in Milwaukee, Cleveland, Philadelphia, Boston, and other nearby cities. There was no longer a need to move to a new, unfamiliar hotel every night.

On the flights to the concerts, the mood on the *Starship* was relatively quiet. But pandemonium reigned on the postconcert flights. No matter what the hour, no matter how tired we may have been, no one slept, not when there were hot meals to eat, beer to drink, and flight attendants and girls to flirt with.

Ironically, at a time when Zeppelin was firmly entrenched as the world's biggest band, there were fewer groupies throwing themselves into our laps than during the early days. One seventeen-year-old blonde who we met at the Riot House in Los Angeles during that '73 tour told me, "My friends didn't even want to try to get to you guys. Your security is becoming so tight that they just figured they'd never get near you."

Many of the old groupies had disappeared. Some had simply grown up. A few had gotten married. Too many had died of drug overdoses. Still, we would meet girls, often in L.A. clubs like the Rainbow Bar and Grill, and few of them ever turned down the invitation for a ride on the *Starship*. When they were willing, the bedroom gave us some privacy, too.

Among its other toys, the *Starship* had an on-board telephone, and whenever we'd be flying into Los Angeles, I'd call from the air to let the Rainbow know we were on the way. I'd usually get Tony or Michael, who ran the

Rainbow, on the phone, and tell them, "We'll be landing at nine-thirty, and then we'll have a twenty-five-minute limo ride from the airport. Please have our tables cleared and some Dom Perignon ready for us." The Rainbow never said no. They spoiled us rotten, but at this point in the band's career, we expected—and almost always got—special treatment.

Linda and Charlotte, who were our favorite Rainbow waitresses and "den mothers," would cordon off an area for Led Zeppelin, and no one got beyond the line of demarcation unless one of us signaled for her safe passage. Usually, adolescent girls with layers of makeup, tight-fitting tops, short skirts, and spike heels had the best chance of winning admission to our asylum.

There were other diversions on the *Starship*. The refrigerators were always well stocked—plenty of champagne, beer, wine, Scotch, Jack Daniels, and gin. The belly of the plane was crammed with cases of Dom Perignon (1964 and 1966 vintage) and Singha beer. We'd drink just about anything, but at times we'd be in the mood for a particular type of alcohol—or drug—and that would become the "substance of choice" for that particular tour.

When he wasn't in a corner playing backgammon, John Paul often would sit at the Thomas, and, with the booze flowing, we'd sing pub songs. We'd encourage the flight attendants—two girls and a guy—to join the partying, and while they took their in-flight responsibilities seriously, they began to feel like part of the Zeppelin family. We didn't fuck around with the stewardesses, Susie and Bianca, because they wouldn't stand for it. But there was a lot of teasing.

Susie was an attractive eighteen-year-old blonde; Bianca was twenty-two years old, with a dark complexion and a good sense of humor. Years later, Susie told me, "Back in nineteen seventy-three, when you guys would get off the plane and we'd be straightening things up, we'd find one-hundred-dollar bills rolled up with cocaine inside them. We knew we weren't on a chartered flight for the Queen of England, but in the beginning I was shocked."

One afternoon, on a flight to Cincinnati for a concert at Riverfront Stadium, the *Starship* had been in the air only fifteen minutes when I heard banging and shouts coming from the bathroom.

"Get me out! Get me out!"

It was Bonzo. The bathroom door was locked. I hit it with a couple of Bruce Lee kicks. The door trembled, then it collapsed. There, before my eyes, sat Bonzo, perched on the can with his pants down, literally unable to move.

"Help me, damn it!"

As hard as he was trying, Bonzo couldn't stand up. Apparently, a mechanic had not properly sealed the vent beneath the toilet, and air pressure was literally sucking him down, keeping his ass anchored to the seat.

I grabbed Bonham by the arms and pulled him free. "Oh, my God!" he gasped, feeling terribly shaken but not hurt. He pulled up his pants and didn't seem the least bit embarrassed by what had happened. He was probably just happy to be alive. As he returned to the main cabin of the plane, he mumbled, "I'm never gonna trust a toilet seat again."

The *Starship* became a symbol of just how high Led Zeppelin was flying. Yes, it was extravagant, pretentious, and snobbish. But the band felt they had earned it. It wasn't the only sign of their belief in their own importance. On those airplane flights, Peter talked to me about his plans to commit the band's life and times to a motion picture. It was another sign of their growing egos.

My first real exposure to the reality of the movie came near the end of the 1973 American tour. When we were at the Sheraton Boston Hotel, I noticed two unfamiliar names on our rooming list. I called Peter and asked, "Who the fuck are these guys?" He invited me over to his room to meet one of them.

"This is Joe Massot," Peter said. "He's a film director, and he's going to be traveling with us on the last few dates."

If the band was going to make a film, Peter and Jimmy wanted it to be something more than just a documentary of the band's concerts. Each member of the band would have input into the film, and it would reflect their personalities.

Massot was one of the filmmakers with whom Peter had talked about the project. Massot was in his forties, tall, dark, and smoked Havana-sized cigars. He was a friend of Charlotte Martin's, which obviously gave him an inside track on the project. Two years earlier, he had been involved in a movie called *Zachariah*, a rock Western that developed into a cult film, thanks in part to appearances by actors like a young Don Johnson and music by Doug Kershaw and Country Joe and the Fish.

A lot of filmmakers had approached the band, but Massot went beyond envisioning just another *Woodstock*. "The movie has to make a statement about rock music and the way that musicians live," Massot said. "I want to include some 'fantasy scenes,' too, with each band member helping to develop the sequences that he appears in."

Initially, Peter was turned off by Massot's idea of fantasy scenes. But the more he thought about it, the more he liked it. He had a few meetings with Massot and after a handshake, unleashed him with a camera and complete access to the band.

Peter insisted that we use Zeppelin's own money to finance the film. "I don't want to feel obligated to anyone," he said. "Let's keep an eye on these guys to make sure they don't spend us dry. But I want it to be *our* movie."

The crew traveled with us into Baltimore, Pittsburgh, and then three days in New York and Madison Square Garden. Massot did some offstage shooting and next set up his cameras to capture all three of the Madison Square Garden performances. The crew used hand-held cameras, as well as dolly shots during the concert filming.

From the beginning, however, the band sometimes had the feeling that the crew not only didn't know what they were doing but were also becoming a real imposition. Some crew members would often bark questionable orders and instructions. "This is very important," Massot once said. "We need everyone in the band to wear the same clothes for all three shows at Madison Square Garden. If your clothes change, there won't be any continuity in the movie."

Robert thought he was kidding. "Is he a filmmaker or a fashion consultant?" he asked me.

Peter, too, was getting nervous. "Do you think they know what they're doing?" he asked as we watched the crew at work. Admittedly, Massot had put his team together in less than a week, but during moments of confusion, some of these guys acted like they would have had trouble with a Brownie Instamatic, much less anything more professional. Fortunately, they shot so much footage that, amid it all, some of it was bound to be good.

Occasionally, we insisted that certain things be kept off limits to the cameras. During the second Madison Square Garden show, Bonzo was in the midst of his "Moby Dick" solo, which gave the other band members twenty or more minutes of rest while he banged and battered the drums. We had a teenage girl from Brooklyn in our dressing room, and as Bonzo took control of the crowd she was performing oral sex on the other band members.

A New York policeman had been assigned to guard our dressing room door, a job that included keeping the camera crew at bay. At one point, the cop shook his head in disbelief at our extracurricular activities. "You guys lead quite a life!" he said. "They don't offer us these kinds of services at the police department."

Those shows at Madison Square Garden were a fitting climax to the 1973 tour. With every seat filled and fans standing and dancing in the aisles, we grossed more than $400,000 for the three nights. If Led Zeppelin had owned printing presses, we couldn't have printed the money any faster.

38

THE ROBBERY

By the Madison Square Garden concerts, I was relieved to see the tour finally coming to an end. Yes, the fan response to the band had been invigorating, and it was always there, night after night. But along with it, there were the usual stresses of touring . . . the hectic rushing from hotels to airports to stadiums . . . the need to deal with overzealous fans who somehow snuck up elevators or stairways, knocking on hotel room doors and showing no sensitivity to our desire for privacy. I was ready for this tour to end.

"It does get to be a real drag after a while," Bonham complained on the last Sunday in July, just hours away from the final concert of the tour, the last of those three nights at Madison Square Garden. Each of the New York performances was a sellout. But everyone was itching to get them over with, climb aboard the plane, and head home.

In New York, we were staying at the Drake on Park Avenue. It was a small, quiet, elegant hotel, a place you'd more likely associate with British royalty than with British rock musicians and their groupies, drugs, and late-night escapades. But the hotel staff patiently put up with middle-of-the-night room service orders and girls wandering through the lobby and navigating their way up via the elevators. Occasionally, the band would escape the confines of the hotel, journeying to Greenwich Village to drink and carouse at Nobody's. But on the whole, by this point in the tour, everyone was usually so tired that we brought in almost everything we wanted, and even passed some idle hours watching the televised Watergate hearings. "No matter how many problems we might have," I chuckled one afternoon, "Nixon's always going to have it a little worse."

At seven o'clock on the night of the final concert, my hotel phone rang.

"Richard, the limos are downstairs. Let's get the boys down here and get moving."

Within three minutes, we had crowded into the elevators. Once in the lobby, we moved briskly toward the pale blue limousines being guarded by two police cars in front of the hotel. I took a detour toward the front desk to clear out our safe-deposit box, where I had stored $203,000 in cash, mostly in $100 bills. We were leaving for London the next morning, and I planned to organize the finances that night.

Of course, $203,000 was a lot of cash to carry. But in those days, I usually had at least $50,000 in my pocket, primarily to satisfy the whims of band members who might venture out for a spontaneous shopping spree. Jimmy often purchased antiques when we were in America. Bonham would sometimes buy a car at the end of a tour, and he always found it easier to negotiate a good deal if he could put cash on the table.

As the 1973 tour wound down, however, I was carrying more cash than usual. Before leaving the country, I would have to pay the movie crew, and I also needed to pay for the *Starship* before we left for home.

At the hotel safe-deposit boxes, I inserted the key into Box 51, pulled the drawer from its slot, and opened the lid.

The money—all $203,000 of it—was gone.

"Oh, no, it can't be," I said to myself. I was absolutely stunned. I gazed blankly at the box for a few seconds and could feel an uncomfortable chill sweeping through my body. I picked up all that remained in the drawer—our passports and Jimmy's American Express card—and then set them down again. I swallowed hard, returned the box to its slot, removed the key, and walked out into the lobby.

Peter Grant and Steve Weiss, our attorney, were waiting there.

"Peter, the money's gone."

Ordinarily, Peter might have thought I was joking. But there was a quiver in my voice and a startled expression on my face.

"What do you mean, it's gone?" he asked.

"Go look in the safe-deposit box. The money's not there."

"Oh, my God." Steve gasped.

The three of us stared at one another for a moment.

"Let's get the band to Madison Square Garden," Steve said. "They don't need to know about this yet."

Steve went outside to release the limos for the five-minute drive to the Garden.

Peter had a violent temper, but at least for the moment he seemed remarkably calm. "When was the last time you were in that box?" he asked.

I explained that at about three o'clock that morning, three fans had ridden up in the hotel elevator to Jimmy's room, four guitars in hand, knocked on his door, and offered the instruments for sale. Jimmy had played each one and, after a few minutes of contemplation, chose a Les Paul model, agreeing to pay for it in cash. He called me and asked for $800 to buy the guitar.

"So I went to the safe-deposit box and took out eight hundred dollars," I told Peter and Steve. "I took the money to Jimmy's suite and gave it to these fellas, asked them to write me a receipt, and then went back to my room. Someone got into the box between then and now."

Steve said, "Well, we better call the police."

As we walked toward the front desk to ask them to summon the police, I suddenly began to panic. Of course, I was concerned that the money had been stolen. But I had an even greater, more pressing worry: In investigating the robbery, the police might decide to search our hotel suites—suites that were filled with illegal drugs, mostly cocaine. If the cops found it, the missing $203,000 would pale in comparison to a drug bust.

For this tour, as with most others, we had drugs that had been given to us by fans and friends. I had made a lot of connections over the years, so I also knew whom to call when we wanted something. The band never turned anything down. Looking back, it was miraculous that we never got busted.

So after the police were called, drugs became my primary concern. I instructed one of our crewmembers to get the drugs out of our suites. "I stashed some cocaine under the carpet in my room by the lamp near the window," I told him. "There's probably cocaine and marijuana in the other rooms, too. Look in Jimmy's suite, Robert's suite, go through all of them. Look under the carpets and under the mattresses. Get rid of everything. Quick."

Minutes later, about a dozen New York policemen arrived from the Midtown North station. Because of the size of the robbery, the FBI was called in, too. Peter, Steve, and I met them in the lobby, and I explained how I had discovered that the money was missing. They listened, took notes, and examined the safe-deposit box.

Because the box hadn't been broken into—and since I supposedly had the only key—I was immediately a prime suspect. For more than an hour, the FBI interrogated me. Yes, I was shaken by the robbery, but if I appeared nervous during the interview it was because I was desperately trying to drag it out for as long as possible to make sure the housecleaning upstairs was completed. Bob Estrada, a young, bright FBI agent, asked most of the questions.

"How much money was in the safe-deposit box, Richard?"

"I can't tell you exactly. I need to figure it out. When one of the band members would want to go shopping or something, I would just grab a handful of cash out of the box and keep track of what was spent. At the end of the tour, I make all the calculations. I think we had about two hundred thousand dollars in there."

"Where did you keep the key?"

"I hid it on the lip of my bed frame, between the box spring and the frame."

"Who else knew it was there?"

"No one."

"Could anyone else have seen you put it there?"

"Well, I had a girl named Diane with me. She spent the night last night. But I know she didn't see me hide it."

"If you had the only key, Richard, how could anyone else get into the box except you?"

"I don't know. I hope you can find that out. The people behind the front desk had seen me go into the box and take out and put in money. If there was a way they could get into it, they knew a lot of money was there. Maybe there's a duplicate key somewhere."

I couldn't tell whether Estrada believed me or not. But by the end of the questioning, I was tired, dazed, and depressed and just wanted to get this entire episode behind us. Later that night, the FBI searched our suites; fortunately, by then, they had been fully "sanitized."

The band had learned about the robbery during the concert that night, while Bonham was performing his drum solo on "Moby Dick." Peter, who had arrived backstage by then, broke the news to Jimmy, Robert, and John Paul. Surprisingly, the band barely flinched. "They were like professionals," Peter told me later. "They weren't happy, of course. How can you be when someone tells you that you're two hundred thousand dollars poorer? But they returned to the stage and finished the concert."

By the time the concert was over, the press had learned about the robbery. Suddenly, Led Zeppelin's music was again overshadowed by offstage events. Reporters swarmed through the lobby of the Drake, but not in search of stories about the band's music. It seemed that Led Zeppelin was about to be crucified anew by the media.

The limousines deposited the band at the hotel entrance, and they made their way toward the elevators. They were already tired at the end of a long tour, and they weren't in any mood to be hounded by the media. But reporters began shouting questions ("Who took the money, Jimmy?") and flashbulbs exploded. "I don't know a thing about it," Jimmy told the journalists. "Maybe we can talk about this later. We'd really like to be left alone for now."

Peter, growing increasingly tense and frustrated, yelled at a *New York Post* photographer, "Stop fucking around with your camera! No pictures!"

The photographer ignored the request. "Just a couple more," he insisted.

Peter flew into a rage. He grabbed the fellow's Nikon and flung it across the lobby. The lens cracked. The flash attachment shattered. The photographer stumbled to the ground in a futile effort to rescue his camera.

The police, who were still at the Drake interviewing the hotel staff, moved in and arrested Peter. The charge was assault. It wasn't our night.

"This is so absurd," Robert said with exasperation. "Is this the way they treat people in this country? Somebody fucking robs us, and they throw one of *us* in jail!"

Peter was taken to the Tombs, although he spent only an hour there. During that time, he was photographed, fingerprinted, and led to a cell filled with hardened criminals. By then, a sympathetic guard—a rock and roll fan who had loved Jimmy Page when he had played with the Yardbirds—recognized Peter and instructed him to take off his turquoise rings, gold bracelet, and chains to avoid any trouble in the cell. "When you get in there," the guard said, "don't even talk to anyone."

As Peter withstood the evil stares from his cell mates, Steve Weiss was working frantically to get him released on bail. In the meantime, the FBI arrived to interrogate Peter about the robbery.

"Grant," yelled the guard.

"Here!" shouted Peter.

"Grant, the FBI is here to see you."

The FBI? Peter's cell mates looked at one another in disbelief. Peter had instantly earned their respect. One of them muttered, "You must be some heavy motherfucker if the FBI wants you." Little did they know that he had been arrested for assaulting a Nikon!

Back at the Drake, the FBI was interrogating the band, one by one. And most of the questions were about me and my character.

"I can't believe that Cole had anything to do with it," Robert told the FBI agent. He was sitting on his bed, sipping a soft drink, growing more impatient with each question.

"He's been our tour manager and handled our money for years," Jimmy said. "He works for us because he's trustworthy. My God, if Richard was going to steal some money, he's smart enough to have waited until there was a hell of a lot more of it to take."

The band knew I wouldn't try to fuck them over. I had managed their money on the road, and the books always balanced—at least they did eventually. Occasionally, my calculations would come up a few hundred dollars short, and I'd ask the band for some help remembering how the money was spent. "Don't you recall," Bonham once said, "that you gave me three hundred dollars for drinks in that bar two nights ago?" Or Jimmy might remind me, "Richard, don't forget about the two hundred I spent on that hooker." Everything balanced out. There was never any dishonesty.

Late on the night of the robbery, after the FBI had finally run out of questions, the band and I headed for a party at the nearby Carlyle Hotel, where they were being honored by Atlantic Records. Atlantic president Ahmet Ertegun planned to present the band with a gold record for *Houses of the Holy*, which by then had been at or near the top of the sales charts for three months.

The party was the first chance I had to talk to the band since the robbery. "I'm sorry for all this commotion tonight," I told them, feeling both embarrassment and dismay. "It sure doesn't end the tour on a high note."

"Don't worry about it, Richard," Bonham said. "With all the guns and the crazy people in America, we should be grateful no one got shot. Have a good time tonight."

In a sense, I already was making the best of it. A friend from the record company had replenished my supply of cocaine, and I was sufficiently numb a few minutes into the party. I shared the drugs with the band—we needed some kind of escape from the evening's events—and all of us were pretty relaxed by the time Ahmet presented us with gold records.

"If we melt this gold down," Bonham chuckled, "how much coke do you think we could buy with it?"

The New York newspapers were filled with stories of the robbery. The *Daily News*'s front-page headline blared, "Led Zeppelin Robbed of 203G." The press was calling it the largest robbery of a safe-deposit box in New York City history.

Danny Goldberg realized that the robbery had instantly undermined his well-planned campaign to focus attention on Led Zeppelin's music. He tried to remain calm, but he showed signs of stress, sometimes answering reporters' questions abruptly, particularly when they were the same questions he had answered a dozen times or more already. He had to deal with dozens of interview requests that day, but not because of our album sales or record gate receipts. Instead, the press was obsessed not only with the robbery itself, but with the band's financial "excesses" and "extravagance," our "bizarre" lifestyle and our "irresponsible" business practices that allowed more than $200,000 in cash to sit in a safe-deposit box. It was a press agent's nightmare.

In light of the robbery, our return to London had been postponed a day, and Danny recommended that Zeppelin face the press—answering questions about the incident in hopes of quickly putting it behind us. The band considered his suggestion, but then ultimately rejected it.

"This is ridiculous!" Robert said. "Can't we just play our music and ignore the rest of this bullshit?"

Peter decided to face the press alone. He walked into a hotel meeting room that had been transformed into a lion's den teeming with two dozen reporters and a row of TV cameras. Dressed in a polka-dot shirt, with a scarf around his neck, Peter showed the strain of the last twenty-four hours while he struggled to keep his composure as the questions escalated to an absurd level:

"Was this just a publicity stunt to get the band's name in the papers?"

"Absolutely not. The only kind of media attention Led Zeppelin is interested in revolves around our music."

"Does the band despise America now? Will you ever come back?"

"This robbery is certainly no indictment of America. We love the country, and we love the people."

Upstairs, the band was becoming increasingly impatient, eager to get home. Jimmy in particular seemed to be feeling the pressure. Pagey always looked a bit pallid and malnourished, but he appeared much more weary than usual. "The fatigue doesn't hurt my playing," he said, "but offstage I have trouble staying on an even keel and keeping the adrenaline and anxiety under control. This robbery doesn't make things easier. When can we get the hell out of here?"

Finally, on July 31, the band piled into limousines and headed for JFK airport and the flight back to London. Even at the airport, however, we couldn't put the robbery completely behind us. As we waited to board the plane, repeatedly ordering rounds of drinks in the Pan Am Clipper Club, Bob Estrada and an FBI colleague unexpectedly walked in.

"Hi, guys," Estrada said. "So you're leaving now?"

"Yeah," I said, bewildered by the FBI's presence.

"Well, have a good flight."

They left as quickly and mysteriously as they had arrived. We exchanged puzzled expressions.

"What was that all about?" Jimmy asked.

"They must still think we have the money," Peter said. "I bet they're going through our luggage right now."

Perhaps they were. When we claimed our baggage and went through customs at Heathrow, the clothes in our suitcases were disheveled, in much greater disarray than when we had packed. A pair of Bonham's brown snakeskin shoes were gone, as if the FBI had confiscated them to rip them apart, searching for the $200,000 inside their custom-made, thick platforms. Two other pairs of Bonzo's shoes—his pink and green ones—were nicked and damaged.

Once we had moved through customs, limousines were waiting for us at curbside. Jimmy had recently bought a beautiful house from actor Richard Harris in the Kensington section of London; he was eager to get home and rode by himself in his own limo. Robert and Bonham, who lived just ten miles apart, shared a limo that took them to their homes. John Paul, Peter, and I each had our own limos.

The drive home, however, was never nonstop. Bonham and I instructed our chauffeurs to stop at pubs along the way. We each had about a two-hour drive, and that was too long to wait for our next drink. No matter what time it was, we could always find open bars with ample English beer: the Copper Kettle . . . the George . . . the Swan.

Perhaps out of frustration with the sour ending to the 1973 tour, Led Zeppelin would not return to the road for eighteen months. I was simply fed up with things and figured it was time to reevaluate my own future. With no new Zeppelin tours on the drawing board, there wasn't much work for me around Peter's office, so I spent a lot of idle time at the local pubs and alone at my house, a seventeenth-century barn that had been converted into a beautiful split-level home. But with my brain fogged by alcohol so much of the time it was hard to do much planning for what might lie ahead.

I took a brief vacation in Romania on the Black Sea, and when I returned to London there was a message for me from Peter, asking me to stop by his house. It was one of the shortest meetings I had ever had with him. "Are you sure you had nothing to do with the robbery in New York?" he asked.

I couldn't believe this was still an unsettled question in his mind. "Absolutely," I said, raising my voice enough to show my frustration. "I don't know who took the money. That's the truth."

"Do you think one of the porters could have gotten the key off of you without your knowledge?"

"No way. The whole thing's a mystery to me."

That was the last time the subject of the robbery ever came up. The band later sued the Drake and won a reasonable settlement. What an ordeal!

39

PUT 'EM IN
THE MOVIES

In October 1973, Joe Massot and his crew were about to begin filming the most creative portions of the Led Zeppelin movie. He was pleased with the concert footage he had shot in New York, and now he was ready to begin developing individual segments with each band member, mostly shot near their homes. Massot told them to let their imaginations run wild and bring their personalities into the filming. John Bonham thought he was out of his mind.

"I'll show him a few of my fucking bulls, but I don't know how he's going to make something interesting out of that," Bonzo said. "We should take him to a bar and he can film us getting blotted out of our minds." Then he asked, "Does this guy really know what he's doing?"

At the same time, the band began making some demands on Massot's patience and abilities. Jimmy wanted to film a segment on a steep rock face, where he would meet a hooded figure who ages a century or more before the camera's eye. Jimmy not only wanted to play both parts in the scene, but he also wanted it filmed at night.

Massot and his crew shook their heads as if to say, "Another spoiled rock star with another crazy idea!" Nevertheless, they erected some scaffolding on the side of the mountain and kept adjusting and readjusting the lighting until the cameras could capture the scene without it looking like a London blackout.

Jimmy, however, soon found out that he himself was in over his head. Massot had to keep reshooting the scene, and after the sixth or seventh take

Jimmy was exhausted from climbing and reclimbing the hill. He tried to recuperate between shots, but just as he would catch his breath, the camera rolled again.

When Bonzo heard about Jimmy's ordeal, he was amused. "If the bastard would just start eating meat, he'd have the energy to climb the Alps. I'll even sacrifice one of my bulls if the guy will just get off this fucking vegetarian kick."

Later in the fall, Peter asked to look at the footage that had been shot. And he didn't like most of what he saw. "Some of this stuff is just fucking ridiculous!" he told me. "I'm fed up! This is turning out to be the most expensive home movie ever made!"

Near the end of 1973, Peter agreed to have his portion of the movie filmed during a large party at his house, celebrating his wife's birthday. Although he was becoming disillusioned about the movie, he was willing to see it through to the end. Peter had a medieval-style home, so for the party he had caterers wearing costumes from the Middle Ages. When they weren't serving food, they were jousting on the lawn for entertainment.

Months later, as the progress of the movie moved at a snail's pace, Peter reached the breaking point. Massot left the project and was replaced with a filmmaker named Peter Clifton. Even so, the movie still had a long way to go. It wouldn't be released for almost another three years. It was a project that wouldn't end.

As the movie took on an unpredictable life of its own, Zeppelin began its first rehearsals for its next album. Jimmy had invited the band to his Plumpton Place home, and they began discussing and writing new material. They still had some unused cuts dating back to the last trip to Headley Grange—most notably, "Houses of the Holy" and "Night Flight." Plant even pulled out a song called "Down by the Seaside" that he and Pagey had written years before at Bron-Yr-Aur.

At about this time, Jimmy was also working on the soundtrack of a movie by Kenneth Anger, an American filmmaker who had made a series of short cult movies—*Scorpio Rising* was probably the best known—that some critics found incomprehensible. Like Pagey, Anger was a devotee of Aleister Crowley. Anger was particularly fascinated that Jimmy had owned a house that once belonged to Crowley. Pagey told him the story about a man being beheaded at the house centuries ago, and how his spirit supposedly continued to live long beyond the time of decapitation. There were also stories of murders and suicides in the house, although no one really knew whether this was just Jimmy's imagination running wild.

Page and Anger became close friends, and as Anger worked on *Lucifer Rising*, a new film with a satanic theme, he asked Jimmy to write the music for it. Jimmy, however, always put his Led Zeppelin work first. Even when he had free time, he procrastinated about finishing the Anger project.

When Pagey finally played Anger some of the music he had written, the filmmaker didn't like what he heard. Anger thought the music was too macabre, and he asked Jimmy to start over again. The process dragged on, and finally Anger began attacking Jimmy's lack of discipline in the press. We heard that Anger was suggesting to friends that Pagey might be a drug addict.

I was shocked by Anger's accusations. After all, if Pagey was a drug addict, that meant I was, too. We were both using a hell of a lot of cocaine. But I wasn't ready to admit that I had a problem, so I figured Jimmy didn't have one, either. If we had been more honest with ourselves and faced up to our addictive behavior, we might have avoided a lot of agony down the road.

40

"HORS D'OEUVRES, ANYONE?"

As the New Year approached, I promised myself that 1974 would be a better time. We seemed to have put the New York robbery behind us, but it was difficult for me. It wasn't something I thought about every day, thanks in part to the escape that booze and cocaine provided. But when it did surface, I would slip into periods of melancholy.

The new year, however, seemed to hold more promise. I had met a young woman named Marilyn, a gorgeous actress and *Playboy* model. She was warm, sensitive, creative, and had a good sense of humor. Her looks didn't hurt, either. I was needy, and she filled a real void in my life. I fell in love quickly, and so did she. Before long, we were talking about marriage.

When I introduced Marilyn to my family, my little Irish mother sized her up and said, "Well, bejesus, Richard, you've had a lot of women in your life, so it's time to settle down. And by the looks of your lady here, she's had quite a few fellows as well! Good luck to both of you!"

Mom never was very diplomatic. Marilyn's face sank so low that it almost struck the floor. I felt so bad for Marilyn. I don't think she ever really liked my mother after that.

As 1973 drew to a close, Marilyn and I set a date for our marriage— January 2. I bought myself a gray suit and arranged to get married at Caxton Hall. I was extremely happy and felt my life was finally getting back on track.

Our wedding reception was held at the Playboy Club in London. Members of Led Zeppelin, the Who, and Bad Company were there, which required that we hire thirty security people to keep the event under control and make sure that the high-profile guests were well protected. The security forces did such an excellent job that they even refused entrance to Victor Lownes, the owner of the Playboy Club, until I had okayed it.

Ironically, as I was signing the register at Caxton Hall, the registrar—a short fellow with a bald head and missing teeth—looked past me at the celebrities in line and shouted, "Oh, can I have your autograph, sir?" I figured he might be talking to Pagey or Plant or Keith Moon. Instead, he walked right past them and handed a pen and paper to Lionel Bart, who had written *Oliver!* "I guess that puts rock musicians in their proper place!" I joked with Peter.

Robert Gaines Cooper, a gaming-machine manufacturer who lived in my village, gave me the use of six Rolls-Royces—Phantoms I through VI—as a wedding gift. The wedding reception itself was a gift from Peter, and as sloshed as I became that day, I repeatedly let him know how grateful I was.

Nevertheless, as a newly married man, I began thinking more seriously that maybe it was time for a new beginning professionally, too. Led Zeppelin, committed to spending the early part of the year in the studio recording their sixth album, still had no touring planned for 1974. Peter asked me to go to the States for six weeks to run Maggie Bell's American tour. I knew that back in London, there was not much work, but I liked living in the U.K., and that's where my friends were. So I decided to keep my ears open for other opportunities there.

In the meantime, just days after my wedding, Peter Grant had called a press conference announcing that Zeppelin was forming its own record company, Swan Song. Their five-year contract with Atlantic Records had expired the previous month, and Jimmy and Peter believed that with their own label the band would have more creative control—and probably even greater financial rewards.

Over the years, other artists—including the Beatles and the Stones—had created record labels of their own. So often it seemed more like an ego trip than anything else, and with Zeppelin it certainly did seem to boost their sense of self-importance. At the press conference, they took the opportunity to sing their own praises and boast of what they hoped to accomplish. Nevertheless, Jimmy said, "It's not going to be an ego thing. We're going to be signing and developing other acts, too. It will be much more than just Led Zeppelin."

Within weeks, their new label had signed Bad Company, Maggie Bell, and the Pretty Things and was looking for other talent to bring into the company.

Danny Goldberg was hired away from Solters, Roskin, and Sabinson to run the new record label from offices in a high-rise on Madison Avenue in New York. A London office was opened on the King's Road as well. And then came the parties. To celebrate the launching of Swan Song, we flew to the States to host receptions at the Four Seasons in New York and the Bel Air Hotel in Los Angeles.

On the plane to New York, all of us were drinking heavily, but Bonzo was setting records in first class. Gin and tonic. Chardonnay. A few glasses of champagne. Almost single-handedly, he kept the stewardesses running during the entire seven-hour journey.

More than midway through the flight, Bonzo was either too drunk or too lazy to get up to use the bathroom. So he did the next best thing—he just pissed in his pants and kept on drinking.

A few minutes later, Bonzo began to feel uncomfortable sitting in his own urine. "I can't take this anymore," he said, leaping up from his window seat, bustling his way past me, and moving toward the coach cabin. As he paraded down the aisle, the large wet spots on his tan pants drew a few stares and snickers from other passengers, although he really didn't seem to care.

Bonham stopped in front of Mick Hinton, who was innocently reading a copy of *Sports Illustrated* in his coach-section seat. "Mick, you're my assistant, right?" Bonzo said.

"Right."

"You're supposed to do whatever I ask you to, right?"

"Right."

"Well, I finally want to return the favor. I'd like to give you my first-class seat for the rest of the flight to New York. You deserve a lot better treatment than you're getting. You fly first class and I'll fly coach! Go sit in seat 3A."

Mick was ecstatic. "That's bloody nice of you, Bonzo. That's just wonderful."

Mick stood up, patted Bonham on the back, and walked to the first-class cabin. "Pardon me, Richard, let me slide in by you," Mick said. "Bonzo is letting me sit in his seat."

"Well, I hope you've got some waterproof pants," I said. "It'll be like swimming in a urinal."

Mick looked at the seat and almost became ill. "Is that what I think it is?" he asked.

Before I could answer, a stewardess announced that all passengers would have to take their seats as the plane entered some turbulence. Mick made himself as comfortable as possible, but he kept squirming during the remainder of the flight. As we got closer to New York, the entire first-class section was reeking from the odor coming from seat 3A.

Once in Manhattan, we checked into the St. Regis Hotel. At the Four Seasons party, I took a plate from the buffet line and poured the contents of my bag of coke on it. "Hors d'oeuvres, anyone?" I said, extending the platter under the noses of the band members.

We were behaving like little kids sneaking candy when no one was looking. Huddled in a corner, we snorted the drug right off the plate, with Jimmy, Bonzo, and I monopolizing most of it.

The Four Seasons party was expensive, but Peter felt it was worth the $10,000 price tag. Even so, not everything went according to plan. The restaurant was supposed to supply white swans to glide elegantly among the guests, representing the Swan Song name. But unfortunately, white swans aren't native to the traffic-congested, crime-infested island of Manhattan. The best they could do was import some aging, asthmatic white geese who could barely honk.

"I think we should fire up the ovens and have those little suckers for dinner," Bonham cackled, sinisterly rubbing his hands together.

We finally got tired of seeing the geese stumble around the party, and Bonham and I began to chase them out onto East 55th Street. Two of them darted into traffic and became instant casualties of the mean streets of New York City.

At the Bel Air, things were much classier. There were man-made lakes on the grounds already stocked with elegant white swans. It was a more beautiful setting, and the party's guest list included an array of Hollywood celebrities, most notably Groucho Marx.

In L.A., we stayed at the Hyatt House on the Sunset Strip. Even though the band was not in town to perform, FM radio jocks were announcing around the clock that Led Zeppelin had invaded the city. Hundreds of Zeppelin fanatics just assumed that we'd be congregating at the Riot House—and so they did, too. The lobby was swarming with photographers with their cameras cocked and excited and with tawdry girls aching for a touch, a pinch, or even more from the band.

Before the trip, Peter and I had sat down and discussed security. Because of the Drake robbery, I felt we needed to heighten our protection. Peter had been thinking the same thing. With all the publicity about the large amounts of cash the band carried, we were afraid some particularly greedy criminals might assume that Zeppelin would be the perfect target for another big hit.

So at the suggestion of Bill Dautrich, our security consultant, we took over and secured the entire ninth floor—and parts of the tenth and eleventh floors—of the Riot House. "You'll have better control of your immediate environment that way," Bill said. Each member of the band had his own corner suite, with a security guard—usually an off-duty Los Angeles policeman—stationed at each door and others positioned at the elevators to keep uninvited guests off the floor.

No one in the band liked those kinds of precautions. Jimmy in particular was perturbed. The cops, he said, made him *more* nervous, constantly reminding him that maybe there really *was* something to be worried about. "We've always had a great relationship with our fans," Jimmy told me. "It's terrible to give the impression that we've surrounded ourselves with a goon squad." Nevertheless, it was hard to argue that the band wasn't becoming more vulnerable as their success and fame grew. Peter and I won this argument.

I loved the Hyatt, but the staff wasn't always very reliable about following through on wake-up calls. So one night, I approached one of our own security guards. "Tell the guard who relieves you to awaken me at noon," I said. "Just have him take the butt of his gun and smash it against my door."

This "alarm clock" worked flawlessly. Once I was up, I decided to invite Bonham to have lunch with me. I called his room repeatedly, but he wasn't answering his phone, so I took the elevator up to his eleventh-floor suite. The security guard in front of Bonzo's door, a Schwarzenegger clone, told me, "Mr. Bonham specifically instructed me that no one is allowed to disturb him."

"Well, I certainly wouldn't want to get you into trouble with Mr. Bonham," I said and strolled back to my own room.

I immediately went out onto my ninth-floor balcony and climbed two floors up the outside of the building, from balcony to balcony, to Bonzo's suite, stopping midway to take a snort of coke from some fans. Bonzo's sliding door was ajar, and I walked in and began to awaken him.

"Get up, ol' boy," I said, shaking him as violently as possible, arousing him cobweb by cobweb. "Let's go get ourselves something to eat."

"What the hell time is it?" he asked in a groggy, barely coherent voice.

"Just meet me in my room in ten minutes."

I exited out the front door of John's suite, choosing to take the stairs back to my room. As I did, Bonzo's security guard took one look at me and his eyes almost popped out of his head.

I politely nodded to him. "Good day," I said.

"How did you get in there?" he asked, scratching his head.

"Hell if I know," I answered as I turned and headed down the hall.

We spent a lot of time at the Rainbow Bar and Grill and would bring girls we met back to the hotel with us. We talked them into sunbathing topless by the rooftop swimming pool during the day. There was something about L.A. that

An overflow audience in Melbourne, Australia, hypnotized by every note from Led Zeppelin, 1972. *(The Richard Cole Collection)*

Jason Bonham looking for attention while his dad and mom snooze by the pool at Bonzo's villa in the South of France, 1972. *(The Richard Cole Collection)*

"Teach me to fly, Uncle Richard!"
(The Richard Cole Collection)

Page *(left)*, Plant *(center)*, and singer Roy Harper disembarking from the *Starship*, 1973. *(The Richard Cole Collection)*

That's me with longtime friend Daniel Markus *(right)*, then with Atlantic Records, aboard the *Caesars Chariot* in 1977.
(© by Neal Preston)

I practice my balancing act while mixing a Brandy Alexander on *Caesars Chariot*, 1977. (© *by Neal Preston*)

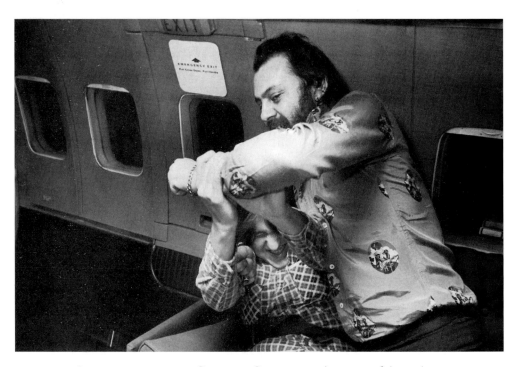

I try to get a young Cameron Crowe to write something nice about me for *Rolling Stone*. (© *by Neal Preston*)

When he wasn't playing music, Bonzo relished being the gentleman farmer. Here he is, cane in hand, at Old Hyde Farm, 1974. *(The Richard Cole Collection)*

My wife, Marilyn, and me during our happier days—just married at Caxton Hall, 1974. That's Lionel Bart, the composer of *Oliver!*, on the right. *(The Richard Cole Collection)*

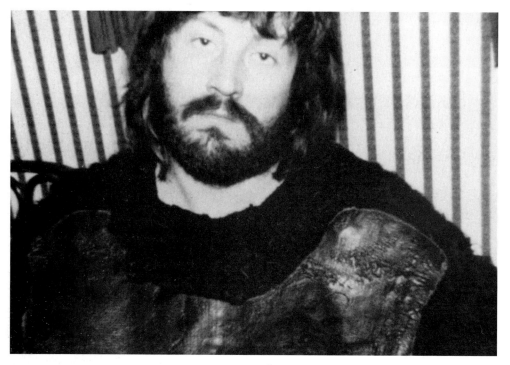

Bonzo, "the adorable beast," homesick (or perhaps seasick) on a Mississippi riverboat party in New Orleans, 1975. *(The Richard Cole Collection)*

John Bonham out and about in New Orleans, 1977. *(The Richard Cole Collection)*

Catching some rays at a hotel in the South of France, 1976.
That's Bonham in the dark outfit; his wife, Pat, sitting next to him;
singer Lulu handing a photograph to Bonzo; and Maurice Gibb of the Bee Gees
readying his camera for the next shot. *(The Richard Cole Collection)*

Robert *(left)*, Jimmy *(center)*, and John Paul *(right)* performing
for a huge crowd in Oakland, 1977. *(The Richard Cole Collection)*

Jimmy is clearly enjoying himself as the band performs in
Oakland in 1977–Led Zeppelin's last concert in the United States.
(The Richard Cole Collection)

Robert *(right)* and Jimmy . . . enjoying the spotlight and the crowd adulation.
(The Richard Cole Collection)

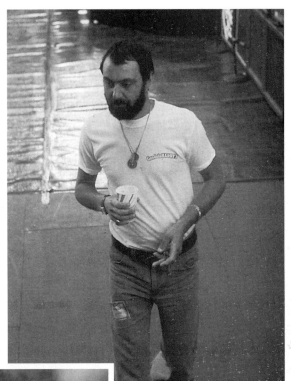

That's me on the edge of the
stage in Oakland, 1977. "Okay,
it's time for a snort."
(The Richard Cole Collection)

John Paul concentrates
on the keyboard during
the 1977 Oakland concert.
*(The Richard Cole
Collection)*

Led Zeppelin takes a quick break onstage in Melbourne, 1972.
(The Richard Cole Collection)

While I slept, Robert seemed pleased with the decorations with which he adorned me in New York, 1977. *(R. E. Aarm)*

Peter *(left)* and Johnny Bindon, one of the band's assistants, at the Edgewater Inn, 1977. "Is that another refrigerator going into Puget Sound?" *(The Richard Cole Collection)*

When I married for the second time, it was a double wedding, including a reception at a well-known pub in Fulham. Front row *(from left)*: Me and my new wife, Tracy, Deseree and Simon Kirke (of Bad Company). Back row *(from left)*: Benji Le Fevre, Robert, Jimmy, Paul Rodgers (of Bad Company), John Paul, and composer Lionel Bart. *(The Richard Cole Collection)*

Here I am reminiscing with old bosses and friends *(from left)*: Carmine Appice (of Vanilla Fudge), Rod Stewart, me, and Robert Plant. The photo was shot at a post-concert party after Robert performed at the L.A. Forum, summer 1982. *(The Richard Cole Collection)*

In 1990, a decade after Led Zeppelin disbanded,
Jimmy *(center)* and I posed for pictures with Spike Gray
(right) of the London Quireboys at the Donnington
Monsters of Rock show. *(Clark Duvall)*

Members of Fem 2 Fem
cuddle their manager in
Texas, 1994 (the girls are,
from left, Alitzah, Julie Ann,
Christina, and Lezlee).
(The Richard Cole Collection)

Here I am relaxing with Crazy Town in Malibu, May 2001 . . . still having the time of my life. (© *Mark Weiss/Angles*)

brought out the decadence in us. And as long as the girls were cooperative, which they always were, who could really complain?

Even without the Rainbow girls, Jimmy already had his hands full. Of course, there was Lori Maddox, but other girls were vying to become one of his "regulars," too. Bebe Buell, a tall blond model once attached to Todd Rundgren, captured some of Jimmy's attention during that tour. So did Krissie Wood, whose marriage to Ronnie Wood of the Rolling Stones was rocked by the mutual attraction between Pagey and Krissie. Even Charlotte Martin flew in for a couple of days from London.

When Ronnie's solo album, *I've Got My Own Album to Do*, reached the record stores, Warner Brothers hosted a party for him, and we were invited to the festivities. Jimmy brought along Charlotte, but was arguing with her most of the night. Their relationship had survived some rocky moments, and I figured this was just another short-lived although heated feud. But when the party finally broke up, Pagey left with Krissie, while Ronnie left with Charlotte. All's fair in love and war, I guess.

Later, however, Ronnie told me how pissed off he was over the swap. "I wasn't real happy with the way things turned out. My end of the deal didn't last too long." I assumed Ronnie didn't get what he wanted out of the bargain.

Lori Maddox, who by this time was barely sixteen years old, couldn't handle this kind of competition. She was a sweet, still somewhat innocent kid who spent half of her time dying to embrace Jimmy and the other half dying to kill him. It was all part of the jealousies that ran rampant among the girls for whom attention from a member of Zeppelin was their Oscar, Pulitzer Prize, and Nobel Prize all in one.

The band members themselves, of course, loved being fawned over. Who wouldn't? No wonder people used to shake their heads when I'd occasionally complain that, even with all the girls and all the booze, things were getting boring at the Riot House. One late afternoon, to relieve the monotony, I suggested that the band dress up in drag. There didn't seem to be anything better to do. "Let's see how pretty you 'girls' really are!" I challenged them. "I'll take a few pictures, and maybe we'll use 'em on the next album cover. I'll put Annie Leibovitz right out of business!"

Without much coaxing, the trio of groupies who were with us that day took off their clothes and Jimmy, Robert, and Bonzo squeezed their way into them, tearing the seams on the dresses and creating runs in the nylons as they did.

"All you guys need now is some makeup," Lori said, helping Jimmy and the others apply lipstick and a little rouge. Interestingly, the boys didn't feel at all awkward or embarrassed as the transformation occurred; in fact, they seemed to enjoy their new look. If only the drag queens in New Orleans could have seen them.

We had become so preoccupied with this impromptu photo session that we almost forgot we were supposed to meet George Harrison for a dinner date. "Let's give George a cheap thrill and let him see how we look," Robert said. When Harrison arrived at the hotel, he had Stevie Wonder with him. George took one look at Bonzo, Robert, and Pagey in drag, and he fell on the floor laughing. The hysterics were contagious, and before long everyone was shrieking—everyone, that is, except Stevie.

"What's so funny?" Stevie kept saying, with a slight grin on his face, knowing something was going on but unsure exactly what it was.

"Shit," I thought. "I hope Stevie doesn't think the joke is on him." Everyone else must have had the same idea, too. The laughter stopped, and we just wanted to crawl into a hole, dresses and all.

There were other uncomfortable moments in Los Angeles, at least for me. Robert and I seemed to be at each other's throats during much of the trip, for no apparent reason. We fought over petty things, like what time the limousines would be arriving. Or who was going to make the calls to room service. Or which girls to bring back with us from the Rainbow. At one point, I asked myself if it was finally time to throw in the towel. I figured I'd be better off doing just about anything other than battling Robert.

Upon reflection, I was upset at more than just Plant. With Swan Song up and running, I thought I might be given a shot at a top position within the new company or perhaps a small percentage of the band's record royalties. After all, I had been exceptionally loyal to them from the beginning. Other than Peter and the band members themselves, no one had given so much of himself to ensure that the organization ran smoothly. But no such offers were ever forthcoming. It just didn't seem fair.

During our last few days in L.A., I was fuming. I just wanted to lash out, to explode. On one of our final nights there, we were having dinner at an elegant Indian restaurant in Westwood Village, just south of UCLA. The members of Bad Company were eating at the adjacent table. There were some good-natured verbal exchanges between the two bands—"When you guys learn how to play, then maybe we can talk about music on the same level," Bonham joked.

About midway through dinner, Bonzo spontaneously heaved a dish of cooked vegetables in the direction of Bad Company. It landed harmlessly on the floor, but it gave me a chance to cut loose. I hurled my entire entrée halfway across the restaurant, where it dive-bombed onto Bad Company's table. That instantly triggered an all-out food fight that lasted for ten minutes.

Curry soared through the air, splattering patrons at other tables. Tandoori chicken coated the carpeting. Rice was smeared on the walls. Both bands thought it was quite hilarious, but I was getting out some of my frustration. The restaurant's staff, however, reacted as though the world were coming to an end. The manager finally stepped into the line of fire and shouted, "I'm calling the police!"

At that moment, two off-duty cops who were part of our entourage stood up at an adjoining table, flashed their badges, and announced, "We're the police!" When the donnybrook finally quieted down, we paid for the damage—$450 in cash—and went on our way.

I knew that I had some thinking to do about whether I could feel good again about continuing to work with Led Zeppelin. But more immediately, there was at least one more event on our L.A. agenda that I was looking forward to—a chance to see Elvis in concert.

41

THE KING

How would you guys like some front-row tickets to see Elvis at the Forum?"

Jerry Weintraub, a promoter for both Elvis and Led Zeppelin, had made us an offer we couldn't refuse. We had seen Elvis perform in Las Vegas years earlier, and it was an extraordinary evening. We weren't going to pass up another night with the King.

Unfortunately, none of us were really in any shape to thoroughly enjoy the concert. We had been partying throughout much of the previous night; in fact, Bonzo and I had been up the entire night drinking and snorting coke. So during the Elvis concert, Bonzo and I were struggling to stay awake. He even dozed off now and then. Fortunately, he didn't snore.

Early in the concert, after Elvis had sung "Love Me Tender," he paused for a moment and told the sellout crowd, "I want to let everyone know that my favorite band, Led Zeppelin, is here tonight. I'd like to have the spotlight put on them, and I hope you'll join me in welcoming them."

As the lights shone down on us, we turned and waved at the cheering audience. All of us, that is, except Bonzo, who slept soundly through the entire introduction. I poked my elbow into his ribs, and he woke up with a start, instinctively shielding his eyes from the bright lights. "You've never made a better first impression," I told him as he fought to stay awake.

Elvis was staying at a suite in a hotel across the street from the Forum, and when the concert ended one of his roadies approached us. "Elvis wants you guys to join him at his hotel," he said. We instantly agreed. When we had seen Elvis perform in Las Vegas, we had left that show out the rear exits with the other fans. Meeting him was going to be a real thrill.

Even though Zeppelin was drawing bigger crowds and selling more records than Elvis, all of us were nervous as we rode the elevator to the top floor of the hotel. Two strapping security guards escorted us down the hall to Elvis's suite. "He's the King," Robert said softly to me. "I don't know what we're going to talk with him about. I hope you can think quickly on your feet."

As we walked in, Elvis came forward to greet us. After shaking hands, all of us felt awkward. Elvis himself seemed unusually cool for the first few minutes. I wondered if we should have stayed home.

Then a smile gradually crept over his face. "Hey," he asked, "are these stories I hear about Led Zeppelin true?"

"What stories?" John Paul said.

"Well, those stories about the things you guys do out on the road. They sound pretty wild!"

If we were quiet before, we were suddenly totally speechless. Finally, Robert nervously said, "Well, a lot of rumors have spread around. We all have families, you know. We're just out there to play music. That's mostly what we do."

Elvis thought for a moment. "Then what do you do for fun?"

"We listen to your music a lot," Robert said. Suddenly, he broke into "Treat me like a fool . . . ," which prompted an ear-to-ear grin from Elvis.

"Good choice of music!" Elvis beamed. "Maybe I'll record that myself someday!"

As the evening progressed, Bonham probably got along better with Elvis than any of us. They talked together about hot rods and Peter Sellers movies ("I've seen those Clouseau gags a thousand times and never get tired of 'em!" Elvis exclaimed).

The conversation rarely weaved its way back to music. Jimmy told me later that he felt uncomfortable talking about Zeppelin's own records with the King. "I didn't know whether he'd be sensitive about it since we're out-selling him," Pagey said. "But the guy's a legend!" So the night was filled mostly with small talk. At one point, Elvis said, "You know, I've never listened to much of your music. My stepbrother once played me 'Stairway to Heaven,' and it was pretty good. But I don't get a chance to listen very much."

Elvis became more relaxed as the night wore on. He offered us drinks. He invited us to visit him if we ever got to Memphis. Before we left, he said, "Let me sign some autographs that you can give to your wives or your kids. And I want you to sign some for me, too."

As Bonzo was scribbling his name on a slip of paper, he whispered to me, "Can you believe it? Elvis wants *my* autograph!"

No, I couldn't believe it, either.

42

CLAPTON

After we returned to England, Led Zeppelin retreated to Headley Grange to record what would eventually become the double-record *Physical Graffiti*. I didn't spend much time at those sessions, either at the Grange or later when the band moved to Olympic Studios. There wasn't much for me to do there, and I was in the midst of my own soul-searching, trying to figure out the direction that was best for me. But during those days that I did visit the Grange, what I did see and hear showed that Zeppelin hadn't lost any momentum.

One of the most engaging cuts created during those sessions was "Kashmir," a song that years later the band would consider one of their classics. Jimmy initially called the song "Driving to Kashmir," and it was inspired by a lengthy, deserted stretch of road connecting Goulimine and Tantan in the Moroccan Sahara, a road Jimmy had driven several times, always with the feeling that it would never end. There was no scenery other than an occasional camel and its rider to break the monotony. Jimmy had written the lyrics to the song, complete with its mystical references, while making that drive alone a few months earlier. The sometimes otherworldly, often dissonant quality to the music merged perfectly with Pagey's words.

Jimmy turned to his Danelectro guitar for the recording of "Kashmir." He had worked and reworked the song's now famous riff, drawing upon a guitar cycle that he had created years before. He was so fascinated and intrigued by its structure that he felt driven to repeatedly fine-tune it. Later, Jonesy added an ascending bass riff and scored a truly magnificent string arrangement.

As always, the band was very conscious of keeping its creativity level at a peak. Jimmy knew that double albums were more vulnerable to criticism, with assaults that basically asked, "Why didn't you cut out the repetition and just put out a single album?" Most critics had never been kind to Zeppelin anyway, and Pagey didn't want to give their wicked pens any extra ammunition.

The band continued to amaze me with its ability to grow. Bonzo's drum playing on "In My Time of Dying" was more gutsy and forceful than I had ever heard it. Robert's vocals on "Down by the Seaside" were painfully sensitive.

As for Jimmy, he was constantly experimenting, spending many hours by himself in the studio, shaping his own guitar solos, laboring to the point of complete fatigue. He claimed that when others were there in the studio with him, he'd sometimes become self-conscious and insecure on those solos, and he preferred to do them in seclusion. When I used to see Jimmy onstage, keeping 30,000, 40,000, or 50,000 fans thoroughly entranced as he nurtured every note, caressed each chord, and somehow exhibited both gentleness and violence with subtle or sudden turns of the wrists or fingers, I found his supposed self-consciousness a tough story to buy. No one ever played the guitar with such finesse. On songs like "Ten Years Gone," he worked endlessly, overdubbing more than a dozen guitar tracks, each harmonizing perfectly with the others.

When I'd hear cuts like that, I didn't know how I could ever seriously consider leaving Zeppelin. "Nobody's any better than they are," I told Marilyn. Those were sentiments I had felt for years.

"Follow your heart," she told me. "But if you have the opportunity to expand your own horizons, don't dismiss it without giving it some thought."

In May, with Zeppelin still at work on *Physical Graffiti*, that opportunity finally materialized. I was talking to Jack Calmes, a friend from Showco. As I described my personal conflict—the sense that I might benefit from getting away from Zeppelin for a while—he said, "Robert Stigwood [Eric Clapton's manager] is looking for a U.S. tour manager for Eric. Robert and Atlantic think that Eric's going to hit the comeback trail with a bang. You'd be perfect for the job."

Jack helped get the word back to Stigwood that I was available. Stigwood was a bit wary about hiring me, concerned about my reputation for creating chaos and worried that he might anger Zeppelin if he "stole" me away. But he invited me to a party at his house, apparently to size me up. Near the end of the evening, he finally approached me and began discussing his need for a tour manager for Clapton.

"Well, if we can work out the numbers, let's give it a try," he said. There was a bit of trepidation in his voice.

The next day, we talked by phone. We agreed on a salary of $15,000 plus bonuses for six weeks of work. When I told Peter and Led Zeppelin about my new gig, none of them had much of a reaction at all.

I had been a fan of Eric's for a long time, so it was a thrill to be invited to work with him. It felt like a new beginning, and I was eager to get started. My first assignment: Arrange the details for the upcoming tour, from making flight and hotel plans to selecting the venues themselves. Upon arriving for work each morning, I'd pour myself a brandy and ginger ale—and then another, and still another. Somehow, the job got done, despite my chronic state of drunkenness. As with Zeppelin, it seemed as though I could somehow override the intoxication and get the work finished without any major mistakes. Looking back, I don't know quite how I managed.

Eric worked on a guarantee against a percentage, so once we were out on the tour itself, I would do the calculations at each venue, making sure the local promoters' math agreed with my own. Repeatedly, I found mistakes in the way they had computed the bottom line.

Eric and his entourage traveled in a customized, twenty-seat private jet and included his five-man band, backup singers, and his girlfriend (and later wife) Patti Harrison. Mick Turner (who had worked with Eric during the Cream days) provided security, although I brought in Bill Dautrich for some advance planning, arranging for police escorts as well as on-site protection at each concert.

Throughout the tour, Eric's guitar work was consistently brilliant, expressing all the joy, all the despair, all the achievements, and all the trials that had been part of his life in recent years. Having watched Pagey for so many years, I was used to guitarists using "super-slinky" strings on their instruments that easily bend. But Eric used ordinary gauge strings that had been traditional with the black blues guitarists. They're murder on the fingers, but Eric had built up incredible strength in those fingers over the years. He had also developed calluses that showed just how long he had been in the business.

His musicianship was particularly astonishing because he was suffering from a bad case of conjunctivitis throughout most of that '74 tour. He simply couldn't see where his fingers were moving. He would stumble around the stage, probably looking as though he were inebriated. Near the end of the tour, the antibiotics finally began to work, and he got back his 20/20 vision and his equilibrium.

The medication, however, did not inhibit Eric from indulging in large amounts of alcohol during the tour. Jack Daniels is sweet and powerful, and Eric would sometimes drink to excess, although it never seemed to affect his ability to perform.

I found touring with Eric to be refreshing, even exhilarating at times. I rarely felt the pressures I had experienced with Led Zeppelin. Maybe that was because I didn't know Eric as well as the boys of Zeppelin, and I knew that any mistakes wouldn't be like letting down my best friend. A lot of responsibility was put on my lap with Clapton, yet I didn't really feel the strain—except for the very first show we did at the Yale Bowl in New Haven, Connecticut.

Because it was my first concert of the tour, I was feeling tense, and those anxieties intensified when it began raining the afternoon of the show. "We may have to cancel this gig," I told Eric a couple of hours beforehand, although I promised to do everything possible to get it underway. We had set up large tents in which a preconcert party was held for record company executives and the press, and I just couldn't see going through the stress of the day all over again.

As the rain continued, I also tried to calm down two city officials who were throwing tantrums backstage, claiming that our equipment trucks had caused $10,000 worth of damage to the grounds when they drove on the rain-soaked grass.

"We're gonna sue!" one of them roared. "You've made a damn shambles of this place!"

"So now it fits in with the rest of New Haven!" I muttered under my breath.

Despite the threat of lawsuits and the continuing intermittent rains, the show went on as scheduled.

When I was in Memphis with Eric, I called Jerry Schilling, one of Elvis's assistants whom I had met in Los Angeles earlier in the year. "Eric would love to meet Elvis," I told Jerry. "Is there any chance we could come by Graceland and see him?"

Jerry said he would check with Elvis, and later that day he called back: "Elvis said, 'Yeah, come and visit.' But he's going to the movies tonight at the Orpheum Theatre. He wants you guys to stop by and join him at the theater."

Then Jerry began to laugh. "Oh, one other thing. Elvis said to me, 'I know who Richard Cole is, but who the hell is Eric Clapton?' "

That night, Eric and I, along with Patti and my wife, Marilyn, arrived at the Orpheum at about 10 P.M. From the front row to the popcorn machine, Elvis had rented the entire theater. When we walked in, the King hadn't yet arrived. The theater manager told us, "Elvis rents the theater a couple nights a month. It's the only way he can get out to see a movie without being mobbed. Oh, once he arrives, no smoking will be permitted."

About ten minutes later, Elvis showed up. He strutted down the aisle of the dimly lit theater surrounded by a retinue of aides and security men. He nodded to us and sat down two rows in front of us. During the evening, we didn't exchange more than a dozen words with one another. Even so, with Elvis there, the screening of the movie—*Murder on the Orient Express*—had the feeling of a command performance.

I finished working for Clapton in August and decided to take a couple of months off. When I had been in New Orleans with Eric and had dinner with Ahmet Ertegun and Earl McGrath of Atlantic Records, Ahmet told me that he hoped I'd be returning to Led Zeppelin for the band's next tour. "You've got to go back and sort out whatever's been left hanging," he said. "You're the only guy who can work with them."

More than anything, however, I was just interested in some time off, although that may have been a big mistake. Marilyn and I had more time to spend with one another, and our marriage began hitting hard times. Some friends gave me some heroin, and I started snorting it about once a week, sometimes less frequently. It was relatively inexpensive in those days, perhaps one-third the price of cocaine, and Marilyn didn't seem to mind that I was using it.

But then I began using heroin more regularly, even daily, and it started driving a wedge between us. Marilyn was much more enamored of alcohol; I was becoming hooked on heroin. We stopped communicating as we once had. And we began to drift apart.

As I sunk deeper into my use of drugs, the gradual deterioration of our relationship didn't disturb me as much as it should have. I had found a new lover of sorts, a new drug that could get me high in seconds.

43

ZEPPELIN REVISITED

In October 1974, I got a call from Peter Grant.

"We're planning a new Led Zeppelin tour," he said. "We're heading to America in January. I'd like to talk about you coming back on the team if you're interested."

I hadn't been looking to return to Led Zeppelin. I had enjoyed the tour with Eric Clapton and realized that I could fit in just about anywhere. Nevertheless, my personal problems—my drug and marital difficulties—were becoming more intrusive, and it was actually nice to hear what sounded like a friendly voice on the other end of the line.

During that phone conversation, Peter made me an attractive offer. It included a company car—a BMW or a Jaguar. And my salary would be about $2\frac{1}{2}$ times what he had previously paid me. At that moment, my bitterness from earlier in the year seemed to have softened. "I'm not going to let the old hard feelings get to me this time," I told myself. I also was already starting to calculate how the increased salary could help keep me supplied with heroin. I accepted the job.

Later that day, Peter, Robert, and Jimmy drove to my house to celebrate, and the four of us went to Ringo Starr's home in Surrey where Maggie Bell was recording a new album. Later, we moved the party to a club called Tramps for some libations.

It didn't take long for me to get back into the Zeppelin way of life. The following week, upon the release of Swan Song's first album in the U.K.—the Pretty

Things' *Silk Torpedo*—Zeppelin hosted a Halloween party at Chislehurst Caves. There was enough food and booze (mostly wine) to meet the needs of the entire British army. Even so, the overflowing buffet tables took a backseat to the entertainment. Live music was provided by a jazz combo, while a couple of magicians and a fire-eater performed.

Much more eye-catching were the topless and, in some cases, fully naked women who mingled among the guests and rolled around in vats of cherry Jell-O. Other nude women played the parts of virgins being sacrificed at makeshift altars. Strippers arrived dressed as nuns and peeled off their habits in an act that, if the Vatican were making the decisions, would have doomed us to an eternity in hell.

I could see that nothing much had changed with Led Zeppelin, at least in terms of their delight in shocking people. They made their surroundings as offensive and titillating as possible. It wasn't an act. It was the kind of environment they relished.

Near the end of November, Led Zeppelin began congregating at a converted theater called Liveware, rehearsing for the upcoming American tour, which would be preceded by two European shows—one in Rotterdam, the other in Brussels. These would be the band's first live performances in eighteen months, and they wanted to get out the kinks as quickly as possible. John Paul, however, was surprised at just how few imperfections there were. Peter agreed, telling the band, "You guys sound as though the hiatus was eighteen hours, not eighteen months."

Meanwhile, my marriage had moved closer to disintegration. In December, Marilyn found out I had had a brief affair. We fought, we made up, but the arguments flared up again and again. One evening, in the heat of battle, she hurled two of my Zeppelin gold records into a roaring fireplace, turning them to ashes. I was incensed.

In the first week of January, it was a relief to get on a plane to Holland. That concert would be the first warm-up for the American tour and the first live performances of songs from the yet-to-be-released *Physical Graffiti* album. The set was scheduled to include "Kashmir," as well as "Trampled Under Foot" and "In My Time of Dying."

It was a joy knowing that I would be hearing Led Zeppelin play again. I was determined that, despite my growing fixation with heroin, I was going to prove myself to Peter and the others that there was no better tour manager around. My spirits were incredibly high—at least until I got my first look at the Rotterdam concert hall, just hours before the performance was scheduled to begin. As soon as I saw it, I realized I had made a mistake in not inspecting it days or weeks earlier. The ceiling was so low that if Robert had leaped into the air during the excitement of performing, he might have self-inflicted a head wound. To make matters worse, there were floor-to-ceiling pillars throughout the building, which would obstruct the view of dozens of fans. I knew the band would make the best of it that night, but I also realized that the shortcomings of the venue would detract from their own enthusiasm.

When I returned to the hotel that afternoon, a local TV news crew was beginning an interview with Led Zeppelin in my suite. A fellow named Van, who was the promoter of the concert, was being interviewed in Dutch. With the cameras rolling, he picked up his Samsonite briefcase and began to open it. Inside, there were 20,000 pounds worth of guldens in cash—the money that he would pay Zeppelin that night. Perhaps the New York robbery was still too fresh in my mind, but I panicked at the thought of publicizing the fact that the band had so much cash in its possession. As Van tilted the briefcase so the TV camera could get a better view, I instinctively leaned over and struck the open lid of the briefcase with a karate chop, which slammed it shut—crushing the index finger of Van's right hand. He began screaming, then cursing in Dutch, which was all captured for posterity by the news camera.

I was off to a rather inauspicious start in my return to the Zeppelin trenches.

Before long, Van wasn't the only one nursing a wounded hand. After the European gigs, we returned to England for three days before flying to the States. During that brief stopover, Jimmy had exited a train at Victoria Station and tried to hold the door open for the passenger behind him. However, the door forced its way shut, with the ring finger of Pagey's left hand bearing most of the brunt. He was in terrible pain, and as soon as he got home he applied ice to the injury. But as the hours passed, the pain didn't subside. Finally, he went to a doctor late that same day. X rays showed he had broken a bone in the tip of the finger.

Jimmy was furious at himself and terribly frustrated. "If it was going to happen, couldn't it have happened sometime during the eighteen months when we weren't performing?" he said.

Immediately, Jimmy began planning how to work around the injury. Having lost the use of a finger, he decided he would try playing with what he called a "three-and-a-half-finger technique." He also realized that certain Zeppelin standards, such as "Since I've Been Loving You" and "Dazed and Confused," would have to be dropped from the act until his finger healed.

Despite the anger and the disappointment, Jimmy's self-confidence wasn't bruised. He told himself that even with the handicap of a broken finger, he could play better than most guitarists at full strength.

"Most fans won't even notice any difference," he proclaimed on the British Airways flight to America.

Although Jimmy was subdued on that long trip from London to New York, his seriousness didn't keep the rest of us from creating commotion and attracting attention. The first-class stewardesses frequently replenished our liquor supply, and as one hour passed into the next the band became increasingly loud and rowdy, caught up in the excitement of the upcoming tour and the fatigue of the lengthy journey. Robert and Bonzo especially were raising their voices loud enough to be heard halfway to Manhattan, and some passengers were looking at one another with expressions that said, "Who the hell are those fellows?" Because Zeppelin made no TV appearances, their faces were still unfamiliar to most people over the age of thirty.

When we finally landed at JFK airport and the plane pulled to a stop at the terminal, we began grabbing our carry-on bags. Just then, the pilot approached us. At a moment when the cabin was relatively quiet, he said, "Your own pilot just radioed a message that he can't get any closer than this." He pointed out the window to the *Starship*. It had been used for a recent Elton John tour and was freshly repainted with stars, stripes, and bright red letters spelling out "Led Zeppelin" on its fuselage. What a sight!

There were stunned looks on the faces of the passengers near us. As we approached the exit doors, Peter told the British Airways cockpit crew and the first-class stewardesses, "Why don't you come over to our jet and have some cocktails and hors d'oeuvres with us."

We had special customs clearance, and so within just a few steps we were inside the *Starship*, where the band proceeded to drain our liquor supply over the next hour and a half until we took off. "So this is what the life of a rock star is like!" one of the crew exclaimed.

The tour helped hype the *Physical Graffiti* double album, which was released while the band was in the States with more than one million advance orders. As record buyers raided music stores to buy the new album, sales of the previous five Zeppelin records also soared. By late March, all six Zeppelin albums were on *Billboard*'s Top 200, making Zeppelin the first rock performers ever to score that achievement.

Even some of the critics seemed to be coming around. When *Rolling Stone* reviewed *Physical Graffiti*, Jim Miller actually offered some praise. But the record sales were what really mattered. That was the kind of validation that counted on this renewal of the touring wars. John Paul said that the fan acceptance inspired them to play with more fury, more intensity, more passion.

During the next few months, Zeppelin proved that they also were still the industry's Number 1 live attraction—and the world's highest-paid band. For that thirty-nine-concert North American tour, more than 700,000 tickets had been sold within hours after they went on sale—and the shows themselves were bigger than ever. At every concert, the music was channeled through an incredible 70,000-watt speaker system and an intricate lighting network that generated 310,000 watts of power. No one ever asked for his money back. Most of them would have paid to see more.

As the tour progressed, we soon had to deal with problems other than Jimmy's injured finger. Less than two weeks into the tour, Robert contracted the flu, with a high fever and a gravelly throat. At one point, he was feeling so ill that he literally couldn't drag himself out of bed.

Peter impressed me with the way he reacted. He still saw Led Zeppelin as a long-term investment, and he insisted that Robert put his health before the tour itself. He called the local promoter in St. Louis and ordered a rescheduling of the forthcoming concert there. That gave Robert a few days to recuperate, which he both needed and appreciated. It also allowed the remaining band members to make an unscheduled invasion of Los Angeles.

At the Ambassador East Hotel in Chicago, Bonham first raised the possibility of leaving town during Robert's recovery. "Let's not hang around here. It's boring as hell. We can have a lot more fun at the Rainbow Bar in L.A."

John Paul protested. He wanted the *Starship* to fly them to the Bahamas, where he could already feel the warm sunshine and fantasize about the girls on the beaches. But Los Angeles held the promise of warm weather, too. We talked about it for an hour and finally reached a consensus. We gave the orders to rev up the engines of the *Starship,* and we headed west.

When the tour resumed, I sometimes felt that Led Zeppelin had become too big, too successful for its own good or at least for its own physical well-being. The audiences were so immense and so enthusiastic that there seemed no way to ensure proper crowd control. Sometimes bedlam broke out days or weeks before the band even reached town.

In Boston, in fact, the concert never got off the ground. Fans had lined up to buy tickets for the performance at Boston Garden, and because the weather was frigid, officials let them camp inside the building. During the night, however, the kids went berserk. They broke into the food stands and got drunk on the beer they had stolen. They ripped seats out of their moorings. They turned on emergency fire hoses. In all, there was more than $30,000 damage to the Garden. As a result, Boston mayor Kevin White ordered the cancellation of the Zeppelin show, fearing even more trouble at the concert itself.

Not knowing quite what to expect, I ordered that security remain extremely tight at those 1975 concerts. At the Philadelphia Spectrum, a fan approaching the stage with a camera during "Stairway to Heaven" was ambushed by two of our hired goons. They battered him with such ferocity that Jimmy nearly became ill watching the brutality in front of him. He moved toward the edge of the stage, as though he was going to intervene in some way. But as he got a closer view of the mayhem, he bowed his head and turned away. It was really more than he could stand.

"What the hell was going on out there tonight?" he shouted at me after the concert. "You have to find a less violent way of controlling these situations!"

I was more sympathetic toward the security team than Jimmy. I had done my time on the front lines at Zeppelin concerts and realized that when security attacked, it was usually for a reason, even if it was in response to their own fears and anxieties. At times, I had felt that crowds were going to overwhelm me, that it was going to be a fight for survival. Late in that same Spectrum concert, when dozens of fans began congregating near the front of the auditorium, I positioned myself underneath the stage and frantically began smashing them on the kneecaps with a hammer.

I learned a lot from the off-duty cops who usually provided the security at the concerts. At the Pittsburgh Civic Arena, one of them was particularly proud of his crowd-control tactics. "Let me loan you a blackjack in case you need to bash in a skull or two tonight!" he said calmly as he handed me one of the metal-laden weapons. He also showed me how to conceal small weights in a pair of gloves, turning them into a potentially lethal weapon. "Some cops here use them to rough people up," he said. I made a mental note to keep a low profile in Pittsburgh.

By the midway point of the tour, I had become possessed with ensuring that the band's safety was never in jeopardy. I never carried a gun in the U.S.— that's where I drew the line. But a knife or a hammer had become a necessity. I just felt more confident with them in certain situations.

One night before our concert at Madison Square Garden, when the stress was starting to overwhelm me, I told Peter, "I feel like a guy working for the secret service, guarding the President and knowing that something terrible could happen in the next tick of the clock. Someday, we're going to reach a point at which all the hassles are not going to be worth it anymore. We're not there yet, but it's gonna happen."

44

DANCING DAYS

When the 1975 tour reached New York for six concerts at Madison Square Garden and the Nassau Coliseum, we parked ourselves at the Plaza Hotel. For Jimmy Page, his suite at the Plaza was much too pretentious, "something comparable to the Versailles Palace," he complained. John Bonham really didn't care whether his suite was gaudy or austere; in fact, as long as there was a pool table in his room (which he always had in New York and Chicago), he could do without just about everything else, including running water.

In New York and everywhere else Led Zeppelin traveled on that 1975 tour, our time clocks were never in sync with the rest of the city. We'd be up all night, still feeling a rush from the excitement and the tension of that evening's concert. By the time we were worn out enough for sleep, the sun was just breaking through.

One night in New York, Mick Jagger called to see if any of us wanted to accompany him and Ronnie Wood to a club in Harlem. Jimmy, Bonzo, and I decided that it sounded better than spending the night in the hotel. I phoned for a couple of limos, and we went downstairs to meet Mick and Ronnie in front of the Plaza. Jimmy climbed into the front limo with the two Stones. Bonzo tried to join them, but they told him to get into the rear car with me, which didn't make him very happy.

As we drove up to Harlem, our two drivers were talking to one another over their radios, chattering about the dangers of going into Harlem late at night. "Don't you think we should stop and get some more armor, or do you think we have enough?" one of them asked. He didn't sound as if he were joking.

As Bonzo listened to this conversation, his eyes lit up. He was still pissed off that he hadn't been allowed to ride in the lead limo, and at a stoplight he told our driver, "Matty, I know you've got some guns up there. Give me one of them after you check to make sure it's unloaded."

Matty inspected a Beretta and handed it back to Bonham.

"Okay," John said. "Now pull alongside their limo."

When the two limos were next to one another, Bonzo signaled to Mick, mouthing the words, "Lower your window." Mick smiled, happy to oblige. When both of their windows were down, John stuck the Beretta out and aimed it right at them. "I'll teach you fuckers to leave me behind," he shouted.

Even though I knew John had an unloaded gun, just the sight of a pointed weapon made me jumpy. In the other limo, they went absolutely berserk. There were screams from the backseat as Mick, Ronnie, and Jimmy simultaneously hit the floor. Their driver slammed down on the accelerator and sped through two red lights, convinced that Bonham's insanity had turned him into a killer.

At the club in Harlem, Bonzo explained that it was all a practical joke. The others were still infuriated, having trouble seeing the humor in it.

A few evenings later, a particularly chilly night in New York, Robert began bitching about the weather. "Who planned this fucking tour anyway?" he grumbled, looking my way. "Whatever happened to *summer* tours? We could have run into warmer weather in Siberia."

"Well," Bonzo said, "let's go back to L.A. tomorrow. We'll sit by the pool and just drink. Or better yet, forget the pool. Let's just spend the whole day at the Rainbow and fly back to New York at night."

With the *Starship*, just about anything was possible. Other than the cost of the fuel, the trip to L.A. wouldn't be too fiscally draining. And we could start drinking during the flight west.

The band assigned me the task of arranging a quick exit to L.A. immediately after the next Madison Square Garden concert. I made plans for the limos to go directly from the Garden to Newark airport, where the *Starship* would be waiting for us. All we needed was a police escort, with sirens and red lights, to speed up the drive to the airport.

But there was a glitch. One of our security men, who we'll call Kenny, told me he was unable to arrange for a police escort: "I'm doing the best I can, Richard, but the cops are telling me that the limos would have to go through the Lincoln Tunnel, and there are different police jurisdictions on either end of the tunnel. The police escort that enters the tunnel can't be the same one that exits it. I don't think it's going to work out."

I knew that Led Zeppelin wasn't used to taking no for an answer. To a man, they could become contemptuous of just about anything that interfered with what they wanted. I could already hear Bonzo exploding in anger ("You really screwed this one up, Cole!").

So I told Kenny to keep trying. "See what you can do," I said. "If it's going to take some money to change their minds, we'll pay whatever they want."

The night of the Madison Square Garden concert, Kenny approached me backstage, accompanied by a uniformed New York policeman. "Richard, let me introduce you to Alan," Kenny said. "He'll be your police escort tonight."

A few minutes later, Kenny took me aside. "Alan's going to need three hundred dollars."

"No problem," I whispered. "How in the hell did you arrange this?"

"Well," Kenny said, "technically, Alan is off duty tonight. He 'borrowed' a police car from his precinct's parking lot, and he's willing to take you through the Lincoln Tunnel and to the airport for an under-the-table payment. Three hundred dollars is what he wants."

"It's worth it," I told him. "For starters, it'll probably save my job."

The band laughed all the way to the airport. "I love getting away with things like this," Jimmy said. "Do you think this cop realizes that we would have paid him one thousand dollars if that's what he had asked for?"

That 1975 trip through America was the first Zeppelin tour in which heroin circulated freely among our entourage. Although alcohol and cocaine were still much more prevalent, I frequently nourished my own smack habit, and at one time or another, Jimmy, Robert, and Bonzo tried some, too. It was the first time I had seen any of them use it, although since I hadn't toured with the band since 1973, they could have been snorting it for months or even years without my knowing. No one was using needles, and none of us really seemed truly hooked in those days, although I'm not really sure about myself. I certainly enjoyed the sensations of smack, although it seemed as though I could go a few days without it and not experience any of the classic withdrawal symptoms.

On some level, I think we all knew the risks associated with heroin. But Led Zeppelin was like a teenager riding a motorcycle without a helmet. We thought we were infalible, that nothing or nobody could topple us from the throne.

Peter knew better, even if we were just experimenting. One afternoon at the Plaza, when he saw me preparing to snort some heroin, he became furious. "You're fucking mad to use that shit," he said, insisting that I flush it down the toilet. I did, just to appease him. Later that day, however, I bought some more.

Before we left New York for the last time during the '75 tour, Zeppelin's attitude toward the media sunk to an all-time low. Bonzo was quietly reading a newspaper in his suite when one of our roadies showed him the results of the new *Playboy* music poll. The magazine had ranked Karen Carpenter as a better rock drummer than Bonzo.

"Oh, my God, no!" Bonham wailed. "Karen Carpenter! *Karen Carpenter!*" He paced his suite. He picked up an ashtray and bounced it off the far wall. "I can't believe it! I give up! If Karen Carpenter is a better drummer, then I'm in the wrong business! I'm gonna get a job driving a taxi! Somebody help me, please!"

All of us were a little apprehensive of what the press would write about us next. When we got word that *Rolling Stone* was sending one of its writers, Cameron Crowe, to travel with the band during part of the '75 tour, we didn't know quite what to expect. And when we met Cameron for the first time, our first thought was, "Geez, he's so young." But as he mingled and talked with everyone in the band, our respect for him grew. All of us were surprised by his knowledge of rock and roll in general and Led Zeppelin in particular. He was obviously someone who did his homework, and knew what he was writing about (of course, he would later go on to direct rock and roll films like *Almost Famous,* and win an Academy Award for his script of that movie, based largely on his travels with bands like Zeppelin). When Cameron's article on Zeppelin was published in *Rolling Stone*, it was quite complimentary of Zeppelin. And to Bonzo's delight, it contained no comparisons of him to Karen Carpenter!

We continued to weave our way across the country, often inviting girls to fly with us on the *Starship*. Sometimes I just liked to see the amazed girls ooh and aah over how lavishly we traveled. Bonzo, however, could only take so much of that ogling. After a concert at the New Orleans Municipal Auditorium, we flew into Texas, accompanied by four girls who had been traveling with us for three days. "I'm getting tired of these birds," Bonham told me. "Can't we find some new ones?"

As we landed in Dallas, Bad Company was at a nearby departure gate, just minutes away from taking off on their own chartered twenty-seater, Viscount turboprop jet. Mick Ralphs, the group's guitarist, ordered the stairs of Bad Company's jet lowered, and we boarded it for a few minutes.

"Hey, can you take these damn chicks off our hands?" Bonzo pleaded.

Mick sounded interested. "I'll make you a deal," he said. "We've got two girls here that we don't want! We'll trade them for your four!"

So we swapped women. Too often, we treated girls like just another commodity, like exchanging one bottle of champagne for another. Plant tried to convince me, "The girls don't seem to mind." And those fresh faces from Bad Company's entourage certainly raised the possibility of making life more interesting for us in Texas.

During our stay in Dallas, however, even those new girls got to be a drag. "Dump 'em!" Bonzo exclaimed. By that point, his interests had shifted across the street from our hotel, where he saw a parked 1966 Corvette Stingray that he instantly fell in love with. "I've got to have it," he thought. "How can I find out who owns the sucker?" he asked me. "I'll pay him anything!"

Back in his hotel suite, Bonzo called Jack Kelly, an ex-FBI agent and one of our security men. "Jack, do whatever you have to do to get that car for me. If you need to, have the owner arrested and don't let him go until he agrees to sell me the fucking car!"

Through the license number, Jack tracked down the car's owner, and Bonzo offered to buy it with cash on the spot. He ultimately paid $18,000 for it, and even though it may not have been worth that much, it really didn't matter to him. It was a toy that he wanted. He drove it into the back of a Ryder rental truck and paid $1,400 for a driver to haul it to L.A., where it would be waiting for him at the Riot House when we arrived.

A week later in L.A., I was returning from the Rainbow Bar one night, driving with three girls in the back of a white limousine that I had nicknamed the "slutmobile." We saw the Ryder parked in front of the Hyatt, with bright lights shining from the back of the truck. I asked the limo driver to pull to the rear of the Ryder, where I could get a better view of what was going on inside. Once I was close enough, I could hear sounds coming from inside.

"Roooar, roooar." It was Bonham, sitting in the front seat of the Stingray, doing his best imitation of a sports car in third gear. Keith Moon was sitting next to him, making almost as much noise. Fortunately, neither of them had the keys to the car, since in their inebriated state they probably would have made a shambles of the L.A. freeways that night.

Los Angeles was our last stop on this American tour. Three nights at the Forum and just as many at the Rainbow. As usual, by this stage of the tour, we were eager for it to end. Nevertheless, the temptations of L.A. made the stay a little more tolerable. We again had staked out the entire ninth floor and part of the tenth and eleventh at the Riot House—we called them the "havoc floors." That gave us plenty of empty hotel rooms in which to stash the girls we had rounded up on any given night and allowed us to play musical beds from one room to the next. Bonzo kept repeating, "It's a tough job, but someone's got to do it!" It was a cliché, but an appropriate one.

One night, Jimmy and I brought a couple of underage girls back to our rooms. Apparently, the father of one of them tracked her down and called up to the ninth floor, where the security guards routinely screened all our calls before deciding whether to put them through.

This particular night, the girl's dad sounded like he was on a rampage. "My daughter's in the hotel with one of your musicians. I'm going to call the police!"

The security guard had a standard reply: "Don't bother. You're talking to an L.A. police officer. There's no one fitting your daughter's description up here. Try another hotel."

We had no qualms about misleading—or was it lying?—to ensure that our party wasn't disturbed. When you had the police covering for you, nothing seemed particularly improper. It just became the way Led Zeppelin operated.

On our last full day at the Riot House, the tedium of touring finally caught up with Bonzo. To fight off the boredom, he decided to shoot jump shots out the windows of his suite—not with basketballs but with television sets. One by one, half a dozen RCA color sets sailed out toward Sunset Boulevard, shattering into slivers of plastic and glass that carpeted the driveway leading up to the hotel entrance.

"I'm not going to get into any trouble this time," Bonzo told me before he began his shooting demonstration. Rather than heave his own TV out his window on the south side of the hotel, he confiscated TV sets from the rooms of our roadies on the north side. When the hotel's assistant manager raced up to the ninth floor to try to catch the troublemaker in the act, he found everything in place in Bonham's suite, including the TV tuned to an early afternoon soap opera.

Bonham tried to act as innocent as possible. "I wondered what all that noise was, too," he told the baffled assistant. Then he raised his voice. "Look, I'm a guest at this hotel, and I sure would appreciate it if you could cut down the noise around here!"

The assistant manager actually apologized to Bonham. As he left, I walked into Bonzo's suite, and we both burst out laughing. "Guess what goes out the window next?" Bonham said. With a malicious grin on his face, he pointed to the white grand piano in the center of the room.

"Nooo, Bonzo, nooo," I told him. Within seconds, however, he and I tried lifting the piano and carrying it to the window. Finally, however, we realized that even if our brawn could handle the challenge, the piano could never fit through the window. "Damn it," he said. "That would have gotten their attention down on Sunset."

THE LEGENDS

There were certain people who Led Zeppelin considered just this side of God. Elvis, of course, probably headed the list. But there were others whose talents we respected, too. Bob Dylan was one of them. No wonder, then, that we were excited when Dylan showed up at a reception we held in L.A. for the press and some of our friends.

The band exchanged cordial greetings with Dylan, but he acted shy and withdrawn. He pretty much kept to himself, staying near the buffet table and politely shaking hands with whomever approached him. If that's what happens when you're famous, Bonzo thought, I don't want to become any better known.

Late in the evening, as I was chatting with Jimmy and Robert, Ronnie Wood staggered over, almost crippled by his own hysterical laughter. "I just heard a killer," he said. "You gotta hear this one."

"Okay, Ron," Robert said. "Calm down and tell us what happened."

Ronnie finally brought his laughter under control. "Peter just walked up to Bob Dylan and introduced himself. He said, 'I'm Peter Grant, and I'm the manager of Led Zeppelin.' And Dylan looked at him and said, 'Don't come to me with your fucking problems!'"

Ronnie was right. It was a killer. It also showed just how far our reputation had spread.

Just before we left L.A., John Paul and I got another opportunity to meet with our *real* folk hero, Elvis. He was staying in a rented house in Bel Air, and when

I called in hopes that I'd be invited to stop by, Jerry Schilling passed along the following message from the King: "Bring John Paul Jones with you because he's so quiet."

We brought a couple of bottles of cold champagne with us, and I had stuffed my pockets with heroin, which was my own drug of choice for the evening. When we arrived, Elvis was sitting in the living room, wearing a very ordinary pair of blue-striped, cotton pajamas, a simple robe, and slippers that had little blue pom-poms on them. There were nearly a dozen aides and bodyguards in the room, too, and not one of them cracked a smile as we moved forward to shake hands with Elvis.

After we had exchanged greetings, the somber mood of the group hadn't changed. Eventually, I remarked, "It's like a fucking morgue in here!"

In an instant, Elvis leaped forward and grabbed me by the lapels. At first, I thought he was kidding. But then I wasn't sure.

"You don't swear and curse in my house, Mr. Cole!"

He pushed me backward, then assumed a karate posture that looked rather intimidating, particularly since I knew Elvis had been studying the martial arts for years. John Paul was standing a few feet from us, stunned by what was unfolding before his eyes.

I was leaner and nimbler than Elvis, but was already stoned by the time we had reached the house. And I didn't want to be remembered as the tour manager who was killed by Elvis.

The King cocked his right arm and took a swing at me. I blocked the blow with my left forearm, but as I did, his hand struck my watch with enough force to snap the watchband. It was an expensive gold Tiffany watch that Ahmet Ertegun had given me, and it bounced on the plush white carpeting.

"Oh, no," Elvis said, dropping to one knee and, at least for the moment, forgetting that he was in the process of trying to spill some of my blood. He picked up the watch, wrapped it around his wrist, and said, "Your wrist must be huge, Richard. This is a great watch! A great watch!"

I didn't know quite how to react. Finally, I said, "Well, please accept it as a gift from me. You can have it, Elvis."

Elvis couldn't take his eyes off the watch. After a while he stood up and, without saying a word, turned and disappeared down the hallway. A minute later, he returned with another gorgeous watch in his hand. "Here," he said, "this one's got thirty-two diamonds. *You* can fuckin' have *this* one!" He was swearing now, too.

The swap meet wasn't over yet.

Elvis turned toward John Paul and asked, "Well, what have you got?"

Jonesy loosened the strap on the cheap Mickey Mouse watch he was wearing and handed it to Elvis. The King laughed and, once again, left the room, returning with a lapis-faced Baume & Mercier watch. He handed it to John Paul.

For the next few minutes, the evening became something akin to a New Guinea tribal ritual in which everyone was trying to prove his manhood—in this case, by giving a bigger and better gift than the last one. I asked Elvis what his sign was, and when he said Capricorn I removed a large amethyst birthstone ring I had bought in Brazil when I was there in 1968 with the New Vaudeville Band. "Go ahead, it's yours," I said.

Elvis left the room again, coming back with a gold ring in the shape of a John Wayne cowboy hat. It had a full carat and a half diamond, surrounded by nine smaller diamonds and was inscribed with the words, "Love, Linda." He handed it to me.

The evening continued like this for the next half hour, with an orgy of gift-giving that Elvis seemed to find exciting.

By the time John Paul and I were ready to leave, Elvis escorted us out his front door, telling his security guards, "I'm okay out here with these guys; Richard will take care of me." As we approached our limousine, Elvis even opened the car door for us. The chauffeur's face registered complete shock. So did mine.

When we returned to England a month later, there was a note waiting for me from Jerry Schilling. "We haven't seen the Boss have such a good time in years," he wrote.

Before we left L.A., a skinny, redheaded girl, covered with freckles and wearing beads and a wrinkled minidress, was meandering through the lobby of the Riot House, pestering the desk clerks and bellhops, insisting that she had to meet with Led Zeppelin, particularly Jimmy. The hotel management finally called Danny Goldberg, who had joined up with us in L.A. He went to talk to the girl.

"I need to see Jimmy Page," she pleaded in a high-pitched, emotional voice. "Something terrible is going to happen to Jimmy, maybe at the concert tonight."

She proceeded to describe a vision she had in which Jimmy's life was in jeopardy. "The last time I had a vision like this," she said, "someone was shot and killed right in front of me!"

Danny let her ramble on for a few minutes, then losing his patience, interrupted her.

"Look, Jimmy isn't available to talk to you now. If you want to write him a note, I'll see that he gets it."

The girl sat down, scribbled a few sentences on a piece of paper, and handed it to Danny. She reluctantly left, whereupon Danny crumbled the note and threw it away.

A few months later, the girl resurfaced—this time on television. The band was staying at a rented beach house in Malibu, working on material for the next album, and the TV was on one evening. They all watched in horror at news reports identifying the freckle-faced girl as Lynette "Squeaky" Fromme, a member of the Charles Manson cult. She had been arrested several days earlier for pointing a loaded gun at President Gerald Ford in Sacramento.

Fromme clearly was a girl with violence on her mind. Fortunately, she and Led Zeppelin never directly crossed paths.

46

TAXED OUT
OF ENGLAND

In April 1975, shortly after the American tour ended, Marilyn and I agreed to work at patching up our marriage. I was still more involved in heroin than she would have liked, but she tried to be understanding. We decided to take a vacation in the Canary Islands, where we could concentrate just on one another for a while.

Nevertheless, I routinely checked in with Led Zeppelin's office. And having me away for two weeks was more than Peter could bear, particularly since he already was plotting the group's next move.

"Here's what I've been thinking," he said. "I want the band to play at Earls Court. I want to go in there for at least three nights, maybe more. How soon can you get back to start arranging those shows?"

"Well, I'm on a holiday," I told him. I didn't want to come back at all.

"Richard, listen to me," he said. "Earls Court is one of the biggest venues in England. It's real important to me. *Real* important."

So Marilyn and I caught a plane to London the next morning. In the days we had spent in the Canary Islands, we seemed to have done some repair work on our relationship. "Let's see how we do back in the real world," I told her on the flight home.

By the following day, I was back in Peter's office, working out details for the Earls Court performances, which were scheduled to begin May 17. Earls Court had a seating capacity of 17,000, and Peter felt we shouldn't cut corners. "I want to stage the entire American production—laser beams, special lighting, and PA equipment, plus adding an oversized video screen," he said. "And I want to keep the ticket prices down."

Of course, we could have charged just about anything and still been assured of sellouts. But even though Peter was very good at making money for the band, he also was sensitive to their image. These would be the first Zeppelin concerts in Britain in more than two years, and after a lot of thought he concluded that the public relations benefits of inexpensive seating would outweigh the financial gains of a much higher price. At his insistence, the ticket prices were kept low—one to two and a half pounds a seat.

On April 19, 51,000 tickets went on sale for three dates. In five hours, they were completely sold out. Two more concerts were added, and those 34,000 tickets were gobbled up instantly, too. Many of the ticket buyers had been Zeppelin fanatics since those earliest days in late 1968. Others had only come aboard with the *Physical Graffiti* album. But their shared enthusiasm transformed the lines at the ticket windows into outdoor festivals in their own right, a celebration of rock music's biggest band.

I chartered a 747 private cargo plane to fly the high-tech equipment from the American tour to London, and we brought in Showco's experienced crew to oversee the entire production. A 20' × 30' video screen was positioned high above the stage. The 70,000-watt speaker system was carefully erected in place. Meanwhile, trains were chartered to bring fans from throughout the country for the five concerts.

The band rehearsed for three days, but after the American tour they knew exactly what they wanted to do. From the first bars of "Rock and Roll," Zeppelin exploded with some of their most energetic, memorable shows. Robert, wearing denim jeans and with his blond curls longer than most British fans remembered them, told the crowds that the band was offering more than music. "This is a journey through some of our experiences—the positive ones and the negative ones—over the last six years."

The band guided the audience through a three-hour Zeppelin retrospective, playing songs from every era, from the early days of *Led Zeppelin* to the gentler acoustic sounds of *Led Zeppelin III* to the most contemporary songs of *Physical Graffiti.* On the final night, after the last encore and the last notes of "Black Dog," Robert shouted a thank-you to the packed house. "We've enjoyed playing for you so much. We'll see you again, maybe in the nineteen eighties."

In fact, the band would only play in the U.K. two more times—both at the Knebworth Festival in Hertfordshire. For many, perhaps most, of the 85,000 who saw them at Earls Court, that was their last live glimpse of Led Zeppelin.

A few weeks later, Peter told me his own reasons for the Earls Court concerts. In a sense, he saw them as "good-bye gifts" to the country. "We're moving out," he said. "The tax man is driving us out of England. These will be the last concerts here for quite a while."

Essentially, Led Zeppelin was just making too much money. And for financial reasons, their accountants had recommended that they become tax exiles. Other rock stars like the Stones had preceded them in seeking refuge outside Great Britain. But even though it made financial sense, it wasn't an easy decision for any member of Led Zeppelin to make. At first, all of them resisted. "This is home," Bonzo told himself. "I'm not going anywhere." Then the numbers were laid out on the table in front of them. It would have been foolish to turn over most of what they made to the government.

Robert had some second thoughts, too. It didn't feel right to abandon his homeland purely because of money. But he and the others had worked like hell for the riches they had accumulated. They felt they might as well keep as much of it as possible.

All the members of Zeppelin maintained their homes in England, but were limited on the number of days they could spend in the country without being gouged by an atrocious tax bite. One by one, they started relocating themselves and their families to Switzerland or France.

Bonzo held out longer than the others. Pat Bonham was pregnant with their second child, and John wanted them to stay together in England, at least until the baby was born. "Fuck the money," he said at one point. "I'm gonna spend time with my wife right here where she needs me."

But once their daughter, Zoe, was born, Bonzo came to his senses. He still had time to start his tax exile that year, which he began in Europe.

Eventually, the entire band ended up in Jersey, the largest of the Channel Islands near the west coast of Normandy. Jersey is a popular tourist spot, but according to Bonham, "The natives here don't seem to do much but drink and wife-swap." For a while, the band rented a big house, and we spent weeks killing time, largely by drinking Pimm's, then Tropical Pimm's, then King Pimm's. It was the next best thing to wife-swapping.

While on Jersey, Bonham had even more time to indulge himself with his passion for cars, particularly luxury models. He had purchased dozens of automobiles over the years—twenty-eight of them in the first eighteen months of Zeppelin's success. After that he stopped counting. He never kept any of them very long; he didn't buy them as investments, but rather because he loved driving fast cars. Still, perhaps not surprisingly, his selection of vehicles sometimes leaned toward the bizarre. Once, he even purchased a Model T bread van, just because he felt in the mood to buy one.

During the time that Bonham owned the bread van, it was one of his most prized possessions. Once while the band was rehearsing at Shepperton Studios, he had parked it in front of the building. A priest from the church down the street paused as he walked by the van. "This is a very *dangerous*-looking automobile," he told Bonzo and me, making a stab at some light humor. "I better bless this car and this boy." Bonham smiled politely while the priest actually fetched some holy water and sprinkled it on the car—and on Bonzo. It was probably the closest Bonzo had been to a religious experience in years.

On Jersey, Bonzo's favorite vehicle was a Rolls-Royce that he used to drive around the island. One afternoon, he had parked the Rolls outside one of his favorite pubs. Dressed in cutoff jeans and a T-shirt, he began washing the car with a sponge and a bucket of soapsuds and was making quite a mess of himself.

An elderly man in a coat and tie walked by and paused a moment to survey Bonzo's efforts. He was clearly amused by what he saw. Finally, the bystander said with an arrogant smirk, "Well, well, well . . . this is the first time I've ever seen a man have to wash his own Rolls-Royce!"

The comment struck Bonzo the wrong way. He gritted his teeth and shouted, "Is that right!" He slammed shut an open door and began furiously kicking the Roll's side panels . . . one kick after another, pounding and pounding again the sides of the car. He'd take a brief break to catch his breath, and then the bizarre outburst would continue, ultimately lasting for several minutes. By the time he was done, there were dozens of dents in the expensive automobile.

Both the elderly man and I stood there, startled by Bonzo's behavior and wondering what he had planned next. But just as quickly as his anger had erupted, Bonzo suddenly calmed down. He turned to the startled onlooker. "I suspect that's the first time you've ever seen a man *smash* his own fucking Rolls-Royce as well! Why don't you fuck off and mind your own business!"

Bonzo strode into the pub and ordered a Pimm's. The passing years had had no sobering effect on his eccentric behavior.

47

THE NIGHTMARE ON RHODES

I've got some horrible news, Richard. There's been a terrible accident. Just terrible."

Charlotte Martin's voice was trembling. She had called Zeppelin's London office from the Greek island of Rhodes, and as I listened to the anxiety in her voice, I developed a queasy feeling in my own gut, expecting the worst as Charlotte continued to talk over the static-filled line. Charlotte had a tendency to exaggerate and panic over even the most minor problems. But this time she sounded as if she was in a daze.

"The Plants' car went off the road," Charlotte said. "Maureen was driving, and it just crashed into a tree. It was horrible. Everyone's been hurt pretty bad."

Maureen Plant had been driving a rented Austin Mini sedan, Charlotte said, and Robert was sitting beside her. Their children were in the backseat, along with Scarlet, the daughter of Charlotte and Jimmy Page. Charlotte was in a second car with Maureen's sister and brother-in-law and was not involved in the accident.

Upon impact, Robert's right ankle and right elbow shattered. So did many of the bones in his right leg. Robert's four-year-old son, Karac, fractured his leg, and seven-year-old Carmen broke her wrist. Scarlet escaped with only a few bruises. Maureen, however, was critically injured. She had broken her pelvis, fractured a leg, suffered cuts on her face, and had a fractured skull. She also had lost large amounts of blood, and because she had a rare blood type, doctors had to rely on her sister, Shirley, for immediate transfusions. A doctor told me later that if Shirley had not been in Rhodes and readily available, Maureen might not have pulled through.

"Can you get here as soon as possible?" Charlotte pleaded. "And, Richard, if you can, bring some British doctors with you. I'm not sure these doctors here know what they're doing. They're having trouble locating more blood for Maureen. I'm going to find out what type of blood it is, and maybe you can bring some of it with you from England."

"I'll be there as soon as I can get a flight," I told her.

"Richard, I'm really scared," she sobbed just before hanging up. "I don't know whether everyone's going to pull through."

In July and August 1975, Robert and Jimmy had taken their families on a vacation to Rhodes by way of Switzerland and Morocco. Jimmy, however, had then left the others on the Greek island to fly to Italy, primarily to look at a farmhouse in Sicily once owned by Aleister Crowley that he was considering buying. From there, he caught a plane to London, where he was overseeing the editing of the "Dazed and Confused" portion of the long-overdue Zeppelin film, now titled *The Song Remains the Same*. Robert and the other globe-trotters were scheduled to return to England later in the week, and the band was due to begin rehearsals for an American tour in the late summer.

After my conversation with Charlotte, I was up most of the night, making phone calls in hopes of tracking down one of the best doctors in London and talking him into flying with me to Rhodes. I ultimately convinced two physicians to make the trip. One of them was Dr. John Baretta, a British physician with an office on Harley Street who provided medical services to the Greek Embassy. He spoke fluent Greek, and I figured he'd be as important a resource for his language skills as for his medical expertise. The other was Dr. Mike Lawrence, one of London's most prominent orthopedic surgeons; from the accounts I was getting of the Plant family's injuries, I figured we could use someone who knew what he was doing in the operating room.

Dr. Baretta had another important asset. He was the personal physician of Sir Robert McAlpine, a successful civil engineer and contractor who owned several private jets, one of which could be turned into a flying ambulance, equipped with special supports for stretchers. I had already tried to charter a private jet for the trip, but Zeppelin's own accountants vetoed the idea. "You fucking asshole," I screamed at one of them. "This is the band's money you're playing with. Robert and his family are badly injured, and now you tell me you're not going to release the money!"

"That's right," he said. "Peter Grant's out of town, and you don't have the authority to do it."

Dr. Baretta quickly arranged for the three of us to fly to Rhodes in one of

McAlpine's jets, leaving late at night. We had stocked the plane's refrigerator with eight pints of blood matching Maureen's type. I was so anxious that I didn't sleep at all on the flight. I didn't even have any booze or drugs to keep me company.

We arrived at six in the morning and took a taxi directly to the hospital, which was really not much more than a little emergency clinic. "I'm not impressed," I told Dr. Baretta as we walked through the front entrance, dodging a few cockroaches crawling on the floor. There were two unattended patients sitting in wheelchairs, looking as though they had given up on ever receiving any medical care.

After evaluating the patients and the hospital conditions, Dr. Baretta and Dr. Lawrence agreed that we should get our patients back to England as soon as possible. They tried reasoning with the Greek physicians—"You are doing a wonderful job, but the patients need to be closer to home," Dr. Baretta told them. The hospital, however, refused to release their patients. "The police are investigating the accident to see if alcohol or drugs were involved," the hospital administrator told us, showing about as much compassion as the Berlin Wall. "Your friends can't leave the country until the police have decided whether they're going to press charges against someone."

We were virtual prisoners. "This fucking hospital staff is behaving like a lynch mob, not health professionals," I complained to Charlotte. In exasperation, I finally began contemplating sneaking Robert and his family out of the hospital in the middle of the night and back to London.

"I think there's only one way out of this," I told Dr. Baretta, "and I don't think you'll like it." He was opposed to my "kidnapping" plot, but by this time I had made up my mind. He had described to me how Robert's leg would have to be reset and how Maureen would need surgery, and I wanted all of it done in England.

As quickly as possible, I hired a private ambulance and rented two station wagons and had them parked at a side entrance. At two in the morning, Charlotte and I wheeled Robert, Maureen, and their children—along with their IV bottles and other medical equipment—down the hospital corridors to the "getaway cars." If anyone saw us leaving, no one said a word.

Later that day, our plane was in the sky, headed for London, with a stop in Rome for refueling. It was a relief just to be in the air.

During the flight, Robert and I had our first real chance to talk. He told me they had been driving to visit Phil May of the Pretty Things and his wife, Electra, who had rented a house on the island from Roger Waters of Pink Floyd. "After the car hit the tree," Robert said, "I looked over at Maureen and thought she was dead." He paused for a moment, fighting back tears.

"Maureen was unconscious and bleeding, and the kids were screaming in the backseat. Charlotte had come up to the car, and she was hysterical."

Robert said that they waited forever for an ambulance, but none ever arrived. "Finally," he explained, "the driver of a fruit truck loaded us onto his open flatbed. He took us to the hospital, but we were bouncing around so much that my leg was dragging on the road for most of the trip."

Word traveled fast around the island. Phil heard about an auto accident involving some Englishmen and assumed it was the Plants. He and Electra went to the hospital and, along with Maureen's sister, helped care for Robert and his family. "In the Greek hospitals, they don't even feed you," Robert said. "If you don't have a relative or a friend to bring you food, they'll let you starve to death! It's completely ridiculous!"

As our plane approached England, I called ahead and had ambulances waiting for us at Heathrow. Although Maureen was sedated, she was still in a lot of pain. The Plants were transported to Guy's Hospital, where Maureen immediately underwent surgery.

There was a bizarre twist to our arrival, however. The plane actually delayed its landing in England, circling at 15,000 feet for thirty minutes, so we wouldn't touch down until shortly after midnight—a new calendar day. Even amid the chaos surrounding the accident, Zeppelin's accountants had the presence of mind to advise me that Robert would need to limit the number of days he spent in Britain because of his "tax exile" status. "If the tax man has any questions, he's going to ask for documentation of the flight schedules," one of the accountants said. "If you land at eleven-thirty at night, that's going to count as a full day that Robert spent in the country. See what you can do to delay the landing here."

I was furious that financial considerations were receiving such top priority. "Forget it," I said. "We're going to get these people to the hospital as soon as possible." But as the jet approached London, Dr. Baretta convinced me that the patients were stable. "If you need to wait another half an hour, they'll be fine," he told me. So I gave permission for the plane to circle outside the three-mile limit until just past midnight. I knew it might save Robert many thousands of pounds in taxes, although I still thought it was more important to save a life.

As a result of the accident, Led Zeppelin was put on hold for months. The mini-U.S. tour covering eight cities in late August and September was canceled. So were European and Far Eastern tours later in the year. All our attention turned to the recovery of Robert and his family.

It was a difficult, tense time for everyone. Maureen spent weeks in the hospital. Robert and his children were released within a few days, but doctors had a sobering message for him. "You probably won't walk again for six months, maybe more," one said. "And there's no guarantee that you'll ever recover completely."

In the back of everyone's mind was the fact that Zeppelin's future was in jeopardy. "This could be the end of Led Zeppelin," Peter said. "We don't know yet, but this might be the end of the line."

48

THE LONG
ROAD HOME

Although Robert was virtually immobilized for months, I was still faced with moving him as quickly as possible away from England for tax reasons. Peter was en route out of the country to protect his own status as a tax exile, so the decision of where to send Robert was left to me. By coincidence, I was having some of my paintings appraised, and Willie Robertson, my insurance broker, was at my house. I explained Robert's dilemma, and he had a suggestion: "My daughter's godfather is Dick Christian, a big lawyer on Jersey. He's a lovely guy. I'm sure he'll let Robert stay at his guest house."

Christian was agreeable to the idea, and when Robert was released from the hospital, an ambulance took him to the British Airways terminal at Heathrow. Robertson, Benji Le Fevre, Marilyn, and I accompanied him on the flight. Because Robert was unable to climb the steps to the plane, I paid a forklift driver twenty-five pounds to raise him and his wheelchair to the jet's doorway. His casts weighed so much that for a while I wondered if the forklift itself might collapse. But he made it onto the plane, where the British Airways crew had removed two first-class seats so Robert could stretch his leg.

When we landed in Jersey, Christian had a limousine and an ambulance with a stretcher waiting at the airport. At the Christian mansion, a butler named Neville greeted us, but appeared horrified as he sized up our long hair. When Dick Christian came to the door, he had the same look—an expression that said, "What have I gotten myself into?"

Nevertheless, Christian was a thoroughly cordial host. He was a tall, middle-aged man with blond hair and glasses. After we exchanged greetings, he said to Neville, "I think my guests need a nice Pimm's." As we moved inside the house, he told the ambulance driver, "You're going to have to leave the stretcher here. Mr. Plant may need it while he's my guest. I'm sure your boss has plenty of others."

For the next few weeks, my assignment was to help take care of this rock-musician-turned-invalid. It was my toughest undertaking in rock music. Robert's cast ran from his hip to his toes. He was uncomfortable and frustrated by his limitations. At times, his attitude was almost intolerable. "I just don't know whether I'm ever going to be the same onstage again," he moaned. "I can't imagine doing three hours in front of an audience, at least not for a long time."

Robert drank a lot of beer, in part to smother his anxiety about his future. At the same time, he further numbed himself with painkilling drugs. He also spent many hours at the piano, a welcome escape from the torturous physical therapy for his leg and ankle that had become part of his daily routine. Eventually, Robert was on his feet, although for months he needed the help of a cane. It was a long, very trying road back.

Dick Christian made us feel as though we could stay as long as we wanted. He offered us the use of the Maserati and the Jensen parked in his garage. "We've all got cars like this Maserati," he said one day, "but I don't know why. You put the damn thing in third gear, and you're already on the next island!"

As the weeks passed, both Peter and Jimmy began to worry about the band becoming stagnant. Pagey felt that as soon as Robert had the energy, they needed to start writing again, with an eye on getting back into the studio. He would call every few days for reports on Robert's progress. "The longer we wait," he told me, "the harder it's gonna be to come back."

In September, Robert finally gave us the thumbs-up. He felt strong enough, he said, both physically and emotionally, to get to work on the band's seventh album, which would ultimately be called *Presence*. I helped Robert pack, and we bid good-bye to Dick Christian. Dick genuinely seemed sad that we were leaving. To show our gratitude, Peter had engraved the names of Dick's children on Led Zeppelin gold records and gave them to the kids as gifts.

Pagey and Plant discussed where to resume their writing. Because of their status as tax exiles, anywhere in England was off limits. They contemplated a number of options before finally deciding upon Malibu, California. They rented a house right on the beach in the Malibu Colony. Between the Pacific Ocean and the bikini-clad girls, they thought the site was gorgeous. Within days of their arrival, Robert talked about how it stimulated his creativity, how he felt so inspired. If the Beach Boys hadn't already done it, Plant might have written a song about California girls then and there.

Page and Plant remained in Malibu for more than a month, and during their stay Bonzo and John Paul flew out to begin rehearsing for the new album. They initially rehearsed in the rented beach house, but then moved into a more formal setting in the SIR Studios in Hollywood.

"Achilles Last Stand" came together during that period in Malibu. As Plant and Page wrote it, the song touched a nerve, expressing their feelings of having been relegated to a nomadic life. Thanks to their tax situation, they felt that they were losing their roots in England and had not found another place where they felt comfortable. Jimmy called the band "technological gypsies," roaming the world, looking for a home.

"Tea for One" had a related theme, in which Robert poured out the loneliness he felt spending so much time away from his wife and children, due to his tax status and the accident. (Maureen's injuries still prevented her from traveling.) As he wrote the lyrics, an avalanche of emotions welled up inside him: Here he was in Malibu, he thought, still away from his family. At that moment, not much about his life made sense.

Benji Le Fevre spent time with the band in Malibu, keeping an eye on Robert and running errands for the band. He later told me there was plenty of heroin there, although he wasn't monitoring who was using it. "We called the house in Malibu 'Henry Hall,' " Benji said. In England, "henry" is a slang word for heroin.

Dr. Lawrence had encouraged Robert to walk as much as possible, so throughout most of his stay in Malibu, he took slow, deliberate strolls along the beach, aided by his cane. The weather was beautiful until the end of their California stay, when a devastating storm ravaged the coastline, almost taking Zeppelin's rented home out to sea. Jimmy, finding hidden messages in much of what nature dealt, figured the storm might be an omen for the band to move on. They began making plans to record again.

The creative process in Malibu had been enormously therapeutic for Robert. Although there were moments early in his recovery when he wondered whether Zeppelin would ever return to full strength, he was now optimistic about the future, both for himself and the band. He wanted to get into the studio.

Jimmy suggested that they fly to Munich to record at the Musicland Studios, a facility located in the basement of the Arabella Hotel. As unglamorous as that sounded, the studio had built quite a reputation as one of the best on the continent.

I checked on Musicland's availability. "They say we can start immediately,"

I told Jimmy, "but we're going to have to work quickly; the Stones have reserved it, beginning in less than three weeks."

The band's goal was to record the entire *Presence* album there. The weather
was bitterly cold in Munich, and we had little else to do but spend most of our
waking hours in the studio—with occasional indulgences in drugs. When we
had arrived in Munich, Bonzo had moaned, "What the hell is there to do in
this godforsaken city?" It was a common refrain of his, no matter where we
were. One of our roadies had the answer. He pulled a bag of smack out of his
coat pocket. "There's a lot of this junk here, and it's good," he said. He helped
keep us well supplied for the next three weeks.

Bonzo, Jimmy, and I used smack during the daytime hours in Munich, and
none of us seemed the worse for it. No one ever talked about the possible
risks, and we probably didn't think much about them, either. We felt trapped
indoors by Munich's frigid air; heroin, it seemed, made the time indoors pass
more quickly.

With the help of one of our roadies, I located a local drug connection
within walking distance of the studio; if I moved briskly, I could purchase the
heroin and get back before frostbite had begun to attack my fingers and toes.
In fact, I experienced many more ill effects from the cold—goose bumps, chattering teeth, the shivers, numb extremities—than I ever did from smack itself.
And I never stopped to think that, eventually, it might catch up with me.

In the late afternoons and into the night, Zeppelin channeled all their
nervous energy into their work, often putting in twelve-hour days. As he had
done from the beginning, Jimmy assumed control over the way the sessions
unfolded. "Hots On For Nowhere" was written in a little more than an hour
right in the studio. So was "Candy Store Rock," a tribute to 1950s rockabilly.
Jimmy recorded all his solos for the album in one fourteen-hour marathon
session, trying to ignore his fatigue, keeping an eye on the calendar and the
date by which they'd have to vacate the studio. He laid down at least six guitar overdubs for "Achilles Last Stand," only stopping when his aching fingers
could no longer move; when the cut was finished, it was more than ten
minutes long.

Jimmy pushed the rest of the group along, determined to finish on time,
but feeling the tension build from one day to the next. At one point during
the sessions, just as he was feeling optimistic about their progress, the entire
album was nearly sabotaged by an accident involving Robert. Though Plant
was out of his wheelchair, the leg cast was such a burden that he always
seemed off balance. "The poor bastard looks like the Leaning Tower of Pisa,"
Bonzo wisecracked. One afternoon, that disequilibrium caught up
with Robert.

"I'll be right back," Plant said, rising from a chair and limping from the engineer's room to one of the recording studios. But barely more than a dozen steps into his journey, he became entangled in an electrical cable. He lost his balance, stumbled, and fell. All his weight landed on his bad leg, accompanied by a horrifying cracking sound. Everyone in the room gasped. It seemed as though Zeppelin itself had crash-landed.

"Fuck!" Robert shouted, sprawled on his stomach on the floor. He began moaning in pain as he rolled onto his side. "Oh, no!" he howled. "Not again! Not again!"

Jimmy was the first to reach Robert, trying to support him with a hand on his shoulder. Initially, we thought about not moving him at all. But he was so uncomfortable, and he wanted to get up onto a chair. It took three of us to help him move there.

That cracking sound was still ringing in my ears. I decided that Robert needed to be examined by a doctor. I summoned an ambulance, and he was taken to a hospital.

"If I broke that leg again, I might as well forget all about walking," Robert grimaced. "Why did this have to happen? Why?"

No work was done the rest of the night, as we waited to see how badly Plant was hurt.

Fortunately, it was a false alarm. There were no new fractures. Everyone heaved a sigh of relief, especially Robert. By the next morning, the band was recording again, although Plant had increased his dose of painkillers.

Jimmy felt as if he were on an emotional roller coaster. "For a while, I thought we were back at square one," he said the following day, still trying to calm down. He shook his head and added, "I'm beginning to wonder if we'll ever get Robert's accident behind us."

Despite that temporary setback, the album continued to come together. Jimmy hated the pressure, but realized that he worked incredibly well when he was under the gun, even when he was tired. He had an ability to focus completely on the project at hand and keep the level of originality high.

Before long, the Stones were just two days away from arriving at Musicland. Jimmy placed a frantic call to Mick Jagger. "All we need is a little more time," he said. "Can you guys come in three days late?"

Mick agreed. He was only too happy to have a legitimate excuse for taking a few extra days off.

When the sessions were finally over, Jimmy was delighted with the finished product. With some of the earlier albums, he would leave the studio feeling pangs of insecurity, convinced that there might have been something else he could have done to make the tracks even better. With *Presence*, however, he seemed perfectly content. Through a frail smile, he told me that not an ounce of energy had gone to waste.

When the Stones finally showed up, we were clearing out our gear. "Thanks for the extra time," Jimmy told Mick.

"No problem," Jagger said. "Did you get a few tracks down while you were here?"

"It was more than a few tracks," Jimmy said. "We've recorded everything for the album and finished the final mixes. The album is done."

Jagger was flabbergasted. "Wait a minute," he said. "But you've been here only three weeks!"

"Yeah, that's all we needed," Jimmy said.

49

THE JINX

Does Jimmy seem anxious and moody to you?"

Peter Grant was sitting across from me at a restaurant in L.A. Not long after the recording session in Munich had ended, Peter and I met in L.A. to take care of some business related to the completion and release of the movie, *The Song Remains the Same.* Jimmy joined us there a few days later. Almost immediately after Pagey's arrival, Peter became concerned.

"Something's different about Jimmy," he said. "He acts nervous and jumpy. Something's not right."

Immediately, heroin came to my mind. Although we had seemed to weather the heroin storm in Munich and Jimmy certainly functioned fine in the studio, I was too preoccupied with my own use of smack to keep an eye on how much he was snorting.

Later during that visit to L.A., Jimmy complained to me about having aches and pains. His nose was running, too, but I wasn't about to give him a lecture about the risks of heroin. I told Peter I'd talk to Jimmy, although I really had no intention of doing so.

Two days later, Jimmy and I flew to London together. He wanted to get back to England to see his daughter in a school play. On the drive to L.A. International, caught in the freeway traffic, he turned to me and said, "Chrissakes, Richard, don't get into this shit."

"What do you mean?" I asked.

"Heroin. I think I'm hooked. It's terrible."

"Have you tried to stop?"

"I've tried, but I can't. It's a real bastard."

That was the last we talked about it during the trip home. At the time, I didn't feel that I had sunk quite as deep as Pagey. I was using heroin regularly, but I still felt I was in control.

After talking to Jimmy, I promised myself that heroin wasn't going to get the best of me. I didn't realize, however, that it probably already had. As soon as we were back in England and I got to my house in Pangbourne, I headed straight for the half gram of heroin that I had hidden in a gold goblet. That Christmas, I was literally out of my head from regularly snorting the stuff. One night, I became so ill at a Christmas party at Peter's house that I spent most of the evening in the bathroom, vomiting repeatedly and praying for the night to end.

Bonzo wasn't doing much better. The last time we had been together in Paris, staying at the George V Hotel, Mick Hinton told me that Bonzo was languishing in bed. "What's wrong with him?" I asked.

"I don't know," Mick said. "He keeps eating Mars candy bars. That's all he wants to eat."

I walked into Bonham's room. "Get up, you fucking bastard," I said.

Bonzo looked pale, disoriented, and almost comatose. He didn't seem to be in any mood to be harassed by me. "I couldn't get out of bed even if I wanted to," he said. "All I feel like doing is eating sweets."

"You know what your problem is, don't you?" I said. "You've got a habit."

I wasn't much help, however. I picked up the phone by the bed and called a dealer I knew in Paris. Within an hour, he had delivered an ounce of smack to Bonham's room. We both snorted some of it and forgot all about the Mars bars for the rest of the day.

Of all of us, John Paul and Robert had come through most successfully. Jonesy was nearly always able to avoid any traps that the rest of us got sucked into; he remained coolheaded enough to know when to jump in and when to back off. Robert was not quite that sensible, but while Bonham, Pagey, and I were struggling with heroin, Robert never really became caught up in it. Maybe after months of painkillers, he had taken enough drugs to last him a lifetime. When he finally got rid of his cane a few days after Christmas 1975— nearly five months after the accident—he felt as if he had been liberated. True, he still was in no shape to challenge Baryshnikov, but most of the healing was behind him. He wanted to get on with his life.

Presence was finally released in late March 1976, but its arrival in the record stores was delayed by (what else!) problems with the cover art. That pillarlike object on the album jacket had fans conjecturing in perpetuity about its meaning. Some thought the obelisk was just an interesting work of art. Many more insisted that there was some symbolism behind it, that it had some link to Jimmy and his black magic rituals. Although Robert was as vague as possible when the press asked about it—"It means whatever you want it to mean"— fans pointed to the accident on Rhodes and figured that Jimmy's fascination with the occult had somehow placed a spell over the band. The object on the cover of *Presence* was supposedly related to it all.

"When you play with the devil, you pay the price," a Los Angeles disc jockey speculated. "Led Zeppelin may be weighted down with a jinx that they can't control."

That was the first time I had ever heard someone use the word "jinx" in reference to Led Zeppelin. It wasn't the last. Jimmy thought that kind of conjecture was bullshit. It angered him, but he tried to ignore it.

"Well," Bonzo once asked me, "does anyone know what Jimmy does behind closed doors with all his supernatural shit?"

Jimmy, of course, didn't talk about it. I suppose it was really no one else's business. But in his continued silence, the rumors started to spread.

Certainly there was no jinx surrounding the new album. *Presence* soared to the top of the sales charts and became the first album in history to earn a platinum record through advance orders alone. Cuts like "Achilles Last Stand" received so much airplay—despite its ten-minute length—that some radio stations got complaints from listeners ("It's a good song, but don't you have anything else to play?").

Jimmy and John Paul felt relieved by the response of record buyers. After Robert's accident, they had talked about just how strong the band could come back. Could Zeppelin rise from the ashes? *Presence*, they agreed, had put those concerns to rest.

Some critics wrote generous reviews of the album. *Rolling Stone*, however, stuck its usual needles into its Zeppelin voodoo doll. Stephen Davis conceded that Led Zeppelin were the "heavy-metal champions of the known universe," but before the review was over, he had digressed into lines like "Give an Englishman 50,000 watts, a chartered jet, a little cocaine, and some groupies and he thinks he's a god. It's getting to be an old story."

The negative reviews were an old story, too.

50

DESPONDENCY

Cole, I need your help! You need to get over here quick!"

I had just pulled my Jaguar up in front of a pub near my house and answered the ringing car phone. It was Peter Grant on the other end of the line. He seemed terribly upset.

"I've got some real problems here," he said. "Gloria has come back for some of her things, and there's a guy downstairs with her."

"What can I do?" I asked.

"Please come over. There might be a problem."

Frankly, I was in no mood to drive over to Peter's house. I had just returned from the latest of several summer '76 trips to New York and Los Angeles, where I had tried to resolve the ongoing problems with *The Song Remains the Same*, most of which centered around its sound and artwork. Peter would have normally handled these responsibilities, but he was despondent about his wife, Gloria, leaving him, and preferred to stay close to home. Fortunately, Frank Wells, head of Warner Brothers Pictures, was overseeing the Zeppelin film, and understood fully what the band wanted to do and say in the picture.

After getting Peter's phone call, I drove first to my home. I went to an upstairs bedroom, collected two guns, put them in the trunk of my car, and drove to Peter's house. When I arrived, he was out front, talking in a raised voice to Gloria and her male friend. They didn't seem on the verge of blows, however, and I decided not to interfere. My presence, I felt, might make things worse.

I drove around to the back of the house. Peter's property had a moat around it, and you could only gain access to the house by walking or driving over a drawbridge. From the back of the property, I was hoping I could somehow jump across the moat and sneak in a rear door. Perhaps I had seen too many Tarzan movies for my own good, but I decided to climb up a tree near one of the narrowest parts of the moat and maneuver out onto one of the branches. "If I can just get far enough out to leap to the other side of the water . . . ," I thought to myself.

Unfortunately, I hadn't noticed that the tree was rotting. As I hovered over the moat, the branch snapped and I belly flopped into the water. To make matters worse, Peter's cesspool was malfunctioning and draining directly into the water. I was suddenly swimming in a sea of shit!

As quickly as I could, I groped my way out of the moat. I was not a pretty sight—or smell. By the time I got cleaned up, Gloria and her friend had left.

Peter was quite distraught that afternoon. He still couldn't accept the fact that his marriage to Gloria was crumbling. Maybe he was overreacting, but I found it easy to be sympathetic. Marilyn and I were having difficulties again, and this time our marriage appeared terminal. She and I had had a terrible fight about the same things we had been arguing over on and off since almost the beginning—drugs, communication, faithfulness. Before long, we each had a lawyer working on dissolving our marriage.

I hoped that with the release of *The Song Remains the Same*, we'd finally get some good news. The world premiere was scheduled for October at Cinema I in New York City, and it was a nerve-racking event for me. I had checked out the sound system at Cinema I, felt it was substandard, and knew the band would be furious with it. This was a movie that needed proper amplification to communicate the power of Zeppelin's music. There were enough other problems with the film itself—occasional out-of-focus and grainy camera work, uneven pacing, a length of more than two hours. I wasn't going to let poor sound quality cause any more difficulties.

"If we can't get a better system in there, I'm going to pull the film," I warned a couple distribution executives at Warner Brothers. "Peter and the band are on a plane to New York right now. If this problem isn't rectified in the next few hours, I will personally cancel the premiere."

The Warner Brothers execs were unhappy, but they took my threat seriously. They finally gave me the go-ahead to contact Showco in Dallas, which flew in one of its sophisticated quadriphonic sound systems. That was exactly what was needed. With that equipment in place, the classic Zeppelin songs—"Stairway to Heaven," "Whole Lotta Love," "Moby Dick"—sounded almost as good as being at a live concert. A few years later, an Atlantic executive told me, "By putting in that big system, you guys did LucasSound years before George Lucas."

However, when the West Coast premieres were held the following week in Los Angeles and San Francisco, the sound was absolutely abysmal. Jimmy was so embarrassed he almost cowered under his seat. "Why are you putting me through this?" he seethed.

The publicity material for the movie promoted the film as the band's "special way of giving their millions of friends what they have been clamoring for—a personal and private tour of Led Zeppelin." It promised that the film would "reveal them as they really are and for the first time the world has a front row seat on Led Zeppelin."

Pagey, however, was never particularly enamored with the film. Even with Showco's sound system, he didn't feel that the Madison Square Garden concerts lived up to the band's capabilities. After a while, he just didn't like looking at the film at all. Bonzo had his complaints, too, and wondered why there wasn't more humor in the film. Peter continued to call it "an expensive home movie." Nevertheless, a soundtrack album from the film was released, and in just a few days it turned platinum.

At the end of the year, Peter bought me an Austin-Healy 3000 as a Christmas present. It was a sign of just how far the band had come. In 1970, my Christmas present from the band was a 750 Triumph Chopper motorcycle. Now they could afford to give me the kind of classic cars that make the covers of magazines.

During December, the band started planning its first live concerts since the Earl's Court performances. Although this new American tour would not begin until the following April at Dallas Memorial Auditorium, rehearsals started four months before that in a refurbished theater in Fulham loaned to us by Emerson, Lake, and Palmer.

From the beginning, everything in those rehearsals jelled. Even months before the American tour, the band was starting to feel the kind of self-confidence it usually reserved for midway through a tour, once everything has fallen into place. Although young bands like the Clash and the Sex Pistols had been trying to steal Zeppelin's thunder, Zeppelin didn't seem worried. They still felt they could create another youth-quake in America. Time would tell.

51

THE
BEGINNING
OF THE END

John Bonham was bored. Led Zeppelin's 1977 North American tour was barely a week old, and yet here he was, sitting alone in his hotel suite at the Ambassador East Hotel in Chicago, yearning for something new, something different to amuse him.

"What's there to do, Cole?" he whined over the phone. "I can't sit still here. Isn't there anything exciting to do in this fucking city?"

Something was different about this tour, the eleventh that Led Zeppelin had made of North America. From the beginning, it just didn't feel right to me. This tour should have been Led Zeppelin's best. Fifty-one dates were on the schedule, the largest Zeppelin tour ever. About 1.3 million fans were expected to see the band in thirty cities. This was also the tour in which the band was rebounding from Robert Plant's accident, and Robert himself felt he had something to prove to the live audiences.

Nevertheless, I told one of our roadies that to me this seemed like the beginning of the end for the band. The soul that had driven Zeppelin since 1968 just seemed to have weakened, and drugs played too much of a role in everyone's life. It wouldn't be fair to say that the music suffered; the sellout crowds never seemed disappointed, at least from my backstage vantage point. But I just felt that the passion and the camaraderie weren't as strong as they had once been. By the end of the tour, the band had performed more than 550 concerts over its life span of nearly nine years. Maybe some burnout was inevitable.

The Zeppelin entourage had grown to ridiculous numbers, which was one of our problems during that spring and summer tour. Each band member traveled with his own personal assistant: Dennis Sheehan, who had been a roadie for Maggie Bell, joined us as Robert's assistant; Dave Northover, a pharmacist and a rugby player, helped John Paul; Rex King, who had one of the meanest right hooks in England, came on board to keep an eye on Bonzo; and Rick Hobbs, Jimmy's chauffeur and butler in London, worked with him. I even had an assistant, Mitchell Fox, who came out of our New York office, and Peter had help from Johnny Bindon. As a result, there were multiple divisions within the organization, with all of us relying less on each other for support and companionship. Mitchell spent most of his time trying to control the other assistants so I could have contact with the band members themselves. Cliques were formed, and a very tight organization became fragmented.

I still tried to make life as tolerable as possible for Led Zeppelin. For instance, I had reserved Bonzo a two-bedroom suite at the Ambassador East, just as he wanted it, with one of the bedrooms furnished with only a pool table, no furniture. But after hours of billiards, the novelty of the pool table had worn thin.

"We're checking out later today," I told him. "Calm down and we'll be out of here before you know it."

Probably more than anyone in the band, Bonham still had difficulty relaxing in the aftermath of a concert. He'd become hyper and fidgety and sometimes feel the need to bang away at something long after he had left his drum kit. This particular afternoon, after I had returned to my own room down the hall, Bonham decided to unwind by methodically demolishing his hotel suite.

Chairs crashed against walls. Couches soared out of shattered windows. So did lamps and end tables. A television set followed close behind, exploding on an airconditioning unit more than a dozen stories below.

Hearing the commotion, I sprinted down the hall, joined by a couple of our own security men. The door to Bonham's suite was ajar, and as we stormed inside he was hovering near the pool table, plotting his next move.

"Well, don't just stand there!" he roared. "This table is as heavy as an elephant. Give me a hand!"

What the hell! There wasn't much in the suite to save by this point. The four of us each gripped a corner of the pool table, lifted it off the ground, tilted it to one side, and then ceremoniously dropped it on the floor, propelling splinters in half a dozen directions. The impact shook the entire room, perhaps the entire city. Before the reverberations had ebbed, there may have been a tidal wave in Lake Michigan.

"Time for an encore?" Bonzo asked, nodding his head in answer to his own question. We repeated the destructive maneuver again and again—raising the table and then letting it explode on the floor—until it resembled firewood.

Of course, in other tours, Bonzo had rarely shown any respect for hotel property. As in the past, maybe it was boredom that was driving him this time, too. But I just felt that it was more, that everything was just coming apart at the seams.

A few minutes after the pool table had crashed into the floor for the last time, the hotel manager showed up at Bonzo's door. He gasped as he surveyed the carnage before him. He hurriedly strode over to the phone and summoned his secretary, who arrived a couple of minutes later with pen in hand. He asked her to note all the damage in the suite, and as she did, Bonzo stood just to her right, playfully helping her make her inventory ("Don't forget the damage to the floor!" he exclaimed). The total bill for the outburst was $5,100.

At one point, when the manager could no longer contain his exasperation, he directed our attention to a mirror that had somehow survived Bonzo's onslaught. With sarcasm oozing from his lips, he exclaimed, "Oh, my God, you missed a mirror!"

Bonham chuckled. "Don't be so sure of that!" he growled. He strutted across the room, lifted the mirror off the wall, and hurled it to the floor. It burst into dozens of pieces.

Despite my own concerns, every concert continued to play to standing-room-only crowds, and the scalpers struck pay dirt, turning six-dollar tickets into seventy-five-dollar sales. In Pontiac, Michigan, 76,229 fans crammed into every breathing space of the Silverdome and the three-hour concert grossed a phenomenal $900,000 for a single night of music. We also sold out four concerts at Chicago Stadium, four at the Capital Centre in Landover, Maryland, six at Madison Square Garden, and six at the Los Angeles Forum. From April through July, Zeppelin showed that it was still the biggest drawing card in rock music.

Peter hadn't lost any of his commitment to the fans. By this point, he could have become hardened to the whole process, developing a "let them eat cake" attitude. After all, he knew that each show would be a sellout, no matter how much extra effort and showmanship he put into it. But even amid the personal problems he had experienced in recent years, he never lost sight of the fact that it was the fans who had made this all possible. As we planned this 1977 tour, he was adamant that every fan would get his money's worth. In large venues, he insisted that an oversized video screen be installed, so that the people sitting in the nosebleed sections would feel just as much a part of the action as those in the front row.

We did without the *Starship* in '77, but we certainly didn't rough it. About ten days before the tour began, I got a call informing me that the jet had been grounded at Long Beach airport when one of the engines nearly came off in flight. With the band already often tied in knots over flying under any circumstances, I figured that giving them a report on the *Starship*'s engine problems would send them running for the nearest Amtrak station. So without going into any great detail as to why the change was made, I went ahead and arranged to use Caesars Chariot, a 707 owned by Caesars Palace. It was just as luxurious as the *Starship*, although it didn't have a Thomas organ.

No one seemed to care about the Thomas, however. Most of us were much more interested in engulfing ourselves in booze and drugs within minutes after the plane was off the ground. For that tour, we consumed Singha beer by the case and drugs as though they were cotton candy.

Robert was taking painkillers as well. His leg, still not fully rebounded from the 1975 accident, was keeping him from functioning at 100 percent. Of course, he was on his feet during most of every concert, strutting like a peacock as the band stampeded over the crowd with "Rock and Roll," "Whole Lotta Love," and "Stairway to Heaven." There were moments, however, when his body seemed to be tied in knots, incapable of emoting the kind of body English that had become a Plant trademark. Sometimes, I could see him grimacing in pain. Pagey tried to pick up the slack, drawing the audience's attention to his own swaggering, straining, and strumming and seeming quite content to lay claim to most of the stage.

Some nights, Robert's leg and ankle literally screamed for mercy from the wear and tear of the grueling concert tour. He appeared relieved as the acoustic set of each three-hour show would begin, when he could actually sit down at center stage next to Bonzo, Robert, and Jimmy and extend his leg in front of him for songs like "Black Country Woman" and "Going to California."

"Sometimes I envy you, Bonzo," Robert said one night, "just sitting on your drummer's stool for the entire concert. Let me know if you ever want to change places."

At one point during the tour, Robert told me that the audiences were sometimes the only thing between him and just throwing in the towel. Their cheering motivated him to grit his teeth and push through the pain as though it didn't exist. The fans were his support, his inspiration.

While Robert never bailed out during the tour, the weather intervened at an outdoor concert in Tampa, forcing a cancellation—a decision that didn't sit well with many fans. Maureen Plant and Mo Jones had traveled to the States with their children to visit Disney World and spend a little time with the band. We had flown into Orlando to pick them up, then headed for Tampa, where 70,000 tickets had been sold for the performance at Tampa Stadium. As Caesars Chariot approached Tampa, it was raining steadily. Peter was gazing out the window near his seat with a concerned expression. I knew his policy was never to let Led Zeppelin go near a stage in damp weather, and to have an alternate rain date available.

In 1972, tragedy had struck Stone the Crows, one of Peter's acts. Maggie Bell was the powerful lead singer of the band, and as the press began comparing her to Janis Joplin, Stone the Crows attracted a growing following. But during one of their performances in Wales, guitarist Les Harvey was electrocuted. Other members of the group, including keyboardist Ronnie Leahy and bass player Steve Thompson, tried desperately to revive Harvey, but he died onstage. Stone the Crows never recovered emotionally from the tragedy. I don't think Peter did, either. In 1973, the band broke up.

An investigation showed that Harvey had been electrocuted when a short occurred in his equipment. After that, Peter decided the risks were too high to let anyone ever perform in circumstances, including rain, that might increase the risks of electrocution. Peter became very protective of his musicians. He spent a lot of money on special transformers capable of absorbing shocks before they could ever cause any harm to Led Zeppelin. Even so, the no-rain policy became an inflexible rule for all of his acts.

Ten minutes before our plane landed in the Tampa rain, I was looking at the tickets for that night's show. "Oh, shit!" I exclaimed. "Peter, look at this. It says that the concert will go on, rain or shine! Who the hell put that on the tickets?"

Peter was outraged. He had never permitted a concert with a rain-or-shine policy, and he had no intention of changing his game plan. Terry Bassett of Concerts West was on the plane with us, and Peter let him know how unhappy he was. "Bassett," he yelled, "what the hell has happened here?"

For the moment, Terry was at a loss for words. Just then, the plane landed with such a jolt that it took everyone's mind off the matter at hand. Peter's fury was put on hold, at least temporarily.

The rain stopped an hour before the show was scheduled to begin, and the skies seemed to be clearing. Peter decided to let the show move ahead as planned. The band opened with "The Song Remains the Same," bringing down the house. But after two more songs and in the middle of "In My Time of Dying," the sky exploded with thunder. Within two minutes, rain began falling in torrents. Peter didn't hesitate. He immediately ordered the band off the stage and the equipment covered with tarps. "If we can, we'll wait it out," he said. The fans didn't budge. A few had brought umbrellas, but most of them were getting drenched. Nevertheless, no one's spirits seemed to be dampened.

We waited backstage patiently for the rain to stop, but it showed no signs of doing so. Finally, Peter grumbled, "Let's get the hell out of here."

Before the crowd was notified of the cancellation, police escorts guided our limos out of the stadium. Then an announcement was made, asking the crowd to disperse peacefully—an announcement that brought a chorus of boos that lasted more than ten minutes. Some of the fans didn't seem to believe it. Others were angry.

Despite the continuing rain, much of the crowd remained at the stadium. They chanted, "We want Zeppelin! We want Zeppelin!" They threw bottles at the stage, where our roadies were trying to dismantle the equipment before the entire stadium became a monsoon.

Then the scene got ugly. Fights broke out in the audience, fans fighting with fans. Forty policemen in riot gear, most of whom had been stationed outside the stadium, dove into the crowd, flailing their billy clubs. The concert had turned into a full-fledged riot. Fists swung and blood flowed. Sirens blared from police cars and ambulances. Sixty fans ended up in the hospital. So did a dozen cops.

When we reached the airport and were boarding Caesars Chariot, one of our security men got word about the mayhem at Tampa Stadium. It brought back memories of the horrifying riot in Milan back in 1971. All of us were crushed, but Robert seemed to take it the hardest. "It's so unbelievable," he said. "People come to hear music and they get their heads bloodied."

Maybe there was something in the air in Florida. When tickets had gone on sale for the concert, hundreds of overzealous fans had forced their way into the Orange Bowl—one of the sites where tickets were being sold—and proceeded to tear out seats, rip apart offices, and steal food from concession stands. A SWAT team from the Miami police department was called and finally brought the disturbance under control by hurling tear gas at the fans. The *Miami Herald* ran the following headline about the disturbance: "Black Sunday for Real at the Orange Bowl: Last Time a Blimp, Now the Zeppelin."

Unfortunately, the Tampa incidents weren't the only violence associated with the '77 tour. After the band's concert at the Summit in Houston, rowdy fans went on a rampage, causing $500,000 worth of damage. Forty of them were arrested for disorderly conduct and drug possession.

52

THE SÉANCE

As the 1977 tour continued, I became increasingly uneasy about how the band was functioning. Onstage, the music continued to be so strong that, at least while they were performing, it eased some of my anxieties about the band's longevity. But offstage, we spent less and less time together as the tour progressed, as though we were staying in different hotels, not just down the hall from one another. When we did socialize, streaks of hostility or maliciousness toward other members of the group sometimes surfaced.

We flew into Atlanta for a concert at the Omni. My girlfriend at the time, Rebecca, was traveling with us. So was another friend, Linda, who had been a waitress at the Rainbow in Los Angeles. On Caesars Chariot, Rebecca was wearing a beautiful Indian-style chamois dress. Someone apparently looked at her and decided to harass me a little. He must have talked one of our security guards into ripping the dress off my girlfriend, probably as a way to drive me nuts.

I was sharing a snort of coke with Jimmy when the security man approached us, grabbed Rebecca's dress at the collar, and jerked his hand downward. The dress tore down the front and, within seconds, she was standing in her bra and panties, screaming and trying to cover herself with her arms.

Pagey burst into laughter. Peter roared with such delight that his voice echoed off the cabin walls. I didn't see anything funny about it.

"You fucking assholes!" I snapped. I leaned back, raised my left leg, and aimed a karate kick at one of the airplane windows, smashing it with my left foot and crumbling two of its three panes. As the window disintegrated, a platter of coke went soaring into the air, creating a snowstorm throughout the plane. Jimmy, who probably hated flying more than any of us, just about fainted. Linda dropped to the floor, figuring that the broken window would cause changes in air pressure and, in seconds, the plane would tumble out of control.

"I'll teach you not to fuck with me!" I screamed, pointing a finger at Jimmy. I had assumed, apparently by mistake, that Pagey was responsible for disrobing Rebecca. "Does this have something to do with your black magic shit? Is this what you're into now—tormenting women?"

Tempers had eased a bit by the time we checked into the Peachtree Plaza Hotel, although I was still pissed off. A short while later, the girls, Jonesy, and I were in Bonzo's suite, sitting around a table, making small talk. I noticed the table had a lever on its underside; by maneuvering a knee and pushing the lever to the side, we could elevate the table.

"Let's stage our own séance," Bonzo suggested. "Jimmy isn't the only one who can get into this supernatural bullshit!"

Jimmy was deeper into Aleister Crowley than ever. He had even opened up a bookstore in London that dealt exclusively with the occult. In general, those interests, however odd they seemed, weren't that big a deal for the rest of us since Pagey still never tried to brainwash us with his own beliefs. But because we occasionally heard stories that Led Zeppelin was a "jinxed" band, they weren't something we could completely ignore, either.

I decided to get back at Jimmy. "Let's have a little fun with Pagey," I said. "In fact, I'd like to scare the shit out of him!"

Jimmy's suite adjoined Bonham's, and the door between them was slightly ajar. I dimmed the lights, and, within earshot of Jimmy, we began chanting as loudly as possible.

"Ooomm . . . ooomm . . . ooomm."

We had linked hands and closed our eyes. Fighting back laughter, we readied ourselves to communicate with the spirits.

"Ooomm . . . ooomm . . . ooomm."

Bonzo whispered, "This stuff really is crap!"

Through squinted eyes, I finally saw Jimmy walking toward us, with Peter a step behind. As they moved closer, Linda gently pushed the lever with her knee. The table began to rise.

Jimmy and Peter were startled. Jimmy flinched and took a step backward. Both had expressions that seemed to say, "It's a fucking miracle!"

The table dipped and then rose two more times. Peter must have finally gotten suspicious. He walked over and flipped on the light switch. With the room fully illuminated, he got down on his hands and knees and spotted the lever. Neither he nor Jimmy seemed to find it very funny.

As the tour proceeded, I wasn't getting along any better with Robert. Of course, he was having problems of his own just making it from one concert to the next without being overwhelmed by his leg pain. He spent a lot of time by himself, whiling away many of his off-hours in his suite, resting his leg, watching TV, and sampling whatever alcohol and drugs happened to be within reach. But during the concerts themselves, he continued to unearth a reserve of energy, clearly thriving on being the center of attention.

Even so, he was more short-tempered than usual offstage, caught up in the frustration of the incomplete recovery of his leg injury. A few minutes before the band took the stage at Landover's Capital Centre, Robert cornered Johnny Bindon and me backstage and began raking us over the coals. "What do you bastards do to earn your money?" Robert boomed, punctuating his sentence by poking his finger into my chest and then into Johnny's. "While I'm singing my ass off onstage, you guys don't do shit."

I didn't appreciate the sentiments, particularly since I had devoted nearly nine years of my life to the band. "I go and collect the fucking money, that's what I do!" I countered. "If I didn't do that, you bastards would be hitchhiking out of here, not taking limos!"

Robert added, "Well, if you guys really want to make yourself useful tonight, go into the audience and get some nice girls for me."

I was pissed. "What an arrogant son of a bitch!" I said to Bindon. Shortly after the concert started, Bindon and I decided to give Robert what he wanted—and drive him a little crazy, too.

We waded into the audience and spotted five gorgeous girls barely in their teens, sitting together in the front row. "How old do you think they are?" I asked Johnny.

"Who gives a shit!" he said. "As long as they're out of diapers, that's good enough for Robert."

I leaned toward the birds, introduced myself, and said, "After the concert, girls, we're going to get you a limousine and take you out to Led Zeppelin's airplane. The band wants to meet you, and they'll give you drinks and autographs."

They started giggling with excitement. The one closest to me, whose braces seemed to be vibrating with the music, said, "Groovy, man!" I knew immediately that we weren't lining the band up with a group of Rhodes scholars.

After the concert, I helped get the girls into the limo. Before I slammed the door shut, I told them, "There's one thing I have to tell you. When you get on the plane, I don't want you to talk to Robert. He gets temperamental some-times, and if you say the wrong thing, you might be sorry. So if he tries to talk to you, don't say a word. Just give him a blank stare. Okay?"

They seemed puzzled, but they all nodded their heads.

Once we had boarded Caesars Chariot, Robert saw the girls and, with a grin on his face, said to me, "They're fucking beautiful. Richard, you're finally earning your damn money!" Robert proceeded to flaunt himself as much as possible in front of the girls. He took his shirt off and smiled as he prome-naded down the aisle.

When the jet took off, however, I suddenly became very alarmed. I had fig-ured that we'd get the girls off the plane before we departed, but I'd been snorting some heroin and got distracted. It was suddenly too late. They were going with us to New York.

One girl in particular looked frightened and started to cry. "Where are you taking us?" she sobbed. "My dad's gonna kill me!" I figured maybe I had gone too far this time. I didn't have the nerve to tell them they'd be coming with us to the Big Apple.

Twenty minutes into the flight, one of the girls, a brunette with false eye-lashes that almost grazed the tip of her nose when she blinked, walked up to me. "As long as we're here, can we at least get Robert's autograph or something?"

Since I had carried my scheme against Plant this far, I saw no reason to back down. "Listen," I said sternly, "I don't want you to have anything to do with him. If you talk to Robert, I'll open the door of the plane and throw all of you out."

She gulped and returned to her seat.

Sure, I was too hard on the girl. I even contemplated apologizing. But just then, Robert came over and tried to flirt with the girls. They kept looking over at me, and I shook my finger at them, warning them to keep quiet.

Just before we landed in New York, Robert finally gave up. "Those are the coldest little bitches I've ever seen. I'm trying to get something going with them, and they just sit there. Who the hell did you round up—a bunch of lesbians?"

When we touched down at J.F.K., I faced another dilemma—what to do with the girls. They had served their purpose in helping me piss off Robert, al-though I was feeling a little guilty about kidnapping them. They couldn't have been any older than thirteen or fourteen, which was too young even for my demented tastes. I finally got them their own room at the Plaza for the night and put them on a flight home the next morning.

Several years later, a beautiful young woman approached me in a bar called the Cat and the Fiddle in Los Angeles. "Hi, Richard, you may not re-member me. When I was fourteen, you kidnapped me and my girlfriends and flew us to New York. I got into terrible trouble for that. The father of one of the girls was a congressman. They had the police and everyone looking for us."

Robert and I remained at odds during the tour. Whenever he was rude to me, I'd try to torment him in some way. I got another chance during one of the band's six concerts at Madison Square Garden. A girl named Audrey had been following Robert from city to city. She was a bit of a pest, but rather harm-less. Before the start of the first New York concert, I saw her in the audience, sitting in an aisle seat about twenty rows from the stage. Audrey, I figured, would be game for just about anything, particularly if it gave her a chance to get close to Plant. Once I had talked to her and looked at the thin, gossamer dress she was wearing, I fantasized about all kinds of possibilities.

I told our lighting crew, "When Robert sings 'Stairway to Heaven,' I'm going to have one of the roadies send this girl down the aisle. When I cue you, shine the spotlights on her. I think we'll be able to see right through her dress."

After "Achilles Last Stand," the band segued into "Stairway to Heaven." As Robert started singing, one spotlight stayed on him while the other four lit up Audrey, parading down the aisle like it was her wedding day. The girl was absolutely beaming. I had already alerted security to let her climb up on the front of the stage. With most of the spots on her, the dress became almost transparent. Nothing much about her figure was left to the imagination.

Everyone on the stage was hysterical—except Robert. Bonzo was laughing so hard he almost stopped drumming. As the girl shyly stood beside him onstage, Plant glared at me with an evil look that said, "Your days are numbered, Cole."

When the show ended, Plant was furious. He chased me through the back-stage dressing rooms, eager to score a knockout punch. He never caught me. With his bad leg, his sprinting was no match for mine.

When he finally cooled down, I asked him, "What makes you think I did it, Robert?"

"I know you well enough, Cole. Who else would it have been?"

When we reached L.A. for concerts at the Forum, I suddenly found myself on a different kind of hot seat over a problem with the band's finances. At first, I thought it was some kind of retaliation by Robert. Then I realized it was more serious than that.

I had always been in charge of the band's petty cash, which in the case of Led Zeppelin, was anything but petty. But my honesty had never really been called into question by the band, even during the '73 robbery in New York. Something during the '77 tour had made Peter suspicious, however, and one day in my hotel room in L.A. I got a call from Shelley Kaye, one of Steve Weiss's associates. "Peter has asked me to make a complete audit of the cash that you've handled during the tour." I was surprised and puzzled when she summoned me to Peter's suite to review all the paperwork, although I knew I had nothing to hide.

We went over the books carefully, item by item. We determined that I had requested a total of $110,000 in cash from local promoters. But as we balanced the incoming and outgoing funds, there was $10,460 unaccounted for. I was baffled by where the money had gone. "Not again," I thought, exasperated and thinking back to the New York robbery.

By this time, Peter had joined us. Like everyone else on this tour, he wasn't in the mood to fuck around. "Where the hell is the money, Richard?"

"I can't imagine," I said. "I really don't know."

At the same time, however, I was becoming paranoid that with all the cocaine and the heroin I had been using, perhaps I had made a major blunder without even realizing it.

Shelley and I went over each financial transaction again. "There has to be a mistake somewhere," I kept saying. Finally, I thought I had found it. "Wait a minute," I said. "It says here that I picked up ten thousand, three hundred dollars in Houston. But I didn't. I remember I had originally requested it and then told the promoter there that I didn't need it after all. You can check that with Bill McKenzie of Concerts West."

There was no way I was going to rip the band off. Shelley called Bill, an accountant with Concerts West, who confirmed my story. Taking that error into account, we did some recalculating. This time, there was just $160 unaccounted for. It was such an insignificant amount that Peter said, "Forget about it, Richard. I guess I owe you an apology." We shook hands. That was the end of the incident.

That night, with the stress of the financial misunderstanding behind me, I felt the need to let off some steam. After the Forum concert, the band, Johnny Bindon, and I decided to go to the Rainbow for some partying. About two hours after we had arrived, one of Rod Stewart's roadies approached me with an invitation. "Rod's having a party tonight. Why don't you stop by? I'm sure he'd be glad to see you."

I hadn't seen Rod in a few years and figured we'd both enjoy reminiscing a little. Even more important, I knew his bar would be brimming with enough booze to give cirrhosis of the liver to half of California. So we got our limo drivers to take us up to Rod's house. When we got there, however, and pressed the buzzer at the iron gate and identified ourselves, we received a rather cool reception: "Mr. Stewart would prefer that you leave."

I was already drunk enough from a couple of hours at the Rainbow that I wasn't interested in taking no for an answer. I got belligerent, and, along with one of our security men, began banging on the gate, finally lifting it off its hinges and tossing it onto the ground. We drove over it on our way up the driveway.

No one answered the doorbell—"Unhospitable bastards, aren't they?" I said to Jonesy—so I began to climb up the drainpipe, figuring that every party needs a gate-crasher or two. But apparently Rod didn't agree. He never opened the front door, but I could hear him screaming from inside: "Cole, I'm gonna call the cops if you and your asshole friends aren't off this property in sixty seconds!"

Normally, I would have taken my chances and tried to burst through the door. This late in the tour, after so many hassles, it wasn't worth pursuing. We turned around and headed back to the Rainbow.

For the last of those six Forum concerts, the band invited Keith Moon to join them onstage during the last encore. The crowd became delirious as Moonie played the congas and the kettle drums for "Whole Lotta Love." In the excitement of the moment, however, none of us realized that Keith was standing directly on the part of the stage where the pyrotechnics crew had positioned the smoke bombs, which were programmed to ignite at the end of the song. As the last note of "Whole Lotta Love" drifted from the stage, the bombs exploded in something resembling a Fourth of July fireworks show—right under Keith's ass. Poor Moonie must have leaped three feet into the air, letting out a scream and running off the stage with a look of absolute terror on his face.

"You cunts!" he screamed at us afterward. "You knew that was going to happen! You wanted to scare the shit out of me, didn't you?"

During a three-week break in the U.S. tour, most of us flew back to London. But Jimmy planned to jet to Cairo with Mick Hinton, apparently to do some Aleister Crowley-related Egyptology research.

On the flight home, Bonzo said to me, "Do you know the reason Jimmy is taking Mick and not you to Egypt? He knows that if he decides to sacrifice someone, he'd find it a lot harder to do away with you than Mick!"

No problem, I thought. I had other plans in England, including renewing my heroin connections. At that point in my life, they were as important to me as anything else. That's how far down I had slipped.

Bonzo stared out the window of the plane and said, "The longer you tour, and the more successful and the bigger you get, the more touring just becomes a fucking chore. It's work. We make a lot of money, but we don't have a life. With the bodyguards, we're imprisoned by our own success. Sometimes I think it's a fucking nightmare."

LAST LEG

After three weeks in England, just a day before Zeppelin was scheduled to return to the States, I fell and broke a cap on one of my front top teeth. It was poor timing, and my dentist couldn't do the repair work before I had to leave. "Why don't you remove the gold stub that's left," he said, "and when the tour's over, I'll do the recapping."

That's what I agreed to do. With a gaping hole in the front of my mouth, I looked even meaner than usual during that last leg of the American tour.

On the polar flight to Seattle, I had taken three Mandrax and was pretty numb for the entire flight. I was probably a little obnoxious, too, and one of the first-class stewardesses took particular offense at a necklace I was wearing—it featured an artist's palette that read, "Fuck off!" It wasn't a gift you'd want to give Mom on Mother's Day.

The flight crew alerted the Seattle police, who took me into custody as I walked off the plane, claiming I had been disturbing the peace on the flight.

"Let's cut the crap!" I told the cops. "Maybe I was a little loud, but you can't arrest me for that."

Still they looked like they were going to—until Bob DeForest, one of our security advisers, stepped in. He was also a Seattle police captain, and he hated to see us get harassed. The whole incident may have been smoothed over behind the scenes, because I never heard anything more about it.

"Over the years, we should have kept count of the number of times we could have been busted but weren't," Bonzo joked. "We probably should have spent more time in prison than on the road!"

Zeppelin stayed at the Edgewater Inn in Seattle. As we had routinely done at the Riot House in L.A., we took over an entire floor of the Edgewater for security reasons. At times, when I'd hear unusual noises, I'd sometimes walk the halls or peer down from our balcony to see if the commotion was directed at us. It eased my anxiety, and, overall, things remained calm.

Late one night, however, I spotted a couple of unfamiliar faces exiting the elevator on our floor, and I cornered them. "I'm Jimmy Page's brother," one of the fellows said. He had a strong Southern twang, which didn't help him make his case.

They didn't realize that I didn't find a breach of our security very amusing. A fan wanting an autograph could be politely turned away, but I saw these guys as troublemakers. They hadn't started off on a good footing by lying about their place in the Page lineage.

"If you assholes know what's good for you, you'll get the fuck out of here!" I shouted at them. One of them began to turn to go, but Pagey's "brother" was apparently insulted by my request. Without warning, he took a wild swing at me, missing by at least two feet. That showed poor judgment on his part. I took a step forward and, with two quick blows, knocked them both to the floor.

By this time, one of our security men, an off-duty cop named Charlie, had raced over to help me. We dragged the intruders out of the hotel and threw them into the parking lot.

"I'm getting tired of this," I told Charlie. Frankly, I was pretty tired of just about everything having to do with this tour. Despite the hiatus in London, things still seemed out of kilter just days into the last leg.

I headed back to my room only to find that the hoodlums apparently hadn't had enough. They had called the police, who arrived at the Edgewater and listened to these fellows explain how I had assaulted them. The cops, however, were aware of Led Zeppelin's presence at the hotel and realized that some of their colleagues were part of our security team. They called me down to the parking lot to confront my accusers.

"So you guys are telling us that Mr. Cole assaulted you!" one of the cops bellowed.

"Yes," one of them said meekly.

"Mr. Cole, show them your front teeth."

I flashed them a big, toothless grin.

"You bastards knocked his tooth out!" the cop said. "You better get the hell out of here before I arrest *you!*"

For the first time in a while, I had something to laugh at. The cops escorted the blokes off the hotel property.

On our last day in Seattle, Bonham and I had wandered into Plant's empty hotel room. We were on the balcony, gazing out on Puget Sound. I was lost in my own thoughts, and Bonzo was bouncing on one leg, either having an anxiety attack or in need of a quick stop at the bathroom. As it turned out, he was plotting a going-away present for Seattle.

"Let's toss the room refrigerator into the ocean!" he snickered. Why not? We picked up the small refrigerator in Plant's room, carried it onto the balcony, and heaved it over the side, sending it splashing into the Sound.

Robert happened to be in Pagey's room down the hall and from his vantage point had seen the refrigerator doing a belly flop. "That's great!" he shouted, moving out onto Jimmy's balcony. Then he spotted us perched outside his own room, laughing hysterically. He suddenly realized that it was *his* refrigerator that had taken the dive.

"You assholes!" he screamed. "There were six bottles of Dom Perignon in that refrigerator! Damn you!"

"Oops!" Bonzo quipped. "Do you sense that Robert is angry? Why is Robert always so angry?"

A few minutes later, we watched two fishermen maneuver toward the floating refrigerator and drag it onto their boat. Once they had it on board, they opened its door and tossed the bottles of champagne into the water. "That's wonderful!" I roared. "That Dom Perignon was nineteen sixty-six vintage. It was worth more than the fucking refrigerator!"

From Seattle, after a sellout performance in the Kingdome, we flew to Tempe, Arizona, for a concert at the Activities Center. As I was checking the band into Marriott's Camelback Inn, two girls approached me in the lobby. One of them reminded me that I had slept with her during the 1973 tour and then added, "We have some gifts. Can we bring them upstairs?"

I helped her carry about a dozen wrapped presents upstairs, and we set them down in my room. I offered the girls some booze, and they spent the afternoon with us. About an hour after they left, Johnny Bindon came in and asked me who the gifts were for.

"Well," I said, "let's open 'em. If there's anything we like, they'll be for us!"

There were Indian string ties, belts, and beautiful jewelry. I figured Johnny and I might divide them between ourselves.

At about that same time, one of the girls had called Robert, who she also apparently knew. "Did you like my presents?" she asked him.

"What presents?" he said.

"The ones I left with Richard."

Robert came storming down the hallway toward my room. He barged in and found Johnny and me sitting on the floor, still admiring the gifts, with torn wrapping paper and boxes everywhere. We must have looked like a couple of kids on Christmas morning.

"You fucking cunts!" Robert screamed. "Those are *my* presents! How could you open *my* presents?"

Oh, brother. The guy's a damn millionaire, I thought to myself, and he's in a rage over things like a couple of string ties.

I handed the gifts over. "I wouldn't want to put a damper on the tour for you, Percy," I said. "The rest of us are having a lot of fun, too."

From Arizona, we flew to Oakland for a pair of concerts in the Coliseum in late July. Judging by the way the rest of the tour had unfolded, I should have guessed that disaster would strike in Oakland, too. Even so, I never expected that some of us would end up in jail.

Problems started during the first show. We rarely stuck around once a concert was over, but promoter Bill Graham had convinced us to stay for a catered dinner, part of his "Day on the Green" program. Backstage, in the middle of the concert itself, Peter Grant's son, Warren, spotted a wood-carved dressing room plaque that read "Led Zeppelin" and asked one of Bill Graham's assistants if he could have it. For no apparent reason, Graham's employee slapped Warren on the side of the head. Bonham, who had come offstage for a few moments, saw the incident, sprinted toward the assailant, and, with a kick that would have made Pele proud, booted him squarely in the balls. The fellow screamed, staggered backward, slumped to the ground, and was out of business for a while. Bonham cursed at him, then returned to the stage, probably figuring the confrontation was over.

Meanwhile, Peter heard about the incident and went looking for the fellow who had slapped his son. The chap was in no shape to defend himself, but Peter and Johnny Bindon cornered him anyway and pushed him into a dressing room trailer to "discuss" the matter. Over the years, I had seen Peter angry from time to time, but never *this* angry. From where I was positioned, it sounded like Grant and Bindon were being a bit physically agressive with the fellow, shouting obscenities all the while. I stood guard outside the trailer to make sure that none of Graham's friends could get inside to put a halt to things. Until later, I didn't realize how bad the situation had gotten in there.

When the concert was over, we climbed into our limousines, having decided not to stay for dinner after all. At the same time, Graham's assistant was being loaded into an ambulance for a ride to the hospital to sew up his face.

The next day, Zeppelin had another Oakland concert to do for Graham, and everyone on both sides of the fracas kept a low profile. But less than twenty hours later, when we were back at our suites at the San Francisco Hyatt, the confrontation escalated again. I was in my hotel room, snorting some cocaine with a local girl whom I had invited to spend a couple of days with me. My phone rang, and it was Peter.

"Come up to my room, Cole, and make it quick. Also, make sure you don't have anything on you."

The floor was swarming with cops. Bill Graham had apparently called out half of the Oakland and San Francisco police departments, including the SWAT team. Some had their guns drawn. Others had their billy clubs poised for action. Bill Graham must have told them that we were Jesse James, John Dillinger, and Baby Face Nelson all rolled into one.

Gregg Beppler, one of our own security men, recognized one of the SWAT team members—someone he had once worked with on the Cleveland Police Department—and tried to intervene on our behalf. "I don't know what you've heard, but these guys with Led Zeppelin are not dangerous. The incident at the Coliseum was blown way out of proportion. Put away your guns."

The cops served arrest warrants on Bonzo, Peter, Bindon, and me. All the while, they were polite and never brought out their handcuffs. But they meant business. The four of us were arrested, read our rights, and taken to police headquarters. More than anything, I was disgusted. "I guess Bill Graham's showing us how much power he has in this city," I told Bonzo.

From the police station, Peter phoned Steve Weiss, who immediately began working to get us released. Within two hours we were out of jail, each freed on $250 bail. Our limousine met us at the jail entrance, and we returned to the Hyatt. "What bullshit!" Peter shouted. "What is Graham trying to prove?"

Bonzo just shook his head. "Did you notice that he waited until the second concert was over to turn the police loose? He didn't want to lose any money by arresting us too early."

"Let's get the hell out of this fucking city," Peter said. Within two hours, we were in the air, heading for New Orleans.

Battery charges were pressed against all of us. The incident ultimately turned into a legal quagmire that dragged on for months. We finally received suspended jail sentences and were put on probation.

Bill Graham was outraged that our sentences were so lenient. "I can't believe that these guys can kick the hell out of somebody, and then a judge tells them, 'Run along now!'" he told the press. The chips usually fell Led Zeppelin's way; this time, they did again.

The following weekend, we were scheduled to play before a sold-out crowd at the New Orleans Superdome. The governor of Louisiana had plans to make us "honorary colonels." That sounded like a lot better treatment than we were getting in California.

Not long after we had checked into the Maison Dupuy Hotel, Robert got a phone call from his wife. I transferred the call to his suite. A few minutes later, Robert appeared in my doorway in a daze.

"What's the matter?" Bonham asked.

"It's Karac," Robert said, shuffling forward and lowering himself into a chair. "My son's dead."

54

MOURNING

All of us were stunned by the news of Karac Plant's death. There was never a question of getting Robert back to England as quickly as possible, even though it meant immediately canceling the last seven concerts of the American tour.

I tried to line up Caesars Chariot to leave right away with Robert on board, but our pilots hadn't had enough time to rest to handle a transcontinental flight. So I called our New York office, discussing the options for getting Robert home. While I waited for a return call, we all tried to comfort him. But it wasn't easy.

Robert somberly told us what little he had learned from his wife about his five-year-old son's death. Karac had become ill with a respiratory infection, and within twenty-four hours his condition deteriorated dramatically. An ambulance was summoned to the family home, but before Karac ever reached the hospital, he died.

"It puts things in perspective, doesn't it?" Robert said. "I've got all this money and all this fame, but I don't have my son anymore. How much is all of this really worth?"

As he talked, tears rolled down his cheeks. He never fully lost control, but he was in terrible emotional pain.

Led Zeppelin wasn't an organization in which any of us easily shared our feelings. Other than "I'm so sorry," there really wasn't much we could think of to say. Robert had just experienced the most devastating loss of his life. We all knew it. Over the next few minutes, we each embraced him, held him, let him know we were there for him.

How ironic, I thought, that this 1977 tour had been so full of turmoil and hostility. The band members had drifted as far apart as they ever had on a tour. There was constant tension. There were arguments and anger. Nevertheless, when a real crisis like this one struck, it deeply affected all of us. All the disagreements and dissension that had seemed so important over the past few weeks suddenly became very insignificant.

Back on the phone, I learned that although Atlantic-Warner Brothers had a corporate jet, it had been loaned to Jimmy Carter. So I made the decision to book Robert on a commercial flight to London, by way of Newark airport. Robert asked Peter if he could take some of us along.

"You name it," Peter said. "Who do you want with you?"

Robert asked John Bonham to make the trip, as well as Dennis Sheehan, his personal assistant, and me. Dennis helped him pack a small bag, and we headed for the airport. Within an hour, we boarded a flight to Newark, which connected with a British Airways flight to Heathrow.

We flew first-class, and there was very little conversation on the flight. Everyone seemed to be lost in thought. I wondered just what would happen to Robert, whether he could rebound from this personal loss. The car crash on Rhodes was not that far in the past. And now this terrible tragedy had happened. Would Robert ever get back on his feet? And even if he did, what would happen to Led Zeppelin?

Robert tried to sleep on the flight, but he was stirring constantly. A couple of times he woke up with a start, then bowed his head, as if grieving over Karac's death. Bonzo, who was sitting next to him, kept one hand on Robert's arm.

When we landed in London, Bonzo and Robert were met by a private jet, which took them to Birmingham. A limo drove them to Robert's home, where they remained until the funeral. I went home, bought a suit the next day, and prepared for the trip to Birmingham for the funeral.

Karac's funeral was held later in the week. Aside from Robert, Bonham was the only member of the band who attended the services; Jimmy, John Paul, and Peter were still in the States. Robert was in terrible anguish through most of the ceremony, and he appeared exhausted. He kept his composure, but his eyes were puffy.

After the services, we went back to Robert's farm. Robert asked me where Peter, John Paul, and Jimmy were. He was clearly disappointed that none of them had attended the funeral, particularly Jimmy, his writing partner.

I was surprised, too, by their absence. Maybe they had business to take care of. Perhaps they didn't like funerals or dealing with death. But Robert clearly had wanted them there.

For about an hour that afternoon, I sat with Robert and Bonzo on the lawn of Plant's farm. We drank some whiskey and tried to talk about the good times, but it was hard. Robert was clearly preoccupied. "It just doesn't make sense," he said. "Why Karac?"

Before I left that day, I told Robert I would be in touch soon. "I just need time to think," he said. "I need to sort things out."

We embraced. I climbed into a limousine and rode back to London.

Almost immediately, the media started reviving the myth of the "Zeppelin jinx." A tabloid in London quoted a psychic as saying that more bad times awaited the band. An FM disc jockey in Chicago claimed that "if Jimmy Page would just lay off all that mystical, hocus-pocus occult stuff, and stop unleashing all those evil forces, Led Zeppelin could just concentrate on making music."

I doubt that Robert ever blamed Jimmy's dabbling in the occult for his own tragedies over the past two years. At least he never told me that. I'm sure he heard the speculation, and he may have even wondered about it from time to time. But curses and jinxes just weren't anything that Robert could relate to.

As for Jimmy, he was angry about all the talk of Zeppelin's bad karma or curse. "The people who say things like that don't know what in the hell they're talking about," he told me, "and Robert sure doesn't need to hear that kind of crap. A lot of negative things have occurred recently, but tragedies happen. Why do they have to make it worse by talking that way? Why don't they let Robert mourn in peace?"

For those who believed in the legend of the Zeppelin jinx, more fuel was added to the fire in September, only two months after Karac's death. Bonzo had been drinking at a pub near his house. Well past midnight, he got into his Jensen to drive home. Less than two miles from his house, he tried to negotiate a curve at an excessive speed. The car veered off the road and careened into a ditch.

Bonzo was hurt. He had terrible pains around his mid-section and was having difficulty breathing. Nevertheless, he somehow made his way to a phone. He didn't call the police, however, or an ambulance. Instead, he phoned a chauffeur who often worked for the band and asked for a ride. He left his car behind and had it towed to a repair yard the next day. When Bonzo was finally checked by a doctor, he had two broken ribs.

As the news of the crash hit the papers, the true believers in the Zeppelin jinx theory had even more ammunition at their disposal.

■ ■ ■

In the aftermath of Karac's death, Robert went into seclusion with his wife and daugher. Not only was the boy's death a devastating blow to the immediate family, but everyone in the Zeppelin organization began to ponder whether the death knell for the band had finally sounded. After Robert's car accident, Zeppelin had been put on hold for months. Now, two years later, it was happening all over again.

Jimmy and Peter had a meeting at the Zeppelin office in London. They felt it was important for the band to give Robert as much time as he needed to decide his own future. "Let's just take things as they come," Peter said. "We're not going to plan anything until Robert feels up to it, whether that's in three months or three years."

Jimmy decided to take a vacation in Guadeloupe in the West Indies with Charlotte Martin and their daughter, Scarlet. "Why don't you join us?" he asked me. Since there was little work for me in London, I agreed. I didn't even back away when Jimmy suggested that we both try to get clean in Guadeloupe. "It means about two weeks without heroin, but with plenty of white rum," he said. I figured if we were both drunk for most of that trip, maybe I wouldn't even miss the smack.

Even so, I still hadn't faced up to the seriousness of my problem. I continued to believe that anytime I wanted to stop, I could, and that I hadn't lost control.

On one Sunday afternoon in Guadeloupe, I left Jimmy at a bar and tried returning to the hotel on my own. Unfortunately, I was so inebriated that I became disoriented on the walk back. I stopped at a store selling Formica coffins and, in a stupor, climbed into one of them by the front window and passed out. I woke up a couple of hours later, aroused by the commotion made by a small crowd of people who had congregated outside, apparently fascinated by what appeared to be a dead body in a casket. My eyes opened, and I sat up with a horrified look on my face. "Where the hell am I?" I thought. "And who the hell are all these people?"

As scared as I was, I wasn't nearly as terrified as the people themselves. When I jumped out of the coffin and ran out of the store and down the street, an elderly lady fainted. I could hear screams for blocks.

Once we returned to England, Jimmy tried to keep active. In September, he performed at a benefit concert in Plumpton for a children's charity called Goaldiggers. He spent time in his home recording studio, listening to tapes of Zeppelin's concerts dating back to 1969. He had talked to Peter about putting out a live album—a retrospective of some of the best concert performances over the years—although it never materialized.

I had heard that Pagey got back into heroin before long, but because I didn't see him for a while, I had no way of knowing for sure. When the band finally re-formed the following year, however, he seemed as immersed in smack as I was. I had returned from Guadeloupe looking and feeling fit, and stopped at Peter's house on my way home. I drank more than forty cans of beer that night. Within two days, I had called my heroin supplier and lapsed back into the habit. Without much work to keep me occupied, I had too much time to fill. And I filled it with drugs.

55

COMING BACK

When 1978 dawned, Led Zeppelin's hiatus was approaching six months. Jimmy desperately wanted to get the band back into the studio, as much for himself as for Led Zeppelin. He wanted to make sure *he* still had it, that he hadn't lost anything, that he could still rev up this band's engines.

He was also anxious about the ongoing rumors—rumors that Robert was still in the depths of despair, that the band was splitting up, that after more than nine years, it was finally all over. "The only way to squelch the rumors is for us to get back to work."

John Paul and Bonzo were ready, but no one felt comfortable pushing Robert. Finally, in May, Peter called them all together for a meeting at Clearwell Castle in the Forest of Dean, near the border with Wales. They brought their instruments with them, and they played music for a few hours. Robert sang a little tentatively, perhaps still searching for the enthusiasm to start all over again. Jimmy told them they needed to get serious about resuming their careers, that it was finally time. Robert, however, wasn't so sure. He knew that once the band got back into motion, there would be no turning back. And he wasn't yet convinced that he was ready, that music was as important to him now as it had been before Karac's death.

Robert eventually decided that if he was going to get back onstage, he needed to ease into it slowly, not by leaping onto a stage before a Zeppelin-sized crowd of 50,000 or more. In July, he asked a band called the Turd Burglars if he could jam with them, and a small, surprised audience at a hall in Worcestershire saw him make his first public appearance in a year, performing songs like "Blue Suede Shoes." He was nervous, he said afterward, but felt good. He had almost forgotten just how much he enjoyed singing for people. The next month, while on vacation on the island of Ibiza, he sang with a band called Dr. Feelgood at the Club Amnesia, and then in September he sat in with Dave Edmunds, a Swan Song act, at a concert in Birmingham.

Throughout most of 1978, however, the band members rarely saw one another. Peter urged the others to continue to give Robert the space he needed and eventually he would come around. Occasionally, they would see each other socially, and Jimmy would try to feel Robert out about his readiness to return to the rock wars. But Pagey refrained from trying to put Robert in a pressure cooker, demanding a commitment on when the music would be reborn.

In September, the entire band attended a reception at the Red Lion, a Fulham pub, to celebrate my wedding. I had gotten married for the second time, at the Chelsea Register Office, on the same day that Simon Kirke, Bad Company's drummer, tied the knot as well. We had a joint reception, which was the last time I did any kind of rejoicing over that marriage. A few years later, a friend told me, "If there ever was such a thing as a 'Zeppelin curse,' your marriage was one of its victims." Maybe he was right.

I had met my new wife, Tracy, while on vacation in Marbella, where I had gone that summer to try once again to clean up from heroin. My first night there, drunk but free of smack, I smashed up my Austin-Healy 3000. It was a total loss, and if I had been smart, I would have cut my losses and gone home. But I hung around long enough to drink a hell of a lot of champagne and meet and bring home with me the young woman I would eventually marry.

My first day back in London, I was already using smack again. And when my heroin dealer, Malcolm, told me he was getting married, Tracy and I decided to get hitched, too, almost on a whim. "I might as well have another crack at marriage," I told myself. But Tracy and I hardly knew each other. It was a big mistake.

Jimmy Page was my best man that day because, he said, "I've never been a best man before." I had a good snort of heroin before the wedding, had a great time at the ceremony, and made love to my new wife that night. But I never had sex with her again. After that, heroin took over. That was all I really cared about.

Nothing really brought me to my senses, not even the death of Keith Moon that same month. I had been out with Keith the night before he passed away. We had gone to a party that Paul McCartney had hosted at the Coconut Grove, celebrating the release of the movie *The Buddy Holly Story* and Paul's involvement with the music in it.

I was strung out on smack at the party. Moonie, on the other hand, was completely sober.

"Richard," he said, "I feel great. I've given up everything . . . drugs, alcohol, everything but women. And I'm getting married again. I'm real happy, Richard. This time it's gonna last."

I wasn't going to be outdone by my old drinking and drugging buddy. "Don't worry," I told him. "I've got everything under control. I enjoy heroin too much to give it up yet. But the day I want to quit, I will!"

By this point, I was starting to wonder whether I believed myself or not. I knew that heroin wasn't doing me any good. But since I had tried and failed to quit before, I didn't know if I could ever pull myself out.

As that night at the Coconut Grove wore on, I decided to drive to another club, Tramps, to start doing some heavier drinking. I didn't feel real comfortable doing it around Moonie. "I'll stay here at the party," he told me. "You go ahead and I'll talk to you soon."

The next day, I heard that Keith had died from a drug overdose—too much of a medication he was taking to help combat his alcoholism.

At Moonie's funeral, Pete Townshend came up to me. He was visibly shaken by the death of his friend. "What the fuck is going on?" he said, shaking his head. "Keith is dead and you're alive. And your drug habits are worse than anyone's."

I just smiled. I never was willing to recognize how much trouble I was in. I got into my car, reached into the glove compartment, and took out a bag of heroin. I took a snort, sat back, and felt relieved, even happy again. I put the key in the ignition, started the car, and drove away.

In December 1978, a reunited Led Zeppelin finally became a reality again. Sixteen months after the death of his son, Robert felt he was ready to go back into the studio. "Maybe I waited too long," he said, "but I just couldn't push myself. I had to let the enthusiasm come back on its own. I'm anxious to get going and see what happens."

The band had begun formal rehearsals for a new album at the EZEE Hire in London. It seemed like an eternity since the Oakland Coliseum concert in July 1977—the last time the band had seriously played together. Even so, they wasted no time recapturing the Zeppelin chemistry. In the first few hours in the studio, they knew Zeppelin was going to come back. John Paul thought to himself, "We're going to be as good as we ever were."

We flew to Stockholm to record a new album—*In Through the Out Door*—at Polar Studios, which was owned by Abba. It seemed like an odd place to go in the dead of winter, but Jimmy and Robert had heard wonderful things about the studio. We spent three weeks there, although we flew home on weekends.

Robert still found it hard to be separated from his family for very long, as though he feared another tragedy might befall them when he was away. Each Friday, Jimmy would take the week's tapes back with him to work on at his studio at home.

At Polar Studios, Jimmy encouraged the band to drive themselves in new directions. So they experimented. Plant and Jonesy incorporated a samba beat into "Fool in the Rain." In "Carouselambra," John Paul took over and directed the ten-minute saga, opening the throttle on his own keyboards only to back away for Pagey's double-neck guitar magic on his Gibson. From cut to cut, John Paul leaped from the Mellotron to the electric piano to the clavinet.

Jonesy and Plant sat down and wrote "All My Love" together, one of the few songs in Zeppelin's history in which Pagey did not receive songwriting credit. When they recorded it, John Paul performed a magnificent classical solo, but it was Robert's singing that brought everyone to a standstill. Some people thought that "All My Love" was Robert's tribute to Karac. Certainly Plant's singing was never more emotional or touching. For that cut, Jimmy ended up using Robert's first vocal track. Bonzo felt it was the best he had ever heard Plant sing.

Pagey was convinced that "In the Evening" would shatter any skepticism that might exist as to whether Led Zeppelin could come back strongly. Robert sneered his way through the song as though he were daring the critics to ever again discount this band. The rest of the album, Jimmy felt, was icing on the cake.

While the band was recording, I spent a lot of time scrounging around Stockholm, trying to find a steady source for heroin. I finally located a dealer whose house was right across the bridge from Polar Studios. When he turned the light on in his living room, that was my signal that he had some stuff for me. Sometimes I felt so desperate that I would dash down the escalator, out the front door, and literally sprint over the bridge to his house.

On occasion, my drug contact didn't have anything available for days at a time. I got by the best I could. Because I seemed to be able to deal with the situation for a while without any serious withdrawal symptoms, I began to feel that maybe I was in control of this drug after all. I never risked carrying drugs with me from London to Stockholm. I was still thinking clearly enough to realize that it was just too dangerous to bring them through customs. So I picked up heroin wherever I could find it and coped as well as I could when it wasn't available. Mercifully, we were home by Christmas and obtaining heroin was no longer a problem.

In May, the rock press began running stories that Zeppelin was planning a return to the stage. The story had leaked that Peter was negotiating with promoter Freddie Bannister for the band to appear at Hertfordshire's open-air Knebworth Festival at Knebworth Park in August. For a time, however, the discussions were stalled by Peter's asking price: An astronomical one million pounds for two performances.

Bannister was shocked by Peter's demand. He didn't think it was possible. But he also knew about Zeppelin's drawing power. He wavered for days. Finally, he agreed. Bannister and Grant shook hands and signed the contract. Tickets went on sale for seven and a half pounds each.

Zeppelin's supporting acts at Knebworth included Fairport Convention, Commander Cody, Keith Richards' New Barbarians, and Todd Rundgren's Utopia. But the crowd—nearly half a million people for the two shows on consecutive Saturdays—was clearly most interested in Led Zeppelin. We didn't cut corners, importing Showco's most powerful outdoor equipment, including a 100,000-watt PA system, a 600,000-watt lighting system, and a complete laser network. Jonesy had his white grand piano, his synthesized Mellotron, and his clavinet trucked to the site, where Brian Condliffe and Andy Ledbetter—who had been flown in from the States—nursed his equipment into perfect shape. Mick Hinton checked and rechecked Bonham's metallic Ludwig kit to ensure that everything was in order and properly miked. Ray Thomas propped five guitars for Jimmy in a line, poised to be pushed to their limits. Benji Le Fevre and Rusty Brutsche came in to run the sound equipment, and Chris Bodger directed the onsite video as he had done at Earls Court. J. J. Jackson had flown in from New York to provide moral support and lend a hand in any way he could.

That first night, I could see the band's tension and anxiety during the opening numbers—"The Song Remains the Same," "Celebration Day," "Black Dog." But once they began to relax, they hit home runs with nearly every song. The show lasted three and a half hours. Robert, wearing charcoal cords and a long-sleeve, polka-dot shirt open almost to the belt, struck lofty poses and created high-voltage vocals like the Robert of old, before the personal tragedies that had crippled his body and mind.

On "Stairway to Heaven," the night became electric as the crowd spontaneously began to sing along—hundreds of thousands of voices harmonizing with one another. With wide eyes, Robert looked at Jimmy as though he could barely believe the incredible sound. It was like an entire city, a small nation, had joined together as one. It was a chilling, memorable moment.

Even as the lengthy show was winding down well past midnight, the crowd pleaded with the band for more. Some had camped out for a week, living in tents and enduring rain showers, to ensure themselves a perfect view for the concert. After multiple encores in which Zeppelin played "Rock and Roll," "Whole Lotta Love," and "Heartbreaker," they finally had spent their last ounce of energy and sprinted toward their limousines that sped them to a pair of waiting helicopters.

Jimmy felt renewed after the Knebworth concerts. It had been four years since the band had last performed in the U.K., and it was as if nothing had changed. Pagey proposed that the band abandon thoughts of any more lengthy, summer-long tours in favor of selected gigs in large venues. "We can still reach our fans without the wear and tear on our own bodies and psyches," he said. No one argued with him.

In Through the Out Door was released in mid-August, about a week after the second Knebworth concert. Fans were starving for some fresh Zeppelin, and in America alone the new album sold a staggering four million copies. That stimulated renewed interest in the band's earlier records as well, and by October all nine Zeppelin albums were in the *Billboard* Top 200. In an era when rock bands rise and fall with the speed of lightning, Led Zeppelin was more popular than ever, over a decade after it had taken flight.

BONZO

I was absolutely furious at Peter.

Here it was, the early months of 1980, and Zeppelin had a European tour planned for the summer through Germany, Holland, Austria, and Switzerland. These would be the first concerts in Europe in three years.

But Peter was worried about me, or at least worried about my capability of still handling the job of tour manager. "Damn it, Cole, you're so fucking wasted on heroin so much of the time, I don't know what you're capable of doing anymore." Then his voice softened. He had made a decision. "I'm not going to put you on this tour. I'm making arrangements for someone else to manage it."

I was stunned, but within seconds the shock had turned to anger. "After more than five hundred and sixty concerts," I thought to myself, "this guy doesn't think I can do the job?" From my drug-warped perspective, Peter was the one who was out of touch, not me.

Although I had spent a little time nearly every day in Peter's office, I was much more dedicated to drinking in the nearby pubs and meeting with the dealers who supplied me with smack. I still loved Led Zeppelin, but my second wife had left me, and my interests were really elsewhere, caught up in a world where drugs were the most important thing in my life. While I floundered, Peter's patience was running thin. He was simply fed up with my heroin habit and warned me repeatedly that I had to get clean or my job was in jeopardy. He even offered to assist me in getting some help.

By then, because I wanted the drugs to work as fast as possible, a dealer had begun to give me heroin injections; I was frightened of using the needle myself, and I'd close my eyes while he did it. He always claimed he was injecting me with only "great stuff," but I never believed him because all these suppliers were liars and crooks, so I'd talk him into giving me a little more smack with every fix. Within a week, I had OD'd twice, ending up in the hospital each time, where they had to pump saline into my system to revive me. If not before, I should have known by then that heroin did not agree with me.

"Look," Peter finally said, "while we're on tour, I want you to go somewhere—whether it's a rehab clinic or just a vacation—and get yourself off drugs. I'll pay for it."

Looking back, I can see Peter had real concerns for my well-being. At the time, however, all I knew was that I was being replaced, that someone else was going to be the band's tour manager, and that my ride with Zeppelin might be over.

I was depressed, pondering just how all this had happened to me and how I was going to get out of it. But figuring my job was on the line, I reluctantly made plans to take a trip to Italy to get clean. In August, I headed for Rome, taking a girl named Susan with me. She was a punk rocker with spiked green and silver hair and a love for miniskirts, garter belts, and fishnet stockings. When we arrived in Rome, we checked into the Excelsior Hotel and immediately went drinking, concentrating on sweet stuff like Brandy Alexanders, which I knew might help me ease off heroin. "I'm really serious about cleaning up this time," I told Susan. "Smack is ruining my life."

The next morning, something else almost ruined my life. Susan and I were awakened by a loud knocking on the door of our hotel room. I tried to ignore it, figuring it was the maid, but the banging got louder, accompanied by a voice shouting, "Police!"

I wrapped a towel around me, opened the door, and a dozen cops with their guns drawn barged inside. "What the hell is going on?" I said.

"Where are the weapons?" they shouted. "Where are the arms?"

"What the hell are you talking about?" I asked. They pushed me against the wall and searched the room. They didn't find anything, but that didn't make them any more polite. They handcuffed Susan and me and led us down the elevators to some waiting police cars.

I was thoroughly baffled and frightened by what was taking place. Down at street level, one of the cops signaled to marksmen on the roof of a nearby building to put down their rifles. In the police car, I told Susan, "Don't worry;

we'll be back in a little while." But I was wrong. Although Susan was released in a few days when the police conceded that there was no reason to hold her, I was taken to the local jail, then transferred to Regina Coeli Prison, a maximum security facility. My cell was divided into catacombs, and my first night there I went to sleep with three cell mates and awoke with twenty-two of them, mostly pick-pockets and other street criminals. "Welcome, boys," I told them. "I hope you have good appetites. The meals here consist of bread and lettuce leaves—all you can eat!"

Ironically, no formal charges were ever brought against me. But under the Napoleonic Code, I was technically "guilty until proven innocent." To make matters worse, all the judges were on vacation in August, and when they returned they went on strike for two months. So in the meantime, I continued to sit in my jail cell, feeling more desperate each day and wondering if I'd ever get out.

My lawyer, Julio, finally found out why I was there: They suspected me of blowing up the Bologna train station, which had been attacked by terrorists the day I had arrived in Italy. The cops and the prison officials desperately tried to get a confession out of me. They roughed me up. They promised me better treatment if I "cooperated." "There's nothing for me to confess to!" I told them repeatedly. "Why am I a suspect? I haven't been to Bologna since nineteen sixty-seven!"

When my luggage was finally sent over from the Excelsior, the prison officials had me go to a bomb-disposal room and unpack the bag myself. I could only think that they were worried there were explosives in it and preferred to have me—rather than one of them—pulverized. In fact, the bag contained only clothes that belonged to both Susan and me. As the prison guards had me unpack, they got quite a chuckle as, one by one, I dangled garter belts, bras, and panties before their eyes. One of the guards told me, "You're the first cross-dressing terrorist we've ever had here!"

As upset as I was about being in prison, particularly on suspicion of something I didn't do, my living conditions at least became tolerable once they transferred me to a third facility, Rebibia Prison. By that time, I had already undergone a forced withdrawal from heroin, which was uncomfortable but not nearly as torturous as I had expected. I was so obsessed with my imprisonment and how I was going to get out that the withdrawal symptoms—the aches and pains, the diarrhea—almost seemed insignificant.

Over the weeks, there were aspects to my imprisonment that kept my spirits up. I shared a cell with some Italian prisoners whose wives used to bring them wonderful meals that they generously shared with me. The Rebibia prison food itself wasn't bad, either, with roast lamb, potatoes, and liters of wine. My cell mates also had their own gas stoves, and I learned to cook some mean pasta dishes while I was imprisoned. They also showed me how to make good use of the stove when it was running low on gas. "There's not enough gas to ignite a flame," one of my buddies said in his broken English, "but you sure can make yourself feel good by sucking a little gas out!" At least I still had one way to get high.

The prison doctors had a very liberal policy about the distribution of sleeping pills. After I had complained to them about insomnia, they prescribed some pills for me, which knocked me out twelve hours a night. I found out that time passes much quicker in prison when you're unconscious.

Once I finally got some messages to the outside world, the Zeppelin organization did their best to help me. Peter figured I was being framed, and he sent me $500 a month and flew a lawyer, Jeff Hoffman, to Italy to meet with me. "They're not going to find anything against me," I told the attorney. "I don't have the cleanest background, but terrorism is one thing I haven't done!"

I also started exchanging letters with Susan, whom I had encouraged to stay at my house back in London and keep an eye on it. At one point, I asked her to send me some cassette tapes, and she innocently shipped me some bizarre selections—the Pink Floyd album, *The Wall*, as if I weren't already surrounded by enough walls to last a lifetime, and the soundtrack of *McVicar*, the Roger Daltrey film about an escape from a high-security prison. Along with the tapes, she enclosed a letter, telling me about a terrible flood at home caused by some burst pipes, leaving my house with about four feet of water in it. "I was so scared because I can't swim," she wrote. It sounded as if the house had suffered enormous damage, and, suddenly, I was in no hurry to get home. Between the sleeping pills and the gas stove, prison seemed almost tolerable.

One afternoon, however, Julio changed all that when he nervously gave me the news that John Bonham had passed away. I felt as if I had been hit in the stomach, as if part of me had died. Maybe part of me had.

Peter heard the news of Bonzo's death from his assistant, Ray Washburn. Peter was at his home in Sussex when Ray fielded the phone call about the tragedy. Ray sat Peter down, handed him a couple of Valium, and insisted he take them.

"Someone is on the phone for you," Ray said.

"Who is it?" Peter said. "What's wrong?"

"It's about John Bonham."

Peter was becoming anxious. "Well, what about him?"

"He's dead."

The word of Bonham's death spread quickly. The wire services flashed the story throughout the world. In the offices of Atlantic Records, which had helped launch the band more than a decade earlier, executives slumped in their seats and secretaries cried. At clubs like the Rainbow in Los Angeles, fans mingled to share their grief, somehow feeling closer to Bonzo by congregating in the places where he had loved hanging out. There was the inevitable talk of the Zeppelin jinx, but, mostly, people shared their pain and sorrow. Even those who didn't know him felt the world had lost someone special.

Bonzo had been my closest friend and ally in the band. I was crushed by the news. I never really knew whether to believe the official cause of his death. John was so caught up in heroin that I wondered if it might have played some role in his passing, even though I had heard that he was telling people that he had finally kicked the habit. I was numb for days, living in denial. Eventually, I realized the full impact of Bonham's death. With his passing, my own life was forever changed. In addition to the loss of a precious friend, I had lost my job as well. Instinctively, I knew that Led Zeppelin had died with Bonzo.

Bonham's funeral was held at Rushock parish church, not far from his farm in Worcestershire. Nearly 300 fellow musicians and fans attended the services. The remaining members of Led Zeppelin were there. They shunned reporters, who were already asking them about Zeppelin's future. The band members had little to say to each other, either. They were all trying to get used to a world without Bonzo and trying to make some sense out of what had happened.

Robert Plant seemed to take it hardest. He had known Bonham since they were struggling musicians still in their teens, aching for a break that might turn them into Somebody. That success happened for both of them. But Robert's life had been marred by tragedy, and now Bonzo was gone. What was it about the life of a musician, Plant wondered, that devours people? He didn't have any answers.

In the fall, I was finally released from prison, never charged with nor convicted of anything. "It was a mistake," one of the prison officials told me. "We're sorry if we inconvenienced you."

When I got out, I didn't feel I had much to go home to, with only a flooded house and uncertainty surrounding Led Zeppelin awaiting me. I ended up going to the Philippines and then to the U.S. for a while, pondering my own future. I was broke, thanks primarily to the enormous amounts of money I had spent on alcohol and drugs. I drank away most of my assets, and the deed to my home in England had been turned over to the bank to pay off my debts. I was unsure where my life was headed, but I knew I had some rebuilding to do.

While I was away, Jimmy, Jonesy, and Robert made the decision to dissolve the band, as I had expected. After Bonzo's death, the rock press reported a flurry of rumors on who might replace Bonham, with Carmine Appice (of Vanilla Fudge) and Cozy Powell most frequently named. But for Robert, Jimmy, and John Paul, that was never part of their game plan. They congregated in Jersey to discuss their futures and then met with Peter at the Savoy Hotel. "We can't go on without Bonham," Plant said. Everyone agreed. They never seriously contemplated looking for another drummer. The twelve-year run of Led Zeppelin was over.

The band released a simple statement through Swan Song that read: "The loss of our dear friend and the deep respect we have for his family, together with the sense of undivided harmony felt by ourselves and our manager, have led us to decide that we could not continue as we were."

Led Zeppelin had enjoyed an incredible flight, but the band had finally touched down for the last time.

GOOD
TIMES,
BAD TIMES

By 1981, those of us who had worked with Led Zeppelin were trying to get used to thinking of the band in the past tense. Clearly, Zeppelin had left an indelible mark on rock music, but I needed to face the reality that there would be no new Zeppelin recordings, no more touring, no more of both the good times and the bad times.

Nevertheless, everyone—from the Zeppelin insiders to their millions of fans—sensed that we hadn't heard the last from the surviving members of the group. For Jimmy, John Paul, and Robert, the band had been their lives for a dozen years, and it took all of them a while to regain their equilibrium after the devastating loss of Bonham. They took some time for soul-searching, not only to ponder their own futures, but to contemplate a blur of philosophical questions, most of which had no answers: Why had so much misfortune struck in such a short period of time? Why had Bonzo died? Why had we lived?

It was a tough recovery period for Jimmy. After all, Led Zeppelin was his creation, his baby. After twelve years, it was difficult for him to think of starting anew. He also continued to live in the house where John Bonham had died and thus had daily reminders that made it almost impossible to put his friend's death behind him. He didn't pick up a guitar for months. He sometimes wondered whether he ever would again.

But time eventually began to heal the wounds. Jimmy produced a final Led

Zeppelin album, *Coda*, which was issued in 1982 and sold more than a million copies around the world. The album consisted of previously unreleased material from the band's earlier studio sessions, dating back as early as 1969, when the group had recorded songs like "We're Gonna Groove" during the *Led Zeppelin II* sessions.

At Eric Clapton's urging, Pagey performed at a charity concert in 1983 at the Royal Albert Hall, overwhelming the audience with a stirring instrumental version of "Stairway to Heaven." Then he decided to assume the laborious, stressful task of assembling a new band. He knew people would compare it to Zeppelin, but eventually he tried to rise above those anxieties. The new group, the Firm, recorded two albums and did some touring. Fans expected a lot more than the band ever produced. The comparisons with Zeppelin never stopped. Eventually, Jimmy disbanded the group.

In 1988, Jimmy recorded a solo album, *Outrider*, and formed a touring band that included John Bonham's son, Jason, on drums. During performances in the U.S. and the U.K., Jimmy didn't shy away from reprising a number of Zeppelin standards, not only "Stairway to Heaven," but also "Kashmir," "Over the Hills and Far Away," and others. If the fans wanted to hear some Zeppelin favorites, he wasn't going to disappoint them. For the first time since Bonham's death, he felt fully confident that he had found a vehicle that worked for him.

Meanwhile, Robert slowly tried to reassemble the pieces of his life. He had suffered so many personal tragedies in the 1970s, culminating in Bonham's death, that it took courage and strength to pull himself together. But he felt that he still had a contribution to make with his music and that music might heal him more quickly than anything else.

Even so, Robert went through a lot of inner turmoil wondering if he was cut out for a solo career. He decided to try singing at a number of small clubs in 1981, intentionally avoiding Zeppelin material, going back instead to an R&B sound. Fans would shout out, "Sing 'Stairway to Heaven' " or "Why didn't you bring Jimmy and John Paul with you?" Plant would just cringe. But he loved being back onstage again, and performing as a solo artist suddenly seemed feasible.

In 1982, Robert recorded his first solo album, *Pictures at Eleven*. Even though the Plant-Page relationship was formally over in 1980, Robert still called upon Jimmy to listen to the tapes that were emerging from his initial solo recording sessions, eager for input from someone whose musical instincts he thoroughly trusted. The solo album was a hit on both sides of the Atlantic. Since then, Robert has released a steady stream of solo albums.

■ ■ ■

John Paul has rarely returned to the stage since 1980. He has been quite content living far away from the spotlight. He performed on and helped piece together the soundtrack for director Michael Winner's 1984 movie, *Scream for Help.* He has produced a few records for other artists, and got involved in Paul McCartney's film, *Give My Regards to Broad Street.* Unlike his Zeppelin colleagues, John Paul has never had a yearning to have a solo act, or a career with high visibility.

For millions of Led Zeppelin fans, however, the individual directions that Page, Plant, and Jones have taken haven't been enough. They want Zeppelin itself back, even though it would mean bringing in a new drummer. If the fans can't have the real thing, they at least want something damn close to it.

Inevitably, throughout the 1980s and into the 1990s, there have been endless rumors about Zeppelin reunions. And, in fact, the band's fans haven't been completely disappointed. In 1985, Robert, Jimmy, and John Paul performed together at the Live-Aid concert at JFK Stadium in Philadelphia, with Tony Thompson and Phil Collins filling in on drums. The act was a little rusty, supported by just a single ninety-minute rehearsal. Plant's voice was a bit hoarse, and Jimmy's Gibson seemed to be slipping out of tune at times. But when they performed "Whole Lotta Love" and "Stairway to Heaven," the fans responded as though everything was well again, as though time had really stood still.

Three years later, the trio performed once more, this time at Atlantic Records' fortieth anniversary concert at Madison Square Garden, joined by Jason Bonham on drums. Jason prepared for the assignment seriously, listening endlessly to the band's albums, playing along with them, and even watching videos of their performances and studying his father's every nuance. The band rehearsed in London without Robert, who was out on tour in the States, but he joined them for a single rehearsal in New York.

At the Garden, the band didn't begin their thirty-minute set until 1 A.M. For more than an hour, Pagey was pacing backstage, second-guessing himself, wondering if this was such a good idea after all. However, despite the late hour, no one at the Garden had left his seat. From the first downbeat of "Kashmir" to the last remnants of "Stairway to Heaven," the sellout crowd— some of whom had paid $1,000 a ticket—were on their feet cheering. Robert muffed a few lyrics, and Jimmy didn't seem quite at home during a solo. But overall even the band members themselves were satisfied. For thirty minutes, Led Zeppelin was back.

Bill Graham staged that show for Atlantic. He put aside the lingering hard feelings from the incident at the Oakland Coliseum in 1977 and recognized that despite the star-studded bill, no one could follow Led Zeppelin. He canceled plans for a grand finale in which everyone in the show (Crosby, Stills, and Nash, Roberta Flack, Ben E. King, Phil Collins, Genesis, the Rascals) would join together to sing some of Atlantic's most memorable hits. Instead, Zeppelin closed out the evening. That was the way it should have been.

I talked to Jimmy just before that New York performance. "It's nerve-racking," he said. "Everyone expects to see the Led Zeppelin that they knew when they went to our concerts. But we've all changed since then. We'll be playing some of the old songs, but it still won't be exactly the same. Everyone has evolved and, of course, it will never be the same without Bonzo. That's why the rumors about the band re-forming are just that—rumors."

I've rebuilt my own life in recent years, while still staying active in the music business. Sharon and Ozzy Osbourne have become my close friends, and Sharon has given me the opportunity to work with a lot of her bands, including the London Quireboys, Lita Ford, and Ozzy himself. In 1990, Sharon asked me to serve as tour manager on the Quireboys' U.S. tour, which turned into a nine-month international tour encompassing 170 concerts in twenty-two countries. In a sense, it was a nostalgic experience for me, as the Quireboys demonstrated the same wonderful spirit and energy that I appreciated so much in the Led Zeppelin tours.

Life on the road, however, has changed in some ways. As these words are written, I have been sober for six years. It took me a long time to realize how drugs and alcohol had ruined so many lives and were taking a terrible toll on mine as well. Bonzo, of course, was the most crushing loss, and I still terribly miss his warm and gentle nature and his incredible zest for living.

Even after Bonham's death, I needed years of introspection to recognize the risks I was subjecting myself to and then some additional time to finally put aside the cocaine, the heroin, and the alcohol for good. I took my last drink on my fortieth birthday in 1986, and, with the help of sober friends, have remained sober and drug-free ever since.

Frankly, I enjoyed the Quireboys tour so much more because of my sobriety, which allowed me to truly appreciate some of the same cities and countries I had visited with Zeppelin, except this time was free of the obsession with drugs and alcohol. The Quireboys enjoyed a few drinks, but drugs weren't part of their lives. Like Zeppelin, they were never late for a concert and made the music their top priority.

As I told Jimmy back in 1988, "Things are so different today; back in the Zeppelin era, we'd all go out and get stoned; now, I'm an example to the young bands of what can happen when you let drugs and alcohol consume you."

"You sure know both sides of it," Jimmy said. And from my perspective to-day, sobriety makes a lot more sense.

Led Zeppelin has secured its place in rock history. Probably more than any other Zeppelin song, "Stairway to Heaven" is considered a classic, still one of the most requested songs on rock radio stations worldwide. In 1991, twenty years after that song was created around a log fireplace at Headley Grange, national magazines like *Esquire* celebrated and dissected it, treating it as one of the great songs of its time, a standard that meant as much to its gener-ation as the works of George Gershwin and Cole Porter meant to theirs.

In 1990, Jimmy produced and Atlantic released a Led Zeppelin retrospec-tive on compact disc—fifty-four tracks digitally remastered at Sterling Sound in New York.

When I listen to Zeppelin's recordings today, I find they have withstood the test of time. The quality and the passion that made Zeppelin the biggest act in rock music are still apparent. And judging by the sales of the CD, the public interest hasn't faded, either. Although ten years had passed since the band had last performed, sales of the new double-boxed CD have been phe-nomenal. There are fans in their thirties and forties who grew up with Led Zeppelin and who haven't lost their fervor for the band; there are others not much older than my own daughter, Claire, who are just beginning to buy records and who have an extraordinary curiosity about a band that con-tributed so much to popular culture.

I take a measure of pride in the role I played with the band. Early in 1992, I was in Europe with Claire, and we had dinner one night in London with Robert Plant, his daughter, and his son-in-law. As we were leaving the restau-rant, Robert turned to Claire and asked, "Is Richard a good daddy to you?"

Claire smiled, nodded her head, and answered, "Yes."

Robert glanced at me and then back at Claire. "He was my dad for many years, too," he said.

That was the way Robert viewed my twelve years as Led Zeppelin's tour manager. Although we had our differences from time to time, Robert seemed to see me as something of a patriarch and a protector and hadn't lost his ap-preciation of the role I played for the band over the years.

Some rock observers have said that Led Zeppelin was ultimately devoured by its own excesses—the "sex, drugs, and rock and roll" that make up much of the music business. Looking back, Zeppelin may have been hedonistic. They may have wrecked hotels and flexed their power and charms with girls, and they may have gone right to the edge with their use and abuse of drugs. Nevertheless, they never allowed their offstage antics to overshadow their craftsmanship onstage and in the studio. They never lost sight of their fans and the debt they owed them. In nearly three decades in the music business, I have never seen anyone else like Led Zeppelin. They were indisputably the greatest rock and roll band in the world.

Looking back, I don't have many regrets. Of course, the band and I misused drugs and paid an awful price for it; drugs were such an important part of the culture at that time, perhaps there was no way we could have avoided them.

The almost instantaneous fame may have been tough for the band to handle, too. Overnight, these young men in their early twenties were turned into international stars. Yes, it may have gone to their heads at times, and they were guilty of the excesses that can accompany fame. But never at the expense of their music.

To a man, the surviving members of Led Zeppelin are rightfully proud of what they accomplished. I don't think they would have done very much differently. The tragedies that befell them were largely out of their control. The band exemplified everything that could go right—and wrong—in the presence of enormous success. A lot of the fun disappeared once we became "big business." The booze and the drugs became a desperate way to keep the fun alive and the boredom from becoming too oppressive. In the end, rather than keeping the fun alive, it destroyed so much of what was good about the band.

We all knew that Led Zeppelin would not go on forever. But none of us were ready for it to end, either. In a way, however, I suppose it hasn't ended at all. Whenever a fourteen-year-old goes into a music store and buys his or her first Zeppelin CD, the band is reborn all over again. In that sense, Led Zeppelin has a long way still to fly.

AFTERWORD

Since *Stairway to Heaven* was published in the early 1990s, I've received many requests from readers and fans of Led Zeppelin to update my own story. Some asked what I've been doing since the book first arrived on bookstore shelves; many wanted more information about my successful battle to overcome years of drug and alcohol abuse. This new edition of the book has given me the opportunity to spend a few pages describing my own life since becoming sober, including the bands I've worked with in recent years, and a glimpse at how the lives of the surviving Zeppelin members have evolved.

In the immediate post-Zeppelin period, you might think that I could have called my own shots. After all, I had spent twelve years as tour manager of the biggest rock band of all time, so it would make sense that I'd be besieged with offers to take over the reins of other major bands during their national and international tours.

But that didn't happen, and I really shouldn't have been surprised. I had taken a vacation in Manila in January 1981, and then flew to Los Angeles to look for work. But I was so wasted by my continuing drug and alcohol use—and still had such a tough gangster image—that no one would touch me. It was frustrating, and left me increasingly anxious, but in those first months, I had no idea how miserable my life was going to become or how hard life would be in the "real world." I had already gone from riding in Cadillac limousines to being "chauffeured" by friends in their battered old Toyotas. I had gone from sleeping in the grandest suites in the world's finest hotels to crashing on the couches of friends.

I remember awakening one morning in a strange house, with no job to go to, and feeling overwhelmed with despair. Immediately I sought solace and escape in a bottle of Jack Daniel's, hoping it would smother my distress and give me the courage to start making phone calls for work. Instead I chose to make a connection for buying some cocaine, then heroin.

It was a terrible time for me. I was living on credit cards and beginning to drown in my own misery and substance abuse. One night at the Rainbow Bar and Grill in West Hollywood, after an evening of drinking too much tequila and sake, a waitress tried to remove a drinking glass from my hand because it was closing time. Infuriated, I bit off a chunk of the glass and spat it at her. Let's face it—I was self-destructing.

Before long, I was in the emergency room at Cedars-Sinai Medical Center in Los Angeles, bleeding from my mouth and rectum, and with a hole in my esophagus. Transferred to Los Angeles County Hospital (because I didn't have insurance), alongside people who were shooting victims, I was treated in the "red room," which one doctor described as a place from which patients usually don't emerge alive. Somehow the doctors there patched me up, but when a friend visited me in my hospital room, my first question to him was, "What drugs have you got?" Within a few seconds, I was snorting speed in my hospital bed.

All I seemed interested in was the next high. Before I was discharged from County Hospital, a doctor asked me what I drank on an average day, and then had the audacity to say, "Do you think you might be an alcoholic?" How dare he! At the time, his question really did offend me, and I let him know in a raised voice and with an onslaught of expletives. Of course, the doctor advised me not to drink again, but seven days after leaving the hospital, I was arrested for drunk driving on Sunset Boulevard.

Amid this personal chaos, there were actually some positive things occurring in my life, although I was too stoned to fully appreciate them. I met Lea Anne, who was working at Barney's Beanery, and she soon became the mother of my beautiful daughter, Claire. But with opportunities to snort heroin and freebase cocaine, I was usually preoccupied with drugs, at the expense of the people in my life.

I had heard many stories of men and women losing everything, including their houses and their families, because of their drug and alcohol habits. But how could that possibly happen to me? Well, one "good" week of drug-taking cost me my beloved Austin Healy 3000, a Christmas present from Peter Grant in 1976, which went up in smoke in just days. Before long, I had received a letter from my accountants in London informing me that they had sold my house there to pay off my debts. I went to my friend Elliott, a pawnbroker on Santa Monica Boulevard, who was willing to let me pawn some of my gold and platinum Zeppelin records, some artwork, a watch or two, a few rings, and anything else I could find in exchange for some beer money.

When Claire was born, I was hoping on some level that this wonderful addition to my life would make me a more responsible person, perhaps encouraging me to stay home more and give up alcohol and drugs. Maybe I'd even become sober enough to hold down a long-term job. But that wouldn't happen for several more years of making myself and the people closest to me miserable.

. . .

Before long, after getting two DUI citations (one in a car, one on a motorcycle) in a single week, I decided that I needed to fly to London to visit my mother, whom I hadn't seen in three years. So with the proceeds from selling my motorcycle to Elliott, I headed to England. My ex-wife, Marilyn, met me at the airport, and I stayed with her for the first couple days of the trip.

During that visit to the U.K., I called Peter Grant at his country estate. After a quick chat, he suggested that I catch a train to Sussex, where he would have a car waiting to take me to Horselunges Manor, his large period house surrounded by a moat that you needed to cross by bridge. When I arrived at the estate, Ray Washburn, Peter's assistant, greeted me with a hug. Peter was sitting in his drawing room, surrounded by his growing collection of art nouveau and art deco paintings and decorative objects. As Peter gave me a hug, Ray asked the question that I yearned to hear: "What would you like to eat and drink?" For a few moments, as Ray went to start the alcohol flowing, I almost felt time-machined back to the Zeppelin days, when I thought I was on top of the world. I told myself that, somehow, I had to get back as an active player in the music business.

But I was a long way from a comeback. In fact, while in England I so desperately needed money that I took a job on the scaffolds, working as an erector—something I hadn't done since 1966 when I had left the Who. My first job was at Amberly Road School, just a couple of bus rides from my mum's home. The best explanation I could invent to tell the other men on the scaffold was that I had gone to live in America and was a little rusty. By the end of the first day, I was also pretty sore, and needed to plaster on the Ben-Gay to soothe my muscle pain.

Actually, I was surprised that I hadn't lost more of my skills to do the job—but my heart still wasn't in it. In fact, at one point, after a day of hard labor, I was feeling unusually desperate. I bought some flowers and put them on my father's grave. As I walked home along the canal bank, I began screaming at God for the life he had given me, wondering why I could not have been like the other kids I had grown up with, ignorant of the glitz and glitter I had once experienced, now with little hope of ever returning to that extravagant lifestyle. There were moments when I wanted to end it all, but that would have broken my mother's heart.

Then there was an unexpected turn of events. After I had been sober for three months, Caesar Danova, an old pal, sent me a telegram, asking me to call him collect in Tokyo about a job in rock and roll. I rushed to a call box as excited as if I were going to score.

Caesar told me, "I'm going to stage a concert on the anniversary of the bombing of Hiroshima, in collaboration with the Japanese government, and I want you to help me." The details were sketchy at the time, but I didn't care. As far as I was concerned, this was a gift from God. Caesar said, "I'll put a few grand in your bank account, and send you a first-class round-trip ticket to Japan. I'll see you soon."

I was ecstatic. I finally thought I had a foot back in the music industry's door.

The Hiroshima concert, however, never worked out—at least not before I re-signed from the project because it seemed so disorganized. But before I left the Far East, I spent a couple of weeks becoming blind drunk in Thailand, and came home penniless. Because I had walked out, Caesar had taken back the home in Mayfair that he had allowed me to live in, so I went back to living with my mum and erecting scaffold. Nevertheless, the whole experience still gave me hope that perhaps I could find other work in rock and roll.

I continued to go through some hard times, however. At one point back in London, my mum threatened to throw me out of her flat, convinced that I had become a "no-good alcoholic" (imagine that!). During the visit, I had even tried (unsuccessfully) to take some money from her purse without her per-mission. That's how desperate I was for a drink.

Then came the day that changed my life. It was January 2, 1986—my fortieth birthday—and I had pawned my Cartier watch and had joined my "villain" friends for a birthday drink at the Adelaide Pub in Chelsea. Halfway through a pint of beer, a voice in my head said, "That's it, Richard. It's over."

I put the beer down and haven't picked one up since! But at that moment, I felt frightened and I quickly called my heroin dealer to buy a gram of heroin. I did half of it at his house, and the other half the next morning—the last time I ever used drugs. I went for a swim and then I called a close friend, composer Lionel Bart, who told me, "I'm going to Chelsea to a meeting of clean drug ad-dicts."

Almost on a whim, I told him, "I think I'll go too. I'll meet you there."

When I walked up the stairs and into the meeting hall, it was like entering a room of old friends with whom I had drank and used drugs over the previ-ous twenty years. I took my coat off and sat down.

As I looked around, I felt as though the weight of the world had been lifted from my shoulders. I somehow knew I was home at last. I felt that I was in a safe place—and I was.

That meeting in 1986 became the launch pad for my sobriety. Yes, at times I've struggled along the way, but have never taken another drink or used cocaine or any other drug since then. That afternoon, I finally recognized how important it was to get my life back on track. And I have. Sobriety has dramatically transformed my life for the better.

Perhaps not surprisingly, once the word spread that I was sober my phone eventually began to ring. No, the ringing wasn't constant, but I began to work again, and at times, the gigs have been steady and rewarding. Yes, I still erected scaffold for a while, and at one point sold some gold records to pay for a plane ticket to Los Angeles to visit Claire on her fourth birthday. But then one night I bumped into Patrick Meehan, a manager and old friend. He was so impressed that I had been clean and sober for almost a year that, on the spot, he offered me a job as tour manager for Black Sabbath. The offer came so quickly that it stunned me, and I actually began to panic a little. But I said yes.

My first shows with Black Sabbath started in Athens, Greece, in 1987, and we then moved on to Sun City, South Africa, for two weekends. Next we were touring Germany and Italy. All the while I was going to plenty of sobriety meetings.

The most surprising part of that tour for me was that everything seemed effortless—so much so that I thought I must have been forgetting things. Then I realized that in the past, most of my time had been taken up looking for and using drugs. Touring while sober was a lot easier and much less time-consuming. Instead of finding a way to score, I used the time to go to sobriety meetings.

After working with Black Sabbath, it was much harder to land another job as a tour manager than I thought it would be. I moved to Los Angeles to be near Claire and to look for a job. Running out of money, I worked for a time for my friend Marcus, who had just launched a messenger service and needed drivers to make deliveries. So I rode a motorcycle all over Los Angeles delivering messages to offices, including those of people with whom I had worked in the Zeppelin days. One delivery was to Danny Goldberg's office. Danny had overseen Zeppelin's publicity for many years, and was now an owner of a management company.

When I told Goldberg's receptionist that I wanted to speak to Danny, she glared at me, figuring that this messenger boy had some nerve asking for the boss. But I gave her a look that said, "It would be in your best interest to tell Mr. Goldberg that I'm here." In a few minutes, Danny came out to greet me, and was surprised to see me delivering messages, but was genuinely thrilled when I told him I was sober. "Call me anytime," he said. "I don't have anything for you at the moment, but please keep in touch, Richard." Like working on the scaffolds, delivering messages was a quick way to learn humility.

As I mentioned in chapter 57, Sharon Osbourne (Ozzy's wife) had become one of my greatest friends in the music business. I had driven Ozzy to a few sobriety meetings, and this reunited me with Sharon, who invited me to help with some of the acts she managed, beginning as tour manager with Lita Ford. I began by working out of the Sunset Marquis Hotel, arranging Lita's twelve-week tour that was intended to promote her new album (which became my first gold record while sober!). It was also my first-ever bus tour in the U.S., and because I was sober for the first time while touring in the States, I got to visit cities I had been to many times, but now saw through fresh eyes.

With Lita, I had to get used to touring without a private Boeing 707 to transport us, and I had to become accustomed to sleeping on the bus so we could travel the distances we needed to cover from one venue to the next. The bus was an Eagle 10, accompanied by a U-Haul truck carrying the band's instruments, and a team of crew members, each of whom had his own title (such as drum tech or guitar tech) and business card. All of us received a per diem for food—a far different situation than my experience with Zeppelin, where I just signed for anything that the band and I wanted.

The tour with Lita was strange because for the first time in many years I was not with the headline band (Lita supported an old friend, Ted Nugent, for part of her tour). But at least I was working and I was very grateful for the job. Times had changed in other ways, too. There was no trashing of hotels and dressing rooms—it just wasn't tolerated anymore. With Zeppelin, I knew from the beginning that the band would become one of the greatest ever, and would never have to visit the small venues and clubs where we started, so I never worried about having to return to places that we had razed and ruined. But with Lita and other acts with whom I soon worked, it seemed sensible to keep on the good side of promoters. At the same time, because I was now sober my ego was not out of control, so it really didn't matter to me that we weren't staying in the best hotels and the fanciest suites in town. Frankly, in 1988—so many years after Led Zeppelin's last concert—it was enough of a treat just to be out on the road again.

Meanwhile, Sharon turned out to be one of the best managers in the business, providing the show contracts and then letting me get on with the job without any interference. Since my last U.S. tour with Zeppelin, however, there had been dramatic changes in the music industry. MTV had become a powerful vehicle for selling records, replacing much of the constant touring of the sixties and seventies that (along with radio promotion) was necessary to build up a fan base.

Midway through Lita's tour, her album turned gold, and its hit single, "Kiss Me Deadly," was flooding the airwaves from coast to coast. But unexpectedly, the tour ended abruptly for me. Two days after returning from a concert in

Montreal, Sharon told me that Lita no longer wanted me as tour manager. The reason? Lita claimed that I was too strict to work with. But Sharon assured me that the dismissal had nothing to do with the quality of my work, and that she would help me whenever she could.

I was crushed by this unexpected news, and I wasn't sure what my next move would be. But while I pondered my future, I needed a job—and went back to life on the seat of a motorcycle, delivering messages to pay the bills. Before my despair became too intense, however, Sharon called again.

"Ozzy really wants to get sober," she said. "He asked me if you would fly to London to hang out with him, keep him company, and go with him on his European press tour to promote his new record." She also wanted me to accompany Ozzy on his American tour down the road.

I was thrilled. It was like being catapulted out of a deep, black hole.

A few days later, Ozzy and his driver, Tony, picked me up at Heathrow Airport in London, and we drove to his beautiful house tucked away behind a high brick wall in the Buckinghamshire countryside. Tony showed me to my room, which had a lovely view of the manicured gardens and the Osbournes' private deer park in the distance. Then we enjoyed a delicious lunch of roast lamb and baked potatoes.

I spent several months working out of Ozzy's home, flying from London to various cities throughout Europe to escort him to press interviews—and attending sobriety meetings with him. Ozzy seemed to be enjoying his new sober life, and I was certainly enjoying working for him.

Before long, Sharon joined us in London (their children were already there with Ozzy). It was a chance for their family to spend time together before we had to return to the States to rehearse for Ozzy's 1988 American tour. When Ozzy and I finally flew to Dallas for a week of rehearsals, he was still committed to staying sober. Every afternoon, just before the rehearsal began, we would attend a sobriety meeting together to put us in the proper mindset for the day. When the week was over, we headed for Pensacola for the opening date on the tour.

That Florida concert was the first time I had ever seen Ozzy perform—and he was quite a showman. His music was masterful. He exploded with energy. He put on an unforgettable concert. He gave the audience everything he had, from the opening moments to the closing number.

We traveled by bus—a new Prevost with nine bunks and elbow room to spare, particularly since the only occupants on the bus were Ozzy, Tony, and me (plus Sharon and the children when they spent a few days with us). Again, this style of touring was different than the Zeppelin days, when we would place our food orders with the pilot of our plane before each show. But on Ozzy's tour, the wardrobe girl would give us a selection of menus to order from, and then the food was waiting for us on the bus as we rode through the night from one city to the next. It actually worked out fine, except that Ozzy and I often ate out of boredom—by the end of the first week, neither of us could zip up our pants, thanks to the weight we had gained. Those extra pounds didn't sit well with Ozzy, and he ordered a Lifecycle (and some barbells) to be placed in his dressing room throughout the rest of the tour. He exercised conscientiously, and dropped the weight in no time. We also canceled the postconcert meals, and he adopted a low-calorie, low-fat diet that kept him slim.

When we arrived in Los Angeles for a New Year's Eve show at Long Beach Arena, I was able to see Claire and Lea Anne, with whom I had not been able to spend time since starting to work with Ozzy four months earlier. I attended plenty of sobriety meetings during those days in L.A., leading and speaking at some of them, and going to sleep clean and drug-free each night. My continuing sobriety was the best holiday present I could have given myself.

Ozzy's tour resumed after the Long Beach concert, taking us to Houston, Shreveport, Dallas, Kansas City, Albuquerque, and San Francisco. When we hit Reno, Ozzy put a silver dollar in a slot machine, and won a $1,000 jackpot. I hoped that was an omen of good things to come, but in Seattle, all the traveling seemed to be taking a toll on Ozzy, and he appeared exhausted. He somehow got through shows in Seattle and then Salt Lake City, but by that point, he was too worn out and sick to carry on. A doctor examined him, and advised Sharon to reschedule the remaining dates, which she did. Ozzy flew to London to recuperate, and I headed back to Los Angeles—and called Marcus to get my messenger job back.

When I wasn't on the seat of a motorcycle weaving through L.A.'s traffic to deliver one envelope or another, I spent as much time as possible in the gym and on the beach—and at sobriety meetings. By mid-1989, I got a gig with Three Dog Night, serving as the group's tour manager through the end of the year. By that point in the band's evolution, there were only two vocalists, Cory Wells and Danny Hutton, but their sound was still there. In the Zeppelin days, we had actually done a couple shows with Three Dog Night, so they weren't altogether unfamiliar to me. At one time, in fact, Danny was Jimmy Page's first choice for the singer for Zeppelin, before Jimmy finally found and settled on Robert Plant.

I returned to L.A. just before Christmas to enjoy a bit of time off. But on my way back from Warner Brothers Studios, where I had met with a friend who wanted to become sober, the unthinkable happened. While riding my motorcycle home, a car speeding in the opposite direction veered into my lane, heading straight at me. I didn't even have time to panic, but instinctively managed to turn my bike to the right, although not fast enough to avoid a collision. The car hit me full force on the left side of my bike, turning both me and the motorcycle into airborne projectiles. The bike and I soared twelve feet before hitting the road, and then I flew another eight feet as my bike split in half nearby. A witness who watched the violent accident told me she couldn't believe that I had survived.

Fortunately, I never lost consciousness. I remember opening my eyes and carefully moving my body to see if all my limbs were intact. Amazingly, although I was wearing only jeans, tennis shoes, and a leather jacket (with no helmet), I had no broken bones or head injuries. But I was terribly battered and bruised, and shaken badly. When an ambulance arrived, it shuttled me to Santa Monica Hospital, and because I complained of pain in my right foot, they took X rays, which revealed that I had a broken toe. The motorcycle didn't fare as well. It was a total loss. In fact, the tow truck driver who picked up the pieces of the bike was stunned to learn that I was alive and not on my way to the morgue.

I considered myself very blessed to have survived. When I left the hospital that night, I limped to a sobriety meeting to count my blessings. Meanwhile, Lea Anne had to fly to Oregon to see her ailing grandmother, and Claire and I decided to spend some time together in Santa Barbara, where I was able to spoil her a little and celebrate the Christmas season with my precious daughter—while also letting my wounded body heal a little.

More than a year later, in February 1990, I returned to working for Ozzy. With Sharon spending time in her London office, I moved into Ozzy's home in the hills of Los Angeles for a couple of months, keeping him company while he wrote and began recording his next album. Shortly thereafter, Sharon asked me to take over as tour manager for her new band, the London Quireboys, who were starting an American (and then a world) tour in mid-May that would last until the end of the year.

I didn't know much about the London Quireboys, except that they had been quite successful everywhere in the world except the U.S. I had heard that they were a wild bunch, and frankly, I was a little uneasy about touring with a band who liked a drink now and then. By this point, I had four years of sobriety under my belt, and remaining sober was my highest priority in life.

There was plenty to organize for the London Quireboys tour (we used two buses and a tractor trailer in the U.S. leg). When I finally flew to Daytona

Beach for the opening concert, I was in for a pleasant surprise. As I mentioned in chapter 57, touring with the London Quireboys turned out to be a joyous experience. Yes, the band members could drink in amounts that were reminiscent of my own boozing in previous times (our bus carried enough alcohol to stock a large nightclub!). And they loved to chase the girls. But I earned their trust and respect, they followed my instructions, and the tour went off with very few hitches.

The only time the band and I were at odds was one night when I became concerned that the rigors of touring might be pushing them to the brink of exhaustion. I knew they had to be in top shape for a pending flight to London, where they were scheduled to play in a huge outdoor festival with the Rolling Stones at the Newcastle football stadium. For the guys, it was the dream of a lifetime, and I was determined not to let them sabotage it. So to help preserve their health, I poured out all the hard liquor that they had accumulated. While the bus was parked, I dumped bottle after bottle down a nearby drain. Midway through the process, two of the band members, Spike and Guy, saw what I was doing, and went berserk.

"What the hell are you doing?!" Spike shouted. "Have you gone nuts?"

The booze continued to flow down the drain, which was more than they could handle. They were absolutely livid, and I was becoming a bit concerned.

Finally, to calm them down I suggested, "Why don't you call Sharon and tell her what I've done?"

They had fire in their eyes, but my comment silenced them. They knew that it wouldn't be a good idea to complain to or mess with Sharon, so they dropped their heads, turned, and walked back to their hotel rooms. All the while, they muttered obscenities about me under their breath.

More than 50,000 people attended the outdoor concert with the Rolling Stones. Since I knew the Stones and their security, I arranged for the Quireboys to meet Mick Jagger and pose for pictures with him. The boys said it was one of the most exciting days of their lives.

From England, the Quireboys headed back to the States, then on to Canada, and finally to Europe, Japan, and back to the U.S. But just three days after returning to the States for a concert in Houston, Capitol Records unexpectedly pulled the plug on its support of the tour. Instantly, the remaining concert dates on the U.S. itinerary had been canceled.

The band members were heartbroken, and I wasn't feeling too good myself. But all was not lost. The Quireboys had already earned a gold record in Canada, and their record company there was convinced that additional touring north of the border could turn the album platinum. So two weeks later we flew to Toronto for a series of concerts, including one on Victoria Island in a club that I had last played with the New Vaudeville Band in 1968, long before McDonald's was a prominent feature on the picturesque island. Sure enough, before leaving Canada the band picked up its platinum record in Vancouver, where Sharon had flown to see the last concert of the tour.

After I returned home, I received photographs taken at the platinum record presentation in Vancouver. I placed those photos next to the pictures taken at the band's gold record presentation six months earlier, and I could see just how much wear and tear all the touring had caused us. We all looked like we had aged a few years—a moving testament to just how brutal touring can be.

When Sharon and Ozzy decided to travel to Switzerland for Christmas, they invited me to spend the holidays in their rented home in the Beverly Glen section of Los Angeles. It was a wonderful Christmas present, and with Sharon's permission, I threw a party for all my sober friends to celebrate my five years of sobriety. I also celebrated the holidays with Claire, buying the biggest Christmas tree I could find and decorating it with her help.

Once I had moved out of Ozzy's home in early 1991, I rented my own apartment in Venice. I didn't have much music memorabilia left to decorate the walls—about a dozen gold and platinum records from Led Zeppelin, a few original Yardbirds and Zeppelin posters, and a couple of photographs—but it was a start and I was excited about having a new apartment. Work was scarce for a few months, and I began to write this book. Then I was hired to tour with a New York band, The Throbs, in the U.S. and England for six weeks, and in 1992 I watched over Alice in Chains for Columbia Records as the band's companion during the recording of a new album. Next, my phone rang to go on the road with Eden, a band whose members included a son of Frankie Avalon and an offspring of one of the Everly Brothers. Eden was a new act on Hollywood Records, and the tour's small budget forced a lot of cutting corners. But at about that time, I had decided to move my career in a new direction—into music management—and with Claire in private school, the Eden tour was an opportunity to add a few dollars to my bank account.

I launched my entry into management with my friends Michael Lewis and Gary Quinn, along with record producer Peter Rafelson. The four of us decided we would put together an all-girl band—an all-lesbian band, to be exact—and we came up with the name Fem 2 Fem. All we needed was to find five beautiful lesbians, and do it in a professional way (we decided it wouldn't look good for us to appear to be aging perverts asking any two girls holding hands if they could sing). So we put the word out on the type of girl we were looking for and held auditions while Michael and Peter began writing songs for the new band.

When I arrived at the auditions, I was amazed at the beauty of most of the young women. Our biggest challenge was to find those with the best voices and attitude—and since we had an offer from *Playboy* for a three-page spread and story, we also needed girls who were uninhibited and willing to take off their clothes. As it turned out, we had no trouble filling the slots for the band. Within days, the girls were in the recording studio, as well as preparing for their *Playboy* photo session and a video shoot. With some help from college students from the UCLA film school, we made one video for MTV and another (with nudity) for the clubs and for European audiences.

Fem 2 Fem's first live show was scheduled at the Dinah Shore Golf Classic in Palm Springs. The promoters wanted only two songs, which was fortunate since the girls didn't know many tunes by then. They were also featured on Geraldo Rivera's TV show, in a program about "lipstick lesbians." Before long we had a record deal, a billboard atop the Virgin Megastore on the Sunset Strip, more TV programs, interviews on radio stations across the country, and a highly publicized appearance on the Howard Stern radio show (during which Howard was more than delighted to get a good look at one of the girl's tits, which everyone agreed were worth their weight in gold).

As we toured radio stations, the girls were plenty of fun to be with, although I did have to raise my voice a few times, particularly when they were all suffering from PMS and were whining and groaning in their bunks. But they always looked drop-dead gorgeous when we arrived at those radio station appearances, even when we had to get there by six in the morning.

From the start, our game plan for the band was to make records, grab some endorsement deals, appear on some radio and TV shows—and that was really all. But then we got a call from a major agency in New York, with an offer for the girls to perform live in concert. I, of course, immediately said yes, told them to send the contract to us—and then nervously asked Michael and Gary, "What the fuck are we going to do now?" When the girls sang on TV and in limited appearances onstage, we kept their own voices low and used backing tracks to give them a well-rounded, professional sound. But now we had to turn the girls into a real singing band. Would it be an impossible task?

Michael took the girls under his wing, and tried to work a miracle. After just a week, he seemed to have succeeded. Fem 2 Fem was ready for prime time. First we tried them out at a gay nightclub in Houston—a city where their first single, *Switch,* was getting plenty of airplay. When our little divas hit the stage, the queens went nuts. While the crowd screamed and shouted, Michael and I looked at each other in amazement, and then just burst out laughing, not believing our good luck.

Almost immediately, offers came in for Fem 2 Fem to perform in Miami, Tampa, Long Island, San Antonio, and again in Houston. The group also made some additional appearances on TV, including on the Maury Povich and Joan Rivers shows.

Even with everything going so well, however, we had to deal with a hurricane of internal turmoil within the band, forcing us to make some personnel changes. One girl started complaining about royalty checks, and would wander aimlessly through the audience before each show. We made the decision to let her go. We gave another girl a leave of absence after her home was badly damaged in the Northridge, California, earthquake. Two others left when they refused to sing some of the lyrics that Michael had written for the band. But we always quickly found new girls to replace the ones who had left.

At the same time, other problems were brewing: We continued to spend more money to keep the band afloat than we were bringing in. Were it not for the $110,000 we received as a publishing advance on the first record, we might have drowned in debt. I was hoping we could survive long enough to release a new record and reap an inflow of publishing cash.

Meanwhile, Michael flew to England with a couple of the girls to publicize the London opening of a stage show built around Fem 2 Fem that the tabloids there were already calling a "singing sex show." Members of the London city council were outraged, insisting that they would shut down the erotic show before it ever opened. As Michael appeared on radio programs, defending freedom of speech and art in the theater, council members turned up at the dress rehearsals (or were they *un*dressed rehearsals?) to get a firsthand look at the onstage nudity. The male councilors seemed to enjoy the show, and wiped their sweating brows with their handkerchiefs. But eventually we decided to take much of the sex and nudity out of the program so the show could go on, even though the girls were still scantily clad in very sexy clothing. When the show opened in London, it drew respectable crowds, including a fair number of men in raincoats who longed to see as much skin as possible.

Eventually, I decided to sever my ties with Fem 2 Fem. It was costing me too much money to stay on, and I felt it would be better to pay for my daughter's school tuition than throw any more dollars into the band.

In the midst of the controversy surrounding Fem 2 Fem in London, I received a call from Terry Rindal, who managed the reggae band Black Uhuru. He needed a tour manager to fly to Jamaica to sort out the band's visas and then accompany them on a tour of Argentina and Brazil. It was just the tonic I needed, and I flew to Kingston to rest in the sun for a week before the tour began. It took me a while to get accustomed to working with the Rastafarian band members, but we soon developed mutual respect for one another, and the tour went so well that Terry asked me to work with the band in their upcoming American tour as well. In fact, I would have a working relationship with Black Uhuru for the next three years, traveling all over the world with them.

In one memorable series of dates with Black Uhuru built around the Ruffles Reggae Festival, we began in Argentina and then spent time in Brazil, including performances in Sao Paulo, Rio de Janeiro, and Brasilia. At Rio's Copacabana Beach, the dark-skinned, topless girls on the sand were absolutely gorgeous, and were only too pleased to entertain us. Nearly every band on the festival tour took time for a bit of girl watching and sunbathing.

Leaving Brazil, we headed to England and then Holland to start the European tour. Our flight to London's Gatwick Airport arrived late, causing us to miss ferry connections to the continent. That left us with some unexpected time to drive to Brixton, a Jamaican community where we could purchase some of the Carribean island's imported goods and vegetables to take with us to Europe (it also gave me a chance to visit my mother for about an hour before heading off).

Touring with Black Uhuru was quite rigorous, and we barely had time to catch our breath. There were shows in Vienna, Brussels, and several cities in Holland, then we moved on to Oslo and down to Berlin (which had changed so much since I drove Ronnie Wood of the Stones there on a Creation tour in 1968—most notably, that awful wall had disappeared). From Berlin, the band traveled to many other European cities, including Hamburg and Florence, and then we headed back to London before jetting to the U.S. for shows in Washington, D.C., and Nashville, followed by dates in the Carolinas, Wisconsin, and Thunder Bay, Canada. We were always moving at breakneck speed, and by the time the band completed its last show of the tour in Chicago, we had covered thirteen countries, sixty-six cities, and 53,000 miles. But before we could even catch a good night's sleep, Terry made an unexpected announcement: He had scheduled more shows for us, forcing us to head immediately for San Juan, then Albuquerque and a long list of other cities and finally end up in Hawaii for a couple performances and a little time to swim and sleep on the beach. I still get tired just thinking about it!

There were more tours with Black Uhuru over the next couple of years, and there was never a scarcity of surprises. At a date in Paris, our soundman never showed up, so we had to make the best of things ourselves. I paid the musicians a little extra cash to set up their own instruments, which kept their moaning and complaining to a minimum.

By the time we reached Toulouse, Terry called with some very bad news. He said that a protracted legal dispute over the ownership of the name Black Uhuru had finally been settled—and not in the current lineup's favor. Duckie Simpson, one of the original members of Black Uhuru, had been awarded rights to the name—forcing an abrupt end to the tour. It was a sad evening for all of us.

When I returned to the States, it finally hit me how much I would miss the boys in this band, who had become such a joy to work with. I still keep in contact with some of them, and occasionally hear from Prince (the band's drummer) and receive photos of his son, who is my godson and growing up wonderfully.

Before long, I went on the road with Miriam Makeba, a dignified artist who was respected worldwide both as a singer and a human-rights activist. In her home country of South Africa, she was considered royalty, and rightfully so. Miriam's band was composed of talented and professional musicians from various parts of Africa, and they put on a wonderful show. It was a pleasure working for her.

But when the tour reached San Jose, I received a message from the hospital in England where my mother was being cared for. When I returned the call, I learned that Mum had passed away that morning, just a few hours after I had tried unsuccessfully to reach her by phone. I flew to London immediately, leaving the Miriam Makeba tour, which was nearing its end anyway, behind me. In London, accompanied by my friend Jenny Fernando, I arranged for a mass to be said for my mum. It was attended by friends, neighbors, relatives, and the kind people from the home who had taken such good care of her during her last years.

In 1997, I received an unusual request: Would I keep an eye on Robert Downey Jr. on a movie set, making sure he complied with a judge's order to refrain from any drug use? Robert had signed an agreement with the court to have someone trustworthy with him at all times, who would inform the judge if he violated any of the drug-related restrictions placed on him. A member of Robert's staff told me that if Robert drank or used drugs, and I didn't report it to the judge, *I* would go to jail for protecting him. Not a pretty thought.

I caught a plane to Boston, where Robert was about to begin filming a Neil Jordan picture, *In Dreams,* with Annette Bening and Aidan Quinn, in Northampton. It was my first time on a film set since Zeppelin made *The Song Remains the Same* about twenty-five years earlier.

Robert turned out to be as pleasant as anyone I ever worked with. True, the early morning starts on the set were not my idea of a good time, and the weather was pretty miserable. But Robert was a joy to be around, and he and I soon reached an understanding of what my job would entail. I gave him a first-edition copy of *Stairway to Heaven* and told him, "As you'll read in my book, I'm not someone who's going to be fucked with. Even though it's not in my nature to want to contribute to putting anyone behind bars, if you start drinking or using drugs, just remember that I'm not going to jail for someone else's mistakes. So make sure you behave yourself while I'm with you, or I'll have no choice but to call the judge."

Robert was very professional on the set, always polite, always kind to fans, often signing dozens of autographs at a time. Everyone in front of and behind the cameras liked him. But it was hard to enjoy the experience too much once I had come down with a bad case of the flu. To compound my own misery, Northampton is not the most exciting town on the map; when I used to visit it with touring bands, we tried to leave as soon as possible after the show to find some happier hunting grounds. Fortunately, after a couple weeks—and quite a few sobriety meetings, which Robert and I attended together—the film's cast and crew moved to the next location, Fontana Village, North Carolina. No one was happier about that change of scenery than I. Next we left the Carolinas for San Diego, where we met up with Robert's wife, Debbie, and his son, Indio, and we settled in for a couple days of rest and relaxation before traveling to Mexico to complete the filming at the same studio where *Titanic* had been shot. Robert and I shared a two-bedroom suite at a Marriott hotel south of the border, and got to know each other a little better. He continued to be enthusiastic about going to sobriety meetings and staying on his recovery track. I was so pleased that he seemed determined to get it right this time. At the end of our trip to Mexico, early in the morning on Thanksgiving Day 1997, I delivered Robert to a treatment center in Malibu, where he would be living until his court appearance the next month.

More than a year later, I worked with Robert again. He called one afternoon to ask if I could travel to Pittsburgh, where he would be working with Michael Douglas on *Wonder Boys*. "I like working with you," he told me, adding that he needed me on the set for about two months. Because the music-touring game had become so slow in early 1999, I figured, Why not?

I flew to Pennsylvania, and checked into the royal suite at the Westin William Penn Hotel, which was certainly much more luxurious than our digs in Northampton in 1997. Our suite had two bedrooms, a lounge, a large dining room, and a kitchen equipped with two coffee machines and a shelf brimming with Starbucks coffee. In those first hours in Pittsburgh, I had forms to fill out and phone calls to make, checking in with the insurance company that had covered Robert for the film. Until the movie was finished, I had to check in with the insurers every week, reporting on whether he was still clean (which he always was).

There wasn't much to do in Pittsburgh except endure the freezing weather during the shooting of the night scenes, which often dragged on until the early hours of morning. Robert and I often slept late, but awoke in enough time to attend sobriety meetings held just a five-minute walk from the hotel.

Michael Douglas was always the gentleman, and on Robert's birthday threw a dinner party for him at an elegant restaurant. At the end of the meal, Michael offered Robert a three-picture deal with his production company as a birthday present—if Robert stayed sober. He handed Robert a beautiful ostrich-skin folder containing a copy of the deal, which was quite a generous and inspirational gift. While I was with him, Robert kept his commitment of sobriety.

When the shooting of *Wonder Boys* finally came to an end, spring had arrived and I was glad to be flying back to Los Angeles. Robert and I caught an 8:30 P.M. flight home, and that was the last time I saw him to this day. He is such a talented actor, has a wonderful sense of humor, and loves his son, Indio, dearly. But I know how difficult it can be to keep this awful disease under control. I wish him well in maintaining his sobriety.

In recent years, I've toured with a number of other musical groups—or at least was prepared to do so in one memorable instance. Eric Wasserman, Diana Ross's business manager, called shortly after an announcement that Diana would soon be touring with two new Supremes. He asked me to shepherd the new girls on the tour, beginning with pre-tour rehearsals at a studio in the San Fernando Valley, and I agreed. (The nicest part was that the rehearsals were next to a studio where Ozzy Osbourne was preparing for his next tour—and Ozzy always had a cup of tea brewing, which was a nice way to start the day or evening.)

During the Supremes' rehearsals, I kept hearing reports that ticket sales for the upcoming tour were lagging behind expectations. Still, it was a job, the money was good, and it sure beat being out of work.

As it turned out, I worked for the girls for only a few days before Diana and the other singers dropped a bombshell: They had decided that they wanted a woman to replace me. I got a call from Lars Brokar, their production manager in London, telling me that Diana had just agreed to a female tour manager for the girls and he would have to let me go. He offered his apologies.

Not long after my ties with Diana Ross and the Supremes were abruptly severed, my friend Jack Carson suggested that I call Dan DeVita, who managed Fu

Manchu and needed a tour manager for the band's European concerts. At almost the same time, I was also asked to work on Paul Rodgers's tour. In looking at their touring schedules, it was clear that I could handle both gigs with no overlap of dates, so I accepted both.

Paul and I had known each other for many years, going back to the days of Swan Song Records and shared management with Peter Grant. It had been at least twenty years since I had last heard Paul perform with Bad Company. I let Chris Crawford, Paul's current manager, know that I had been sober for fourteen years by then, quieting any anxieties he may have had that I was still the wild man of old. But although I took the job, I also felt disappointment knowing that we'd be touring during Claire's graduation from high school. Claire understood that there was no way I could get home, and this was where the money for her future education would come from. (I was able to speak with Claire by phone when she graduated, and she was thrilled with the flowers I had sent; I was clearly a proud papa, with Claire not only winning many first-place awards upon graduation [for English literature, creative writing, and journalism], but also earning a scholarship to a top art college in Los Angeles.)

The dates in Paul's tour were pretty much London-based, so to reduce hotel costs, my ex-wife Marilyn let me stay at her London home. (Most of the band members, including old friend guitarist Jeff Whitethorn, stayed at their own homes, and I would usually rent a car to take us to most of our performances in and around London.) There was plenty of nostalgia on that tour, including a show at the Cavern Club, the old home of the Beatles and a place I had not played since 1965 with the Who (when their incredibly loud music caused plaster to fall off the walls and ceiling!).

The day after Paul Rodger's last performance, I got some rest and then headed for my gig with Fu Manchu and its tour of Europe, making some last-minute changes in hotels and travel arrangements during my first hours on the job. From the start, there were the usual snafus that seem part of any major tour, and that are well beyond anyone's control. Early on, all nonlocal flights in and out of the London airports were canceled due to a major breakdown of the radar system, so the band couldn't make its way to London from the U.S., necessitating canceling the opening show in Manchester. Fu Manchu ended up catching a flight to Dublin, and then boarding a commuter plane to Gatwick Airport, where I met them and got the gears in motion for a show in Southampton. Before long, we were in Germany, after which we drove over the Alps to the Milan airport to catch a plane to Lisbon. Thank God we used two drivers for this leg of the tour, or it simply couldn't have been done safely (as it was, the bus broke down once during the trip).

Fu Manchu eventually made its way to Switzerland for a festival, then on to Bonn, Leeds, Liverpool, and Belfast. We had plenty of good times on that tour, but it wasn't all fun and games. We were in Belfast at the time of the Orange Day parade in Northern Ireland, and there were bonfires in the street and extra police patrols right in front of the club where we were playing. In fear for our safety, the police closed the club early, cutting our set short for fear that the show would be impolitely interrupted by a petrol bomb thrown through a window. So it turned out to be an early night for us. All in a day's work of a rock and roll tour manager.

Not long thereafter, I went to work for the Gipsy Kings, a group of brothers and cousins hailing from the South of France. On the tour, I oversaw their road transportation and hotels, and made sure all of their needs were met. It was a great five weeks living it up at the finest hotels—Ritz-Carltons, Meridians, and Four Seasons—not to mention almost a full week at the Rihga Royal in New York. I certainly enjoyed working with the Gipsys, even though they did not speak English very well and thus it was a challenge for us to communicate.

It took a little time for the Gipsy Kings to develop trust and faith in me, but after the first week, they asked Pascal, one of their managers, why they hadn't had me on their team in the past, since under my guidance, their life on the road ran very smoothly. Pascal also asked me to look after their merchandise—a part of the job that I always found thoroughly unenjoyable—but almost everything else on the tour worked out fine. I was sorry it didn't last longer.

By the way, it was amazing that I didn't lose control of my waistline during the tour, since Pascal often had me take the band members to lunch before their siesta—and then there were dinner parties after each show that were always held at the best restaurants in town. It's all part of the job.

As I write these final pages, I've been working as the tour manager for Crazy Town since the fall of 2000. My friend Tony Morehead had done a couple shows for this Los Angeles band, but had made a commitment to another group, so he asked if I'd be interested in taking over. The band's manager, H. M. Wollman, a charming young man, seemed delighted when I spoke with him and told him about my fifteen years of sobriety. After all, some members of Crazy Town were newly sober, and he hoped I'd be a positive influence on them. So with his blessing, I went to work preparing for a tour set to begin in November. At the time, I knew almost nothing about Crazy Town, including the type of music they played.

Nevertheless, the band seemed pleased that I was on the job. Only a week earlier, I had spoken at a sobriety meeting that the recovering band members attended, so when they heard that I had been hired, apparently no one complained.

A week later, I went to the rehearsal studio to meet the band. But as I shook their hands, my first thought was, "What have I gotten myself into?" The band members had so many tattoos on their bodies that it was hard to see any skin. When they started to play, the music was so loud in that small room that my ears began to ache. I finally excused myself and left to get a cup of coffee, all the while wondering if I was really up to this anymore.

An hour later, I went back to the rehearsal studio, where only two of the band members—Squirrel (the guitarist) and JBJ (the drummer)—remained. We chatted for a while, and I gradually got to know them and the other boys. They were a few days away from shooting the video for their new single, "Butterfly," and then we'd be heading for Oklahoma, the first stop on their tour.

In that initial concert in Tulsa, Crazy Town was very impressive. I remember thinking, "I don't know anything about hip-hop or whatever kind of music they're playing, but the audience sure loves them."

On the band's website, one of the vocalists, Epic Mazur, says, "I don't know what you would classify our music as. Sometimes you may think it's purely rock, sometimes just hip-hop. But listening to the whole album, we're expressing whatever kind of music through a hip-hop mentality. We're some hip-hop kids that needed to rock, rather than some rock kids that needed to rap."

That first tour with Crazy Town went smoothly from Tulsa to Atlanta, to Norfolk, supporting Orgy, and then on to Knoxville where we started a headline tour with Shuvel and Slaves on Dope. Crazy Town turned out to be a great bunch of guys, and the newly sober musicians among them went to meetings with me regularly. They seemed to get along well with one another, and would sometimes write and practice music in a studio set up in the back of our bus. Although I learned that the band hadn't earned any gold stars for congeniality and good behavior on their previous tour, those antics had occurred when the group was using drugs, before they cleaned up. Since I've been with them, I've had no complaints about their behavior, nor has anyone else.

Next, the tour arrived in Lawrence, Kansas, which turned out to be a sweet little town with a sobriety meeting just minutes from our hotel that got us all on the right track. Then we moved on to a concert in St. Louis, which was the hometown of Trouble, one of the band members. While we were there, Trouble got to spend a few hours with his dad and show him how sobriety had changed him. I could see how proud his dad was (that's always nice, since most of us junkies and drunks always end up hurting the ones closest to us).

Next it was on to Cincinnati, and then for a couple of days to Detroit, where I had hoped to see Kate, my old girlfriend, but she was at an ashram for the weekend. Of course, when you're young, you have plenty of girls to choose from on the road if you so desire, although some band members are quite content just calling their girlfriends back home in Los Angeles or wherever they're living. As for me, my days of chasing and catching women like I used to are over, unless a blast from the past shows up and rekindles the old days. It's usually off to bed early for me, unless I break down on the odd occasion and accompany some of the guys to a strip joint—but not getting much attention from the strippers, I often wonder why I didn't just put the money toward a new pair of Gucci loafers or something else I wanted. (The boys in Crazy Town sometimes called me "Dad"—what does that say about my age?)

Crazy Town continued to play major cities through the East and Midwest, including Cleveland, Philadelphia, Boston, Hartford, Pittsburgh, Columbus, Baltimore, and Milwaukee. Most days seemed like the one before, with a slew of phone-ins, visits to radio stations, press interviews, and anything else to get the band in the public eye and ears. When we arrived in New York, I made some time for a visit to Saint Patrick's Cathedral, where I lit candles and said a few prayers for my family.

As the tour continued, "Butterfly" was getting more and more airplay, and the crowds grew in size. Some promoters asked us to headline shows, even when we had originally been scheduled to open them.

During that particular tour, one of the biggest challenges was the weather. Guided by forecasts on the Weather Channel, I realized we might have a harrowing drive from Chicago to Portland, Oregon, with a major snowstorm predicted on part of the route; Chicago itself was nearly snowed in, and making it to the West Coast for the Portland show appeared doubtful. Production manager Eddie Oetella and I, along with our bus driver, decided to go south, look for a clearing in the weather, and then head to San Francisco. But once we hit the road, even that route was treacherous, although our driver, Jim Wiggins from Coast to Coast Coaches, did a great job of keeping the bus on the icy roads.

The good news was that the "Butterfly" video was getting played on MTV, and the single was selling extremely well—and still growing in popularity. The band's CD was selling about 3,000 copies a week when the U.S. tour started; by the end of 2000, sales had soared to 75,000 a week. The band played its last three shows of the tour—San Bernardino, Fresno, and its hometown, Hollywood—to large, enthusiastic crowds. Because L.A. was our home base, families and friends of the band showed up at the Hollywood show at the Palace, which was a wonderful way to finish the tour.

Crazy Town had worked very hard, never complaining about the early morning wakeup calls and all the promotion we had them do. For me, returning to the Hollywood Palace was rather nostalgic, recalling 1967 when I had arrived there with the New Vaudeville Band, appeared on *The Milton Berle Show,* and spent time on the corner of Hollywood and Vine at Wallach's Music City, where you could listen to albums in a private booth to see if you liked the tracks before making a purchase.

I had a month off before Crazy Town would begin touring again, and I spent time with Claire as well as some friends. Meanwhile, "Butterfly" was spreading its wings on TV and radio, and earned the band a platinum album. The band got short-notice calls to perform at Universal City Walk, as well as in Hollywood and Denver, and they headlined at the Hard Rock Hotel, where we were accompanied by a *Rolling Stone* writer and photographer.

In late February 2001, we left for New York for the band's appearance on *Total Request Live* on MTV. Then there were shows in Atlanta, Gettysburg, Seattle, and Canada, after which we finally escaped the snow (thank God!) for a flight to Cancun for MTV's *Spring Break* and five days in the sun. Three of the band members—Seth, Doug, and Trouble—flew their girlfriends to Cancun, knowing they would soon be spending a lot of time on the road away from their ladies. Next we caught a plane to Europe for promotion, TV appearances, and live shows (one of which MTV taped) in five countries. In Europe, "Butterfly" was the number one record in most of the cities we visited, and we collected even more gold records. For the most part, it was all work and no play, but the band members were riding a tidal wave of excitement that kept their energy levels soaring. For me, I had not experienced anything quite like this since the days of Led Zeppelin.

We finally made our way back to L.A., regained some strength, and then the band performed at the ESPN Awards at the Universal Amphitheater, where my old pals, Black Sabbath with Ozzy Osbourne, were also on the bill. A week later, our bus rolled out of Los Angeles at 2 A.M. to Phoenix for the first stop of another five weeks of performances in the U.S. The Phoenix show was with Linkin Park, and then we began another headline tour with Saliva and Stereo Mud. In midtour, we flew on a private jet back to L.A. to shoot the video for the band's new single, "Revolving Door." (So many girls had been hired to appear in the video that the set looked like Caligula's palace!) Two days later, we flew to Nashville for the first of more concert dates, eventually completing the tour in Birmingham, Myrtle Beach, and Chicago—and then went back to Europe for another ten grueling days of promotion and shows. And the tours go on. . . .

As for Led Zeppelin, I haven't seen much of the three surviving band members lately, although I do bump into them from time to time. Since the first edition of the book was published, they have remained active to one degree or another. Plant and Page, of course, released *Walking into Clarksdale* in 1998, and performed in a long-awaited reunion tour. They also appeared on MTV's *Unplugged* in 1997. Jimmy toured, and performed with the Black Crowes as recently as the year 2000, although some of their dates had to be canceled because of Pagey's ongoing back problems.

John Paul has kept as busy as he's wanted to, arranging and composing classical music and motion picture scores, and producing albums for Heart and Ben E. King. He has also done arranging for artists such as R.E.M. and Peter Gabriel.

Led Zeppelin did reunite onstage when they were inducted into the Rock and Roll Hall of Fame in 1995, but the surviving members of Zeppelin have all moved on, and times change. When Page and Plant released their joint CD, Robert told *Time* magazine that although the "best place to find us is in a bar," he admitted that they no longer partied as hard as they once did. "We control it now," he said. "Before, it was rather amorphous—we couldn't stop it." I'm glad we've all grown up a little.

The Zeppelin music itself lives on. In 1997, the Recording Industry of America certified ten of Led Zeppelin's albums as multiplatinum, with cumulative certified sales totaling nearly 64 million copies. Two years later, just one of those albums—*Led Zeppelin IV*—had racked up certified sales of 21 million. Each new generation of young people seems to embrace Zeppelin as their own, and thus the band's CD sales continue to soar. Only the Beatles have sold more albums than Zeppelin.

Since my days with Led Zeppelin, Crazy Town has really been the first hugely successful band I've worked with from its beginning. It's been wonderful to see this young band take off so fast and go so far, but times are certainly different now than in the Zeppelin era. I remember how Led Zeppelin worked themselves to death for almost two years, making the first album for $2,500 and financing the first tour out of the pockets of Jimmy, John Paul, and Peter. From the start, they owed nothing to anyone, including their record company, and were on their way to the bank after the first U.S. tour. Because Zeppelin never made TV appearances, the band's live shows were instant sellouts the moment they were advertised. By contrast, the cost of making videos is so high these days, and the exposure on MTV can become so saturated, it's a lot harder now for bands to get ahead financially early in their careers.

For me, it's still fun being on the road, working with a band like Crazy Town with a great management team and record company behind them, even if the rigors of touring does knock the crap out of me at times. It's a much better life than I would have had if I had not been a skillful enough liar to get my first job with Ronnie Jones and Mick Eves back in 1964. As I write this,

I've spent the last thirty-eight years working with some wonderful bands, and I've profited from the valuable advice of great managers like Peter Grant and Sharon Osbourne.

Next it's off to Europe for a three week record promotion trip, followed by Ozzfest. I'm looking forward to spending time with Sharon Osbourne and Ozzy, along with my old band, Black Sabbath, at Ozzfest, as it's always nice to see old friends with whom you have history in these days of revolving bands. Then, for me, it's back to working on my movie script about how to make rock stars, with writer Christopher Crowe and Julie Anne Park at Paramount Pictures.

What could be better than sitting on the balcony of the Embassy Suites in Myrtle Beach, watching the waves crash on the shore while I type this chapter? For a while, I can even forget that I am really fifty-five years old, not twenty-five—and I'm still having the time of my life.

—Richard Cole
June 2001

LED ZEPPELIN
DISCOGRAPHY

Album, year of release, and contents:

Led Zeppelin, Atlantic Records, 1969
"Good Times Bad Times," "Babe I'm Gonna Leave You," "You Shook Me," "Dazed and Confused," "Your Time Is Gonna Come," "Black Mountain Side," "Communication Breakdown," "I Can't Quit You Baby," "How Many More Times."

Led Zeppelin II, Atlantic Records, 1969
"Whole Lotta Love," "What Is and What Should Never Be," "The Lemon Song," "Thank You," "Heartbreaker," "Living Loving Maid (She's Just a Woman)," "Ramble On," "Moby Dick," "Bring It On Home."

Led Zeppelin III, Atlantic Records, 1970
"Immigrant Song," "Friends," "Celebration Day," "Since I've Been Loving You," "Out On the Tiles," "Gallows Pole," "Tangerine," "That's the Way," "Bron-Y-Aur Stomp," "Hats Off to (Roy) Harper."

Untitled, Atlantic Records, 1971
"Black Dog," "Rock and Roll," "The Battle of Evermore," "Stairway to Heaven," "Misty Mountain Hop," "Four Sticks," "Going to California," "When the Levee Breaks."

Houses of the Holy, Atlantic Records, 1973
"The Song Remains the Same," "The Rain Song," "Over the Hills and Far Away," "The Crunge," "Dancing Days," "D'yer Mak'er," "No Quarter," "The Ocean."

Physical Graffiti, Swan Song, 1975
"Custard Pie," "The Rover," "In My Time of Dying," "Houses of the Holy," "Trampled Under Foot," "Kashmir," "In the Light," "Bron-Yr-Aur," "Down by the Seaside," "Ten Years Gone," "Night Flight," "The Wanton Song," "Boogie with Stu," "Black Country Woman," "Sick Again."

Presence, Swan Song, 1976
"Achilles Last Stand," "For Your Life," "Royal Orleans," "Nobody's Fault But Mine," "Candy Store Rock," "Hots On for Nowhere," "Tea For One."

The Song Remains the Same, Swan Song, 1976
"Rock and Roll," "Celebration Day," "The Song Remains the Same," "Rain Song," "Dazed and Confused," "No Quarter," "Stairway to Heaven," "Moby Dick," "Whole Lotta Love."

In Through the Out Door, Swan Song, 1979
"In the Evening," "South Bound Saurez," "Fool In the Rain," "Hot Dog," "Carouselambra," "All My Love," "I'm Gonna Crawl."

Coda, Swan Song, 1982
"We're Gonna Groove," "Poor Tom," "I Can't Quit You Baby," "Walter's Walk," "Ozone Baby," "Darlene," "Bonzo's Montreux," "Wearing and Tearing."

Led Zeppelin, Atlantic Records, 1990 (digitally remastered, boxed set)
"Whole Lotta Love," "Heartbreaker," "Communication Breakdown," "Babe I'm Gonna Leave You," "What Is and What Should Never Be," "Thank You," "I Can't Quit You Baby," "Dazed and Confused," "Your Time Is Gonna Come," "Ramble On," "Travelling Riverside Blues," "Friends," "Celebration Day," "Hey Hey What Can I Do," "White Summer/Black Mountain Side," "Black Dog," "Over the Hills and Far Away," "Immigrant Song," "The Battle of Evermore," "Bron-Y-Aur Stomp," "Tangerine," "Going to California," "Since I've Been Loving You," "D'yer Mak'er," "Gallows Pole," "Custard Pie," "Misty Mountain Hop," "Rock and Roll," "The Rain Song," "Stairway to Heaven," "Kashmir," "Trampled Under Foot," "For Your Life," "No Quarter," "Dancing Days," "When the Levee Breaks," "Achilles Last Stand," "The Song Remains the Same," "Ten Years Gone," "In My Time of Dying," "In the Evening," "Candy Store Rock," "The Ocean," "Ozone Baby," "Houses of the Holy," "Wearing and Tearing," "Poor Tom," "Nobody's Fault But Mine," "Fool In the Rain," "In the Light," "The Wanton Song," "Moby Dick/Bonzo's Montreux," "I'm Gonna Crawl," "All My Love."

INDEX